# Que's Computer User's Dictionary

## Third Edition

**Bryan Pfaffenberger, Ph.D.**

School of Engineering
and Applied Science

University of Virginia

*Que's Computer User's Dictionary,* 3rd Edition

## Copyright ©1992 by Que Corporation

Library of Congress Catalog Number: 92-64024

ISBN: 1-56529-023-2

95 94 93 92          4 3 2

Interpretation of the printing code: the rightmost double-digit number is the year of the book's printing; the rightmost single-digit number is the number of the book's printing. For example, a printing code of 92-1 shows that the first printing of the book occurred in 1992.

*Publisher:* Lloyd J. Short

*Associate Publisher:* Rick Ranucci

*Product Development Manager:* Thomas H. Bennett

*Book Designer:* Scott Cook

*Acquisitions Editor:* Patricia J. Brooks

*Production Team:* Jeff Baker, Claudia Bell, Laurie Casey, Michelle Cleary, Jerry Ellis, Kate Godfrey, Bob LaRoche, Jay Lesandrini, Linda Seifert, Sandra Shay, Dennis Sheehan, Susan VandeWalle, MaryBeth Wakefield, Christine Young

Screen reproductions in this book were created using Collage Plus from Inner Media, Inc., Hollis, NH.

## Product Director

Charles O. Stewart, III

## Production Editor

Barbara K. Koenig

## Editors

J. Christopher Nelson
Heather Northrup
Pamela Wampler

## Technical Editors

Rolf Crozier
Doug White

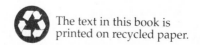

# Dedication

To Suzanne

# About the Author

Bryan Pfaffenberger, Ph.D., is a Charlottesville, Virginia–based author who has written more than 30 books on personal computer applications. He currently is an associate professor in the School of Engineering and Applied Science, University of Virginia, where he teaches technical writing, the history and sociology of technology, and computer applications. His book *Democratizing Information: Online Databases and the Rise of End-User Searching* (G. K. Hall, 1990) won the Best Book of the Year award from the American Society for Information Science. His research and consulting interests currently include the impact of computers on organizations and the role of personal computing technology in business process reengineering.

# Acknowledgments

The language of personal computing is changing as fast as the technology, and that's why Que is publishing a third edition of *Computer User's Dictionary*. In this edition, you find expanded coverage of memory management, Microsoft Windows, desktop publishing, multimedia, and other exciting, new areas of personal computing hardware and applications. Every definition has been checked, revised, or expanded to ensure that this edition reflects the current language of personal computing.

I would like to thank Lloyd Short once again for encouraging me to undertake this project—thanks, Lloyd, for your confidence in me. I also thank Charles Stewart, the project director, for guidance that was as intelligent as it was good-humored. Praise is due to Que's world-class editorial team for their usual superb job: Heather Northrup, Pamela Wampler, Chris Nelson, and Melissa Keegan. The technical editors for this project were Rolf Crozier and Doug White. Very special thanks are owed to Barbara Koenig, whose enthusiasm, hard work, and humor have helped to make this revision effort as pleasant as it is comprehensive.

Que gave me the freedom to attempt a totally new kind of dictionary, a user's dictionary: it's a dictionary written from the personal computer user's viewpoint. Terms are included only if they're relevant to personal computer users—and they're defined with the user's needs in mind. Academic types and lexicographers may find this approach wrong-headed or even to pose a danger to civilization for having obfuscated nice, tidy academic distinctions, but *I* am the proper target for their ire, not those who aided me so much while I pursued my goal. If computer users find this dictionary of value in defining the world of computing as they see it, I will be more than satisfied.

—B. P.

# Preface

Personal computing technology brings computing tools to ordinary people. Personal computing, however, also brings a new and daunting terminology to daily life.

These terms aren't just the unfamiliar terms of data processing and management information science—the kind of words defined in other computer dictionaries. These terms are the unfamiliar terms of personal computing, such as *paging memory, interleaved memory, parameter RAM*, and *wait state*. Personal computer users are faced with seemingly unanswerable questions every day: Do you want your new 386 to use cache memory or will a disk cache do? Do you prefer an ST506 hard disk over a SCSI-compatible drive?

The language of personal computing is distinct for reasons other than the arrival of complicated new hardware. Today's user also must learn terms derived from new applications of computing technology, such as desktop publishing and presentation graphics.

To use a page layout program effectively, for example, you should understand at least some of the terms of professional typesetting, such as the difference between *points* and *picas*. To use a presentation graphics package, you should understand the difference between the *x-axis* and the *y-axis*. In both cases, understanding these distinctions is all but essential to using these programs productively and intelligently.

Terms like these often are not defined in other computer dictionaries, which have two aims. First, other computer dictionaries include any and all computer terms, even if they derive from academic computer science and mainframe computing. Second, these dictionaries exclude terms not intrinsically computer-related, even if some of these terms (such as *pica* or *y-axis*) are relevant to computer applications. These aims stem from the academic purpose of such dictionaries; they strive to define the scope of computer science by a comprehensive survey of its distinctive language.

*Que's Computer User's Dictionary,* Third Edition, is different; the purpose of this book is practical, and the focus is personal computing. Its principle of inclusion is simple:  if the term is relevant to the user, it belongs in the dictionary. If the term is relevant to academic computer science, electrical engineering, data processing, scientific computing, or corporate mainframe computing, but is not relevant to users, it does not belong in this dictionary. (Other dictionaries cover such terms but do not do a comprehensive job of covering the language of user computing.) Any and all terms relevant to Macintosh and IBM personal computing are included, even if some of these terms are not intrinsically computer-related. Mainframe data processing or academic computer science terms that personal computer users are not likely to encounter are excluded. This dictionary is a user's dictionary.

The emphasis on practicality leads to another unique feature of this dictionary: the many tips and cautions. What is the point of learning what ASCII sort order means, unless you are warned that this sort order violates standard publication guidelines and that you may have to move some sorted items if you let the computer sort text for you? This dictionary's aims are practical. The information contained should be of practical value to you, the user.

Any attempt to define the language of user computing is akin to trying to change a tire on a moving truck. Hardly a week goes by without the introduction—replete with talk of "revolution"—of some new computer system based on a new microprocessor, or a self-described "path-breaking" new program that will turn the entire industry on its ear. No doubt you will find the names of some chips, computers, and programs are missing from this dictionary. This dictionary is necessarily an artifact of its history, and I have not attempted to include most of today's software packages and systems; I have tried to include only the best-sellers or programs that are innovative or important in some way.

The concepts of user computing change more slowly than the changing faces of systems and software packages. One of the most widely hyped "new" applications, hypertext, was envisioned more than twenty years ago. Even if this dictionary doesn't list your favorite new application or the snazziest new microprocessor, you will find that the underlying concepts are surprisingly stable, and this dictionary should prove of lasting value to you.

# Using This Dictionary To Learn Computer Concepts

If you are new to personal computing, you can use this dictionary to learn the fundamental concepts of user computing. Disregarding specific brands and products, the following list is a quick overview of some of the more important conceptual entries, broken down by subject category.

- *Adapters and buses*: adapter, address bus, bus, expanded memory, expansion slot, Extended Industry Standard Architecture (EISA), Micro Channel Bus, network interface card, open architecture, open bus system, and video adapter

- *Applications*: communications program, database management, database management program, desktop publishing (DTP), draw program, paint program, presentation graphics, spreadsheet program, and word processing program

- *Artificial intelligence and expert systems*: expert system, knowledge base, and knowledge representation

- *Communications*: asynchronous communication, communications program, electronic mail, modem, and terminal emulation

- *Database management*: database, database design, database management, database management program, database management system (DBMS), database structure, data field, data independence, data integrity, data manipulation, data record, record-oriented database management program, relational database management, relational database management program, and table-oriented database management program

- *Desktop publishing*: page description language (PDL), page layout program, and PostScript

- *Disks, disk drives, and secondary storage*: CD-ROM, disk drive, floppy disk, hard disk, optical disk, and secondary storage

- *Display adapters and monitors*: analog monitor, Color Graphics Adapter (CGA), color monitor, digital monitor, Enhanced Graphics Adapter (EGA), Hercules Graphics Adapter, monitor, monochrome display adapter (MDA), monochrome monitor, and Video Graphics Array (VGA)

- *Files and file formats*: binary file, file, file format, file name, graphics file format, and text file

- *Fonts and typography*: bit-mapped font, body type, display type, font, font family, outline font, printer font, screen font, and typeface

- *Graphics*: analytical graphics, animation, bit-mapped graphic, draw program, multimedia, paint program, and presentation graphics program

- *Keyboards, mice, and other input devices*: character, cursor-movement keys, extended character set, input, keyboard, keyboard layout, mouse, and trackball

- *Macintosh*: desktop, Finder, graphical user interface (GUI), icon, and System

- *Measurements*: access time, benchmark, dots per inch (dpi), kilobyte, megabyte, megahertz (MHz), pica, point, response time, and transfer rate

- *Memory*: base memory, bit, byte, cache memory, dynamic random-access memory (DRAM), expanded memory, extended memory, firmware, memory, primary storage, random access, random-access memory (RAM), read-only memory (ROM), secondary storage, sequential access, storage, and virtual memory

- *Microprocessors*: 8-bit computer, 16-bit computer, 32-bit computer, central processing unit (CPU), chip, digital, digital computer, instruction cycle, instruction set, integrated circuit, microprocessor, numeric coprocessor, protected mode, real mode, and wait state

- *Microsoft Windows*: application program interface (API), graphical user interface (GUI), Microsoft Windows, TrueType, Windowing environment

- *Multimedia*: base-level synthesizer, CD-ROM, extended-level synthesizer, General MIDI (GM), Multimedia Personal Computer (MPC), Musical Instrument Digital Interface (MIDI), and synthesizer

- *Networks*: baseband, broadband, bus network, connectivity, connectivity platform, contention, distributed processing system, electronic mail (e-mail), file server, local area network (LAN), multiplexing, network architecture, network interface card, network operating system, peer-to-peer network, platform independence, ring network, star network, token-ring network, workgroup, and workstation

- *Operating systems and utilities*: argument, argument separator, background, backup, backup utility, basic input/output system (BIOS), batch file, boot, cold boot, command-line operating system, command processor, context switching, crash, current directory, current drive, delimiter, extension, file name, graphical user interface (GUI), hard disk backup program, interactive processing, load, multitasking, system disk, system file, system prompt, system software, tree structure, warm boot, and wild card

- *Ports and interfaces*: interface, parallel port, port, RS-232C, and serial port

- *Printers*: built-in font, cartridge, continuous paper, daisywheel printer, dot-matrix printer, downloadable font, friction feed, imagesetter, laser printer, letter-quality printer, nonimpact printer, page description language (PDL), parallel printer, plotter, PostScript, PostScript laser printer, print engine, printer driver, printer font, resolution, serial printer, thermal printer, toner, and tractor feed

- *Programming*: algorithm, assembly language, branch control structure, case branch, control structure, conventional programming, debugging, DO/WHILE loop, extensible, FOR/NEXT loop, high-level programming language, IF/THEN/ELSE, instruction, interpreter, loop,

loop control structure, low-level programming language, machine language, macro, modular programming, nested structure, object code, object-oriented programming language, procedural language, program, sequence control structure, software command language, source code, structured programming, subroutine, and variable

- *Programming languages*: BASIC, bundled software, C, character-based program, command-driven program, copy protection, default setting, documentation, freeware, graphics-based program, groupware, integrated program, menu-driven program, Pascal, public domain software, run-time version, shareware, SmallTalk, software, and vaporware

- *Spreadsheets*: absolute cell reference, active cell, automatic recalculation, built-in function, cell, cell address, cell pointer, cell protection, constant, Edit mode, entry line, forecasting, formula, key variable, label, macro, mixed cell reference, model, range, range expression, range name, recalculation method, relative cell reference, spreadsheet program, value, what-if analysis, worksheet, and worksheet window

- *Systems and system vendors*: clone, closed bus system, compatibility, desktop computer, hardware, hardware platform, high end, home computer, laptop computer, low end, mainframe, microcomputer, minicomputer, multiuser system, open architecture, open bus system, personal computer, portable computer, and professional workstation

- *User interface and windowing systems*: application program interface, graphical user interface (GUI), mouse, pull-down menu, scroll bar/scroll box, user interface, window, and windowing environment

- *Word processing*: attribute, base font, block, block move, boilerplate, document base font, document format, embedded formatting command, emphasis, forced page break, format, hanging indent, hard space, hidden codes, indentation, initial base font, Insert

mode, justification, leading, mail merge, off-screen
formatting, on-screen formatting, Overtype mode,
proportional spacing, scroll, selection, soft page break,
soft return, style sheet, what-you-see-is-what-you-get
(WYSIWYG), word processing, word processing program, and word wrap

**100% column graph**  See *one hundred percent column graph*.

**1-2-3**  See *Lotus 1-2-3*.

**3-D graph**  See *three-dimensional graph*.

**3-D spreadsheet program**  See *three-dimensional spreadsheet*.

**3 1/2-inch disk**  A floppy disk originally developed by Sony Corporation and used as a secondary storage medium for personal computers. The magnetic disk is enclosed in a hard plastic case.

Introduced to personal computing by the Apple Macintosh computer and later used in IBM's Personal System/2 machines, 3 1/2-inch disks represent a significant improvement over 5 1/4-inch floppies, which are susceptible to fingerprint damage because of the open access hole. Unlike their larger predecessors, 3 1/2-inch disks cover the access holes with an aluminum gate, which the disk drive opens only after you insert the disk. 3 1/2-inch disks also are easier to write-protect; instead of covering up a notch hole with a piece of tape, you move a little plastic lever on the back of the disk.

Under MS-DOS, 3 1/2-inch disk drives offer storage capacities of 720K (double density) or 1.44M (high density). MS-DOS 3.2 began supporting the 720K disks, and MS-DOS 3.3 began supporting the 1.44M disks. Macintosh computers format 3 1/2-inch disks with a storage capacity of 800K (double density) or 1.4M (high density).

If your IBM PC–compatible computer has 3 1/2-inch disk drives, specify 3 1/2-inch disks when purchasing software. Ordinarily, software publishers distribute their products on 5 1/4-inch disks, but 3 1/2-inch disks often are made available—if you ask for them. In some cases, the only way you can get 3 1/2-inch disks from a software publisher is to send in a coupon, but some companies are faster than others in sending the 3 1/2-inch disks to you. Because computers with 3 1/2-inch disk drives prevent you from exchanging data with colleagues who have 5 1/4-inch drives, many computers are sold with a 5 1/4-inch drive and a 3 1/2-inch drive. Organizations find that having such a computer around the office is convenient.

**4th Dimension** A relational database program developed by Acius, Inc., for Macintosh computers.

A sophisticated product with networking capabilities, 4th Dimension is of special interest to organizations with large mainframe databases. A special version of Oracle, a connectivity platform, enables 4th Dimension to search Oracle, DB2, and SQL databases. See *connectivity platform* and *ORACLE*.

**5 1/4-inch disk** A floppy disk enclosed in a flexible plastic envelope and used as a secondary storage medium for personal computers. Synonymous with *minifloppy*.

The most widely used secondary storage technology medium in personal computing, 5 1/4-inch disks are inexpensive and used as a distribution medium for commercial software.

 The open access hole of 5 1/4-inch disks is an invitation for fingerprints, which can make the disk unreadable. Handle 5 1/4-inch disks with caution, and when you are not using them, store them in the protective envelope.

**8-bit computer** A computer that uses a central processing unit (CPU) with an 8-bit data bus and processes one byte (eight bits) of information at a time.

An 8-bit computer represents the minimal configuration of computing equipment; in binary numbers, eight bits represent all letters of the alphabet and the numbers 0 through 9. The first microprocessors used in personal computers, such as the MOS Technology 6502, Intel 8080, and Zilog Z-80, found their way into 8-bit computers such as the Apple II, the MSAI 8080, and the Commodore 64.

Millions of these computers are still in use for educational and home-computing applications, but the best business and professional software is available for 16-bit and 32-bit personal computers such as the IBM Personal Computer and the Apple Macintosh. See *central processing unit (CPU)*, *CP/M*, *data bus*, and *microprocessor*.

**8-bit video adapter**   A color video adapter that can display 256 colors simultaneously. See *video adapter*.

**16-bit computer**   A computer that uses a central processing unit (CPU) with a 16-bit data bus and processes two bytes (16 bits) of information at a time.

 Many computers, such as the original IBM Personal Computer and IBM Personal Computer XT and compatibles, which are often described as 16-bit computers, do not use a true 16-bit structure. These machines use the Intel 8088, which is technologically outmoded. The 8088 can process two bytes at a time internally, but the external data bus is only eight bits wide. IBM chose to use the Intel 8088 to take advantage of the many inexpensive, off-the-shelf peripherals developed for 8-bit computers. The IBM Personal Computer AT, introduced in 1984, used a microprocessor with a true 16-bit structure; the data bus that extends beyond the microprocessor also is 16 bits wide. To run Microsoft Windows, you are wise to purchase a computer with an Intel 80386 (or more recent) microprocessor. See *Intel 8088*, *Intel 8086*, *Intel 80286*, *Intel 80386DX*, and *Intel 80386SX*.

**24-bit video adapter**   A Macintosh color video adapter that can display more than 16 million colors simultaneously—from 216 to 16,777,216 colors. With a 24-bit video card and monitor, a personal computer can display beautiful, photographic-quality images on-screen. A 24-bit video card and full-color monitor, however, can add as much as $7,000 to the cost of a Macintosh system.

**32-bit computer**   A computer that uses a central processing unit (CPU) with a 32-bit data bus and processes four bytes (32 bits) of information at a time.

Personal computers advertised as 32-bit machines, such as the Macintosh Plus, the Macintosh SE, and IBM PC compatibles based on the 80386SX microprocessor, are not true 32-bit computers. These computers use microprocessors (such as the Motorola 68000 and Intel 80386SX) that can process four bytes at a time internally, but the external data bus is only 16 bits wide. The designers of these machines chose the external 16-bit data bus so that they could take advantage of inexpensive, off-the-shelf peripherals developed for 16-bit computers. True 32-bit microprocessors, such as the Motorola 68030 and the Intel 80386DX, use a true 32-bit data bus and 32-bit peripherals, and they cost slightly more than computers that do not extend the 32-bit structure beyond the bounds of the microprocessor. See *Intel 80386DX*, *Intel 80386SX*, *Intel 80486DX*, *Intel 80486SX*, *Motorola 68000*, *Motorola 68020*, *Motorola 68030*, and *Motorola 68040*.

**286**   See *Intel 80286*.

**386DX**   See *Intel 80386DX*.

**386 Enhanced mode**   An operating mode of Microsoft Windows that takes full advantage of the technical capabilities of Intel 80386 and later microprocessors (such as multitasking, virtual memory, and Protected mode). To use the 386 Enhanced mode, your computer must have an 80386 or higher microprocessor and at least 2M of random-access memory (RAM).

The Intel 8088 and 8086 microprocessors, employed in the earliest IBM PCs and compatibles, run DOS programs using a direct memory-addressing scheme called *real mode*. In real mode, programs have direct access to actual memory locations. This memory access technique is straightforward, but it causes problems when you try to run more than one program at a time. In real mode, nothing prevents a poorly designed program from invading another program's memory space, resulting in a system crash and lost work. In addition, the 1M RAM limit of these chips, coupled with a DOS design decision that limits to 640K the RAM accessible to programs, has proven insufficient.

The Intel 80386 microprocessor introduced several technical improvements that directly tackled these problems. For compatibility, an 80386 can run in real mode, with the attendant 640K RAM limit and the possibility of memory conflicts. But the 80386 also offers protected mode. In protected mode, the 80386 can address far more than 1M of memory directly—up to 4 gigabytes, in fact—far more than you can install in any PC. The chip also is capable of simulating more than one 8086 "machine" in this vast, undifferentiated ocean of RAM. These machines, called *virtual machines*, are protected from one another, preventing memory conflicts.

Running a DOS program in the protected mode of an 80386 computer requires software to manage the memory. This software stands between the computer and DOS programs, which try to address memory and peripherals directly. Like a traffic policeman, this software—called a *memory-management program*—channels DOS programs into their own 640K virtual machines, where they execute happily without interfering with other programs. Many memory-management programs are available for 80386 and 80486 computers, but by far the most popular is Microsoft Windows. Windows is much more than a memory-management program; it's a complete application program interface for personal computing. And its memory-management capabilities have given DOS a new lease on life.

Windows doesn't automatically use protected mode in 80386 and higher machines. To run in 386 Enhanced mode, which switches on the microprocessor's protected mode, your system must have at least 2M of RAM installed; you need more RAM (at least 4M) to take full advantage of multitasking. Because each DOS program is able to run in its own virtual machine, Windows is capable of true multitasking in 386 Enhanced mode (as opposed to the pseudo-multitasking characteristic of Windows' Standard mode and the Mac's Multifinder, which are capable of loading several programs at once but not of running more than one at a time).

In 386 Enhanced mode, Windows also takes advantage of the 80386 microprocessor's virtual memory capabilities. Virtual memory is a way of extending RAM by configuring part of the hard disk as if it were RAM. Most DOS applications swap program instructions and data back and forth from disk rather than keeping them in memory. For personal computing, the 80386 has pioneered the implementation of virtual memory at the system level, rather than letting each program worry about virtual memory individually. As far as the memory management software is concerned, an unlimited amount of RAM in which to run programs appears to be available; however, disks are significantly slower than RAM. If you frequently run more than one program with Windows, you would be wise to increase the amount of extended memory in your computer. See *extended memory, memory-management program, Microsoft Windows, multiple program loading, multitasking, protected mode, random-access memory (RAM)*, and *real mode*.

**386SX**   See *Intel 80386SX*.

**486DX**   See *Intel 80486DX*.

**486SX**   See *Intel 80486SX*.

**8086**   See *Intel 8086*.

**8088**   See *Intel 8088*.

**8514/A**   Originally intended for professional graphics workstations, an IBM video standard that offers a high-resolution display (1,024 pixels horizontally by 768 lines vertically).

The earliest of IBM's high-resolution video standards, 8514/A failed to attract much of a market, due to IBM's choice of interlacing technology to achieve high resolution. Interlacing is a display technique in which the monitor's electron gun draws only half the horizontal lines on each pass, drawing the rest of them on the next pass. For this reason, interlaced monitors require phosphorescent materials that remain illuminated longer than those used in non-interlaced monitors. The persistence causes screen flicker when images change quickly. Flicker is an undesirable quality in a monitor.

 If you're looking for a high-resolution video system, choose an Extended VGA or Super VGA video card (1,024 by 768 resolution) and a non-interlaced monitor. See *flicker, non-interlaced monitor,* and *Super VGA.*

**68000**   See *Motorola 68000.*

**68020**   See *Motorola 68020.*

**68030**   See *Motorola 68030.*

**68040**   See *Motorola 68040.*

**@function**   See *built-in function.*

**A-B roll editing**   In multimedia, a method for creating a master edited videotape by directing selected portions of video signals from two video sources (VCRs or camcorders) to a destination recording device, usually a VCR.

**abandon**   To clear a document, spreadsheet, or other work from the computer's memory without saving it to disk. The work is irretrievably lost.

**abort**   To cancel, or terminate, a program, command, or procedure while it is in progress.

**Abs key**   In Lotus 1-2-3, the F4 function key, which cycles a cell reference through four possible combinations: an absolute cell reference ($A$1), two types of mixed cell references ($A1 and A$1), and a relative cell reference (A1). See *absolute cell reference*, *mixed cell reference*, and *relative cell reference*.

**absolute cell reference**   A spreadsheet cell reference that does not adjust when you copy a formula.

Use an absolute cell reference to keep the reference the same when you copy it. For example, the following Lotus 1-2-3 formula contains a relative cell reference (B12) and an absolute cell reference ($A$6). The formula tells 1-2-3 to multiply B12 by the contents of cell $A$6 and place the result in the current cell:

    +B12*$A$6

When you copy this formula to the next row down and the next column to the right, 1-2-3 changes the formula to +C13*$A$6. The relative cell reference is adjusted, but the absolute cell reference stays the same.

Use absolute cell references to establish
a fixed place for key variables for your
worksheet. A key variable is a constant, such
as a tax rate. See *key variable*, *low-level
format*, and *relative cell reference*.

**absolute value**   The magnitude of a number, regardless of
its algebraic sign (positive or negative), equal to the
positive value of a number. The absolute value of –357,
for example, is 357. In Lotus 1-2-3 and similar spreadsheet programs, the @ABS built-in function returns the
absolute value of a number.

**accelerator board**   An adapter containing a microprocessor
faster or more advanced than the one that powers your
computer. If you have a Macintosh based on the
Motorola 68000 chip, for example, you can purchase
an accelerator board containing the faster 68030 chip.
If you have an IBM PC–compatible computer based on
the Intel 8088 microprocessor, you can purchase an
accelerator board containing the faster 80286 or 80386
microprocessor.

 Adding an accelerator board can speed a
sluggish computer, but the speed gains are
most apparent for tasks carried out within
the microprocessor, such as sorting or calculating. An accelerator board does little to improve
the speed of disk-related operations, such as retrieving
a file. If you frequently use a program (such as a database program) that makes heavy use of the disk drive,
a faster hard disk probably leads to a more noticeable
speed improvement than an accelerator board. If you
are using an IBM PC–compatible computer based on
the Intel 8088 chip, you cannot use the faster drives
designed for the 16-bit data bus of the AT-class computers. Therefore, 8088 users are advised to forget accelerator boards—save your money for an 80386-based
computer. See *hard disk*.

**accent**   A mark that forms one of the accented characters of many languages other than English. The following accents are used frequently:

| ´ Acute | ˘ Breve | ç Cedilla |
|---------|---------|-----------|
| ^ Circumflex | ¨ Diaeresis | ` Grave |
| ¯ Macron | ~ Tilde | ¨ Umlaut |

You enter accents in two ways. First, you can use a dead key, which enters the accent character without advancing the cursor to the next character. You then press the letter, and the two keystrokes form the ac-cented character. Second, you can use a key code to enter the character and the accent at the same time. On a Macintosh computer, you can use both techniques. To enter the vowel *e* with an acute accent, you press Option-E (a dead key that enters an acute accent char-acter) and then press the E key; the accented character (é) appears.

**access**   To retrieve data or program instructions from a secondary storage device or some other on-line com-puter device.

To the dismay of English teachers everywhere, the noun *access* is now used as a verb, as in "I cannot access that file." English usage authorities usually disparage the conversion of nouns into verbs, but this usage is sufficiently common to be included in a dictio-nary such as this one.

**access arm**   In a disk drive, the mechanical device that moves the magnetic read/write heads back and forth across the surface of the disk.

Without an access arm, the disk drive would act like a record player's arm as it moves sequentially along the grooves of an LP record and would take a long time to reach information stored away from the head's current location. See *random access* and *sequential access*.

**access code**   An identification number or password you use to gain access to a computer system.

**access hole**   An opening in a floppy disk's case. The access hole enables the disk drive's read/write head to make contact with the surface of the disk. Only when this contact occurs can the drive perform read/write operations, in which the computer retrieves information from or stores new information on the disk.

**access mechanism**   In a disk drive, the mechanism used for moving the read/write head over the surface of the disk so that data can be accessed. Synonymous with *actuator*. See *disk drive* and *read/write head*.

**access privileges**   In a local area network, the ability to open and modify directories, files, and programs located on another computer. In AppleTalk and other peer-to-peer (democratic) networks, access privileges are granted by the owner of the computer resources, and determine who can access this information and what they can do with it. See *local area network (LAN)*.

**Access System menu**   In Lotus 1-2-3, the menu that appears when you type the word *lotus* at the DOS prompt. This menu enables you to start Lotus 1-2-3, install the program, or choose the Translate option (see fig. A.1).

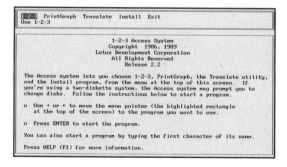

**Fig. A.1.** The Access System menu of Lotus 1-2-3.

You can bypass the Access System menu by typing *123* at the DOS prompt.

**access time**   The time that elapses between the time the operating system issues an order for data retrieval and the time the data is ready for transfer from the disk.

For hard disks, access times usually are measured in microseconds (ms). Typical access times for personal computer hard disks range between 9 ms (fast) and 100 ms (slow). For disk-intensive applications like database management programs or book-length word processing projects, the difference between a fast and slow disk drive is noticeable to the user. The access time of a disk drive is determined by the following: seek time (the time the disk heads take to move to the correct track), settle time (the time the heads take to settle down after reaching the correct track), and latency (the time required for the correct sector to swing around under the head).

If you are using an IBM PC–compatible computer based on an 80286, 80386, or 80486 microprocessor, make sure that the hard disk's access time is 28 ms or better. When you run these computers under MS-DOS, much of the speed improvement over earlier 8088-based machines is attributable to the faster hard disk. See *hard disk* and *operating system*.

**accounting package**   A set of personal computer programs intended to help a small-business owner automate a firm's accounting functions.

Accounting packages do not comprise a large share of the total market for personal computer software for a couple of reasons. First, most small-business owners have none of the accounting knowledge required to use most available programs and therefore prefer to leave the accounting to a professional. Second, using these programs without a point-of-sale system that automatically posts receipts to the ledgers is too tedious. You would have to type all the figures over again at the end of the day.

Despite these drawbacks, you may have good reasons to use a simple accounting program. Even if you don't perform all accounting functions yourself, your accountant needs to see a ledger showing all your business transactions. If some of these transactions can be posted automatically to a computer ledger from PCs that handle sales invoices and other transactions, you have simplified your life immensely. See *integrated accounting package* and *modular accounting package*.

**accumulator**    A temporary storage location in a central processing unit (CPU). The accumulator holds intermediary values during a computation, or it stores input/output information.

Many processing operations require an accumulator. Computer multiplication, for example, frequently is done by a series of additions; the accumulator holds the intermediate values until the process is completed. See *central processing unit (CPU)*.

**accuracy**    The correctness of a measurement, unlike precision (the number of decimal places to which the accuracy is computed).

A computer-based statistical analysis may report, for instance, that a device is likely to operate for 8,025 hours without failure, with an error margin of +25 and –25 hours. Such a measurement is accurate, but not precise.

**acoustical sound enclosure**    A sound insulation cabinet designed to accommodate noisy impact printers and reduce the noise such printers release into the environment. See *impact printer*.

**acoustic coupler**    A modem with cups that fit around the earpiece and mouthpiece of a standard telephone headset. The cups contain a microphone and a speaker that convert the computer's digital signals into sound, and vice versa. With the increasing use of modular telephone connections, direct-connect modems have supplanted acoustic modems in general use. See *direct-connect modem* and *modem*.

**acronym**  A word formed by joining the first letters (sometimes other letters) of a series of words, such as BASIC (Beginners' All-Purpose Symbolic Instruction Code) and WYSIWYG (what-you-see-is-what-you-get).

**active area**  In a Lotus 1-2-3 worksheet, the area bounded by cell A1 and the lowest rightmost cell containing data.

**active cell**  In a spreadsheet, the cell in which the cursor currently is positioned. Synonymous with *current cell*.

**active database**  In database management, the database file currently in use and present in random-access memory (RAM).

**active file**  The worksheet currently in memory when working with Lotus 1-2-3 and other spreadsheet programs.

Versions of Lotus 1-2-3 before Release 2.2 do not warn you when you leave the active file without saving your work. Lotus 1-2-3 does not update the disk file until you issue the File Save command. If you quit 1-2-3 without saving your work, the file on disk remains unchanged.

In some cases, leaving the file unchanged is desirable. For example, many users like to perform what-if analyses, which involve entering hypothetical values as the key variables of the worksheet. You don't want to save these changes because the data is imaginary. Early versions of Lotus 1-2-3 and other spreadsheet programs left the decision of whether to save a session's changes to the user. Most users, however, want to be reminded when they are about to lose changes. Versions of Lotus since Release 2.2, therefore, detect changes and warn you at the end of a session that you are about to lose those changes. See *what-if analysis*.

**active index**   In database management programs, the index file currently being used to determine the order in which data records are displayed on-screen. See *index*.

**active sensing**   In multimedia, a MIDI message that commands a device to monitor its channels to determine whether messages occur on the channels within a predetermined maximum time (called a *time window*). See *Musical Instrument Digital Interface (MIDI)*.

**active window**   In an application program or operating system that displays multiple windows, the window in which the cursor is positioned and text appears when you type.

Early windowing environments tiled the windows so that none overlapped, but too often the windows were too small for convenient use. In more recent windowing applications, the active window floats above the others (see fig. A.2).

**Fig. A.2.** An active window (Windows Applications) superimposed on other windows.

  In Microsoft Windows, the color of the active window's title bar is different from the other windows' title bars. Similarly, the color of the active icon's label is different from the other icons' labels. See *windowing environment*.

**activity light**   A small red or yellow light on the computer's front panel that signals when a disk drive is reading or writing data.

**actuator**   See *access mechanism*.

**Ada**   A high-level programming language developed by the U.S. Department of Defense and required for all military programming applications.

Named for Lady Augusta Ada Byron, a friend of Charles Babbage and arguably the world's first female computer scientist, the Ada language stems from the military's need for a standard computer language capable of real-time process control (the operation of a highly complex device like a missile). In the early 1970s, more than 400 languages were being used to develop systems acquired by the military, and the expense of maintaining so many incompatible systems was mounting. A committee was appointed to create a new standard language, and the final specification was published in 1980.

With roots in Pascal and Modula-2, Ada uses the principles of structured programming, such as program modules that can be compiled separately (like those of Modula-2). Ada programs are designed to be highly readable so that they are easier to maintain.

Ada has attracted a great deal of criticism from computer scientists who believe that no single programming language can succeed at all tasks. Ada is a highly structured language for general-purpose programming and a specialized language for real-time process control. As a result, Ada is an extremely large language; the compiler requires several hundreds of thousands of code lines. To critics, Ada's unmanageable size is an invitation to disaster because large programs are likely to contain errors that cannot be detected. However, the language's success is ensured. The U.S. Department of Defense requires contractors to use Ada or demonstrate why they cannot use the language.

Ada is now available for personal computers, but if you decide to learn the language,
make sure that you choose a compiler that
the Department of Defense has certified.
This agency rigidly controls the Ada standard and
accepts no code that has not been created by a compiler that meets the department's standards. See
*compiler, Modula-2, Pascal, real time*, and *structured
programming*.

**adapter**   A circuit board that plugs into a computer's expansion bus and gives the computer additional capabilities.

Popular adapters for personal computers include display adapters that produce video output; memory
expansion adapters; input/output adapters that provide
the computer with serial ports, parallel ports, and game
ports; internal modems; and clock/calendar boards.
Increasingly, this circuitry is being included on the
motherboard of personal computer systems. The
motherboard of IBM's PS/2 computer, for example,
includes ports and a VGA display adapter for high-
resolution video output. See *circuit board, clock/
calendar board, expansion bus, internal modem,
motherboard, open bus system, parallel port, serial
port*, and *video adapter*.

**adapter segment**   See *upper memory area*.

**Adaptive Differential Pulse Code Modulation (ADPCM)**
In multimedia, a method of digital waveform sampling
where the difference between successive samples is
encoded rather than their actual values. This technique
provides higher fidelity sound with fewer bits of resolution than conventional pulse code modulation (PCM)
encoding techniques. Using ADPCM, you can increase
the quantity of audio information that can be stored on
a single compact disk from 1 hour to about 16 hours.
ADPCM is the storage technique used by CD-ROM XA
and CD-I disks. See *CD-I, CD-ROM XA,* and *pulse code
modulation (PCM)*.

**ADB**   See *Apple Desktop Bus.*

**add-in program**   An accessory or utility program designed to work with and extend the capabilities of an application program.

A popular add-in program for Lotus 1-2-3 is Allways (Funk Software), which adds desktop publishing features to 1-2-3's report capabilities. Allways prints Lotus spreadsheets with a variety of fonts, lines, shadings, and other formatting features, such as boldface and underline. See *Allways* and *ORACLE.*

**address**   A computer system location identified by a name, number, or code label. The address can be specified by the user or by a program. See *memory address.*

**address bus**   An internal electronic channel from the microprocessor to random-access memory (RAM), along which the addresses of memory storage locations are transmitted.

The address bus is necessary so that the microprocessor can locate program instructions and data stored in memory. Like a post office box, each memory location has a distinct number or address; the address bus provides the means by which every location in the memory can be activated independently.

 The width of the address bus determines the maximum size of the computer's main memory because the number of wires in the address bus determines the maximum number of possible memory locations. Computers use binary numbers internally, and because address information is sent along the address bus in parallel (one number per lane of the freeway), the address bus needs many wires to handle a big binary number. Early IBM personal computers used address buses 20 bits wide (20 wires); these computers could identify and use a maximum of $2^{20}$ memory locations (1M of RAM). With an address bus width of 24 bits, more recent IBM PC–compatible computers can address a maximum of 16M of RAM. However, the standard operating system of IBM PC–compatible computers, DOS, cannot use more than 640K of RAM. See *bus*, *expanded memory*, *extended memory*, *Microsoft Windows*, and *Operating System/2 (OS/2)*.

**ADM3A**   A terminal developed by Lear Siegler and used in the late 1970s and early 1980s. The ADM3A is included in the list of terminals that communications programs can emulate. See *communications program*, *terminal*, and *terminal emulation*.

**Adobe Illustrator**   A professional illustration program for Macintosh and IBM PC–compatible computers. Adobe Illustrator produces object-oriented images and prints them on PostScript laser printers.

Introduced in 1987, this highly regarded program went several steps beyond existing painting and drawing programs, such as MacPaint and MacDraw, by offering PostScript output, Bézier curves, an autotrace tool, precision coding for color printing, and many other features for professional illustration. See *autotrace*, *Bézier curve*, *Freehand*, *object-oriented graphic*, and *PostScript*.

**Adobe PostScript**   See *PostScript*.

**Adobe Type Manager (ATM)**   For Macintosh computers, a utility program that displays outline fonts without distortion.

The Macintosh normally uses bit-mapped fonts for the screen display. For desktop publishing applications, however, this display technique has drawbacks. If you try to display a font in a size not matched by a complete set of bit-mapped characters in the System Folder, you see grossly distorted characters on-screen. Adobe Type Manager tackles this problem by using outline font technology to display fonts. Because outline fonts are constructed from mathematical formulas, you can scale them to any size without distorting them.

Adobe Type Manager has its drawbacks.
The program affects the appearance of only
Adobe fonts. Even Adobe fonts are not
affected unless you have in the System
Folder a special screen-display file for each font you
want to display. The program comes with Times Roman
and Helvetica; you must purchase an expensive add-in
program to obtain screen fonts for the rest of the typefaces usually included with PostScript laser printers.

**ADPCM**   See *Adaptive Differential Pulse Code Modulation*.

**Advanced Run-Length Limited (ARLL)**   A method of
storing and retrieving information on a hard disk that
increases the density of Run-Length Limited (RLL)
storage by more than 25 percent and offers a faster
data-transfer rate (9 megabits per second). See *data-
encoding scheme* and *Run-Length Limited (RLL)*.

**aftermarket**   The market for software and peripherals
created by the sale of large numbers of a specific brand
of computer.

**agate**   A 5.5-point type size frequently used in newspaper
classified advertising but too small for most other uses.

**aggregate function**   In database management programs,
a command that performs arithmetic operations on all
of a field's values in all the records within a database or
in one view of the database. dBASE, for example, performs the following aggregate functions:

| Function | Description |
| --- | --- |
| Average | Computes the arithmetic mean of the values |
| Sum | Adds all the values |
| Minimum | Finds the smallest value |
| Maximum | Finds the largest value |
| Count | Counts the number of records that meet the specified criteria |

**aggregate operator**   In a database management program, a
command that instructs the program to perform an
aggregate function.

Suppose that you are the owner of a video tape rental
store and want to know how many tapes are more than
two weeks late. Because the date is May 19, you want
to know how many rentals were due on or before
May 5 (less than 05/06/93). The following dBASE
expression finds the information:

```
COUNT FOR due_date <05/06/93
```

You will see a response such as

```
2 records
```

See *aggregate function*.

**AI**   See *artificial intelligence*.

**AIX**   An IBM version of the UNIX operating system. AIX
runs on PS/2 computers equipped with the Intel 80386
microprocessor, IBM workstations, minicomputers, and
mainframes.

**Aldus PageMaker**   See *PageMaker*.

**alert box**   In a graphical user interface, a cautionary window
that appears on-screen to warn you that the command
you have given may result in lost work or other errors
(see fig. A.3).

**algorithm**   A specific set of well-defined, simple mathematical and logical procedures that can be followed to solve
a problem in a finite number of steps.

An algorithm is a recipe for finding the right answer to
a difficult problem by breaking down the problem into
simple, easy steps. The steps allow you to perform the
action successfully, even though you do not fully understand what you are doing. You already have learned
many algorithms—for example, the ones you learned
for grade-school arithmetic. You use algorithms every
day when following recipes, mowing the lawn, placing
long-distance telephone calls, or packing grocery bags.

For example, the steps you take to start a weed trimmer
probably include manipulating the machine's choke and

**algorithm** 22

throttle, even though you may have no idea exactly what these parts do or why you manipulate them the way you do. Algorithms, in short, provide a way to encode competence and distribute it throughout society.

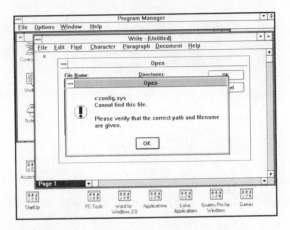

**Fig. A.3.** An alert box.

Not every list of instructions constitutes an algorithm, however. An algorithm must satisfy the following three basic criteria:

- The list of instructions must be finite and short enough that you can complete them.

- Each instruction must be executable; you must be able to perform the actions or operations named.

- The algorithm must enable execution to end at some point.

The British logician Alan Turing proved that any mathematical or logical problem capable of a solution, and for which a solution is known to exist, can be solved by the algorithmic approach. Every known solvable problem can be attacked by a computer; the solution is a matter of finding the correct algorithm.

The computer programs you use every day embody one or more algorithms. Someone, somewhere, had to sit down and puzzle through the problem of how to get that font to appear on-screen and print with typographical beauty on your laser printer. At one time, the problem was unsolved, and many people thought that it never would be solved. A good deal of thought and work went into expressing the procedure as a computer-readable algorithm.

**alias**    A secondary or symbolic name for a file or computer device. In a spreadsheet, for example, a range name, such as *Income*, is an alias for a range, such as A3..K3. In computer networks, group aliases provide a handy way to send a message to two or more people simultaneously.

 With the Macintosh System 7 software, you can create aliases for commonly accessed program and document icons. If you drag an alias to the Apple Menu Items folder within the System Folder, the alias appears on the Apple pull-down menu, allowing fast access to this item.

**aliasing**    In computer graphics, the undesirable jagged or stair-stepped appearance of diagonal lines in computer-generated graphic images. Synonymous with the *jaggies*. See *antialiasing*.

**alignment**    In personal computing, the adjustment of tolerances within a disk drive's mechanism so that read/write operations occur without error. In word processing, the horizontal arrangement of lines on the page with respect to the left and right margins (flush left, centered, flush right, or justified).

 Because a jolt can knock a floppy disk drive out of alignment, be careful not to drop or knock your computer around when moving the machine. A drive that is slightly out of alignment may have trouble reading floppy disks, especially those formatted by a different computer. If your machine cannot read an important floppy disk, don't assume that the disk is bad—possibly another computer can read the disk.

**allocate**   To reserve memory that is sufficient for a program's application. For example, Microsoft Word 5.0
for the Macintosh requires 1M of memory space (2M if
you want to use the program's grammar-checking
capabilities).

 Macintosh users should make sure that the
System has allocated enough memory for
each program. To find out how much
memory has been allocated for a specific
program, switch to the Finder and highlight the
program's icon. Then choose Get Info from the File
menu. You'll see the program's Info dialog box, which
shows the suggested memory size and the current
memory allocation. With some programs, you get better performance, fewer crashes, and more available
features when you increase the suggested memory
allocation by 256K or 512K.

**all points addressable (APA) graphic**   See *bit-mapped
graphic*.

**Allways**   A Lotus 1-2-3 add-in program (Funk Software, Inc.)
that adds desktop publishing capabilities to the popular spreadsheet program's report functions.

**alphanumeric characters**   Any character you can type,
including upper- and lowercase letters A through Z,
numbers 0 through 9, punctuation marks, and special
keyboard symbols. See *data type*.

**alpha test**   The first stage in the testing of computer software before commercial release. Alpha tests usually are
conducted by the software publisher. Later tests, called
*beta tests*, are conducted by users. See *beta test*.

**Alt key**   On IBM PC–compatible keyboards, a key that
programs frequently use in combination with other
keys to generate commands. In Microsoft Word, for
example, pressing Alt-B boldfaces the selected text.

**ALU**   See *arithmetic logic unit*.

**Am386**   A 32-bit microprocessor developed by Advanced
Micro Devices that is 100 percent compatible with the

Intel 80386DX microprocessor. A version of the chip designed for portable computers, the Am386DXL, uses only one-third the power required to fuel the 80386 in the 20MHz and 25MHz versions and two-thirds the power in the 33MHz version. The microprocessor offers advantages for laptop and notebook computers. See *Intel 80386DX*.

**American National Standards Institute (ANSI)**   An organization devoted to the development of voluntary standards that will enhance the productivity and international competitiveness of American industrial enterprises. ANSI committees have developed standard versions of computer languages such as COBOL and FORTRAN.

**American Standard Code for Information Interchange**   See *ASCII*.

**Amiga**   A personal computer developed by Commodore International and based on the Motorola 68000 microprocessor.

The Amiga is used for home computing applications. With outstanding color graphics and multichannel stereo sound, the Amiga is considered by some to be the computer of choice for playing computer games and composing music. The machine has found little acceptance as a business computer, however, because of the lack of business software for the machine.

The Amiga is not compatible with the Macintosh computer, which uses the same microprocessor but a different operating system. See *Musical Instrument Digital Interface (MIDI)*.

**Ami Pro**   A full-featured professional word processing program developed for Microsoft Windows and marketed by Lotus Development Corporation. With its many features that enhance the integration of text and graphics, Ami Pro is suitable for many desktop publishing applications.

**ampersand**   A character (&) sometimes used in place of the English *and*; originally a ligature of *et*, which is Latin for *and*.

**analog**   A form of measurement or representation in which an indicator is varied continuously, often to reflect ongoing changes in the phenomenon being measured or represented.

Analog representation is used, for example, in a thermometer: the hotter the patient becomes, the higher the mercury rises. Analog techniques also are used for the reproduction of music in standard LP records and audio cassettes. See *digital*.

**analog computer**   A computer that draws a comparison, or analogy, between the computer representation and the object being represented, making the object easy to measure. Analog computation is used widely in laboratory settings to monitor ongoing, continuous changes and to record these changes in charts or graphs. See *digital computer*.

**analog device**   A computer peripheral that handles information in continuously variable quantities rather than digitizing the information into discrete, digital representations. An analog monitor, for example, can display thousands of colors with smooth, continuous gradations.

**analog/digital converter**   An adapter that enables a digital computer (such as an IBM Personal Computer) to accept analog input from laboratory instruments. Analog/digital converters are frequently used for the real-time monitoring of temperature, movement, and other continuously varied conditions. See *analog*, *digital*, and *real time*.

**analogical reasoning**   A form of understanding in which the dynamics of something in the real world—such as the aerodynamics of a proposed airplane—are understood by building a model and exploring its behavior. One of the computer's greatest contributions has been to lower the cost (and increase the convenience) of analogical reasoning.

Analogic reasoning was common before the computer, as shown by the use of airplane models in wind tunnels. Because computers greatly lower the cost of analogical

reasoning, computers have led to an unprecedented
explosion of analogical discovery—and, arguably, just
in time. Scientists increasingly concede that most of the
phenomena in the universe are not characterized by
the kind of simple, f=ma relationships that distinguish
the greatest discoveries of physics; in contrast, complex
systems—the human immune system, human societies,
ecologies, the world's weather, and the interaction of
large-scale cosmological structures—are characterized
by nonlinear or chaotic behavior, which cannot be
described by a simple equation. Such systems cannot
be understood through any means other than analogical reasoning. By allowing humanity to create analogical models of unprecedented scope, computers have
enabled a new kind of science: a science of complexity.

**analog monitor**   A monitor that accepts a continuously
varied video input signal and consequently can display
a continuous range and infinite number of colors. In
contrast, a digital monitor can display only a finite
number of colors. EGA monitors are digital and VGA
monitors are analog, which is why VGA monitors have all
but driven EGA technology out of the marketplace. Most
analog monitors are designed to accept input signals at
a precise frequency; however, developments in display
adapter technology ensure that, in the future, higher
frequencies will be required to carry higher-resolution
images to the monitor (the higher the frequency, the
greater the on-screen resolution). For this reason,
multisynch monitors have been developed that automatically adjust themselves to the incoming frequency.

If you're shopping for a Windows system,
don't buy an outmoded EGA adapter and
monitor. Although most Windows applications support EGA technology, VGA is now
considered the entry-level display technology for
Windows computing. Usually, you can get a VGA
adapter and monitor for just a few dollars more than
their "bargain" EGA counterparts. See *digital monitor,
Enhanced Graphics Adapter (EGA), multisynch monitor,* and *Video Graphics Array (VGA).*

**analog transmission**   A communications scheme that uses a continuous signal varied by amplification. See *broadband* and *digital transmission*.

**analysis**   A method of discovery that proceeds by breaking down a situation or a problem to its component parts and trying to understand how they affect one another. In personal computing, a common form of analysis is sensitivity testing or "what if" analysis using an electronic spreadsheet program. In sensitivity testing, you alter fundamental (key) variables to see how changing these variables affects the outcome of the spreadsheet model.

**analytical graphics**   The preparation of charts and graphs to aid a professional in the interpretation of data.

Many spreadsheet programs' graphs fall into this category: they are useful for clarifying trends in worksheet numbers, but you don't want to show them to the company's stockholders. Presentation graphics packages can accept and enhance graphs created by spreadsheet programs. See *presentation graphics*.

**anchor cell**   In Lotus 1-2-3, the cell in which the pointer is anchored as you press the cursor-movement keys to define a range.

**anchored graphic**   A graph or picture fixed in an absolute position on the page so that text flows around it. See *floating graphic* and *wrap-around type*.

**animation**   The creation of the illusion of movement in a computer program by recording a series of images that show slight incremental changes in one of the displayed objects, and by playing these images back fast enough that the eye perceives smooth movement. See *cell animation* and *MacroMind Director*.

**annotation**   An explanatory note or comment you can insert into a document such as a business report or analytical worksheet. With some applications, you can insert an annotation as an icon that, when clicked by the person who reads the document, opens a separate window that contains the note. Users of Macintosh systems equipped with digital sound and microphones, such as the Macintosh LC II, can add voice annotations to Microsoft Word 5.0 documents; the annotation—a brief voice explanation, in this case—appears in the document as an icon. When the reader double-clicks the icon, the Mac plays back the recording.

 Windows 3.1 users can add comments to the Help documents using the Annotate command on the Edit menu. If you discover something important about the way Windows works, don't scribble a note to yourself on a slip of paper—use the Annotate command instead.

**ANSI**   See *American National Standards Institute*.

**ANSI screen control**   A set of standards developed by the American National Standards Institute (ANSI) to control the display of information on computer screens. See *ANSI.SYS*.

**ANSI.SYS**   In MS-DOS, a configuration file containing instructions needed to display information, following the recommendations of the American National Standards Institute.

 Some programs require that you include the instruction DEVICE=ANSI.SYS in a CONFIG.SYS file, which must be present on the disk you use to start your computer. See *CONFIG.SYS*.

**answer mode**   See *auto-dial/auto-answer modem*.

**answer/originate**   In data communications, the property of a communications device such that the device can receive (answer) and send (originate) messages.

**antialiasing**   The automatic removal or reduction of stair-step distortions in a computer-generated graphic image. See *aliasing*.

**antistatic mat**   A mat or pad placed on or near a computer device. This pad absorbs static electricity, which can damage semiconductor devices if the devices are not properly grounded.

**antivirus program**   See *vaccine*.

**APA graphic**   See *bit-mapped graphic*.

**API**   See *application program interface*.

**APL (A Programming Language)**   A high-level programming language well suited for scientific and mathematical applications.

APL uses Greek letters and requires a display device that can display these letters. Used on IBM mainframes, the language is now available for IBM PC–compatible computers. See *high-level programming language*.

**append**   To add data at the end of a file or a database. In database management, for example, to append a record is to add a new record, which is placed after all existing records (preserving the chronological order of data entry).

**Apple Computer**   A major manufacturer of personal computers, located in Cupertino, CA.

Founded by Steve Wozniak and Steve Jobs in 1976, Apple Computer grew out of the activities of the San Francisco Bay Area hobbyists to become one of the largest corporations in the United States. Wozniak, a member of the Homebrew Computer Club and a Hewlett-Packard engineer, worked with Jobs to develop the Apple I, a hobbyists' computer packaged as a technically challenging kit.

This machine sold far more successfully than they had hoped, and Wozniak and Jobs developed its successor, the Apple II—one of the first complete, ready-to-run personal computer systems made available to the public. Wozniak chose the MOS Technology 6502, an 8-bit microprocessor for the Apple I and II, because this chip was available for significantly less money than the chip most hobbyists preferred, the Intel 8080.

Equipped with sound and color graphics, the Apple II was welcomed not only by home computer hobbyists, but also by educators, and the machine soon became the personal computer of choice for elementary and secondary school applications in computer-assisted instruction.

Featuring an open architecture design, the Apple II demonstrated that such a system can increase its own chances of success by encouraging third-party firms to develop adapter boards and peripherals. By 1979, dozens of firms were manufacturing such equipment, which broadened the computer's range of applications. VisiCalc, the first electronic spreadsheet program, was released for the Apple II, and equipped with this program, thousands of Apple II computers found their way into large and small businesses.

The Apple II's success was followed by what most analysts agree was a major design and manufacturing misstep, the Apple III, released in 1980. The Apple III, which also used the MOS Technology 6502 microprocessor, did not represent a significant technological advance over its predecessor. Worse, the machine was released without proper testing and had serious manufacturing flaws. This machine was not even fully compatible with Apple II software.

Although the manufacturing problems were corrected, the Apple III damaged the company's reputation. Fortunately for the company, Apple II computers continued to sell well in home and educational markets. Apple's failure to develop an innovative computer for business applications, however, created a vacuum in the marketplace, into which IBM stepped with its 1981 Personal Computer, the open architecture design which is reminiscent of the Apple II. Apple could not respond to the IBM PC's challenge, and in the years to follow, its market share eroded as IBM and IBM PC–compatible computers grew in popularity.

Searching for innovative technology, Jobs learned of the remarkable team of computer scientists and electrical engineers assembled at Xerox's Palo Alto Research

Laboratory (PARC). The PARC researchers developed a sophisticated approach to human/computer interaction that includes virtually all the components of a graphical user interface: the use of the mouse as an editing and control device; the representation of computer functions using on-screen icons, pull-down menus, and dialog boxes; the on-screen display of typefaces and graphics; and the use of laser printers for high-quality personal computer output.

Industry analysts, however, believe that Xerox's management did not fully comprehend the significance of the technology the PARC researchers developed, and the company failed to market the technology effectively. Correctly sensing the promise of PARC technology, Jobs lured away several PARC researchers and assigned them to the development of a new business computer, the Lisa.

Released in 1983, the Lisa was a pioneer personal computer that featured a graphical user interface and a set of integrated application programs. Critically acclaimed, the machine (priced in excess of $10,000) was far too expensive for its market, and sales were disappointing.

In 1984, however, Apple released the Macintosh, which for $2,500 offered a significant fraction of Lisa technology at highly competitive prices. Technically innovative in many respects, the Macintosh soon proved to have significant design defects: the machine was equipped originally with only 128K of random-access memory (RAM) and one 400K disk drive, making the machine unsuitable for business applications. In addition, the Mac used a closed architecture, a significant—and unwise—departure from the open architectural principles that Apple had pioneered (and which had contributed strongly to the success of the IBM Personal Computer). As computer industry experience has repeatedly demonstrated, open architecture designs are more likely to succeed because third-party suppliers can develop a rich range of accessories, each appealing to key niche markets.

Subsequently, Jobs recruited John Sculley, formerly the CEO of Pepsi, to head the firm. Internal conflict, partly over the Macintosh and issues regarding the company's direction, resulted in Sculley's expulsion of Jobs from Apple Computer in 1986, and the firm's future seemed uncertain. But help was to come from the unanticipated rise of a new application for computing technology: desktop publishing.

With the release of Aldus PageMaker—the first page layout program for personal computers—and the development of the Apple LaserWriter, Apple's graphical user interface was positioned to place the Macintosh in the forefront of desktop computing. The LaserWriter established the Macintosh as a computer for serious business enterprises.

Subsequent product releases—such as the Macintosh SE with a hard disk—and the open-architecture Macintosh II renewed Apple's fortunes, but the company failed to regain the market share lost to IBM in the early 1980s.

By 1990, however, Apple's focus on sophisticated, high-end desktop publishing systems contributed to a neglect of low-end systems, and as Apple II sales declined, the company waited too long to develop an inexpensive Macintosh for the home and educational markets. Apple lost sales to inexpensive IBM PC–compatible machines. In 1991, Apple corrected this deficiency by releasing the Macintosh Classic and the Macintosh LC, but the budget pricing led to a substantial drop in the company's earnings. The 1992 introduction of the PowerBook notebook computers remedied another serious product deficiency.

Inexpensive Windows systems continue to challenge Apple. IBM PC–compatible computers based on the Intel 80386 and 80486 microprocessors can run Microsoft Windows, which provides a graphical user interface akin to the Macintosh system software. In an attempt to fend off Windows' challenge, Apple sued Microsoft, claiming that Windows infringes on Apple's copyrighted interface technology, but the court battle has yet to be resolved. Industry experts agree that Apple has all but lost its technological edge in the high end of the marketplace, except in the area of sound. Most new Macs come equipped with digital sound capabilities. In 1992, Apple announced the purchase of a voice-recognition algorithm, which will allow future Macintoshes to recognize human speech for command purposes.

Apple's periodic problems make for business headlines and best-selling tell-all books, but the company's achievements should not be forgotten. With its motto of developing computers for the rest of us, Apple has played a leading role in bringing computing technology to people who would not otherwise have access to that technology.

The Macintosh user interface, in particular, is one of the great achievements of U.S. industrial design, and this achievement came during a period that has witnessed the steady erosion of American innovativeness and competitiveness in world markets. See *graphical user interface (GUI)*, *Macintosh*, and *open architecture*.

**Apple Desktop Bus (ADB)**   An interface standard for connecting keyboards, mice, trackballs, and other input devices to Apple's Macintosh SE, Macintosh II, and Macintosh IIGS computers. These computers come with an ADB port capable of a maximum data transfer rate of 4.5 kilobits per second. You can connect up to 16 devices to one ADB port.

**Apple Desktop Interface**   A set of user-interface guidelines, developed by Apple Computer and published by Addison-Wesley, intended to ensure that all Macintosh applications appear and work in similar ways. See *user interface*.

**Apple File Exchange**   A utility program provided with each Macintosh computer that enables Macs equipped with suitable disk drives to exchange data with IBM PC–compatible computers.

**Apple Macintosh**   See *Macintosh*.

**AppleShare**   A network operating system developed by
Apple Computer, Inc. AppleShare transforms a
Macintosh computer into a file server for an AppleTalk
network. The Macintosh being used as the server
cannot be used for other applications; that computer
becomes a "slave" of the network.

After installing AppleShare, you see a virtual device—an
additional hard disk icon on the desktop—which you
can access just as if the drive were present in your
system. See *AppleTalk*, *local area network (LAN)*,
*LocalTalk*, and *virtual device*.

**AppleShare file server**   In an AppleTalk local area network,
a Macintosh computer that runs AppleShare File Server
software so that network users can employ this machine to store and retrieve shared programs and data.
See *local area network (LAN)*.

**AppleTalk**   A local area network standard developed by
Apple Computer, Inc. AppleTalk is capable of linking as
many as 32 Macintosh computers, IBM PC–compatible
computers, and peripherals such as laser printers.
Every Macintosh computer has an AppleTalk port,
through which you can connect the machine to an
AppleTalk network using a bus topology. Most
AppleTalk networks are simple; they link a few
Macintosh computers with a LaserWriter printer.

A significant advantage of AppleTalk is that the network
also can accommodate IBM PC–compatible computers;
several companies manufacture adapters that provide
AppleTalk ports for IBM PC–compatible computers.
Microsoft Mail, an application developed by Microsoft
Corporation, enables you to send electronic mail to all
users of an AppleTalk network, including users of IBM
PC compatibles.

Another advantage of AppleTalk is that almost anyone
can quickly set up an AppleTalk network. In many
offices, AppleTalk networks are used for sharing access
to a laser printer.

AppleTalk also is priced right. Because every Macintosh includes an AppleTalk network port, the only hardware required for an AppleTalk network is connectors and cable. Apple's LocalTalk hardware makes the physical connections among the computers and peripherals. Each device has a LocalTalk connector, a small box containing a transformer that insulates the computer or peripheral from electrical interference and provides plugs for the network interface. The LocalTalk boxes are connected by ordinary telephone wire (called *twisted-pair cable*) with standard modular connectors.

AppleTalk networks are slow compared to high-speed systems like EtherNet. AppleTalk is capable of transmitting up to 320 bits per second, but EtherNet and other networks using network interface cards that connect directly to the computer's high-speed internal bus are capable of speeds of up to 20 million bits per second. However, AppleTalk's simplicity and low cost make it an attractive option for networks of modest size and use.

 If you are considering an AppleTalk installation, you can save money and extend an AppleTalk network's capabilities by using PhoneNet hardware (Farallon Computing, Inc.). After equipping each node with a PhoneNet connector (instead of the LocalTalk connector), you can wire the network by using ordinary telephone cabling, considerably cheaper than LocalTalk cable. In some circumstances, you can use existing telephone wiring to create the network. A PhoneNet network can transmit data 3,000 feet, three times the extent of a LocalTalk network; Farallon also offers repeaters and other devices that make even larger networks possible. See *AppleShare*, *bus network*, *local area network (LAN)*, *LocalTalk*, *node*, *repeater*, and *twisted-pair cable*.

**AppleWorks**   A popular integrated software package developed by Apple Computer for the Apple II series. The program includes a word processor, a spreadsheet, a file manager, business graphics, and a telecommunications package.

**application**   The use of a computer for a specific purpose, such as writing a novel, printing payroll checks, or laying out the text and graphics of a newsletter.

Application software is collectively distinguished from system software, the programs needed to make the computer run, and system utilities, the programs provided to assist you with system maintenance tasks, such as backing up your work.

The history of application software amply demonstrates the monumental influence that paper wields over our lives. Despite all the experts' predictions of a "paperless office," one that would take full advantage of the computer's technological implications for office work and office communication, people buy programs that help them create ever-increasing mountains of paper. Every major application software advance has occurred because people found that it helped them deal with paper more efficiently: word processing documents replaced typed letters, memos, and reports; database management programs replaced index cards; electronic spreadsheet programs replaced accountants' worksheets; and desktop publishing programs replaced the layout artist's studio. Electronic mail is the latest victim in paper's unending series of victories over the paperless office. Although electronic mail provides a paperless communication medium that improves organizations' efficiency, people still prefer fax! As if conceding the inevitable, peripheral manufacturers are now marketing combination fax/modem boards, which let you send and receive faxes as well as electronic mail.

By any logic, our continued fixation with paper is irrational. Paper-based documents certainly have many advantages, but the amount of waste they produce should pause any environmentally conscious organization. Getting the full benefit from computers may depend on breaking the paper habit and using the computer as an alternative to long bouts of paper shuffling.

A midwestern manufacturing corporation realized a huge payoff through a strategic computer application—and tellingly, one that eliminated one entire class of paper-based documents. The firm's receiving department found that the company's suppliers rarely sent a full shipment, which meant that packing slips had to be marked to show what was actually received. The packing slips were then hand-carried to the accounting department, where clerks typed the information into the accounts payable database, generated checks (but only for what was actually received), and then spent arduous hours filing the packing slips. Suppliers claimed that the firm was slow to pay its bills—and no wonder! One of the firm's managers decided to cut out the packing slips entirely by placing personal computers in the receiving department. Instead of marking up the packing slip, the receiving department personnel used the personal computers to access the accounting package, and they generated the checks right on the spot. The result? Lowered costs, happier suppliers, greater efficiency, and improved productivity—and all because one wasteful, inefficient paper form was eliminated.

Despite all such efforts, though, no one expects paper to disappear. Paper-based documents are light and easily transported. Unlike computer files, which can be all but lost on a 133M hard disk, paper documents sit on your desk, glaring at you, until you decide to do something about them: read them, file them, make confetti out of them, or consign them to the round file. They demand action. Moreover, unlike computer documents, they contain visual and tactile cues that help us retrieve information ("I'm looking for that letter that was printed on that nice, thick paper," or "Where's that report with the big coffee stain on the cover?"). And like it or not, today's Windows and Macintosh systems include font technology that allows individuals a considerable amount of expressiveness, even if—on balance—the expression is sometimes regrettable from the point of view of taste and readability. (Just look at any of your colleagues' documents that employ more than four fonts.)

**application control menu**   In Microsoft Windows and
Windows applications, a menu that appears on the
extreme left of the menu bar. You use this menu to
copy and paste information among Windows applications, to minimize and maximize the application window, to move the application window or icon, and to
switch to other active Windows applications.

 PC Tools Version 7 comes with a Windows
application launcher that modifies the application control menu in a useful way. When
this menu is modified, you can use it to
launch nonactive Windows applications without returning to the File Manager.

**application development system**   A coordinated set of
program development tools, typically including a full-
screen editor, a programming language with a compiler, and an extensive library of ready-to-use program
modules. The use of an application development system substantially lowers the effort required to develop
a stand-alone application, especially compared to the
more primitive tools typically provided as part of an
operating system's programming environment.

 The makers of some application development systems claim that little or no programming skills are needed to develop
applications with the systems. Generally,
these systems can create only a limited range of database management applications and are not well suited
to the development of other kinds of programs. See
*programming environment.*

**application heap**   In a Macintosh computer, the area of
memory set aside for user programs. Synonymous with
*base memory.*

**application icon**   In Microsoft Windows, an on-screen,
graphic representation of a minimized program. The
icon appears on the desktop.

In Windows, you can work with more than one application program at a time. After you click the Minimize button to shrink the active window, the application remains in your computer's memory, even though it is no longer visible in an on-screen window. To remind you that the application is still present in memory, Windows places an application icon on the desktop (see fig. A.4). See *icon* and *Microsoft Windows*.

Application icons

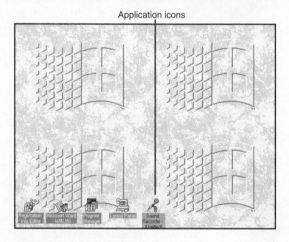

**Fig. A.4.** Application icons of several minimized applications (Microsoft Windows).

**application program**   A computer program designed to help you perform tasks such as analyzing stock data, writing a report, or creating a presentation. Application programs are distinguished from system programs, such as operating systems and system utilities, which help you control and maintain your computer.

**application program interface (API)**   System software that provides resources on which programmers can draw to create user interface features, such as pull-down menus and windows, and to route programs or data to local area networks (LANs).

An application program interface greatly benefits the user. With an API, all programs written for a computer can draw from a common repertoire of command names, menus, windows, dialog boxes, keyboard commands, and other interface features. Such standards substantially lower the cost of learning a new program and lead to measurable increases in the number of programs a typical user is likely to use. For example, Macintosh users typically use more programs and use their computers for longer portions of the workday than do users of DOS systems. The Macintosh was the first personal computer to use the API concept. See *DESQview* and *Presentation Manager*.

**application shortcut key**   In Microsoft Windows' 386 Enhanced mode, a shortcut key you assign to bring an application to the foreground. If you assign the shortcut key Ctrl-Alt-W to Word for Windows, for example, pressing this key combination brings Word to the foreground if the program is running. You assign the keyboard shortcut using the Advanced options in the PIF Editor dialog box. You also can use application shortcut keys with the MS-DOS 5 task switcher. See *386 Enhanced mode* and *Microsoft Windows*.

**application software**   Programs that perform specific tasks, such as word processing or database management; unlike system software that maintains and organizes the computer system and utilities that assist you in maintaining and organizing the system. Synonymous with *read-only memory (ROM)*. See *application*, *database management program*, *page layout program*, *spreadsheet program*, *system software*, *utility program*, and *word processing program*.

**application window**   In Microsoft Windows, an application's main window, which contains the application's menu bar and work area. The work area can contain one or more document windows. See *document window* and *Microsoft Windows*.

**A Programming Language**   See *APL*.

**architecture**   The overall design by which the individual hardware components of a computer system are interrelated.

The term *architecture* is frequently used to describe the internal data-handling capacity of a computer. The 8-bit architecture of the Intel 8088 microprocessor, for example, is determined by the 8-bit data bus that transmits only one byte of data at a time. See *microprocessor*.

**archival backup**   A backup procedure in which a hard disk backup program backs up all files on the hard disk by copying them to floppy disks or some other backup medium. See *hard disk backup program* and *incremental backup*.

**archive**   A compressed file that is designed for space-efficient backup storage and that contains one or more files.

A program for compressing and decompressing IBM PC–compatible files is ARC, a shareware program created by Systems Enhancement Associates. The program is available from many bulletin board systems; look for files named ARC*xxx*, where *xxx* is the version number. A recent version is ARC500. The Macintosh file compression utility of choice is Stuffit, a shareware program created by Raymond Lau.

Almost all bulletin board systems store files in archives, because archived files take up considerably less space. You must use the file compression program to extract archived files. See *file compression utility*.

**archive attribute**   In DOS, a hidden code, stored with a file's directory entry, that indicates whether the file has been changed since the last backup operation.

When you archive a file by using the BACKUP command, DOS turns off the archive attribute. When the archive attribute is off, these commands ignore the file; however, when you use an application program to modify the file after the archive attribute has been turned off, DOS turns on the archive attribute. The next time you use the BACKUP command, therefore, you can instruct the command to back up only the modified file. A file's archive attribute enables you to back up or copy only the files you have changed since the last backup procedure.

You can view and modify a file's archive attribute by using the ATTRIB command.

**ARCnet**   See *Attached Resource Computer Network*.

**area graph**   In presentation graphics, a line graph in which the area below the line is filled in to emphasize the change in volume from one time period to the next. The x-axis (categories axis) is the horizontal axis, and the y-axis (values axis) is the vertical axis.

When more than one data series is displayed, each series is shown in a distinctive cross-hatching pattern (see fig. A.5). See *column graph*, *line graph*, *presentation graphics*, *x-axis*, and *y-axis*.

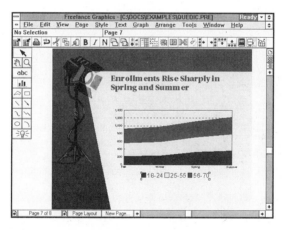

**Fig. A.5.** An area graph.

**argument**   Words, phrases, or numbers you enter on the same line as a command or a statement to expand or modify that command or statement. The command acts on the argument.

In the dBASE expression, USE customer, *USE* is the command and *customer* is the argument. In Lotus 1-2-3, the arguments of built-in functions are enclosed in parentheses, as in @SUM(B1..B3).

Think of the command as a verb and the argument as an object of the verb. See *argument separator* and *parameter*.

**argument separator**   In spreadsheet programs and programming languages, a comma or other punctuation mark that sets off one argument from another in a command or statement.

Many commands, such as the built-in functions of spreadsheet programs, require you to provide information, called an *argument*, that the program needs to execute the command. For example, the function @CTERM in Lotus 1-2-3 requires three arguments: interest, future value, and present value. You must specify all three arguments, separated by commas:

   @CTERM(.012,14000,9000)

The argument separator is essential in commands that take more than one argument. Without the separator, the program cannot tell one argument from another.

 If you are having trouble getting a command or function to work, make sure that you know exactly how many arguments the command or function requires and that you have separated the arguments with the correct separator. Some programs don't allow spaces after the separator. If you are used to pressing the space bar after typing a comma, you may have to delete unnecessary spaces.

**arithmetic-logic unit (ALU)**   The portion of the central processing unit (CPU) devoted to the execution of fundamental arithmetic and logical operations on data.

**arithmetic operator**   A symbol that tells the program how to perform an arithmetic operation, such as addition, subtraction, multiplication, and division.

In almost all computer programs, addition is represented by a plus sign (+), subtraction by a hyphen (–), multiplication by an asterisk (*), and division by a slash ( / ). See *logical operator* and *relational operator*.

**ARPANET**   A wide-area network supported by the U.S. Defense Advanced Research Projects Agency (DARPA) and intended to support advanced scientific research.

Access to ARPANET is restricted to a small group of advanced researchers because its broader communication functions are being taken over by NSFNET. See *wide-area network*.

**array**   One of the fundamental data structures in computer programming; a single- or multidimensional table that the program treats as one data item. Any element in the array can be referenced by naming the array and the element's location within the array.

**arrow keys**   See *cursor-movement keys*.

**artificial intelligence (AI)**   A computer science field that attempts to improve computers by endowing them with some of the characteristics associated with human intelligence, such as the capability to understand natural language and to reason under conditions of uncertainty.

Artificial intelligence researchers generally concede that AI has failed to achieve its objectives, and the problems that prevent further progress are so difficult that solutions may be decades—or even centuries—away. Ironically, the AI applications that were thought to be too difficult (such as programming a computer to play world-class chess) have proven to be easily achieved, and those that were thought to be easy (such as machine translation from one human language to another) have proven to be very difficult. The latter point was proven when, after the expenditure of very large amounts of taxpayers' money, a U.S. Defense Department computer system translated the Russian phrase "The spirit is willing but the flesh is weak" as follows: "The vodka is excellent but the meat is rotten."

Attempts to endow computers with intelligence have
paid off, though, in one respect: They have amply demonstrated the unbelievable amount of knowledge that
humans bring to bear on everyday activities, such as
decoding the meaning of a spoken sentence. Douglas
Lenat, an artificial intelligence researcher who is trying
to provide a computer with much of this background
knowledge, points out that the computer cannot fully
decode (and work with) a sentence, such as "Mr. Lin-
coln is in Washington, D.C.," without recording a
plethora of additional information, such as "When a
person is in a city, his or her left foot is also in the city."
If you have ever wondered whether you're smarter than
a computer, this example should put all doubts to rest.
See *expert system*.

**ascender**   In typography, the portion of the lowercase letters *b, d, f, h, k, l,* and *t* that rises above the height of
the letter *x*. The height of the ascender varies in different typefaces. See *descender*.

**ascending order**   A sort in which items are arranged from
smallest to largest (1, 2, 3) or from first to last (a, b, c).
Ascending order is the default sort order for virtually
all applications that perform sorting operations. See
*descending sort*.

**ASCII**   Pronounced "ask'-ee." Acronym for *American Standard Code for Information Interchange*, a standard
computer character set devised in 1968 to enable efficient data communication and to achieve compatibility
among different computer devices.

The standard ASCII code consists of 96 displayed
upper- and lowercase letters, plus 32 non-displayed
control characters. An individual character code is
composed of seven bits plus one parity bit for error
checking. The code enables the expression of English-
language textual data, but is inadequate for many
foreign languages and technical applications. Because
ASCII code includes no graphics characters, most
modern computers use an extended character set containing needed characters. See *extended character set*.

**ASCII character set**  A character set consisting only of the characters included in the original 128-character ASCII standard. See *extended character set*.

**ASCII file**  A file that contains only characters drawn from the ASCII character set. See *binary file*.

**ASCII sort order**  A sort order determined by the sequence used to number the standard ASCII character set. Words or lines that begin with spaces or punctuation come first, followed by words or lines that begin with numbers. Next sorted are words or lines that begin with uppercase letters, followed by words or lines that begin with lowercase letters.

Programs that sort data in ASCII sort order may violate publication guidelines—all capitalized words, for instance, come before words beginning with lowercase letters—so you may have to perform some manual rearrangement of the data. In addition, an ASCII sort does not alphabetize foreign language characters properly. See *dictionary sort*.

**aspect ratio**  In computer graphics, the ratio of the horizontal dimension of an image to the vertical dimension. In sizing a graphic, maintaining the height-to-width ratio is important to avoid distortions.

**assembler**  A program that transforms an assembly language program into machine language so that the computer can execute the program. See *assembly language* and *compiler*.

**assembly language**  A low-level programming language in which each program statement corresponds to an instruction that the processing unit can carry out.

Assembly languages are procedural languages; they tell the computer what to do in precise detail. They are only one level removed in abstraction from machine language, the language of 0s and 1s that the processing unit actually reads to carry out its operations. Assembly language differs from machine language only in the use of codes that represent the major functions the machine carries out.

Assembly languages have many disadvantages. Programming in assembly language is tedious; the programmer must specify in detail exactly what procedure is to be followed to accomplish a task, and as many as two dozen lines of code may be required to add two numbers. Assembly language programs are extremely difficult to write, and they exhibit no obvious structure or modularity beyond that imposed by the procedure and dictated by the processing unit. Assembly language programs also are not transferred easily from one type of computer to another. They are designed for the specific capabilities and instruction sets of a given processing unit.

If you program in assembly language, the code is compact and operates quickly. If you program in a high-level language, such as BASIC or Pascal, when the compiler translates the code into assembly language code, it does not do so as efficiently as an operator would. Some programs, such as operating systems, must run at the maximum speed possible. By programming in assembly language, a programmer can ensure that a program performs efficiently. Most operating system programs, therefore, are written in assembly language. Assembly language programs also consume less memory space than compiled programs written in a high-level language.

For application program development, assembly language has the advantage of producing fast programs. Lack of portability, however, limits the market for these programs. Professional software developers, therefore, prefer to develop programs in C, which combines the structure of a modern high-level language with the speed and efficiency of assembly language programming. See *BASIC*, *C*, *compiler*, *high-level programming language*, *machine language*, *Pascal*, and *procedural language*.

**assign**   To give a value to a named variable.

**assignment statement**   In computer programming, a program statement that places a value into a variable. In
BASIC, for example, the statement LET A=10 places the
value 10 into the variable A. See *BASIC*.

**associate**   In Microsoft Windows and MS-DOS 5.0, to create
a link between a data file's extension (such as DOC)
and a specific application program. You can open an
associated file and start the application that created it
by double-clicking the document's icon in the File
Manager. When you install a Windows application, the
installation utility tells Windows which extension—
such as DOC or WB1—the program uses.

You can tell whether a file has been associated with an application by looking at the
file name in the File Manager's directory
window. Associated files are shown with
a document icon—a page with writing on it. If an
application's files are not automatically associated,
you can use the Associate command from the File
Manager's File menu to create an association.

**associated document**   A file linked at the system level with
the application that created it. You can start an application by choosing one of its associated documents.

MS-DOS doesn't have any facilities for associated documents; you can't start Lotus 1-2-3, for example, by
choosing the document FALLQTR.WK1. In Microsoft
Windows, Windows applications automatically establish
associations with their documents, but you must manually associate non-Windows applications and documents. In the Macintosh Finder and Multifinder, all
documents are associated with the applications that
created them. The association is controlled by the creator type code, a four-letter code that identifies the
application used to create the file. See *creator type*,
*Finder*, *Microsoft Windows*, and *Multifinder*.

**asterisk**   In DOS, the wild-card symbol (*) that stands for one or more characters, unlike the question mark (?) wild card, which stands for only one character.

**Asymetrix ToolBook**   A program development environment and hypertext authoring tool for Microsoft Windows that enables nonprogrammers to develop Windows applications quickly. The program, which resembles the HyperCard application in the Macintosh environment, is published by Asymetrix Corporation. See *HyperCard, hypertext,* and *Microsoft Windows.*

**asynchronous communication**   A method of data communication in which the transmission of bits of data is not synchronized by a clock signal but is accomplished by sending the bits one after another, with a start bit and a stop bit to mark the beginning and end, respectively, of the data unit.

Asynchronous communication is popular among personal computer developers. Because of the lower communication speeds, you can use normal telephone lines for asynchronous communication. See *baud rate, bus, modem, synchronous communication,* and *Universal Asynchronous Receiver/Transmitter (UART).*

**AT**   See *IBM Personal Computer AT.*

**AT bus**   The 16-bit expansion bus used in the IBM Personal Computer AT, as distinguished from the 8-bit bus of the original IBM Personal Computer and the 32-bit bus of computers using the Intel 80386 and 80486 microprocessors. Most 80386 and 80486 machines contain AT-compatible slots. See *expansion bus, IBM Personal Computer, IBM Personal Computer AT, Intel 80386DX, Intel 80386SX, Intel 80486DX, Intel 80486SX,* and *Micro Channel Bus.*

**AT command set**   A standard for software control of modems developed by Hayes Microcomputer Products, and initially offered in its SmartModems. The AT command set has become the de facto standard for personal computer modems and is widely emulated by so-called "Hayes-compatible" modems.

**AT keyboard**   An 84-key keyboard introduced with the IBM
Personal Computer AT (Advanced Technology) in response to complaints about the original IBM Personal
Computer keyboard, which used a keyboard layout
dissimilar to that of office typewriters. The AT keyboard
is considered a minimal standard today; most IBM and
IBM-compatible computers come equipped with an
enhanced 101-key layout. See *keyboard layout*.

**ATM**   See *Adobe Type Manager*.

**Attached Resource Computer Network (ARCnet)**   A
popular local area network for IBM Personal Computers and compatibles originally developed by Datapoint
Corporation and now available from several vendors.
ARCnet interface cards are inexpensive and easily installed. ARCnet networks employ a star topology, a
token-passing protocol, and coaxial or twisted-pair
cable. The network is capable of transmitting data at
speeds of 2.5M per second. See *coaxial cable, local
area network (LAN), network interface card, network
protocol, network topology,* and *twisted-pair cable*.

**attenuation**   In local area networks, the loss of signal
strength when the system's cables exceed the maximum range stated in the network's specifications. The
attenuation of a signal prevents successful data communications. You can use a device called a *repeater* to
extend the maximum length of a network's cable. See
*local area network (LAN)* and *repeater*.

**attribute**   In many word processing and graphics programs,
a character emphasis, such as boldface and italic, and
other characteristics of character formatting, such as
typeface and type size. In WordPerfect, for example,
attributes include appearance attributes (boldface,
underline, double underline, italic, outline, shadow,
small caps, strikeout, and redline) and size attributes.

In MS-DOS and Microsoft Windows, the term *attribute*
refers to information about a file that indicates whether
the file is a read-only file, a hidden file, or a system file.
See *archive attribute* and *file attribute*.

**audit trail**   In an accounting program, an automatic program feature that keeps a record of transactions so that
you can locate the origin of specific figures that appear
on reports.

**authoring language**   A computer-assisted instruction (CAI)
application that provides tools for creating instructional or presentation software.

A popular authoring language for Macintosh computers
is HyperCard, provided free with every Macintosh
computer. Using HyperCard, educators can develop
instructional programs quickly and easily. HyperCard
applications can control video disk players and CD-
ROM drives, making the application useful as a front
end for large text or video databases.

**AutoCAD**   A computer-aided design (CAD) program developed by AutoDesk and widely used for professional
CAD applications. See *computer-aided design (CAD)*.

**auto-dial/auto-answer modem**   A modem capable of generating tones to dial the receiving computer and of
answering a ringing telephone to establish a connection when a call is received. See *modem*.

**AUTOEXEC.BAT**   In DOS, a batch file that DOS consults
when you start or restart the system.

AUTOEXEC.BAT is not mandatory for IBM PC–
compatible computers, but when you are running a
hard disk loaded with several applications and a computer to which you have attached several peripherals,
the file is all but essential for efficient operation.
Commonly found in an AUTOEXEC.BAT file are PATH
command statements that tell DOS where to find application programs and the names of system-configuration
programs, such as MODE, that set up your computer
for the use of peripherals, such as a serial printer and
mouse. Such commands and programs do not remain
in your computer's memory when you shut off the
power. All this information must be entered manually
at the start of every operating session; AUTOEXEC.BAT
does the task for you.

In the early days of DOS computing, you had to create AUTOEXEC.BAT manually so that your programs would run, typing commands such as FILES=30 or DEVICE=ANSI.SYS. These commands were needed so that the programs would function correctly. Today, however, most programs come with installation utilities that add the needed commands to AUTOEXEC.BAT; they even create the file, if necessary.

 Be very careful to leave AUTOEXEC.BAT undisturbed. Should you accidentally erase the file, your computer may not function normally. If you want to modify AUTOEXEC.BAT manually, be sure to save the file as an ASCII or DOS text file that does not contain any of your word processing program's formatting codes. See *batch file*, *CONFIG.SYS*, and *path*.

**automatic backup**   An application program feature that saves a document automatically at a period the user specifies, such as every five or ten minutes. After a power outage or system crash, you see your work on-screen (up to the last time it was backed up) when you restart the application. This feature can help you avoid catastrophic work losses.

 If your program supports automatic backup, by all means use it, but be sure to distinguish the files created by automatic backup from the files your program creates when you save your work in the normal way. In most programs, the backup files are intended for use only after an abnormal termination caused by a power outage or a system crash and usually cannot be accessed with the normal procedures for opening and editing files. Use automatic backup, but save your work at frequent intervals as you otherwise would.

**automatic font downloading**   The transmission of disk-based, downloadable printer fonts to the printer, done by an application program as the fonts are needed to complete a printing job. See *downloading utility* and *printer font*.

**automatic hyphenation**   See *hyphenation*.

**automatic mode switching**   The automatic detection and adjustment of a display adapter's internal circuitry to adjust the video output of a program on an IBM PC–compatible computer. Most Video Graphics Array (VGA) adapters, for example, switch to adjust to CGA, MDA, EGA, or VGA output from applications.

**automatic recalculation**   In a spreadsheet, a mode in which cell values are recalculated every time any cell is changed in the worksheet.

Automatic recalculation slows your work because the program recalculates the worksheet every time you add a new label, value, or formula. Unless you are working with a large spreadsheet, automatic recalculation is still better than manual recalculation. After you switch to manual recalculation, the computed values become inaccurate as you add new data to the worksheet. If you forget to recalculate (or to turn automatic recalculation back on), you could print a spreadsheet with erroneous results. See *background recalculation* and *manual recalculation*.

**automation**   The replacement of human skill by automatic machine operations.

Automation brings the specter of technological job displacement, in which skilled humans suddenly find themselves without employment as machines take over the jobs they once performed. You can look at automation in another way, however. Automation also can distribute the skills formerly possessed only by highly paid experts and make those skills available to many.

Word processing software is an excellent example of the potential of automation to distribute skills; a secretary can expertly center text on the page and proofread spelling so that letters and reports contain no spelling or typographical errors. A high-quality word processing program such as WordPerfect is, in part, an automated secretary, and its economic significance lies partly in the fact that the program brings secretarial expertise to people and small businesses that could not afford such expertise in the past.

Using such technology, a small firm can compete more effectively. In academia, for example, to get tenure, you sometimes need a research grant. Hiring a secretary used to be the only way you could keep up with the mass of paperwork involved in networking effectively, getting grants, and building a solid case for tenure. Personal computer technology has altered the power equation in the academic game and is performing the same role for small businesses and entrepreneurs.

The potential of personal computing technology to distribute expert skill is one of the major reasons for its success in the marketplace. Equipped with a desktop computer and a variety of application programs, virtually anyone can carry out a sophisticated financial analysis, create a presentation-quality business chart, and publish an attractive newsletter or brochure.

Why pay an artist and typesetter $2,000 every six months to produce a newsletter, when the same job can be done by adding the one-time expense of a $400 page layout program and a $2,000 laser printer to an existing desktop computer system? Experts are quick to point out that untrained people often make mistakes when they attempt such applications. Learning basic guidelines for producing quality output sometimes is easier than mastering layout and design skills, such as the use of an X-ACTO knife and a T-square.

**autorepeat key**   A key that repeatedly enters a character as long as you press and hold down that key.

**autosave**   See *timed backup*.

**autostart routine**   A set of instructions contained in ROM that tells the computer how to proceed when you switch on the power.

In most personal computers, the operating system must be loaded from disk at the beginning of every operating session. One of the autostart routine's instructions tells the disk drive how to position the read/write head over the portion of the disk on which the operating system is stored.

**autotrace**   In a graphics program, such as Adobe Illustrator, a command that transforms an imported bit-mapped image into its object-oriented counterpart.

The bit-mapped images created by a paint program, such as MacPaint, can print at the maximum resolution of the Macintosh screen (72 dots per inch). Object-oriented graphics, however, print at the printer's maximum resolution (up to 300 dots per inch for laser printers). Using the autotrace tool, you can transform low-resolution graphics into art that prints at a substantially higher resolution. See *bit-mapped graphic*, *object-oriented graphic*, and *paint program*.

**A/UX**   Apple Computer's version of the UNIX operating system. To use A/UX, you need a Macintosh with a Motorola 68020 or 68030 microprocessor and 4M of random-access memory (RAM). See *UNIX*.

**AUX**   In DOS, an abbreviation for *auxiliary port*, the communications (COM) port DOS uses by default—normally COM1.

**auxiliary storage**   See *secondary storage*.

**axis**   See *x-axis*, *y-axis*, and *z-axis*.

**back end** The portion of a program that does not interact with the user and that accomplishes the processing job that the program is designed to perform. In a local area network, the back-end application may be stored on the file server; front-end programs handle the user interface on each workstation. See *client/server architecture* and *front end*.

**background** In computers that can do more than one task at a time, the environment in which low-priority operations (such as printing a document or downloading a file) are carried out while the user works with an application in the foreground.

In a computer system that lacks multitasking capabilities, the background task is carried out during brief pauses in the execution of the system's primary (foreground) tasks. Many word processing programs use this technique to provide background printing. See *multitasking*.

**background communication** Data communication, such as downloading a file, accomplished in the background while the user concentrates on another application in the foreground. See *multitasking*.

**background noise** The random or extraneous signals that infiltrate a communications channel, unlike the signals that convey information.

**background pagination** See *pagination*.

**background printing** The printing of a document in the background while a program is active in the foreground.

Background printing can bring major productivity benefits if you frequently print long documents or use a slow printer. Without background printing, you cannot use your computer system while the document is printing. With background printing, you can continue to work while the document prints.

Background printing can work four ways. First, some word processing programs, such as Microsoft Word, provide a background printing command that enables you to print one document while editing another. Second, commercially available print spooling programs extend background printing to all or most of your applications. Third, some operating systems, such as OS/2, provide background printing (bringing another application to the foreground while printing in the background). Fourth, you can add a print buffer to your system. A print buffer is a hardware device that connects your computer and the printer. The buffer contains memory chips that store the computer's output until the printer is ready. The computer thinks that it is hooked up to a super-fast printer and sends the output at maximum speed. You return to your work, and the buffer feeds the output to the printer. See *multitasking*, *print queue*, and *print spooling program*.

**background processes**   In a multitasking operating system, the operations occurring in the background (such as printing or downloading a program from a bulletin board) while you work with an application program in the foreground.

**background recalculation**   In spreadsheet programs, such as Lotus 1-2-3, an option that enables you to make changes to a large spreadsheet while the program performs recalculations in the background.

**backlit display**   A liquid crystal display (LCD) commonly used in notebook and laptop computers. The back of the screen is illuminated to improve the screen's legibility, but at the cost of decreased battery endurance. See *liquid crystal display (LCD)*.

**backplane**   The rear panel of a computing device where you find receptacles for peripheral devices and power cords.

**backspace**   A key that deletes the character to the left of the cursor's position, or the act of moving one space to the left by using the cursor-movement keys.

**backup**   A copy of a program or document file made for archival purposes. Also, the act of copying a data or program file to a removable secondary storage device so that you can keep it in a safe off-site location.

Hard disks fail, and when they do, they often take some or all of the data and documents with them. Regular backup procedures are required for successful use of a hard disk system. See *archival backup*, *backup procedure*, *global backup*, and *incremental backup*.

**backup procedure**   A regular system maintenance procedure that copies all new or altered files to a backup storage medium, such as floppy disks or a tape drive.

If you have ever thought about the time loss, anxiety, and business disruption that a hard disk failure could cause, you realize the need for a regular backup procedure. Hard disks do fail, and a catastrophic disk failure could eradicate every last bit of data you have saved. The conclusion is simple: If you use your computer for business or professional purposes, you should back up your hard disk on a regular basis—at least weekly. If you do not, you expose yourself to the possibility of professional embarrassment, lost clients, and lost profits.

You can manually back up important files to floppy disks, but this approach is inconvenient, time-consuming, and liable to error. Will you remember to back up every new file and every file you have changed since your last backup? Sooner or later, you will encounter a file that's larger than the floppy disk media you're using for your backups. What will you do then? And what if you accidentally back up several versions of the same file? Which is the correct one? Backing up your work manually is a temporary solution, at best.

The best solution to the backup dilemma is to purchase a backup utility, such as Norton Utilities, FastBack Plus, or Central Point Backup. Your first step with one of these programs is to perform a full backup of your entire disk. This procedure is very tedious and can consume as many as 50 or more floppy disks; however, after you accomplish it, the rest is simple. At an interval you choose, such as once a week, you perform an incremental backup, in which the backup utility automatically detects any files you have created or altered since your last backup. The backup utility automatically prompts you to insert the correct disk and to add more disks to the backup disk set if necessary.

Because performing a full backup is so tedious, some users prefer to back up only those subdirectories that contain the data they have created. This choice saves time when performing the initial full backup, because fewer disks are involved. They argue that, if their hard disk fails, they can restore their programs from the original program distribution disks; backing up all their software seems pointless. Two flaws mar this reasoning. First, if your hard disk fails, you will lose all your program configuration choices. When you reinstall your software on your new (or repaired) disk, you must choose all these configuration options again. Second, installing programs can be a very tedious process; for example, installing Windows 3.1 takes about one hour. If you back up your entire hard disk, you can use the restore operation to re-create your entire hard disk— program files and configuration files included—in about the time it would take to install one, huge application.

 Quarter-inch cartridge tape drives are now available for $300 or less, and you should consider equipping your system with a drive whose capacity matches that of your hard disk. Backing up with a tape drive is much more convenient than backing up to a floppy: you don't have to sit there, swapping disks in and out. Moreover, most backup utilities include a scheduler program that lets you schedule automatic, background backup operations. What could be more convenient? Every Friday at

4 P.M., if that's the time you choose, the operation occurs automatically. Two backup utilities that include
automatic backup features are Central Point Backup
for Windows and Norton Desktop for Windows. See
*archival backup, backup utility, incremental backup,
quarter-inch cartridge (QIC),* and *save.*

**backup utility**   A utility program that makes it easier to
back up program and data files from a hard disk to a
backup medium such as floppy disks.

A good backup utility can back up an entire hard disk
on a series of floppies; the program prompts you when
one disk is full and the next one is needed.

Experienced computer users don't waste time regularly
backing up an entire hard disk, because most of its
contents are applications and the many support files—
such as printer drivers—that these applications require.
In the event of a disk failure, you can recover these
applications and files by reinstalling the programs after
repairing or replacing the disk. (You can recover your
hard disk more quickly, however, if at one time you
*have* performed a full backup of your entire disk; using
the restore operation to re-create your hard disk usually is faster than reinstalling program and configuration files.) A good backup utility allows you to back up
selected directories—the directories that contain your
irreplaceable documents.

 By default, most Windows applications save
their documents to their own directories,
forcing you to back up all the application's
files in addition to the document files. You
can avoid this problem in two ways. The first way is to
use a backup utility that allows you to specify the extensions of files you want to back up. If you specify the
extensions that your applications automatically assign
to documents, such as DOC, WB1, or WB3, those
files—and no others—will be backed up. The second
way is to configure all your Windows applications to
save your files to a single directory called DOCS. To
do so, create the DOCS directory. Then highlight an
application's icon in the Program Manager, and choose

Properties from the File menu. Type the directory's path name in the Working Directory dialog box. Repeat this procedure for all your applications, and then configure your backup utility to backup from only the DOCS directory. See *backup*, *backup procedure*, and *incremental backup*.

**backward chaining**  In an expert system, a commonly used method of drawing inferences from IF/THEN rules. A backward chaining system starts with a question and searches through the system's rules to determine which ones enable the system to solve the problem and what data is needed.

Expert systems simulate the expertise of a professional in fields like medical diagnosis, property assessment, identification of an unknown substance's toxicity, and acceptability of life insurance applications. These programs engage the user, who is not an expert in these fields, in a dialog.

In a backward chaining system, you begin with a question, such as "How much is this property worth?" The program then searches the IF/THEN rules stored in the knowledge base. As the search goes on, the program prompts you to supply additional data by asking questions such as "Does the house need a new roof?" (Unlike a database, a knowledge base contains more than data—a knowledge base contains propositions about the subject, phrased in IF/THEN rules, such as "IF the house needs a new roof, THEN deduct $3,000 from the asking price.")

This technique is backward because you begin with the question and supply the necessary data in response to the program's queries. In a forward chaining system, you begin by supplying all the data. Because backward chaining systems are more interactive, they are preferred for applications designed for people who aren't computer experts. See *forward chaining* and *knowledge base*.

**backward compatible**  Compatible with earlier versions of a program or earlier models of a computer. Windows 3.1, for example, is backward compatible with applications

designed to run on Windows 3.0. Microsoft Word 5.0
for the Macintosh is backward compatible with some
Macintoshes that are no longer in production, such as
the Macintosh Plus or Macintosh SE (provided they are
equipped with sufficient memory). The program also
will run on System 6, the predecessor of the current
Apple system software (System 7), at the same time
that it can take full advantage of System 7's advanced
features.

Software and hardware developers may sacrifice backward compatibility to take advantage of important
technological advances or to add complexity. Today's
Windows applications will not run on IBM PCs and
PC-compatibles equipped with the Intel 8088 microprocessor, even though millions of these machines are
in existence.

**backward search**   In database management or word processing, a search that begins at the cursor's location
and proceeds backward toward the beginning of a
database or document (rather than the default forward
search).

**bad break**   An improperly hyphenated line break. See
*hyphenation*.

**bad page break**   In word processing and desktop publishing, an inappropriate or unattractive soft page break
that the word processing or page layout program has
inserted.

A common flaw in documents produced on computers,
bad page breaks should be caught by a final, careful
proofreading before a document goes out the door.
Headings can be widowed at the bottom of pages; units
of text that should be kept together (such as tables) can
be split; and single lines of text (orphans) can be left at
the top of pages.

The best policy is to use block protection features that
prevent bad page breaks from occurring. These features are found in high-quality word processing programs, such as WordPerfect and Microsoft Word.

Don't fix bad page breaks by inserting hard page breaks. Suppose that you place a hard page break just before a heading so that it prints with the text below. If you later revise your document, adding a great deal of text before the hard page break, the break is no longer needed but is forcing a bad page break. Use Block Protect or a similar feature. Block protection is used only if the program would place a soft page break within that block. See *block protection*, *orphan*, *soft page break,* and *widow*.

**bad sector**  An area of a floppy or hard disk that will not reliably record data.

Almost all hard disks have some bad sectors as a result of manufacturing defects. If you run a disk diagnostic program such as CHKDSK and the diagnostic program reports a few bad sectors, don't worry. The operating system locks these sectors out of reading and writing operations. Aside from the loss of a few bytes of storage, you can use the disk as if the bad sectors did not exist.

Bad sectors on floppy disks present serious problems. Most operating systems reject new disks containing bad sectors. If an attempt to format a floppy disk fails, discard the disk. If a bad sector appears after you have used the disk, you can be almost certain that the data on that sector has been corrupted, probably by dust or a fingerprint. The entire disk may be unusable. Users of IBM PC–compatible computers may be able to salvage a portion of the disk by using utility programs such as Norton Utilities or PC Tools. As a last resort, users may use the DOS RECOVER command if the file that corrupted the bad sector is a text file. See *bad track table*.

**bad track table**  A list attached to or packaged with a hard disk. The bad track table lists the bad sectors or the defective areas of the disk.

Almost every hard disk comes off the assembly line with some defects. During the low-level format, these defective areas of the disk are locked out so that system software cannot access them. See *low-level format*.

**bandwidth**  A measurement, expressed in cycles per second (hertz) or bits per second (bps), of the amount of information that can flow through a channel. The higher the frequency, the higher the bandwidth.

**bank switching**  A way of expanding memory beyond an operating system's or microprocessor's limitations by switching rapidly between two banks of memory chips. See *expanded memory*.

**bar code**  A printed pattern of wide and narrow vertical bars used to represent numerical codes in machine-readable form.

Bar codes are printed on almost every product sold in supermarkets. These bar codes conform to the Universal Product Code (UPS), a standard bar code format that lists the product maker's identification number and a product number. When the bar code is dragged past an optical scanner at the check-out counter, the point-of-sale computer matches the product number with its database of price lists and rings up the correct amount.

Equipped with a bar code reader and the appropriate software, personal computers can be used for the development of bar code applications. For example, an audio-visual office can attach bar code labels to all pieces of equipment so that checking out this equipment becomes a simple matter. You pass the reader over the bar code label, and the equipment number is posted to the database of checked-out equipment. Bar code applications can be major time savers when you need to maintain inventory control. See *bar code reader*.

**bar code reader**  An input device equipped with a stylus that scans bar codes; the device then converts the bar code into a number displayed on-screen. See *bar code*.

**bar graph**   In presentation graphics, a graph with horizontal bars, commonly used to show the values of independent items. The x-axis (categories axis) is the vertical axis, and the y-axis (values axis) is the horizontal axis.

Properly, the term *bar graph* is used only for graphs with horizontal bars (see fig. B.1). If the bars are vertical, the graph is a column graph. In practice, however, *bar graph* is used for both. In professional presentation graphics, bar graphs are used to display the values of discrete items (such as apples, oranges, grapefruit, and papaya), and column graphs are used to show the changes in one or more items over time (for example, apples vs. oranges in January, February, March, and so on). See *column graph*, *line graph*, *paired bar graph*, *x-axis*, and *y-axis*.

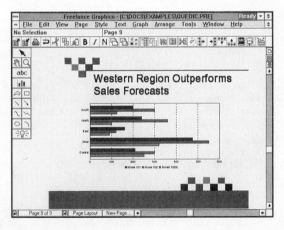

**Fig. B.1.** A bar graph.

**baseband**   In local area networks, a communications method in which the information-bearing signal is placed directly on the cable in digital form without modulation.

A computer's signals can be conveyed over cables in two ways: by analog signals or by digital signals. Analog signals, such as the signals that travel from a high-fidelity amplifier to its speakers, are continuous signals that vary in a wave-like pattern. The number of variations or cycles per second is the signal's frequency, measured in hertz (Hz). Digital signals are discrete signals that alternate between high current or low current.

Because a computer's signals are digital signals, they must be transformed by a process called *modulation* before they can be conveyed over an analog-signal network. A modem performs this task. An analog communication network is called a *broadband network*.

Digital communication networks are called *baseband networks*. The advantage of a baseband network is that considerably less circuitry is required to convey the signal to and from the computer. In addition, because many baseband networks can use twisted-pair (ordinary telephone) cables, baseband networks are cheaper to install than broadband networks that require coaxial cable. However, a baseband system is limited in its geographic extent and provides only one channel of communication at a time. Most personal computer local area networks are baseband networks. See *broadband*.

**base font**   The default font that a word processing program uses for a document unless you specifically instruct the program otherwise. You can choose a default base font for all documents or for just the document you are currently editing.

 If your word processing program enables you to use many fonts, you should understand how the base font is selected. In WordPerfect 5.1, you can set the base font in three ways. The primary way is to choose an initial base font from the Select Printer Edit menu. You can override this setting, however, by choosing a document base font from the Format Document menu or by placing a base font code in your document. Establishing base fonts doesn't mean that you cannot change fonts within the document; the base font is the default font, the one the program uses unless you give explicit commands to the contrary. In Microsoft Word 5.0 (DOS version), the base font for laser printers is monospaced Courier. You can override the base font by redefining the Normal style in each document's style sheet. See *default font*, *document base font*, and *initial base font*.

**base-level synthesizer**   In multimedia, the minimal music synthesizer supported by Microsoft Windows 3.1 and its Multimedia Personal Computer (MPC) specifications. The synthesizer must be capable of playing a minimum of six simultaneous notes on three melodic instruments, and three simultaneous notes on three percussion instruments. See *Multimedia Personal Computer (MPC)*.

**baseline**   In typography, the lowest point that characters reach (excluding descenders). For example, the baseline of a line of text is the lowermost point of letters like *a* and *x*, excluding the lowest points of *p* and *q*.

**base memory**   See *conventional memory*.

**BASIC**   An easy-to-use (but widely criticized) high-level programming language available on personal computers.

Developed in 1964 by John G. Kemeny and Thomas E. Kurtz, two Dartmouth College professors, BASIC (Beginner's All-Purpose Symbolic Instruction Code) was designed to make computer programming accessible to people who are not computer scientists. Like predecessors FORTRAN and ALGOL (the forerunner of Pascal), BASIC is a procedural language that tells the computer what to do step-by-step. A program consists of lines of text, with each line containing one or more statements. Unlike its predecessors, BASIC programs run in an interactive environment, complete with a text editor, debugger, and interpreter that translates and executes the BASIC source code line-by-line. You develop a program interactively, trying alternatives and testing program integrity each step of the way. The result is a process of program construction highly conducive to learning. More recently created compilers transform BASIC code into stand-alone executable programs.

BASIC may be easy to learn, but many computer scientists question whether the language is worth the effort. Like other interpreted languages, BASIC programs execute slowly, making the language a poor choice for professional applications. Some computer scientists argue that BASIC is a poor choice even for educational purposes. Early versions of BASIC lacked the control structures needed for structured programming. Students who learned BASIC also were learning bad programming techniques, such as the use of the GOTO statement, which in early versions was the fundamental building block for the control of program flow. A GOTO statement transfers program control to a specified line number, producing spaghetti code in which even the programmer has difficulty visualizing all the interlinks. The result is a program that most people find impossible to read if the program is longer than two or three dozen lines.

Newer versions that include modern control structures and named subroutines have appeared. These subroutines make GOTO statements superfluous. Line numbers are optional in these newer versions of BASIC. Examples of modernized BASIC include Microsoft's QuickBASIC and Borland's TurboBASIC. Both versions include compilers that make the production of professional executable object code programs possible. Although these modern versions of BASIC are hardly the language of choice for professional program development, some commercially viable software (and a great many shareware programs) are written in a compiled BASIC. C is far more popular for professional program development.

New programming techniques are giving BASIC a new lease on life. Microsoft's Visual BASIC, designed for Windows programming, greatly simplifies the task of creating Windows applications by allowing the programmer to visually create the program's on-screen appearance by using graphics tools; the programmer then writes a small amount of BASIC code that specifies how these on-screen objects work and interact with each other. The result is that a modest amount of programming can create an impressive-looking application, one that would have taken much more time to develop in other languages. Visual BASIC, moreover, is an event-oriented language: the programmer writes code to make something happen only when the user manipulates one of the objects. See *C, compiler, control structure, debugger, interpreter, Pascal, procedural language, QuickBASIC, spaghetti code,* and *structured programming.*

**BASICA**  An interpreter for the Microsoft BASIC programming language. BASICA is supplied on the MS-DOS disk provided with IBM personal computers. See *GW-BASIC.*

**basic input/output system (BIOS)**  A set of programs encoded in read-only memory (ROM) on IBM PC–compatible computers. These programs facilitate the transfer of data and control instructions between the computer and peripherals, such as disk drives.

The BIOS programs of IBM PCs, XTs, ATs, and PS/2s are copyrighted. Companies that manufacture IBM PC–compatible computers must create a BIOS that emulates the IBM BIOS without actually using IBM's code. Such companies can choose to create the BIOS emulation themselves or purchase an emulation from another company, such as Phoenix Technologies.

**batch file**  A file containing a series of DOS commands executed one after the other, as if you had typed them. Batch files are useful when you need to type the same series of DOS commands repeatedly. Almost all hard disk users have an AUTOEXEC.BAT file, a batch file that DOS loads at the start of every operating session.

The following example shows how a simple batch file can help you avoid a major disaster: accidentally reformatting your hard drive. Normally, the FORMAT.COM program is activated when you type the word *FORMAT* at the prompt. You can disguise this program by renaming it XFORMAT.COM with the following command:

RENAME FORMAT.COM XFORMAT.COM

If someone types *FORMAT*, DOS displays an error message because no program is named FORMAT. Instead of FORMAT, you use the following batch file, FORMAT.BAT:

```
ECHO OFF
IF %1. == . GOTO :NONE
IF %1 == C: GOTO :NOCAN
IF %1 == c: GOTO :NOCAN
XFORMAT %1
GOTO END
:NONE
ECHO You did not specify the drive (B:)
ECHO e.g. FORMAT B:
ECHO Please try the command again.
GOTO END
:NOCAN
ECHO You don't really mean to do that--format
ECHO the C drive--do you?
:END
```

With the renamed file and batch file in place, typing *FORMAT B:* causes DOS to use the batch file, not FORMAT.COM. See *AUTOEXEC.BAT*.

**batch processing**   A mode of computer operation in which program instructions are executed one after the other without user intervention.

Batch processing efficiently uses computer resources in a multiuser system, but batch processing is not convenient. You often discover a programming or data input error only after the computer has run the job and spewed out reams of useless printout. In interactive processing, you see the results of your commands onscreen so that you can correct errors and make necessary adjustments before completing the operation. See *interactive processing* and *multiuser system*.

**baud**   Pronounced "bawd." A measure of the number of times per second that switching can occur in a communications channel. See *baud rate* and *bits per second (bps)*.

**baud rate**   The transmission speed of an asynchronous communications channel.

Technically, baud rate refers to the maximum number of changes that can occur per second in the electrical state of a communications circuit. Under RS-232C communications protocols, 300 baud is likely to equal 300 bits per second (bps), but at higher baud rates, the number of bits per second transmitted is actually higher than the baud rate because one change can represent more than one bit of data. For example, 1200 bps is usually sent at 600 baud by sending two bits of information with each change in the electrical state of the circuit.

In personal computing, baud rates are frequently cited to measure the speed of modems. Although 1200-baud modems are standard, most frequent users of telecommunications prefer 2400-baud modems. With serial printers, you must set up your computer's serial port so that the computer sends the printer signals at the correct speed. The Apple LaserWriter, for example, requires serial transmissions at 9600 baud. Under DOS, you use the MODE command to set the serial transmission speed. See *asynchronous communication*, *bits per second (bps)*, *LaserWriter*, *modem*, *serial port*, *serial printer*, and *telecommunications*.

**bay**   See *drive bay*.

**BBS**   See *bulletin board system*.

**BCD**   See *binary coded decimal*.

**bed**   In multimedia, the instrumental music that provides the enveloping background for a presentation.

**bells and whistles**   An application program's or computer system's advanced features.

Many people say that bells and whistles, such as mail-merging capabilities in a word processing program, aren't desirable for novices, and they recommend programs that lack such features. If advanced features do not clutter the user interface, however, you should buy full-featured software you can grow into. A feature that seems hopelessly advanced right now may turn out to be vital. See *mail merge*.

**benchmark**   A standard measurement used to test the performance of different brands of equipment.

In computing, standard benchmark tests (such as Dhrystones and Whetstones) do not provide accurate measures of a system's actual performance in an end-user computing environment. Most of these tests are CPU-intensive; that is, they put the central processing unit (CPU) through a mix of instructions, such as floating-point calculations, but do not test the performance of system components such as disk drives and internal communications.

The speed of these components greatly affects the performance of end-user application programs. Benchmarks developed for personal computers, such as the Norton SI, include the performance of peripherals. See *Norton SI* and *throughput*.

**benchmark program**   A utility program used to measure a computer's processing speed so that its performance can be compared to that of other computers running the same program.

Benchmark programs provide some indication of the number-crunching prowess of a central processing unit (CPU), but the results they generate may be close to meaningless. What counts for users is a system's throughput, its capability to push data not only through the CPU but also through all the system's peripheral components, including its disk drives. A computer with a fast processor (and a numeric coprocessor) performs well on benchmarks, but if the computer is equipped with a sluggish hard disk and lacks cache memory, the performance may disappoint the user. See *cache memory*, *central processing unit (CPU)*, *throughput*, and *utility program*.

**Berkeley UNIX**   A version of the UNIX operating system, developed by the University of California at Berkeley, that takes full advantage of the virtual memory capabilities of Digital Equipment Corporation (DEC) minicomputers.

The Berkeley version of UNIX, often called BSD (Berkeley System Distribution) UNIX, was initially developed to take full advantage of the technical capabilities of VAX minicomputers. Enhancements also were added, and many thought that Berkeley UNIX would become a standard. AT&T's promotion of its own UNIX System 5, however, has relegated Berkeley UNIX to a subsidiary role. Berkeley UNIX still is preferred in technical, academic, and educational environments, in which the system's features meet special needs. See *UNIX*.

**Bernoulli box**   An innovative removable mass storage system developed by Iomega Corporation for IBM PC–compatible and Macintosh computers.

Bernoulli boxes have removable cartridges containing flexible disks capable of holding up to 44M of programs and data. Unlike floppy disk drives, however, these disks spin at high speeds; the latest Bernoulli boxes are capable of up to 22-millisecond access times. The Bernoulli box is named for the Swiss scientist who discovered the principle of aerodynamic lift. Owing to the force of air pressure, the disk bends around the object (read/write head) just enough to maintain a slight space between the object and the disk. Unlike hard disks, which use a massive, fixed platter, this design is resistant to head crashes, in which the read/write head collides with and ruins the disk. Crashes often are caused by shock, but you can drop a Bernoulli cartridge to the floor without damaging the disk or data. Bernoulli cartridges also are removable and relatively inexpensive; therefore, you can use Bernoulli boxes to create a virtually unlimited mass storage system. See *hard disk* and *secondary storage*.

**beta site**   The place where a beta test occurs. When developing a program or a version of an existing program, a company chooses beta sites where the program is subjected to demanding, heavy-duty usage. This process reveals the program's remaining bugs and shortcomings.

**beta software**   In computer software testing, a preliminary version of a program that is widely distributed to users who attempt to operate the program under realistic conditions. See *alpha test, beta site,* and *beta test.*

**beta test**   The second stage in the testing of computer software, before the commercial release. Beta tests usually are conducted outside the company manufacturing the software. See *alpha test.*

**Bézier curve**   Pronounced "bez'-ee-ay." A mathematically generated line that can display nonuniform curves.

Bézier curves are named after the French mathematician Pierre Bézier, who first described their properties. In a Bézier curve, the location of two midpoints—called *control handles*—is sufficient to describe the overall shape of an irregular curve. In computer graphics applications, you manipulate the control handles, usually shown as small boxes on-screen. By clicking on these points and dragging with the mouse, you manipulate the complexity and shape of the curve.

**bibliographic retrieval service**   An on-line information service that specializes in maintaining huge computerized indexes to scholarly, scientific, medical, and technical literature.

The databases offered by these services are almost identical to the indexes available in the reference section of major university libraries. Most databases do not contain the text of the works cited—only the bibliographic citation and an abstract that may not contain useful information. To get the full benefit of the literature, you have to retrieve the original document. These service firms offer the original documents, but the price is stiff.

The two leading information firms are BRS Information Technologies (Latham, NY) and DIALOG Information Services (Menlo Park, CA). Serving mainly corporate and institutional customers, these companies' fees are steep—well over an average of $1 per minute. Personal computer users can access, at substantially lower rates, special menu-driven night and weekend versions of these services, BRS/After Dark and Knowledge Index.

Before signing on, find out whether your local library makes databases available on CD-ROM disks. If so, you can search these databases for free. Because no clock is ticking away, you can make full use of the interactive searching potential of this information. See *on-line information service*.

**Big Blue**   Slang for International Business Machines (IBM) Corporation, which uses blue as its corporate color.

**binary coded decimal (BCD)**   A method of coding long decimal numbers so that they can be processed with precision in a computer, which uses a fixed number of places—such as 8 or 16—to code numerical values.

Most personal computers process data in 8-bit chunks called *bytes*, but that size causes problems for number crunching. When working with binary numbers, the biggest number that can be represented with 8 bits is 256. Some programs get around this limitation by using BCD notation, a way of coding decimal numbers in binary form without really translating them into binary. You cannot fit the binary equivalent of the number 260 into 8 bits, but you can fit the codes for 2, 6, and 0 into 3 adjacent bytes. A 3-digit decimal number takes up 3 bytes of storage; larger numbers can be accommodated by increasing the number of bytes set aside in memory to store the number. Therefore, you have no limit to the precision that can be achieved in coding and processing numbers. See *precision*.

**binary file**   A file containing data or program instructions in a computer-readable format. You cannot display the contents of a binary file using the DOS TYPE command or a word processing program.

Don't panic if you open a strangely named file and see an appalling collection of happy faces, spades, clubs, and other odd symbols: chances are that you have opened a binary file by accident. Just close the file and try again.

**binary numbers**   A number system with a base (or radix) of 2, unlike the number systems most people use, which have bases of 10 (decimal numbers), 12 (measurement in feet and inches), and 60 (time).

Binary numbers are preferred for computers for precision and economy. Constructing an electronic circuit that can detect the difference between two states (high current and low current) is easy and inexpensive; building a circuit that detects the difference among ten states is much more difficult and expensive.

**binary search**   A search algorithm that avoids a slow sequential search by starting in the middle of the sorted database and determining whether the desired record is above or below the midpoint. Having reduced the number of records to be searched by 50 percent, the search proceeds to the middle of the remaining records, and so on, until the desired record is found. See *algorithm*.

**binary transfer**   In Microsoft Windows, a file transfer protocol that enables you to transfer binary (compiled) files to a remote computer via the Windows Terminal accessory.

**binding offset**   An extra-wide margin that shifts text away from the edge of the page, leaving room for the document's binding.

You use binding offsets only for documents printed or reproduced on both sides of the page (duplex printing); the margin is increased on the right side of verso (left, even-numbered) pages and the left side of recto (right, odd-numbered) pages.

 If you are planning to bind a document printed or reproduced on only one side of the page, don't use a binding offset. Just increase the left margin to make room for the binding. See *gutter*.

**BIOS**   See *basic input/output system*.

**bit**   The basic unit of information in a binary numbering system (BInary digiT).

Computers work with binary numbers, and the internal circuit can represent one of the two numbers in a binary system: 1 or 0. These basic either/or, yes/no units of information are called *bits*. Because building a reliable circuit that tells the difference between a 1 (represented by high current) and a 0 (represented by low current) is easy and inexpensive, computers are accurate in their internal processing capabilities. Computers typically make fewer than one internal error in every 100 billion processing operations. Note, however, that such internal errors have nothing to do with programming errors, which are much more common and account for almost all computer glitches. See *byte*.

**bit map**   The representation of a video image stored in a computer's memory. Each picture element (pixel), corresponding to a tiny dot on-screen, is controlled by an on or off code stored as a bit in the computer's memory.

Bit-mapped graphics are notorious consumers of memory. Up to 1M of video memory may be required to store a map of all the tiny dots needed to form a high-resolution graphic image. See *bit*, *bit-mapped graphic*, *block graphics*, and *pixel*.

**bit-mapped font**   A screen or printer font in which each character is composed of a pattern of dots. Bit-mapped fonts represent characters with a matrix of dots. To display or print bit-mapped fonts, the computer or printer must keep a full representation of each character in memory.

When referring to bit-mapped fonts, the term *font* should be taken literally as a complete set of characters of a given typeface, weight, posture, and size. For example, if you want to use Palatino (Roman) 12 and Palatino Italic 14, you must load two complete sets of characters into memory. You cannot scale bit-mapped fonts up or down without introducing grotesque staircase distortions, called *aliasing*. Distortions are clearly visible when you attempt to scale Macintosh bit-mapped screen fonts to a size not represented by a corresponding font in the System Folder.

Because the computer's or printer's memory must contain a complete set of characters for each font you use, bit-mapped fonts consume enormous amounts of disk and memory space; however, outline fonts (also called *scalable fonts*) are constructed from mathematical formulas and can be scaled up or down without distortion.

 Outline fonts are technically superior because you can choose any font size without needing a corresponding file of bit-mapped characters on disk. Outline fonts, however, place heavy demands on your computer's processing circuitry, because each character must be generated from a mathematical formula. If your computer seems to scroll documents more slowly after you format your text with an outline font, switch to a bit-mapped font (such as Microsoft Windows' MS Serif or MS Sans Serif) while you're editing. Performance should improve. Switch back to the outline font just prior to printing. See *aliasing*, *LaserJet*, *LaserWriter*, *outline font*, *printer font*, and *screen font*.

**bit-mapped graphic**   A graphic image formed by a pattern of pixels (screen dots) and limited in resolution to the maximum screen resolution of the device being used. Bit-mapped graphics are produced by paint programs, such as MacPaint, SuperPaint, GEM Paint, PC Paintbrush, and some scanners.

Considered inferior to object-oriented graphics for most applications, bit-mapped graphics tie the printed resolution to the resolution of the video display currently in use, even if the printer is capable of a higher resolution. Macintosh systems, for example, display bit-mapped graphics with a resolution of 72 dpi, even though LaserWriter printers can print at 300 dpi. Such graphics may be afflicted with aliasing—rough diagonal lines attributable to the square shape of the pixels. The irregular patterns are visible when the image includes a straight diagonal line (see fig. B.2). However, a skillful illustrator can create beautiful airbrush effects with paint packages.

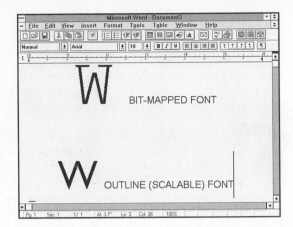

**Fig. B.2.** Aliasing visible in the diagonal lines of a
bit-mapped graphic.

Bit-mapped graphics have other drawbacks. Unlike
object-oriented and Encapsulated PostScript (EPS)
graphics, bit-mapped graphics consume considerable
memory and disk space. Resizing a bit-mapped graphic
image without introducing distortions is almost impossible. Scaling up the graphic produces a chunky effect
because the lines thicken proportionately; scaling
down causes the bits to run together, resulting in an
inky effect. Unlike object-oriented graphics, in which
each object, such as a line, can be edited or moved
independently, bit-mapped graphic images are difficult
to edit or modify. See *aliasing*, *Encapsulated
PostScript (EPS) file*, *object-oriented graphic*, *paint
program*, *pixel*, *resolution*, and *scanner*.

**BITNET**   A wide-area network that links over 1,000 colleges
and universities in the U.S., Canada, and Europe.

BITNET (Because It's Time Network) was developed by
EDUCOM, a nonprofit educational consortium, for
scholarly communication. Services provided include
electronic mail and file transfer. BITNET is used heavily
by geographically separated scholars who are working
jointly in a narrowly defined research area.

The service is used by scholars fortunate enough to work at host institutions, but scholars at institutions that are not BITNET members frequently complain that they are shut out of an important network of informal scholarly communication.

**bits per second (bps)**   In asynchronous communications, a measurement of data transmission speed.

In personal computing, bps rates frequently are used to measure the performance of modems and other serial communications devices, such as serial ports. The bps rates are enumerated incrementally: 110 bps; 150 bps; 300 bps; 600 bps; 1200 bps; 2400 bps; 4800 bps; 9600 bps; 19200 bps; 38400 bps; 57600 bps, and 115200 bps. See *asynchronous communication*, *baud*, and *modem*.

**black letter**   In typography, a family of typefaces derived from German handwriting of the medieval era.

Black letter typefaces often are called *Fraktur* (after the Latin word *fractus*, meaning *broken*) because the medieval scribes who created this design lifted their pens from the line to form the next character— fracturing the continuous flow of handwriting.

**blank cell**   In a spreadsheet program, a cell that contains no values, labels, or formatting different from the worksheet's global formats.

**blessed folder**   The Macintosh's System Folder, equivalent to a DOS subdirectory and containing files loaded at the beginning of an operating session.

The Macintosh operating system—the System— consults this folder when the computer cannot locate a program file. The blessed folder is like a DOS directory named in the PATH command. A major limitation of the Macintosh operating system, however, is that the System Folder is the only folder the System consults when it cannot find a file. Macintosh users, therefore, are obliged to place all the configuration files required by their application programs in this folder, which can quickly grow so large that keeping track of its contents is difficult. See *System* and *System Folder*.

**block**   A unit of information processed or transferred. The unit may vary in size. In communications, a unit of information passed from one computer to another is a block. For example, using XMODEM, a communications protocol for transferring files, 128 bytes is considered a block. Under DOS, a block transferred from a disk drive is 512 bytes. In word processing, a block is a unit of text that you mark so that you can use a block operation to move, copy, or otherwise affect that text.

In word processing, techniques for marking blocks vary. The earliest word processing programs required you to enter a keyboard command at the beginning and end of the block. More recent programs enable you to mark the block using a process called *selection*, in which you use the cursor-movement keys to highlight the marked text so that it is displayed in reverse video. After you mark a block, you can perform block operations, such as copying, moving, deleting, formatting, or saving the block to a named file. See *block operation*.

**block definition**   See *selection*.

**block graphics**   When working with IBM PC–compatible computers, graphics formed on-screen by graphics characters in the extended character set.

The graphics characters in the IBM extended character set are suitable for creating on-screen rectangles but not for fine detail. Because the block graphics characters are handled the same way as ordinary characters, the computer can display block graphics considerably faster than bit-mapped graphics. See *bit-mapped graphic* and *graphics character*.

**block move**   A fundamental editing technique in word processing in which a marked block of text is cut from one location and inserted in another. Synonymous with *cut and paste*.

Writing experts agree that the major determinant of a written work's quality is its logical coherence: the ideas and facts must be presented in a logical progression. To achieve coherence, restructuring large amounts of text is often necessary.

Because word processing software allows a writer to restructure large text domains with ease, some writing teachers thought the technology would lead to improved writing. After all, the coherence of large-scale text domains, such as paragraphs and sections, determines the overall quality of one's writing. But the predicted improvement has not materialized, largely because writers do not take advantage of the increased ease of revision that word processing software offers. Instead, they typically concentrate on the minor details of words and sentences. In a misguided attempt to improve a poorly phrased sentence, for example, they insert more words into it. The resulting phenomenon, well known to publishing houses, is "word-processor bloat." This malady is partly responsible for the last decade's huge and pointless increase in the average length of Ph.D. dissertations, which—fortunately—attract only a tiny audience. Also, rather than encouraging quality revisions, word processing may actually discourage it by focusing the writer's attention on only one-third of a page at a time.

 Learn how to carry out a block move with the word processing software you are using. The technique should be second nature so that you do not hesitate to use it. Remember that a well-organized document, in which the ideas and facts are presented in logical order, impresses people.

If you write with the computer, develop a strategy that enables you to envision your document's overall structure. The cheapest and simplest solution is to print your document and revise it on paper. Seeing the overall structure of your writing is much easier on those big, bright sheets of bleached wood pulp. Other strategies are to purchase a full-page monitor and to use a word processing program such as Microsoft Word, which enables you to display and manipulate an outline of your document.

**block operation**   The act of transferring a chunk, or block, of information from one area to another. In word processing, an editing or formatting operation—such as copying, deleting, moving, or underlining—performed on a marked block of text. See *block move*.

**block protection**   In word processing and page layout programs, the prevention of soft page breaks within a block of text. See *bad page break* and *soft page break*.

**BMP**   In Microsoft Windows, an extension indicating that the file contains a Windows-compatible bit-mapped graphic.

**board**   See *adapter* and *circuit board*.

**body type**   The font (usually 8- to 12-point) used to set paragraphs of text (distinguished from the typefaces used to set headings, subheadings, captions, and other typographical elements).

 Serif typefaces, such as Century, Garamond, and Times Roman, are preferred over sans serif typefaces for body type because they are more legible. See *display type*, *sans serif*, and *serif*.

**boilerplate**   A standard passage of text used over and over in letters, memos, or reports.

 Use boilerplate to achieve big gains in your writing productivity. If your job involves answering routine inquiry letters, develop boilerplate responses to questions on such matters as warranty, sales terms, and the like, and attach these passages to glossaries—named storage areas for boilerplate text and other frequently used items, such as logos. Then you can write a letter just by inserting two or three glossaries and adding a few personalized touches. See *glossary*.

**boldface**   A character emphasis visibly darker and heavier in weight than normal type. Each entry word in this dictionary is in boldface type. See *emphasis* and *weight*.

**bomb**   See *crash*.

**Boolean operator**   See *logical operator*.

**boot**   To initiate an automatic routine that clears the
memory, loads the operating system, and prepares the
computer for use.

The term *boot* is derived from the saying "pulling yourself up by your own bootstraps." Personal computers
must do just that because random-access memory
(RAM) does not retain program instructions when the
power is shut off.

Buried within the computer's read-only memory (ROM)
circuits is an autostart program that comes into play
when the power is switched on (a cold boot). Unlike
RAM, ROM circuits retain data and program instructions without requiring power. The autostart program
instructs the computer's disk drives to search for the
disk containing the computer's operating system.

After a system crash occurs, you usually must reboot
the computer. With most systems, you can perform a
warm boot that restarts the system without the stress
on electronic components caused by switching the
power off and on again. See *cold boot* and *warm boot*.

**boot record**   The first track on an IBM PC–compatible disk
(track 0). After you turn on the power, the boot-up
software in ROM instructs the computer to read this
track to begin loading MS-DOS. See *boot*.

**bowl**   In typography, the curved strokes that enclose or
partially enclose the counter, such as the blank space
inside the letter *a* or *o*.

**bps**   See *bits per second*.

**branch**   In Microsoft Windows' File Manager, a segment of
the directory tree that represents a subdirectory and
any further subdirectories it contains (see fig. B.3).

Branch

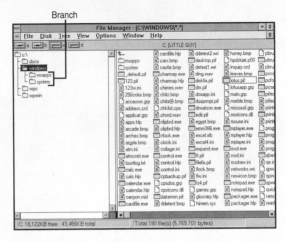

**Fig. B.3.** Directory tree with branch (Microsoft Windows).

**branch control structure** A control structure that tells a program to branch to a set of optional instructions, which come into play only if a specified condition is met. For example, if a program detects that a vital data file has been irretrievably corrupted, the program branches to an on-screen message that says The file you want to open is corrupted. Don't worry, be happy! Synonymous with *selection*. See *case branch*, *control structure*, and *IF/THEN/ELSE*.

**break** A user-initiated signal that interrupts processing or the reception of data. See *Ctrl-Break*.

**breakout box** A testing device inserted into a communications cable that enables each electrical line to be tested independently.

**breakpoint** In Microsoft Excel, a location in a macro where the macro pauses to display a dialog box with three options; you can step through each formula, continue the macro, or stop the macro's execution.

If you're writing a complex macro, include several breakpoints so that you can pause the macro's execution and examine the intermediate values.

**bridge**   In local area networks, a device that enables two networks (even ones dissimilar in topology, wiring, or communications protocols) to exchange data.

**broadband**   In local area networks, an analog communications method characterized by high bandwidth. The signal usually is split, or multiplexed, to provide multiple communications channels.

A broadband system uses analog transmissions. Because the microcomputer is a digital device, a device similar to a modem is required at either end of the transmission cable to convert the signal from digital to analog and back again.

Broadband communications can extend over great distances and operate at extremely high speeds. A broadband network can, like a cable TV network, convey two or more communication channels at a time (the channels are separated by frequency). Therefore, a broadband network can handle voice and data communications. See *analog, analog transmission, bandwidth, baseband, digital,* and *local area network (LAN)*.

**brownout**   A period of low-voltage electrical power caused by unusually heavy demand.

Brownouts can cause computers to operate erratically or to crash. If brownouts frequently cause your computer to crash, you may need to purchase an uninterruptible power supply (UPS) to work with your machine. See *uninterruptible power supply (UPS)*.

**browse**   To use a dialog or list box to look for a document (see fig. B.4). In a database management program, to use a dialog or list box to look for a data record.

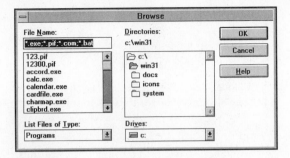

**Fig. B.4.** Browse dialog box.

When using the Browse dialog box, restrict the display of files by choosing an appropriate option in the List Files of Type list box.

**Browse mode**  In a database management program, a program mode in which data records are displayed in a columnar format for quick, on-screen review (see fig. B.5). Synonymous with *list view* or *table view* in some programs. See *Edit mode*.

```
 Records   Organize   Fields   Go To   Exit
 FIRST_NAME  LAST_NAME  AREA_CODE  PHONE_NO  MALE  BIRTH_DATE  ANNUAL_PAY
 James C.    Smith      206        123-4567  T     07/04/60      34500.00
 Albert K.   Zeller     212        457-9801  T     09/28/59      27900.00
 Doris A.    Gregory    503        204-8567  F     07/04/62      16900.00
 Harry M.    Nelson     315        576-8235  T     02/15/58      29000.00
 Tina B.     Baker      415        787-3154  F     10/12/56      25900.00
 Kirk D.     Chapman    618        625-7845  T     08/04/61      19750.00
 Mary W.     Thompson   213        432-6783  F     06/18/55      24500.00
 Charles M.  Duff       206        456-9873  T     07/22/64      13500.00
 Winston E.  Lee        503        365-8512  T     05/14/39      34900.00
 Thomas T.   Hanson     206        573-5005  T     12/24/45      28950.00


 Browse    C:\data\dbdata\EMPLOYEE   Rec 1/10        File          NumCaps
```

**Fig. B.5.** Records displayed in Browse mode.

**brush style**  In typography, a typeface design that simulates script drawn with a brush or broad-pointed pen.

**buffer**   A unit of memory given the task of holding information temporarily, especially when such temporary storage is needed to compensate for differences in speed
between computer components.

 A major incentive to run Microsoft Windows
exists even for those who steadfastly cling to
their DOS applications: in Windows' 386
Enhanced mode, Windows sets up a portion
of your computer's memory to act as a buffer for printing. When you print your file, your program dishes out
the print instructions as fast as your computer's
memory can accept them—and that's much faster than
your printer can. You quickly regain control of your
application, and as you continue to work, Windows
operates in the background, doling out information to
the printer at the requisite, glacial pace.

**bug**   A programming error that causes a program or a computer system to perform erratically, produce incorrect
results, or crash.

Bugs can have serious consequences. Five days before
the first manned moon attempt, a bug was discovered
in NASA's program. This bug would have performed
trajectory calculations based on the assumption that
the moon's gravity was repulsive rather than attractive.
If the bug had not been discovered, the astronauts
probably would not have returned to earth safely.

The term *bug* was coined when a real insect was discovered to have fouled up one of the circuits of the first
electronic digital computer, the ENIAC.

**built-in font**   A printer font encoded permanently in the
printer's read-only memory (ROM).

All laser printers offer at least one built-in font family.
You should purchase a printer with a range of built-in
fonts, including (at the minimum) a Roman-style serif
font such as Times Roman or Dutch and an attractive,
clean sans serif font such as Helvetica or Swiss.
PostScript-compatible laser printers have a nice range

of built-in fonts from Adobe Systems, Inc. These fonts include Avant Garde, Bookman, New Century Schoolbook, Palatino, and Zapf Chancery. See *cartridge font*, *downloadable font*, and *screen font*.

**built-in function**   In a spreadsheet program, a ready-to-use formula that performs mathematical, statistical, trigonometric, financial, and other calculations.

A built-in function is prefaced by a special symbol (usually @) and followed by a keyword, such as AVG or SUM, that describes the formula's purpose. Most built-in functions require one or more arguments. In Lotus 1-2-3, for example, the @ROUND function requires you to provide the number to be rounded (or a cell reference) and the number of decimal places to which the number should be rounded. The following built-in function rounds the value in cell C5 to two decimal places: @ROUND(C5,2).

When a built-in function has more than one argument, you must use argument separators, such as the comma in the preceding example, so that the program can tell one part of the expression from the others. Synonymous with *@function*. See *argument*, *argument separator*, *function*, and *keyword*.

**bulk storage**   A secondary storage device (usually using magnetic tape) that can store data. Synonymous with *mass storage*.

**bullet**   An open (○) or closed circle (•), about the height of a lowercase letter, used to set off items in a list.

Often combined with a hanging indent, bullets are effective for listing items whose content is roughly equal in emphasis or significance. If you want to list items that vary in their significance or are arranged chronologically, choose a numbered list. See *hanging indent*.

**bulleted list chart**   In presentation graphics, a text chart used to communicate a series of ideas or to enumerate items of equal weight (see fig. B.6). See *presentation graphics*.

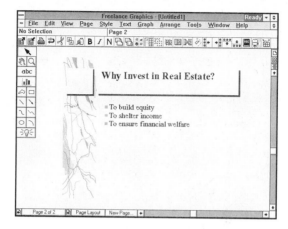

**Fig. B.6.** A bulleted list chart.

**bulletin board system (BBS)**   A private telecommunications utility, usually set up by a personal computer
hobbyist for the enjoyment of other hobbyists.

Bulletin boards used to be great fun. Late at night, you
loaded your communications software, dialed a BBS,
left messages, uploaded and downloaded public domain software and shareware, and played Space
Invaders. The advent of computer viruses took away a
great deal of the BBS's appeal. Anyone using a personal
computer with a hard disk for professional purposes
should download software from a BBS with great caution. If you want to explore bulletin boards, use a dual-
floppy computer and keep the downloaded software
away from your main system. See *communications
program*, *telecommunications*, and *virus*.

**bundled software**   Software included with a computer
system as part of the system's total price.

**burn-in**   A power-on test of a computer system, performed
on behalf of the customer.

Semiconductor components such as memory chips and
microprocessors tend to fail either early or late in their

lives, but seldom during the middle. Responsible computer retailers, therefore, test systems for 24 to 48 hours before releasing the systems to customers. Defective chips are likely to fail during the burn-in period.

**bus**  An internal pathway along which signals are sent from one part of the computer to another.

Personal computers have a bus design with three pathways:

- The data bus sends data back and forth between the memory and the microprocessor.

- The address bus identifies which memory location will come into play.

- The control bus carries the control unit's signals.

The data bus and address bus are wired in parallel rows so that all the bits in a binary number can travel simultaneously, like eight cars side by side on a 16-lane freeway.

Three bus architectures are commonly found in today's IBM PC and PC-compatible marketplace:

- *Industry Standard Architecture (ISA) bus.* This bus is the 16-bit bus initially developed for IBM's AT (Advanced Technology) computers; indeed, the term ISA bus is synonymous with AT bus. The bus includes 8-bit slots for downward compatibility with earlier adapters, but includes 16-bit slots for improved, AT-compatible adapters such as 16-bit VGA adapters.

- *Micro Channel Architecture (MCA) bus.* A proprietary, 32-bit bus used in high-end IBM PS/2 computers.

- *Enhanced Industry Standard Architecture (EISA) bus.* A 32-bit bus that, unlike the MCA bus, is backward compatible with ISA adapters.

See *expansion bus.*

**bus mouse**  A mouse connected to the computer by an adapter inserted into an available expansion slot. See *serial mouse.*

**bus network**   In local area networks, a decentralized network in which a single connecting line, the bus, is shared by a number of nodes, including workstations, shared peripherals, and file servers (see fig. B.7).

**Fig. B.7.** An illustration of a bus network.

In a bus network, a workstation sends a message to all other workstations. Each node in the network, however, has a unique address, and its reception circuitry constantly monitors the bus to determine whether a message is being sent to the node. A message sent to the Laser Printer node, for example, is ignored by the other nodes in the network.

 Bus networks have a significant advantage over competing network designs (star networks and ring networks); the failure of a single node does not disrupt the rest of the network. Most commercial local area networks, such as AppleTalk and EtherNet, use a bus network. Extending a bus network also is a simple matter. You lengthen the bus and add nodes, up to the system's maximum. The signal, however, cannot travel more than about 1,000 feet without an added device called a *repeater*. See *node* and *repeater*.

**button**   In graphical user interfaces, a dialog box option you can choose to determine how a command will function. See *Cancel button, default button, OK button, pushbutton,* and *radio button.*

**byte**   Eight contiguous bits, the fundamental data unit of personal computers.

Storing the equivalent of one character, the byte provides a basic comprehensible unit of measurement for computer storage. Because a single page of double-spaced text contains about 1,375 characters, approximately 1,500 bytes are required to store the page (allowing for spaces, control characters, and other needed information). Because many bytes of memory are required to store information in a computer, byte counts tend to involve very large numbers—many personal computers have millions of bytes of memory. Because computer architecture is based (for the most part) on binary numbers, bytes are counted in powers of two. The most frequently used units are kilobyte (K), which is approximately one thousand bytes, and megabyte (M), approximately one million bytes.

The terms *kilo* (in kilobyte) and *mega* (in megabyte) are misleading: they derive from decimal (base 10) numbers. Kilo suggests 1,000 and mega suggests 1,000,000; however, kilobyte actually is 1,024 bytes, and megabyte is 1,048,576 bytes. Many computer scientists criticize these terms for their inherent inaccuracy and irrelevance to computer architecture. However, $2^{10}$ and $2^{20}$ are logical places to establish benchmarks for measurement, and the fact that they are close to 1,000 and 1,000,000 (respectively) gives those who think in decimal numbers a nice handle on the measurement of memory. See *bit* and *kilobyte (K)*.

**C** A high-level programming language widely used for professional programming. C is highly portable and produces efficient, fast-running programs.

Developed by Dennis Ritchie of Bell Laboratories in 1972, C is a descendant of an earlier language called B. Most major professional software companies prefer C over other programming languages. A general-purpose procedural language like FORTRAN, BASIC, and Pascal, C combines the virtues of high-level programming languages with the efficiency of an assembly language.

The program's syntax encourages the creation of well-structured programs using modern control structures. At the same time, the programmer can embed instructions that directly address the processor's internal management of individual data bits. Because these instructions perform computations at the processing unit's highest speed, compiled C programs run significantly faster than programs written in other high-level programming languages. You can think of C, in fact, as a modular and structured framework for the expression of assembly language instructions. The framework of the program expresses the algorithm for the application; the assembly language instructions reach the bit-by-bit representation of data inside the processing unit to enhance the speed and efficiency of the program's operations.

Assembly language programs usually are not portable to other processing environments because assembly language programs are tied to a specific processing unit's design. A C program is rewritten easily and quickly so that the program runs on a new computer, if the target environment has a C compiler. The language's portability is an important factor in its widespread adoption by professional programmers who hope to find the widest possible market for their products. The portability of C is evident in UNIX. This operating system (also developed at Bell Laboratories) was written in C and is portable across all processor architectures. Most UNIX systems include C compilers.

Despite C's many advantages, the language is formidable for beginners. Unlike BASIC and Pascal, which originated as teaching languages, C was designed as a tool for advanced professional programmers. Therefore, the syntax and terminology are designed for efficiency rather than readability.

C's dominance in the professional programming world is all but ensured and not merely because of its efficiency and portability. AT&T's Bell Laboratories was prohibited from copyrighting C or UNIX because of the antitrust regulations in effect before the breakup of the Bell System. Therefore, C compilers and UNIX are in the public domain and have been adopted by virtually all colleges and universities. The result is a steady stream of computer science graduates well versed in the C language and the UNIX operating system. See *algorithm*, *assembly language*, *control structure*, *high-level programming language*, *portable computer*, *procedural language*, *syntax*, and *UNIX*.

**C++** A high-level programming language developed by Bjarne Stroustrup at AT&T's Bell Laboratories. Combining all the advantages of the C language with those of object-oriented programming, C++ has been adopted as the standard house programming language by several major software vendors, such as Apple Computer. See *C* and *object-oriented programming language*.

**cache** Pronounced "cash." A storage area that keeps frequently accessed data or program instructions readily available so that you do not have to retrieve them repeatedly. Two kinds of memory caches are frequently used in personal computing: cache memory, in which a special section of high-speed RAM is set aside for cache purposes, and disk caching, in which part of the hard disk is used for cache purposes. Of the two, cache memory is significantly faster. Disk caching capabilities are built into the Macintosh and its system software. See *cache memory* and *disk cache*.

**cache controller**   A hard disk controller that includes its own disk cache (pronounced "cash") memory. The cache memory stores frequently accessed program instructions and data in random-access memory (RAM) chips, which your computer can access much faster than it can access the disk.

 If you are putting together a high-performance system, look for drive circuitry that includes a cache controller. Because the controller contains its own random-access memory (RAM) chips and processing circuitry for the cache memory, you do not need to set aside the computer's RAM or occupy the microprocessor's time for this purpose. See *disk cache* and *disk drive controller*.

**cache memory**   A special fast section of random-access memory (RAM) set aside to store the most frequently accessed information stored in RAM.

A cache (pronounced "cash") memory is a special section of ultra-fast RAM chips, such as static RAM chips. This section is controlled by a cache controller chip, such as the Intel 82385. Cache memory dramatically improves the speed of a computer because the microprocessor need not wait for the slower dynamic random-access memory chips (DRAM) to catch up. With a cache memory and cache controller, even a fast 80386 microprocessor can operate without wait states. Cache memory is distinguished from a disk cache, an area of ordinary RAM set aside to store information frequently accessed from disk drives.

 To assemble a very fast computer system, choose a system with the Intel 82385 cache controller and at least 32K of static cache memory (64K is preferable). See *disk cache*, *static random-access memory (RAM)*, and *wait state*.

**CAD**   See *computer-aided design*.

**CADD**   See *computer-aided design and drafting*.

**CAI** See *computer-assisted instruction*.

**calculated field** In a database management program, a data field that contains the results of calculations performed on other fields.

In a database that stores students' grades for a training course, for example, you can create a field that totals the scores of tests and quizzes. You can place the calculated field on the on-screen data form or on the report form so that the calculated total appears when you print a report. Synonymous with *derived field*. See *data field*.

**call** In programming, a statement that directs the flow of program control to a subroutine, procedure, or function.

**callout** The text (often accompanied by arrows) used to point out and identify parts of an illustration.

**camera-ready copy** A printed and finished manuscript or illustration ready to be photographed by the printer for reproduction.

**Cancel button** In the industry-standard and graphical user interfaces, a pushbutton in a dialog box that you can activate to cancel a command and return to the active document.

 With most programs, you can press Esc to activate the Cancel button. See *pushbutton*.

**cap height** The height of a capital letter from the baseline. See *baseline*.

**Caps Lock key** A toggle key that locks the keyboard so that you can enter uppercase letters without pressing the Shift key.

Some keyboards have a light that illuminates when you toggle the keyboard into the uppercase mode. If the keyboard has no light, you must look at what you are typing before you know which mode you have selected. Some programs display a message, such as CAPS LOCK, when you are in uppercase mode.

Unlike the Caps Lock key of a typewriter, the keyboard's Caps Lock key has no effect on the number and punctuation keys. To use the punctuation marks on the row of number keys, you must press Shift, regardless of whether or not you have pressed Caps Lock.

**capture**   To write to a disk file a graphic image corresponding to the current screen display.

**card**   An electronic circuit board designed to fit into the slots of a computer's expansion bus. Synonymous with *adapter*. See *expansion bus*.

**caret**   A symbol ( ^ ) commonly found over the 6 key on computer keyboards. The caret sometimes is used to stand for the Ctrl key in computer documentation, as in "Press ^ C."

**carpal tunnel syndrome**   See *repetitive strain injury (RSI)*.

**carriage return**   See *Enter/Return*.

**carrier sense multiple access with collision detection (CSMA/CD)**   In local area networks, a widely used method for controlling a computer's access to the communication channel. With CSMA/CD, each component of the network (called a *node*) has an equal right to access the communication channel. If two computers try to access the network at the same time (an unlikely occurrence), the network uses a random number to decide which computer gets to use the network.

This channel access method works well with relatively small- to medium-sized networks (two or three dozen nodes). This method is used by the two most popular network architectures: EtherNet and AppleTalk. Note that when you have many workstations and network traffic volume is high, many data collisions occur. The entire system can become overloaded and lock up, with each station behaving as if it were trying to access the system and failing because the system is in use. Large networks, therefore, use alternative channel access methods, such as polling and token passing. See *AppleTalk*, *EtherNet*, *local area network (LAN)*, *node*, *polling*, and *token passing*.

**Cartesian coordinate system**   A method, created by the seventeenth-century French mathematician René Descartes, of locating a point in a two-dimensional space by defining a vertical axis and a horizontal axis.

A mouse uses the Cartesian coordinate system to locate the pointer on-screen. In some graphics applications, you can display the coordinates so that the pointer can be located precisely.

**cartridge**   In secondary storage, a removable module containing secondary storage media such as magnetic tape and magnetic disks. In computer printers, a removable module that expands the printer's memory or font capabilities.

**cartridge font**   A printer font supplied in the form of a read-only memory (ROM) cartridge that plugs into a receptacle on Hewlett-Packard LaserJet printers and clones.

Hewlett-Packard LaserJet printers rely heavily on cartridge fonts that have some merits over their chief competition: downloadable fonts. Unlike downloadable fonts, the ROM-based cartridge font is immediately available to the printer and does not consume space in the printer's random-access memory (RAM), which can be used up quickly when printing documents loaded with graphics.

Hewlett-Packard's cartridges generally contain only two to four typefaces, but other firms have cartridges available with as many as 25 fonts in several typefaces.

 If you plan to print documents containing several typefaces, buying one cartridge that contains all the typefaces you use is better than buying several cartridges, each of which

contains only one or two typefaces. With the
multitypeface cartridge, you do not need to change
cartridges in the middle of a printing operation. See
*font* and *typeface*.

**cascading windows**   In a user interface, a mode in which
two or more on-screen windows overlap so that you
can see the title bars of the hidden windows. This mode
is convenient because although the topmost window
occupies much of the screen, you still can see the titles
of all the other windows you have opened (see fig. C.1).
See *overlaid windows* and *tiled windows.*

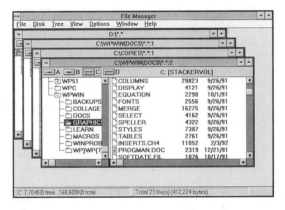

**Fig. C.1.** Cascading windows (Microsoft Windows).

**case branch**   In programming, a branch control structure
that specifically enumerates several IF/THEN/ELSE
branch options.

The following example demonstrates how a menu with
three options can be kept on-screen until the user gives
one of the three correct responses. It is written in
pseudocode, a mock computer language intended to
simulate how a real program would look.

```
WHILE response = false
   ASK choice "Load (R)eport, (L)etter, or
      (M)emo template?"
   BEGIN CASE
      CASE choice = "R"
         LOAD REPORT.DOC
         SET response = true
      CASE choice = "L"
         LOAD LETTER.DOC
         SET response = true
      CASE choice = "M"
         LOAD MEMO.DOC
         SET response = true
   END CASE
ENDWHILE
```

In English, the program reads as follows: "Define a new variable called *response* and set the variable to false. Create a variable called *choice* and show an on-screen message asking whether the user wants to load a report, letter, or memo template. Place the user's typed response in the choice variable. If the response is equal to false, examine the user input. If the user types *R*, load the REPORT.DOC file and set the response to true. If the user types *L*, load the LETTER.DOC file and set the response to true. If the user types *M*, load the MEMO.DOC file and set the response to true. When the response is equal to true, quit."

The menu in the ASK statement stays on-screen until the user types one of the three acceptable inputs: *R*, *L*, or *M* (upper- or lowercase). Any other input doesn't match one of the cases and doesn't set the response to true. As long as the response remains false, the menu stays on-screen. See *control structure* and *pseudocode*.

**case-sensitive**  Responsive to the difference between upper- and lowercase letters. DOS is not case-sensitive; you can type DOS commands in upper- or lowercase letters.

**case-sensitive search**  A search in which the program attempts to match the exact pattern of upper- and lowercase letters in the search string. A case-sensitive search for *Porter*, for example, matches *Porter* but not *PORTER*, *porter*, or *pOrter*.

**cast-based animation**   In multimedia, an animation methodology in which each object in a production is treated as an individual graphic image (a cast member). You can manipulate each cast member individually by means of a script. See *script*.

**catalog**   In dBASE, a list of related database files you have grouped together so that you can easily distinguish them from others.

Like all relational database management programs, dBASE can work with more than one file at a time. Frequently, the results of relational operations (such as a join) produce a new file. In addition, you create several indexes and other files that support the application. The Catalog menu helps you track all these related files in a unit. See *dBASE*, *join*, and *relational database management system (RDBMS)*.

**cathode ray tube (CRT)**   A computer monitor that uses an electron gun (cathode) to emit a beam of electrons that illuminate phosphors on-screen as the beam sweeps across the screen repeatedly. The same technology is used in television. See *monitor*, *phosphor*, and *refresh*.

**CAV**   See *constant angular velocity*.

**CBT**   See *computer-based training*.

**CCITT**   See *Comité Consultatif International Téléphonique et Télégraphique*.

**CD**   See *compact disk*.

**CDEV**   See *control panel device*.

**CD-I**   See *Compact Disk–Interactive*.

**CD-ROM**   A read-only optical storage technology that uses compact disks.

CD-ROM disks can store up to 650M of data, all of which can be made available interactively on the computer's display. CD-ROM currently is used to produce encyclopedias, dictionaries, and software libraries available to personal computer users. New compression techniques enable you to pack up to 250,000 text pages on one CD-ROM disk.

Like all electronic devices, CD-ROM drives and disks are getting cheaper. Because prices have fallen significantly, you may want to consider equipping your computer with a CD-ROM drive. Doing so makes excellent sense if you're expanding a home computer system; the cost of a CD-ROM drive and a high-quality CD-based encyclopedia is considerably less than a traditional, print-based encyclopedia. Examples of currently available compact disks include the New Grolier Electronic Encyclopedia (which includes the full text of the *Academic American Encyclopedia*, thousands of illustrations, more than 250 maps, and sounds of birds, mammals, musical compositions, musical instruments, and excerpts from famous speeches) and the CD-ROM version of *Webster's Ninth New Collegiate Dictionary* (which not only defines the words, but also pronounces them).

CD-ROM technology is also an excellent choice for desktop publishers who need access to large numbers of fonts and clip art images. Most font publishers make their entire font collections available on CD-ROM; the fonts are "locked," but you can unlock one or more of them by calling the firm, paying a fee, and getting the access code. Currently available clip art disks include SunShine's Visual Delights CD-ROM, which contains over 5,800 TIFF images of men, women, plants, flowers, music, art objects, trees, balloons, designs, borders, and much more.

 You probably will not find much CD-ROM equipment locally, but several mail-order firms are specializing in this area. Excellent sources of budget-priced CD-ROM drives and compact disks are DAK Industries (8200 Remmet Avenue, Canoga Park, CA 91304) and EDUCORP Computer Services (7434 Trade Street, San Diego, CA 92121-2410). If you're buying a CD-ROM drive for a Windows-compatible system, be sure to look for a drive that conforms to the Multimedia Personal Computer (MPC) standard. See *compact disk (CD)*, *Multimedia Personal Computer (MPC)*, and *optical disk*.

**CD-ROM disk drive**   A read-only disk drive designed to
   access and read the data encoded on compact disks
   and to transfer this data to a computer.

   With audio compact disk players selling for as little as
   $99, personal computer users often are appalled at the
   high price of CD-ROM drives. The two devices, however, are dissimilar. A CD-ROM disk drive contains
   circuitry optimized to locate data at high speeds; CD
   players need to locate only the beginning of audio
   tracks, which they play sequentially. As the number of
   these drives increases, the prices of CD-ROM drives will
   drop to more reasonable levels.

    CD-ROM drives retrieve data much more
   slowly than computer disk drives. If you
   don't like waiting for the screen to update,
   you should spend more money to get one of
   the faster CD-ROM drives. An access time of 320 ms to
   400 ms is considered relatively fast for currently available drives and is well worth the additional cost. Avoid
   drives with 800-ms access times. If you're buying your
   drive for a Windows-compatible MPC system, make
   sure that the CD-ROM drive can play CDs that store up
   to 600M of data; transfer data at rates of at least 150
   kbits per second; and access data in at least 400 ms. In
   addition, make sure that the drive has headphone
   jacks, external speaker jacks, and a volume control. See
   *access time*, *compact disk (CD)*, and *millisecond (ms)*.

**CD-ROM eXtended Architecture (CD-ROM XA)**   A compact disk data storage standard jointly developed by
   Philips, Sony, and Microsoft for the storage of audio
   and visual data on compact disks so that you can simultaneously access the audio and visual portions.

**CD-ROM XA**   See *CD-ROM eXtended Architecture*.

**cell**   In a spreadsheet, the rectangle formed by the intersection of a row and column. You can place constants,
   labels, or formulas in cells. See *constant*, *formula*, and
   *label*.

**cell address**   In a spreadsheet, a code that identifies a cell's location on the worksheet by specifying the cell's row and column (A3, B9, C2, and so on). When used in a formula, the cell address becomes a cell reference. See *cell reference* and *formula*.

**cell animation**   An animation technique in which a background painting is held in place while transparent sheets of celluloid are moved over the background painting, producing the illusion of movement.

Cell animation is much easier than drawing a new background for every frame in the animation sequence. A Macintosh animation program that uses a computerized version of cell animation is MacroMind Director. See *MacroMind Director*.

**cell definition**   The actual contents of a cell in a spreadsheet, as displayed on the entry line.

The cell definition may differ from what is displayed in the worksheet. If you place a formula in the cell, the program displays the value generated by the formula rather than the formula itself.

You easily can corrupt a spreadsheet by typing a value in a cell that contains a formula. As you look at the worksheet, unless the pointer is resting on the cell, you have no way to tell whether a cell's value is a constant (a number you typed directly into the cell) or a value produced by a formula. If you mistakenly think that the value is a constant, you may change the value and erase the formula stored in the cell. As a result, the worksheet may not generate the correct answer—but you won't know why. This mistake is a common source of incorrect results.

You can guard against this problem by using cell protection and by keeping your eye on the entry line as you move the cursor through the worksheet. The entry line always shows the current cell definition, displaying precisely what is in the cell—including any formula. See *cell protection*, *entry line*, *formula*, and *value*.

**cell format**   In a spreadsheet, the way the program displays values and labels on-screen.

You can format labels and values two ways: first, by choosing a global format that affects all the cells of a worksheet; second, by choosing a range format that affects one or more cells in a rectangular block. Label formats for character-based programs like Lotus 1-2-3 are limited to label alignment; graphics spreadsheets can use multiple typefaces and type sizes. Numeric formats include currency (displays dollar signs, commas, and two decimal places), fixed (displays a user-specified number of decimal places), and general (displays only the number). See *character-based program*, *current cell*, *global format*, *graphics spreadsheet*, *label*, *label alignment*, *numeric format*, *range format*, and *value*.

**cell pointer**   In Lotus 1-2-3, the rectangular highlight that indicates the location on-screen of the current cell, where values and labels appear after you type them and press Enter. Synonymous with *cursor*.

**cell protection**   In a spreadsheet program, a format applied to a cell, a range of cells, or an entire file. The format prevents you from altering the contents of protected cells.

**cell reference**   In a spreadsheet formula, a cell address that specifies the location of a value to be used to solve the formula. Cell references are the keys to a spreadsheet program's power and usefulness. A spreadsheet program would not be very useful if you had to write formulas with constants, such as 2+2. Because formulas are not visible on the worksheet, you would have to edit the formula to perform the exploratory what-if recalculations that make spreadsheets useful. Using cell references instead of values, you write the formula as B1+B2. B1 and B2 are cell addresses. When used in a formula, they instruct the program to go to the named cell (such as B1) and to use the value appearing in that cell. If you want to change the constants, you don't have to edit the formula; you type a new constant in cell B1 or cell B2.

Cell references enable you to create an intricate pattern of links among the cells in a worksheet. A cell reference also can refer to a cell containing a formula. The value produced by the formula is referenced. Because the formula may contain its own cell references to other cells, which can themselves contain formulas, the worksheet can contain an unbroken chain of mathematical links. A change made to any constant in such a worksheet affects intermediate values and, ultimately, the bottom line. See *cell address*, *constant*, *formula*, *recalculation*, *value*, and *what-if analysis*.

**central mass storage**   See *file server*.

**central processing unit (CPU)**   The computer's internal storage, processing, and control circuitry, including the arithmetic-logic unit (ALU), the control unit, and the primary storage.

Only the ALU and control unit are wholly contained on the microprocessor chip; the primary storage is elsewhere on the motherboard or an adapter on the expansion bus. See *adapter*, *arithmetic-logic unit (ALU)*, *control unit*, *expansion bus*, *microprocessor*, *motherboard*, and *primary storage*.

**Centronics interface**   The standard parallel printing port of IBM PC and PC-compatible computers, named after the company (Centronics) that designed a predecessor to this interface standard. Synonymous with *parallel port*.

**Centronics printer**   An archaic term (if such a thing *can* be in so new a field) for *parallel printer*.

**CGA**   See *Color Graphics Adapter*.

**CGM**   See *Computer Graphics Metafile*.

**chain printing**   The printing of separate files as a unit by placing at the end of the first file commands that direct the program to continue printing the second file, and so on.

Full-featured word processing programs such as Microsoft Word enable chained printing with continuous pagination and, in some cases, the generation of a complete table of contents and index for the linked files.

**chamfer**   In desktop publishing and presentation graphics, a beveled edge between two intersecting lines.

**channel access**   In local area networks, the method used to gain access to the data communication channel that links the computers. Three common methods are contention, polling, and token ring. See *contention*, *local area network (LAN)*, *polling*, and *token-ring network*.

**character**   Any letter, number, punctuation mark, or symbol that can be produced on-screen by pressing a key on the keyboard.

**character-based program**   A program that relies on the IBM PC's built-in character set and block graphics rather than taking advantage of a windowing environment to display on-screen fonts and bit-mapped graphics. Figure C.2 shows Lotus 1-2-3, a character-based DOS program, running with Norton Desktop for Windows, a graphics-based program. See *Lotus 1-2-3*, *Microsoft Windows*, and *windowing environment*.

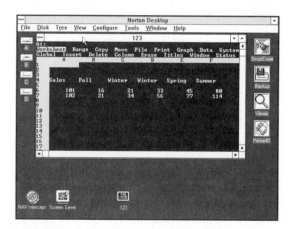

**Fig. C.2.** A character-based program (1-2-3) and a graphics-based program (Norton Desktop).

**character graphics**   See *block graphics*.

**character-mapped display**   A method of displaying characters in which a special section of memory is set aside to represent the display; programs generate a display by inserting characters into the memory-based representation of the screen. The whole screen, therefore, remains active, not just one line, and the user or the program can modify characters anywhere on-screen. See *teletype (TTY) display*.

**character mode**   In IBM and IBM-compatible computers, a display adapter mode in which the computer displays only those characters contained in its built-in character set. Synonymous with *text mode*.

 If you're using an older DOS machine, you probably will get the best performance from programs (such as Microsoft Word) that allow you to choose between character mode and graphics mode. Switch to graphics mode only when you need to preview formatting or graphics before printing. See *character set, character view,* and *graphics mode*.

**character set**   The fixed set of keyboard codes that a particular computer system uses. See *ASCII, code page,* and *extended character set*.

**characters per inch (cpi)**   The number of characters that fit within a linear inch in a given font. Standard units drawn from typewriting are pica (10 cpi) and elite (12 cpi).

**characters per second (cps)**   A measurement of the speed of a communications or printing device.

**character string**   Any series of characters that the program treats as a group. In programming and database management, you distinguish character strings from reserved words (command names) by enclosing strings in quotation marks; as a result, the characters in the string give no instructions to the computer. In a database management query language, for example, the expression *FIND "Wyoming"* causes the computer to search for the first record that exactly matches the character string *Wyoming*. Synonymous with *string*.

**character view** In some DOS applications, a mode in which the program switches the display adapter circuitry to character mode. In character mode, the computer is capable of displaying only those characters contained in the computer's built-in character set.

 On all but the fastest machines, character view is noticeably faster than graphics view. Unless you need to see graphics and fonts on-screen, work in character view and switch to graphics view before printing. See *character mode* and *graphics view*.

**check box** In a graphical user interface, a square box that appears in a dialog box and that you choose to toggle an option on or off. When the option is turned on, an *X* appears in the check box. A check box may appear alone or with other check boxes in a list of items. Unlike radio buttons, you can choose more than one check box.

 In Windows applications that employ dialog boxes, you usually can toggle a check box on or off in three ways. If the option has a boldfaced letter, such as Replace without Confirmation, you can hold down the Alt key and press the option's boldfaced letter (Alt-C). You also can position the cursor in the check box and press the space bar. If you have a mouse, you place the pointer in the check box and click the button. See *graphical user interface (GUI)*, *dialog box*, and *radio button*.

**checksum** In data communications, an error-checking technique in which the number of bits in a unit of data is summed and transmitted along with the data. The receiving computer then checks the sum.

If the sum differs, an error probably occurred in transmission. A commonly used personal computer communications protocol called XMODEM uses the checksum technique. See *XMODEM*.

**checkwriting program**  A program designed to help individuals and small-business owners keep track of checking accounts, credit card accounts, tax records, and budgets. The industry leader is Quicken (Intuit).

**child**  In a windowing system such as X Windows or an outlining utility such as ThinkTank, a unit—such as a window or outline heading—that is subordinate to a higher-level unit, called a *parent*. In the following outline, the subheading *Cardinal* is a child of its parent, the major heading.

> ABUNDANT BIRDS OF WEST VIRGINIA [parent]
>     Bluejay [child]
>     Cardinal [child]
>     Goldfinch [child]

See *family* and *parent*.

**chip**  A miniaturized electronic circuit mass-produced on a tiny chip or wafer of silicon.

The electronic age began in earnest with the 1947 invention of the transistor, a switching and amplifying device that replaces huge, power-hungry, and unreliable vacuum tubes. As important as the transistor was, it did not solve the biggest problem facing any firm that wanted to manufacture complex electronic components: the necessity of wiring all those components together.

Various automated procedures were devised, but in the end, at least some of the wiring and soldering had to be done manually. Complex electronic devices, therefore, were very expensive.

In the late 1950s, Jack Kilby (an engineer at Texas Instruments) and Robert Noyce (an engineer at Fairchild Semiconductor) discovered that they could create an integrated circuit, a chip made out of semiconducting materials that could duplicate the function of several transistors and other electronic components.

Semiconductors—materials such as silicon—can be chemically altered in a process called *doping* so that their conductive properties are improved or reduced.

Doping a chip of silicon in a series of layers, each with differing conductive properties, creates the equivalent of one or more transistors.

The first integrated circuits contained only a few components, but an impressive and sustained drive of technological development created chips containing thousands, tens of thousands, and more components on one tiny chip. The same techniques now can generate 16 million components on a chip so tiny that you can place it on the tip of your finger.

Of even greater economic and social significance than the chip's miniaturization is the fact that it can be mass-produced. After a chip is designed, the circuit pattern is transferred to a series of lithographic plates called *photomasks*. The photomasks then are used to coat the chip with materials that, when exposed to light, lay down a pattern of hardened and unhardened areas. Acid is applied to etch out the unhardened areas, and then chemicals are forced into these areas to alter the silicon's conductive properties.

Through multiple applications of the photomask, a chip with several layers of silicon with varying conductive properties is created, and the result is the equivalent of a complex electronic circuit. The process is largely automated, and chips can be produced at low prices.

Today's Intel 80486 microprocessor, for example, sells for a few hundred dollars, but this microprocessor is the electronic equivalent of a mainframe computer priced at several million dollars just 20 years ago. The achievement of chip-manufacturing technology has made possible the diffusion of computer technology throughout society.

Memory chips and microprocessors are the two chips most applicable to users' needs, but many kinds of special-purpose chips are manufactured for a variety of applications. These chips include microprocessor support chips, chips for the control of disk drives, and chips for generating video displays. See *integrated circuit* and *microprocessor*.

**choose**  In a program that uses menus and dialog boxes, to pick an option that begins an action.

*Highlighting* an option is often different from *choosing* it. In many programs, you can use the arrow keys to highlight a menu option without choosing it. To choose the highlighted option, you press Enter. In Microsoft Windows, *to choose* means to use the keyboard or mouse to pick a button, menu option, or icon that begins an action. In this sense, choosing differs from merely highlighting an option in that it also initiates action, such as confirming choices in a dialog box by choosing the OK button. See *highlighting*.

 If you use a mouse, investigate the ways you can save time by double-clicking an option. In many applications, double-clicking an option highlights and chooses it in one quick action. To double-click, press the mouse button twice in rapid succession.

**Chooser**  A Macintosh desktop accessory (DA) supplied by Apple Computer with the Mac's operating system—the System. The Chooser governs the selection of printer drivers, the programs that control communication with the printer. The Chooser displays the icons of the printer drivers currently installed in the System Folder.

A major contrast between character-based DOS and the Macintosh operating system is that the Macintosh provides printer drivers at the operating system level, but in DOS computers, character-based programs must provide their own printer drivers. This arrangement is inconvenient for the user (not all programs offer a wide range of drivers) and costly for software developers, who must develop dozens of drivers for each application program. A Chooser printer driver works with any Mac application. Following the Mac's lead, Microsoft Windows provides printer drivers for all programs designed to take advantage of its graphical user interface. See *character-based program*, *Microsoft Windows*, *printer driver*, *System*, and *System Folder*.

**chord**  In desktop publishing and presentation graphics, a line segment that connects the end points of an arc.

**chrominance**   In multimedia, the portion of a composite video signal that contains color information.

**circuit board**   A flat plastic board on which electrically conductive circuits have been laminated. Synonymous with *printed circuit board*. See *adapter* and *motherboard*.

**circular reference**   In a spreadsheet, an error condition caused by two or more formulas that reference each other. For example, a circular reference occurs when the formula +B5 is placed in cell A1 and the formula +A1 is placed in cell B5.

Circular references do not always result in errors. They can be used deliberately, for example, to create an iterative function in a spreadsheet: each recalculation increases the values of the two formulas. However, circular references frequently arise from unintentional typing errors. Unintended circular references may produce erroneous results.

 If you see an error message informing you that a circular reference exists in your worksheet, track down the circular reference. Eliminate any unwanted circular references before placing confidence in the spreadsheet's accuracy.

**CISC**   See *complex instruction set computer*.

**Class A certification**   A Federal Communications Commission (FCC) certification that a given make and model of computer meets the FCC's "Class A" limits for radio frequency emissions, designed for commercial and industrial environments.

 In terms of competition, *A* is usually better than *B*, but not so with the FCC. The Class B standards (for computers to be used in homes and home offices) are actually tougher; computers used at home are more likely to interfere with radio and television signal reception. If you plan to use your computer at home, avoid computers that have only Class A certification (that is, they failed Class B).

**Class B certification**   A Federal Communications Commission (FCC) certification that a given make and model of
computer meets the FCC's "Class B" limits for radio
frequency emissions, which are designed for homes
and home offices. Class B standards are tougher than
Class A and are designed to protect radio and television
reception in residential neighborhoods from excessive
radio frequency interference (RFI) generated by computer usage. Class B computers also are shielded more
efficiently from external interference.

**clear**   To remove data from a document without being able
undo the deletion. In the Windows and Macintosh
environments, the Clear command (Edit menu) completely wipes out the selection, as opposed to Cut,
which removes the selection to the Clipboard (from
which you can retrieve the selection, if you later discover that you deleted it by mistake).

 Most applications can recover a cleared
deletion if you choose Undo (Edit menu)
immediately after performing the clear.
Don't move the pointer, choose another
command, or type any other text before choosing
Undo, or the deletion may be lost irretrievably.

**click**   To press and quickly release a mouse button. You
frequently see this term in instructions such as, "Click
the Bold check box in the Fonts dialog box." This instruction means, "Move the mouse pointer so that its
tip touches the Bold check box, and click the mouse
button."

With many Macintosh and Windows applications, you
also can double-click, which performs varying functions.
In dialog boxes, double-clicking an option is the same
as choosing the option and clicking the OK button. In
documents, double-clicking highlights an entire word.
Double-clicking a program icon launches the application.

Most applications also support Shift-clicking, which
extends a selection. With the selection on-screen, hold
down the Shift key and use the mouse to extend the
selection in the direction you want. See *double-click*
and *Shift-click*.

**client**   In a local area network, a workstation with processing capabilities, such as a personal computer, that can
request information or applications from the network's
file server. See *client/server network*, *file server*, and
*local area network (LAN)*.

**client application**   In object linking and embedding (OLE),
an application capable of functioning as the destination
of linked or embedded objects. See *object linking and
embedding (OLE)* and *server application*.

**client-based application**   In a local area network, an application that resides on a personal computer workstation
and is not available for use by others on the network.

Client-based applications do not make sharing common data easy, but they are resistant to the system-wide
failure that occurs when a server-based application
becomes unavailable after the file server crashes. See
*client/server network*, *file server*, *local area network
(LAN)*, and *server-based application*.

**client/server architecture**   A design model for applications
running on a local area network, in which the bulk of
the back-end processing, such as performing a physical
search of a database, takes place on the file server. The
front-end processing, which involves communicating
with the user, is handled by smaller programs distributed
to the client workstations. See *local area network (LAN)*.

**client/server network**   A method of allocating resources in
a local area network so that computing power is distributed among the personal computers in the network, but some shared resources are centralized in a
file server. See *file server* and *peer-to-peer network*.

**clip art**   A collection of graphic images, stored on disk
and available for use in a page layout or presentation
graphics program.

The term *clip art* is derived from graphics design tradition; portfolios of printed clip art are sold and actually
clipped out by layout artists to enhance newsletters,
brochures, and presentation graphics. Now available
on disk, clip art collections can be read by most page
layout or presentation graphics programs (see fig. C.3).

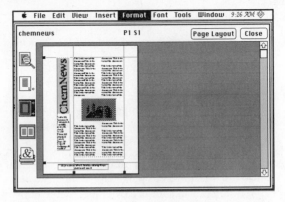

**Fig. C.3.** Print preview of a document employing clip art.

**Clipboard**   In a windowing environment such as Microsoft
Windows or the Macintosh Finder, a temporary storage
area in memory where text or graphics, or both, are
stored as you copy or move them (see fig. C.4).

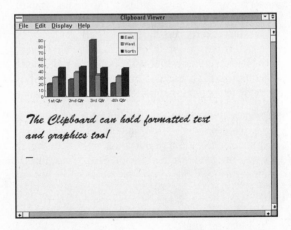

**Fig. C.4.** The Clipboard window (Microsoft Windows).

Because the Clipboard can hold only one unit of cut or copied text at a time, moving text with the Clipboard can be risky. Suppose that you cut a brilliant paragraph to the Clipboard, planning to paste it elsewhere in your document. As you examine the text where you want to insert the paragraph, you see a misbegotten sentence and delete it using the same Cut command that you used to cut the brilliant paragraph. Unfortunately, you just replaced the Clipboard's contents—the brilliant paragraph—with the misbegotten sentence. If this accident occurs, choose Undo immediately, which may restore the sentence to the screen (and the paragraph to the Clipboard). To avoid this accident, always delete text using the command (usually called Clear) that erases text permanently without placing it in the Clipboard; use Cut only to move text.

**Clipper**   A compiler developed by Nantucket Systems, Inc., for the dBASE software command language. Many application developers consider Clipper superior to the compiler offered by dBASE's publisher, Ashton-Tate. See *compiler* and *dBASE*.

**clock**   An electronic circuit that generates evenly spaced pulses at speeds of millions of cycles per second; the pulses are used to synchronize the flow of information through the computer's internal communication channels.

Some computers also contain a circuit that tracks hours, minutes, and seconds. See *clock speed* and *clock/calendar board*.

**clock/calendar board**   An adapter that includes a battery-powered clock for tracking the system time and date and is used in computers that lack such facilities on their motherboards. See *adapter* and *motherboard*.

**clock speed**   The speed of the internal clock of a microprocessor that sets the pace—measured in megahertz (MHz)—at which operations proceed within the computer's internal processing circuitry.

Each successive model of microprocessor has produced a faster clock speed. The original microprocessor of

IBM Personal Computers, the Intel 8088, operated at a speed of 4.77 MHz. The chip powering the original IBM Personal Computer AT, the Intel 80286, operated at 6 MHz, with more recent versions operating at up to 25 MHz. The Intel 80386 microprocessor operates at speeds ranging from 16 to 50 MHz.

Clock speed affects performance but is not the only determinant. Faster clock speeds bring noticeable gains in CPU-intensive tasks, such as recalculating a spreadsheet. Disk-intensive application programs perform slowly, however, if the disk drives are sluggish.

Another determinant of speed is the use of wait states. A wait state is an idle period in which the microprocessor waits for slower components to catch up with it. A computer with zero wait states has components fast enough that the microprocessor does not have to wait for these components to catch up. A zero wait state computer running at 16 MHz may be faster than a machine nominally rated at 20 MHz but employing one wait state.

When comparing clock speeds, you also should bear in mind that speeds are comparable only between computers that employ the same microprocessor. For example, you can safely bet that a 25 MHz 80386SX computer is faster than a 16 MHz 80386SX; however, a 16 MHz 80486DX is faster than a 20 MHz 80386DX.

Some computers come with two or more clock speeds you can select using the keyboard or a button located on the computer's front panel. These computers offer this feature to accommodate certain older programs that cannot run at faster clock speeds. Most Windows applications are designed to run at the fastest speed of which your system is capable.

 If you're planning to run Windows applications, you need an 80386-based system that runs at a minimum of 16 MHz with zero wait states. Experienced Windows users prefer 80386 systems that run at 20 MHz or more. See *Intel 80386DX, Intel 80386SX, Intel 80486DX, Intel 80486SX,* and *wait state.*

**clone**    A functional copy of a hardware device, such as
a non–IBM PC–compatible computer that runs software and uses peripherals intended for an IBM PC–
compatible computer, or of a program, such as a
spreadsheet program that reads Lotus 1-2-3 files and
recognizes most or all of the commands.

Only one year after the IBM PC hit the market, a Texas
company, COMPAQ, released the first IBM PC–
compatible computer. The COMPAQ was designed to
be 100-percent compatible with IBM software and
accessory devices, such as displays and printers. Additional companies followed COMPAQ with 100-percent
compatible computers; these companies, including
AT&T, Tandy, Zenith, Epson, and Dell, experienced
great success. At first, these computers were known
collectively as *clones*, conveying the connotation of a
cheap imitation. Many IBM PC–compatible computers
actually improved on the original, however, so the term
*clone* is no longer fair.

Why did IBM permit so many companies to copy its
personal computer? The original IBM PC was designed
to use off-the-shelf components—such as disk drives,
microprocessors, and power supplies—that non-IBM
companies had developed already for earlier personal
computers. These same components could be assembled
by anyone with the requisite technical know-how. In
addition, IBM purchased the PC's operating system,
PC DOS, from Microsoft Corporation, which was free
to sell virtually the same system (MS-DOS) to clone
manufacturers. The only part of the computer that IBM
actually copyrighted was a small amount of internal
programming code, which other computer companies
could emulate without actually copying. In 1987, IBM
threatened to sue several small clone makers who,
according to IBM, actually had copied the code verbatim.

Partly to counter the compatible market, IBM attempted to close the architecture of its personal computers by the 1986 release of the PS/2 series. A key
feature of the PS/2 line is its Micro Channel Bus architecture, which has certain technical advantages over the

method used to communicate data within previous PCs. However, the Micro Channel Bus created a closed environment for PC add-on boards and accessories; the older boards and accessories do not work on a Micro Channel machine, and any company developing products for Micro Channel machines needs a license from IBM.

Compatible makers have not emulated the Micro Channel standard, preferring instead to stick with the tried-and-true PC architecture. To take full advantage of the 32-bit bus structure of the Intel 80386 and 80486 microprocessors, these manufacturers (dubbed the "Gang of Nine") have created a bus standard called *Extended Industry Standard Architecture* (EISA). Computers conforming to the EISA standard can accept existing adapters while taking full advantage of these powerful new microprocessors.

Clones also exist in the software world, but unlike hardware clones, software clones have attracted a great deal of litigation. In early cases, the courts tended to support clone makers as long as the program code was not a verbatim copy of the original. More recently, however, some software companies have taken the view that a copyright infringement occurs if a program emulates the "look and feel" of another program, even if the code differs. On this basis, Lotus Development Corporation sued Paperback Software International, claiming that Paperback's VP-Planner copied the look and feel of Lotus 1-2-3. In a move that astonished industry observers, Apple Computer sued Microsoft Corporation, claiming that Microsoft Windows copied the look and feel of the Macintosh user interface. These and other cases will require years of litigation to resolve, but few firms have attempted software clones recently. The cost of litigation can ruin a small company, even if that company wins. See *Extended Industry Standard Architecture (EISA)*, *IBM Personal System/2*, and *Micro Channel Bus*.

**close**   In a program that can display more than one document window, to remove a window from the display.

In many applications, you must save your work before you close a window. If you haven't saved your work, the program probably will display an alert box warning you to save. To abandon your work, confirm that you don't want to save the document. See *document window*.

**closed bus system**   A computer design in which the computer's internal data bus does not contain receptacles and is not easily upgraded by users. See *open bus system*.

**cluster**   In a floppy disk or hard disk, a unit of storage that includes one or more sectors.

When DOS stores a file on disk, DOS breaks down the file's contents and distributes them among dozens or even hundreds of clusters drawn from hither and thither all over the disk. The file allocation table (FAT) tracks how all the sectors on a disk are connected. See *file allocation table (FAT)*, *file fragmentation*, and *sector*.

**CLV**   See *constant linear velocity*.

**CMOS**   See *Complementary Metal-Oxide Semiconductor*.

**coaxial cable**   In local area networks, a high-bandwidth connecting cable in which an insulated wire runs through the middle of the cable. Surrounding the insulated wire is a second wire made of solid or mesh metal.

Coaxial cable is much more expensive than twisted-pair cable (ordinary telephone wire), but coaxial cable can carry more data. Coaxial cables are required for high-bandwidth broadband systems and for fast baseband systems such as EtherNet. See *bandwidth*, *broadband*, *local area network (LAN)*, and *twisted-pair cable*.

**COBOL**   A high-level programming language specially designed for business applications.

Short for COmmon Business Oriented Language, COBOL is a compiled language that originated in a 1959 committee representing business, government, defense, and academic organizations. Released in 1964, the language was the first to introduce the data record as a principal data structure. Because COBOL is designed to store, retrieve, and process corporate accounting information and to automate such functions as inventory control, billing, and payroll, the language quickly became the language of choice in businesses. COBOL programs are verbose but easy to read because most commands resemble English. The programmer, therefore, hardly can help documenting the program, and program maintenance and enhancement are easy even if personnel change frequently. COBOL is the most widely used programming language in corporate mainframe environments.

Versions of COBOL are available for personal computers, but the language's strengths for corporate computing are of little relevance to stand-alone workstations. Business applications for personal computers far more frequently are created and maintained in the dBASE command language that taps the flexible data record capabilities of this popular database management system. See *dBASE* and *high-level programming language*.

**code**   To express a problem-solving algorithm in a programming language. See *algorithm*.

**code page**   In DOS, a table of 256 codes for an IBM PC–compatible computer's character set. Code pages are classed as two kinds:

- *Hardware code page*. The character set built into the computer's ROM.

- *Prepared code page*. A disk-based character set you can use to override the hardware code page.

Prepared code pages contain character sets appropriate for foreign languages. (Supported by MS-DOS 4.0, for example, are Canadian French, Danish, Finnish, French, German, Italian, Latin American Spanish, Dutch, Norwegian, Portuguese, Peninsular Spanish, U.K. English, and U.S. English.) To override the hardware code page, use the CHANGE CODE PAGE (CHCP) command. See *character set*.

**codes**   See *hidden codes*.

**cold boot**   A system start-up initiated by turning on the
system's power switch. See *boot* and *warm boot*.

**cold link**   A method of copying information from one document (the source document) to another (the target
document) so that the link can be updated. To update
the link, you choose a command that opens the source
document, reads the information, and recopies the
information if it has changed. See *dynamic data
exchange (DDE)*, *hot link*, *inter-application communication (IAC)*, and *System 7*.

**collapse**   In an outlining utility or a graphical disk directory
(such as Microsoft Windows' File Manager), to hide all
the subordinate entries below the selected outline
heading or directory.

 In File Manager (Microsoft Windows),
you can double-click the directory icon to
collapse a directory quickly.

**collate**   See *sort*.

**collating sequence**   See *sort order*.

**collision**   In local area networks, a garbled transmission
that results from simultaneous transmissions by two or
more workstations to the same network cable. See
*local area network (LAN)*.

**color**   In typography, the tone quality of the printed portion
of the page, which should be perceived by the eye as an
overall shade of gray without interruption from rivers,
bad word breaks, poor character spacing, or uneven
line spacing.

To maintain good color, use consistent word spacing,
avoid widows and orphans, use kerning as necessary
(especially for display type), and avoid hyphen ladders.
See *hyphen ladder*, *kerning*, *orphan*, *river*, and *widow*.

**Color Graphics Adapter (CGA)**   A bit-mapped graphics
display adapter for IBM PC–compatible computers.

This adapter displays four colors simultaneously with a resolution of 200 pixels horizontally and 320 lines vertically or displays one color with a resolution of 640 pixels horizontally and 200 lines vertically.

CGAs can drive composite color monitors and RGB monitors, but screen resolution produced by CGA adapters is inferior to that of EGA and VGA adapters. See *bit-mapped graphic*, *composite color monitor*, *Enhanced Graphics Adapter (EGA)*, *RGB monitor*, and *Video Graphics Array (VGA)*.

**color monitor**    A computer display device that can display an image in multiple colors, unlike a monochrome monitor that displays one color on a black or white background.

**color scheme**    A named collection of screen colors you can select from a menu to customize a program's on-screen appearance.

In Microsoft Windows, you can choose Colors from the Control Panel to display the Color dialog box (see fig. C.5). You can choose from a variety of preset color schemes, which range from understated to gaudy. If Microsoft's color schemes don't suit you, you can individually paint the screen to your liking.

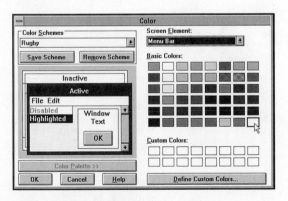

**Fig. C.5.** The Color dialog box.

**color separation**    The creation of a multicolor graphic by creating several layers, with each layer corresponding

to one of the colors that will be printed when a professional printer reproduces the graphic. See *Pantone
Matching System (PMS)*.

**column**   In character-based video displays, a vertical one-
character-wide line down the screen. In a spreadsheet,
a vertical block of cells, identified (in most programs)
by a unique alphabetical letter. In a database management program, the terms *column* and *field* are sometimes used synonymously.

**column graph**   In presentation and analytical graphics, a
graph with vertical columns. Column graphs are commonly used to show the values of items as they vary at
precise intervals over a period of time (see fig. C.6).
The x-axis (categories axis) is the horizontal axis, and
the y-axis (values axis) is the vertical axis. Such graphs
are often called *bar graphs*, but technically speaking,
bar graphs have horizontal bars.

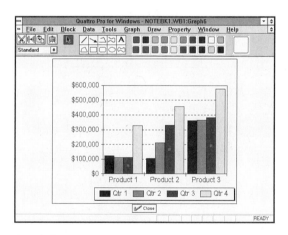

**Fig. C.6.** A column graph.

Column graphs should be differentiated from line
graphs, which suggest a continuous change over time.
Column graphs suggest that the information was obtained at intervals. In this sense, column graphs are more
honest than line graphs in some cases, because a line
graph suggests that you are making data observations all
along instead of once a month or once every two weeks.

When displaying more than one data series, clustering
the columns (see fig. C.7) or overlapping them (see
fig. C.8) is helpful. With caution, you also can create a
three-dimensional effect to differentiate the columns,
if it really helps clarify the data (see fig. C.9). See *bar
graph*, *histogram*, *line graph*, *stacked column graph*,
*x-axis*, and *y-axis*.

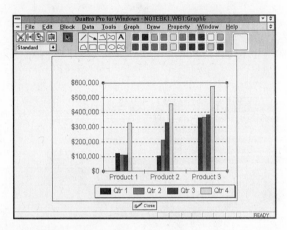

**Fig. C.7.** Clustered columns.

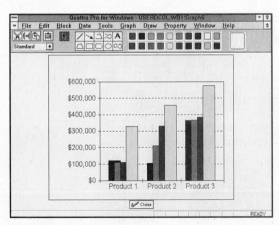

**Fig. C.8.** Overlapped columns.

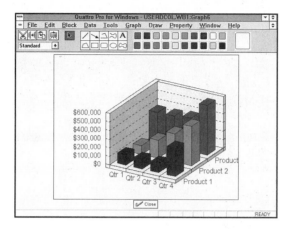

**Fig. C.9.** A three-dimensional column graph.

**column indicator** In word processing programs, an on-screen status message that shows the current number of horizontal spaces, or columns, the cursor has moved across the screen.

**column text chart** In presentation graphics, a text chart used to show related text items side by side in two or three columns (see fig. C.10).

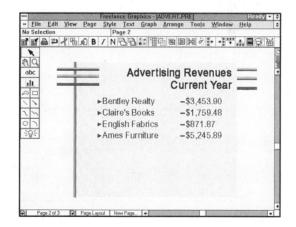

**Fig. C.10.** A column text chart.

**column-wise recalculation**   In spreadsheet programs, a
   recalculation order that calculates all the values in
   column A before moving to column B, and so on.

 If your spreadsheet program does not offer
   natural recalculation, use column-wise
   recalculation for worksheets in which
   columns are summed and the totals are
   forwarded. Row-wise recalculation may produce erroneous results. See *natural recalculation*, *optimal
   recalculation*, and *row-wise recalculation*.

**COM**   In DOS, a device name that refers to as many as four
   serial communications ports (COM1, COM2, COM3,
   and COM4). When used as an extension to a file name,
   COM indicates an executable program file limited to
   64K. To run a COM file, you type the file name (but not
   the extension) and press Enter.

**combinatorial explosion**   A barrier to the solution of a
   problem that occurs when the possibilities that have to
   be computed are too numerous.

   Combinatorial explosions vex the designers of chess
   software, which must frequently compute and analyze
   tens of thousands of alternative moves in a turn. People
   are better than computers at solving such problems,
   because they rely on as yet poorly understood intuitive
   processes that narrow down the range of possibilities
   to a manageable number, which is why the best chess
   champions can still beat the best chess programs.

**Comité Consultatif International Téléphonique et
   Télégraphique (CCITT)**   An international organization that sets standards for analog and digital
   communications involving modems, computer networks, digital signal transmission, and fax machines. In
   the United States, early modem communications standards were proprietary standards, such as the use of
   the Bell 103 standard for 300-baud telecommunications
   in place of the CCITT V. 21 standard. Increasingly, U.S.
   firms are switching to CCITT standards. Commonly

used, for example, is the V.22 standard, which governs modem telecommunications at 2400 baud. CCITT standards are also evident in fax machines, which conform to the CCITT Group 3 standards.

**comma-delimited file**   A data file, usually in ASCII file format, in which a user or program has separated the data items by commas to facilitate the transfer of data to another program. See *ASCII*, *file format*, and *tab-delimited file*.

**command**   A user-initiated signal given to a computer program that initiates, terminates, or otherwise controls the execution of a specific operation.

In command-driven programs, you have to memorize the command statement and its associated syntax and type the command. In a menu-driven program, you choose a command from an on-screen menu. See *command-driven program*, *graphical user interface (GUI)*, and *menu-driven program*.

**command button**   In graphical user interfaces such as Microsoft Windows or the Macintosh Finder, a button in a dialog box that initiates an action such as carrying out a command with the options you have chosen, cancelling a command, or displaying another dialog box.

You can quickly choose the default button just by pressing Return (Macintoshes) or Enter (Windows systems). See *pushbutton*.

**COMMAND.COM**   In DOS, an essential system disk file that contains the command processor. This file must be present on the start-up disk for DOS to run. See *command processor*.

**command-driven program**   A system, utility, or application program that requires you to memorize keyboard commands and to rely on your memory to type command statements with the correct syntax and nomenclature. See *graphical user interface (GUI)* and *menu-driven program*.

**command key**  On Macintosh keyboards, a key marked
with ⌘ that is frequently used in combination with
alphabetical keys to provide keyboard shortcuts for
menu options. Apple has standardized these shortcuts
so that all Macintosh applications support them. Note
the following standard Macintosh keyboard shortcuts:

| *Keyboard Shortcut* | *Menu Equivalent* |
| --- | --- |
| ⌘-A | Select All |
| ⌘-C | Copy |
| ⌘-N | New |
| ⌘-O | Open |
| ⌘-P | Print |
| ⌘-Q | Quit |
| ⌘-S | Save |
| ⌘-V | Paste |
| ⌘-W | Close |
| ⌘-X | Cut |
| ⌘-Z | Undo |

**command language**  See *software command language*.

**command-line operating system**  A command-driven
operating system, such as MS-DOS, that requires you to
type commands at the keyboard. See *graphical user
interface (GUI)*.

**command processor**  The portion of a command-line
operating system that handles user input and
displays prompts and messages such as confirmation
messages and error messages. See *COMMAND.COM*
and *command-line operating system*.

**comment**  See *remark*.

**communications parameters**  In telecommunications and
serial printing, the settings (parameters) that customize

serial communications for the hardware you are contacting. See *baud rate*, *communications protocol*, *full
duplex*, *half duplex*, *parameter*, *parity bit*, and *stop bit*.

**communications program**   An application program that
turns your computer into a terminal for transmitting
data to and receiving data from distant computers
through the telephone system.

A good communications program includes a software
command language you can use to automate cumbersome log-on procedures, the support of two or more
file-transfer protocols (such as XMODEM and Kermit),
terminal emulation of two or more popular mainframe
terminals (such as the DEC VT100), and on-screen
timing so that you can keep track of time charges and
facilities for storing and retrieving telephone numbers.

 For communications software, most users
need not fork over big bucks for a commercial program; several excellent shareware
communications programs are available.
Examples include PC-Talk and QMODEM for IBM PC–
compatible computers. See *terminal* and *terminal
emulation*.

**communications protocol**   A list of communications
parameters (settings) and standards that govern the
transfer of information among computers using telecommunications. Both computers must have the same
settings and follow the same standards to avoid errors.

When you use a modem to access a bulletin board or
information service, such as CompuServe, you must
choose the correct communications protocol—the one
established by the host computer system. Your communications program enables you to choose the necessary
parameters, including baud rate, data bits, duplex, parity,
and stop bits. The baud rate usually is determined by
your modem's capabilities. Most communications services use eight data bits and one stop bit; full duplex is
also common. Before you attempt to establish communication with an on-line service, read the documentation

to find out which communications parameters to use. The settings are prominently displayed at the beginning of the documentation.

You may have to specify an additional parameter called *handshaking*. This parameter establishes the way one computer tells the other device when to wait. Almost all computers and many peripheral devices use XON/XOFF handshaking, the default for most communications programs.

 If you are having trouble establishing communication with an on-line service, press Enter twice and try these settings:

Parity: No
Data bits: 8
Stop bits: 1
Duplex: Full

If you cannot see what you are typing, switch to half duplex. If the preceding settings don't work, hang up and dial again with these settings:

Parity: Even
Data bits: 7
Stop bits: 1
Duplex: Full or half

If you are using half duplex and see the echoed characters HHEELLOO, switch to full duplex. See *asynchronous communication, baud rate, communications parameters, communications program, file transfer protocol, handshaking, mode, modem, parity, stop bit,* and *terminal emulation*.

**communications settings**  See *communications parameters* and *communications protocol*.

**comp**  In desktop publishing, a complete mock-up of a page layout design, showing what the final printed page will look like.

**compact disk (CD)**   A plastic disk, 4.75 inches in diameter, that uses optical storage techniques to store up to 72 minutes of music or 650M of digitally encoded computer data.

In an optical storage medium, digital data is stored as microscopic pits and smooth areas with different reflective properties. A precisely controlled beam of laser light shines on the disk so that the reflections can be detected and translated into digital data.

Compact disks provide read-only secondary storage. The computer can read information from the disk, but you cannot change this information or write new information to the disk. Therefore, this storage medium accurately is termed *CD-ROM* (read-only memory). Erasable optical disk drives are now available and are expected to have a major impact on secondary storage techniques in the 1990s. In the meantime, however, compact disks are expected to become popular for the distribution of huge databases to personal computer users who have systems equipped with CD-ROM disk drives. Currently, the disks tend to be very expensive because the market is small, but as CD-ROM disk drives become available at lower prices, the price of the disks also should drop. The average computer user eventually may work with a system capable of displaying, in an on-screen window, the contents of huge databases, such as the complete works of William Shakespeare or the *Encyclopedia of Science and Technology*. See *CD-ROM disk drive, erasable optical disk drive, optical disk,* and *secondary storage*.

**Compact Disk–Interactive (CD-I)**   A compact-disk standard designed for interactive viewing of audio/visual compact disks using a television set and a CD-I player. Designed for education, training, and entertainment, CD-I has been slow to find a market.

**company network**   A wide-area computer network, such as DEC ENET (the internal engineering network of Digital Equipment Corporation), that often has automatic gateways to cooperative networks such as ARPANET or BITNET for functions such as electronic mail and file transfer.

**COMPAQ Computer Corporation**   A Houston company that manufacturers high-performance IBM PC–compatible desktop and portable computers.

COMPAQ was the first maker of IBM Personal Computer clones, and their first computers were portable versions of the popular PC. The company sold over $100 million worth of computers in its first year in business (1983), setting a U.S. record. Subsequently, the firm became known as the maker of technically sophisticated, high-end machines that featured fast clock speeds and other technical improvements.

COMPAQ also was the first manufacturer to develop and market a desktop computer based on the Intel 80386 microprocessor, and the firm played a leading role in the development of the Extended Industry Standard Architecture (EISA), an alternative to IBM's proprietary Micro Channel Bus. COMPAQ's fortunes declined in 1991 because the firm failed to distinguish its pricey products from cheaper clones. A 1992 price cut resulted in reduced profits and the departure of the firm's founder and CEO. See *Extended Industry Standard Architecture (EISA)*.

**comparison operator**   See *relational operator*.

**compatibility**   The capability of a peripheral, a program, or an adapter to function with or substitute for a given make and model of computer. Also, the capability of one computer to run the software of another company's computer.

To be truly compatible, a program or device should operate on a given system without modification; all features should operate as intended, and a computer claiming to be compatible with another should run all the other computer's software without modification.

 In IBM PC–compatible computing, a frequently used index of 100-percent IBM compatibility is a computer's capability to run Microsoft Flight Simulator. See *clone*.

**compiler**   A program that reads the statements written in a human-readable programming language, such as Pascal or Modula-2, and translates the statements into a machine-readable executable program.

Compiled programs run significantly faster than interpreted ones because the entire program has been translated into machine language and need not share memory space with the interpreter. See *interpreter* and *machine language*.

**Complementary Metal-Oxide Semiconductor (CMOS)**
An energy-saving chip fabricated to duplicate the functions of other chips, such as memory chips or microprocessors. CMOS chips are used in battery-powered portable computers and in other applications where reduced electrical consumption is desired. See *chip*.

**complex instruction set computer (CISC)**   A central processing unit (CPU) that can recognize as many as 100 or more instructions, enough to carry out most computations directly.

Most microprocessors are CISC chips. The use of RISC technology is becoming increasingly common, however, in professional workstations and is expected to migrate to personal computers in the mid-1990s. See *central processing unit (CPU)* and *reduced instruction set computer (RISC)*.

**compose sequence**   A series of keystrokes that enables you to enter a character not found on the computer's keyboard. In Lotus 1-2-3, for example, you can enter *é* by pressing Alt-F1 and then typing *233*.

**composite**   See *comp*.

**composite color monitor**   A monitor that accepts a standard analog video signal that mixes red, green, and blue signals to produce the color image. Display quality is inferior to that of RGB monitors. See *composite video* and *RGB monitor*.

**composite video**   A method for broadcasting video signals in which the red, green, and blue signals are mixed together.

Composite video, regulated by the U.S. National Television Standards Committee (NTSC), is used for television. Some computers have composite video outputs that use a standard RCA phono plug and cable such as on the backplane of a high-fidelity system. See *composite color monitor* and *RGB monitor*.

**compound device**   In multimedia, a device (such as a MIDI sequencer) that reproduces sound or other output that you record in a specific media file, such as a MIDI file. See *Musical Instrument Digital Interface (MIDI)*.

**compound document**   In object linking and embedding (OLE), a single file created by two or more applications. When you use OLE to embed a Microsoft Excel chart into a Microsoft Word document, the resulting file contains the Word text as well as the Excel object, which contains all the information Excel needs to open the file and make the chart available for editing. Compound documents are considerably larger than normal files because they must contain the information needed by all the applications that created them. See *object linking and embedding (OLE)*.

**compressed file**   A file that a file compression utility has written to a special disk format that minimizes the storage space required. See *file compression utility*.

**CompuServe**   The largest and most successful personal computer information service.

Essentially a for-profit version of a bulletin board system (BBS) coupled with the resources of an on-line information service, CompuServe offers file downloading, electronic mail, current news, up-to-the-minute stock quotes, an on-line encyclopedia, and conferences on a variety of topics. However, the character-based command-line user interface is outmoded and challenging to novice users. If you are interested in using CompuServe, consider using a front-end program like CompuServe Navigator or TAPCIS. See *bulletin board system (BBS)*, *on-line information service*, and *Prodigy*.

**computation**   The successful execution of an algorithm whose steps are finite, executable, and capable of termination. By this definition, a computation can be a successfully completed textual search or sort, as well as a calculation. See *algorithm*.

**computer**   A machine capable of following instructions to alter data in a desirable way and to perform at least some of these operations without human intervention.

Do not think that computers are devices for performing only calculations, although that function is one of many computer tasks. Computers represent and manipulate text, graphics, symbols, and music, as well as numbers. See *analog computer* and *digital computer*.

**computer addiction**   The compulsive use of the computer, such that other activities recede in importance and primary relationships deteriorate.

Are computers addictive? A few minutes spent late at night in the computer room of a university will suffice to sensitize anyone to this question. Inevitably in such locales, you encounter hackers who have allowed virtually everything else in their lives—including their personal cleanliness and their grade point averages—to deteriorate as they become involved in a self-destructive quest for mastery of the computer. A recent study of British university hackers suggests, however, that the people who become addicted to computing in this way show signs of compulsive disorders *before* they discover the computer; for them, computing becomes an avenue by which they can satisfy compulsive drives, while at the same time acquiring highly marketable skills and knowledge. It appears unlikely that a person lacking compulsive disorders would become addicted to the computer in this way.

**computer-aided design (CAD)**   The use of the computer and a computer-aided design program as the environment for the design of a wide range of industrial artifacts, ranging from machine parts to modern homes.

CAD has become a mainstay in a variety of design-related fields, such as architecture, civil engineering, electrical engineering, mechanical engineering, and interior design; however, computer-aided design has been dominated until recently by expensive dedicated minicomputer systems. CAD applications are graphics- and calculation-intensive, requiring fast processors and high-resolution video displays. CAD programs often include sophisticated statistical analysis routines that help designers optimize their applications, as well as their extensive symbol libraries. All these features require huge amounts of processing power—a requirement that kept CAD off early personal computers.

Like many other professional computer applications based on expensive mainframe or minicomputer systems, however, CAD is migrating to powerful personal computers, such as those based on the Intel 80386, Intel 80486, Motorola 68030, and Motorola 68040 microprocessors. CAD software for personal computers blends the object-oriented graphics found in draw programs with precision scaling in two and three dimensions. Drawings can be produced with an intricate level of detail. See *draw program* and *object-oriented graphic*.

**computer-aided design and drafting (CADD)**   The use of a computer system for industrial design and technical drawing.

CADD software closely resembles computer-aided design (CAD) software but has additional features that enable the artist to produce drawings conforming to engineering conventions.

**computer-assisted instruction (CAI)**   The use of instructional programs to perform instructional tasks, such as drill and practice, tutorials, and tests.

Unlike human teachers, a CAI program doesn't get bored or frustrated with a slow student and is blind to distinctions of gender and race. Ideally, CAI could use sound, graphics, and on-screen rewards to engage a student in learning—with huge payoffs. In practice, however, a great deal of CAI software is badly designed: the software is stilted and boring and emphasizes drill and practice, often in a way that suggests remedial instruction.

With standard programming techniques, creating quality instructional software is a big job, which accounts for the scarcity of high-quality CAI software. With the advent of multimedia, however, CAI may be entering a new era. Standard computer configurations, such as a character-based PC equipped with a printer, reduce the appeal of CAI programs; they are visually drab and lack information density. Multimedia machines equipped with compact disks, video, and sound, however, may function to open new worlds to students by placing immense reservoirs of knowledge and experience in every classroom. Authoring languages, such as HyperTalk, make developing high-quality instructional software much easier. By using techniques that enable interactive exploration of a subject, multimedia promises to engage learners in a kind of creative exploration not possible with standard computer configurations. See *authoring language*, *HyperTalk*, and *multimedia*.

**computer-based training (CBT)**   The use of computer-aided instruction (CAI) techniques to train adults for specific skills, such as operating a numerically controlled lathe.

**Computer Graphics Metafile (CGM)**   An international graphics file format that stores object-oriented graphics in device-independent form so that you can exchange CGM files among users of different systems (and different programs).

Personal computer programs that can read and write to CGM file formats include Harvard Graphics and Ventura Publisher.

CGM is a loose standard and, as many users have discovered, a CGM file created by one application may not be readable by another. Industry analysts believe CGM will be supplanted by the Microsoft Windows vector graphics standard, the Windows Metafile Format (WMF). See *object-oriented graphic* and *Windows Metafile Format (WMF)*.

**computer system** A complete computer installation— including peripherals, such as disk drives, a monitor, and a printer—in which all the components are designed to work with each other.

**CON** In DOS, the device name that refers to the keyboard and monitor.

The command COPY CON C:AUTOEXEC.BAT, for example, creates a file called AUTOEXEC.BAT and stores in this file all the characters you type after giving the command. To finish copying text from the keyboard, press Ctrl-Z and then press Enter.

**concatenation** The combination of two or more units of information, such as text or files, so that they form one unit.

In DOS, you easily can combine two or more files by using a straightforward (but little-known) variation of the COPY command. Normally, the COPY command copies the source file (the first file named) to the target file (the second file named). To combine files, you list all the source files, using plus signs to separate them. The following command combines all the DOC files into one backup file (REPORT.BAK):

```
COPY REPORT1.DOC+REPORT2.DOC
+REPORT3.DOC REPORT.BAK
```

**concordance file** A file containing the words you want a word processing program to include in the index the program constructs.

To index a document, you have only one choice with most programs: you must mark each occurrence of each word throughout the manuscript. The program includes those words (with page references) in the index, constructed and appended to the document. This operation is tedious because an important word may appear on more than one page.

The best word processing programs, such as WordPerfect, use a concordance file to simplify the manual part of indexing. Instead of marking the words manually throughout the document (many of them more than once), you create a file that contains one sample of each word you want indexed. When you give the command that starts the indexing operation, the program uses the concordance file as a guide and performs the marking operation.

**concurrency control**   In a local area network (LAN) version of an application program, the features built into the program that govern what happens when two or more people try to access the same program feature or data file.

Many application programs that are not designed for networks can run on a network and enable more than one person to access a document, but the results may be catastrophic: nothing prevents one person from inadvertently destroying another person's work. Concurrency control addresses this problem by enabling multiple access where such access can occur without loss of data and by restricting multiple access where such access could result in destroyed work. See *file locking*, *LAN-aware program,* and *LAN-ignorant program.*

**concurrency management**   The capability of an application written for use on a local area network (LAN) to ensure that data files are not corrupted by simultaneous modification or multiple input.

**concurrent processing**   See *multitasking.*

**condensed type**   Type narrowed in width so that more characters will fit into a linear inch. In dot-matrix printers, condensed type usually is set to print 17 characters per inch (cpi). See *characters per inch (cpi).*

**CONFIG.SYS**   In DOS, an ASCII text file that contains configuration commands.

DOS consults this file at system start-up. If no CONFIG.SYS file is on the start-up disk, DOS uses the default configuration values. Most programs work well with the default configuration settings. Nonstandard peripherals and some application programs, however, may require the presence of a CONFIG.SYS file in the root directory so that these configurations are modified.

The following list is an overview of the most frequently used configuration commands:

- DEVICE. Specifies the driver DOS requires to use a peripheral device. If you are using a mouse, for example, you need to create a CONFIG.SYS file with a statement such as DEVICE=MOUSE.SYS. The root directory must contain a file called MOUSE.SYS. If your mouse doesn't work, check to see whether you have erased CONFIG.SYS. If you recently installed another program, you may have erased your old CONFIG.SYS; you will have to put the DEVICE statement back into the file by using your word processing program.

  Some programs require you to place the following command in your configuration file: DEVICE=ANSI.SYS. ANSI is an acronym for American National Standards Institute, and the file ANSI.SYS (on every DOS disk) contains procedures for controlling the display of information. The file called ANSI.SYS must be present in the root directory.

- DOS=HIGH. Loads most of the transient portion of DOS into High Memory. This procedure results in more of the precious 640K of RAM being available for application programs. (Only MS-DOS 5.0 and later.)

- DEVICEHIGH. Replaces the traditional DEVICE= statement for most devices. This command loads a particular device into High Memory, freeing more of the lower 640K. For example, to load a mouse driver into high memory, you could use a statement such as DEVICEHIGH=MOUSE.SYS. (Only MS-DOS 5.0 or later.)

- BUFFERS. Determines the number of areas DOS sets aside in memory to store disk data temporarily. The default setting varies according to the version of DOS you are using. Some application programs require you to specify more buffers than the DOS default number. You may need to add a statement such as BUFFERS=15 before these programs will work.

- FILES. Determines the number of files that can be open at the same time. The default setting is eight files.

If the preceding material seems too technical, do not worry: the peripherals and programs that require CONFIG.SYS statements usually create them automatically when you follow the standard installation procedure. Knowing about these commands is worthwhile, however, especially if you accidentally erase CONFIG.SYS or, as sometimes happens, if an installation program erases the existing CONFIG.SYS and substitutes its own.

 If an application program you are using has written a CONFIG.SYS file to your start-up disk, do not erase the CONFIG.SYS file. If you do, the program may not run, or some features may be disabled. If you erase CONFIG.SYS accidentally, repeat the program's installation procedure. See *American National Standards Institute (ANSI), ANSI.SYS, ASCII, buffer, driver, mouse, peripheral,* and *root directory.*

**configuration**   The choices made in setting up a computer system or an application program so that it meets the user's needs.

Properly configuring your system or program is one of the more onerous tasks of personal computing and, sad to say, it has not been eliminated by the arrival of windowing environments. Microsoft Windows, for example, is equipped with sophisticated installation software that analyzes your system's capabilities and chooses an appropriate configuration, but often you must perform some manual configuration to obtain maximum performance from Windows and to take full advantage of the memory available on your system. Along the way, you may be obliged to distinguish among upper memory, high memory, extended memory, and expanded memory, in addition to the usual kinds of memory: memory, more memory, and not enough memory.

Once established, the configuration is saved to a configuration file, where it is vulnerable to accidental erasure. Windows, for example, stores the user's configuration choices in a file called WIN.INI, which you should be very careful not to erase. In addition to creating configuration files, programs also frequently perform surreptitious modifications to AUTOEXEC.BAT and CONFIG.SYS, the two files that DOS consults when you start your system. If you delete these files, your system may not perform as you expect, and applications—if they run at all—may revert to their preconfigured states or prevent you from choosing certain commands.

**configuration file**    A file, created by an application program, that stores the choices you make when you install the program so that they are available the next time you start the program. In Microsoft Word, for example, the file MW.INI stores the choices you make from the Options menu.

More than a few users have inadvertently erased configuration files by erasing unidentifiable files in an attempt to free up disk space. Avoid erasing the configuration file your program creates (beware of files with extensions such as CFG, INI, or SET). If you erase the configuration file, the program probably will revert to the default settings chosen by its programmers. These settings may or may not prove suitable for your system and application needs. In the extreme, the program may not function at all, and you may have to reinstall it.

To avoid disturbing configuration and other vital program files, don't store your documents in your application's directory. If you store them elsewhere, you will be less likely to erase vital application files when you are deleting unwanted documents.

**confirmation message**   An on-screen message asking you to confirm a potentially destructive action, such as closing a window without saving your work. See *alert box.*

**connectivity**   The extent to which a given computer or program can function in a network setting.

**connectivity platform**   A program or utility designed to enhance another program's capability to exchange data with other programs through a local area network. Oracle for the Macintosh, for example, provides HyperCard with the connectivity required to search for and retrieve information from large corporate databases. See *HyperCard* and *local area network (LAN).*

**console**   A display terminal, consisting of a monitor and keyboard.

In multiuser systems, *console* is synonymous with *terminal*, but *console* also is used in personal computer operating systems to refer to the keyboard and display.

**constant**   In a spreadsheet program, a number you type directly into a cell or place in a formula.

You see two kinds of numbers in a worksheet's cells. Constants are numbers you type on the entry line. These numbers do not change unless you edit the cell contents or type a new value in the cell. The second kind of number is the value produced by a hidden formula. You cannot tell the difference between a constant and a value produced by a formula just by looking at the worksheet. If you place the pointer on the cell, however, the actual cell definition—including a formula, if present—appears on the entry line.

If you type a constant in a cell containing a value produced by a formula, you erase the formula in the cell. This mistake is a common cause of major errors in spreadsheet calculations.

You should avoid entering constants in formulas. Suppose that you have created a worksheet in which each column computes a commission of 5 percent. You enter this constant into 15 formulas. If you decide to compute the commission at 6 percent, you must change all 15 formulas.

A better solution is to place the constant in one cell, called a *key*, and place this cell at the top of the worksheet. You then reference this cell in the formulas. That way, if you change the constant, you make only one change instead of fifteen. See *cell definition* and *key variable*.

**constant angular velocity (CAV)**   In auxiliary storage media such as disk drives, a playback technique in which the disk rotates at a constant speed. This technique results in faster data retrieval times as the read/write head nears the spindle; retrieval times slow as the read/write head moves toward the perimeter of the disk. See *constant linear velocity (CLV)*.

**constant linear velocity (CLV)**   In compact disk players, a playback technique that speeds or slows the rotation of the disk to ensure that the velocity of the disk at the reading point remains constant. To achieve constant linear velocity, the rotational speed of the spindle motor must be inversely proportional to the distance of the read point from the spindle. The closer to the spindle, the slower the speed. In contrast to CLV devices, constant angular velocity (CAV) devices such as hard disks access data at differing rates, depending on the distance of the read/write head from the drive spindle. See *constant angular velocity (CAV)*.

**contention**   In local area networks, a channel access method in which access to the communication channel is based on a first-come, first-served policy. See *carrier sense multiple access with collision detection (CSMA/CD)*.

**context-sensitive help**   In an application package, a user-assistance mode that displays on-screen documentation relevant to the command, mode, or action you currently are performing.

Context-sensitive help is a desirable program feature because it reduces the time and keystrokes needed to get on-screen help. In WordPerfect, for example, if you press Help (F3) after pressing Format (Shift-F8), you see a help screen explaining the options available on the Format menu. Without context-sensitive help, you have to locate the desired information manually from an index or menu.

**context switching**   The immediate activation of a program loaded into random-access memory (RAM) along with one or more other programs in a multiple loading operating system.

Unlike true multitasking, a multiple loading operating system, such as the Macintosh System equipped with MultiFinder, enables you to load more than one program at a time, but while you are using the foreground program, the background program stops executing. For a stand-alone computer, multiple-loading operating systems provide a high level of functionality: they allow you to switch rapidly from one program to another. When combined with a graphical user interface and cut-and-paste facilities provided by the Clipboard, context switching enables you to move data rapidly and easily from one application to another. See *DESQview, multiple program loading,* and *multitasking*.

**contiguous**   Adjacent; placed one after the other. In Microsoft Windows, for instance, the permanent swap file must occupy contiguous sectors on the disk. The file's maximum size—and, in consequence, Windows' ability to create virtual memory for your system—is limited by the number of contiguous sectors available.

Before creating a permanent swap file for Microsoft Windows, run a file defragmentation utility to free up the maximum number of contiguous free sectors.

**continuous paper**   Paper manufactured in one long strip, with perforations separating the pages, so that you can feed the paper into a printer that has a tractor-feed mechanism. Synonymous with *continuous-feed paper*.

**continuous tone**   An illustration, whether black-and-white or color, in which tones change smoothly and continuously from the darkest to the lightest, without noticeable gradations.

**Control-Break**   In DOS, a keyboard command that suspends the execution of a program at the next available break point.

**control code**   In the American Standard Code for Information Interchange (ASCII), a code reserved for hardware-control purposes, such as advancing a page on the printer. ASCII has 32 control codes. See *ASCII*.

**Control (Ctrl) key**   In IBM PC–compatible computing, a key frequently pressed with other keys for program commands. In WordStar, for example, pressing Ctrl-Y deletes a line.

**controller**   See *disk drive controller*.

**controller card**   An adapter that connects disk drives to the computer. Most personal computer controller cards contain circuitry to connect one or more floppy disks and hard disks. See *adapter*.

**control menu**   In Microsoft Windows, a pull-down menu found in most windows and dialog boxes that contains options for managing the active window (see fig C.11). The control menu icon, shaped like a hyphen, is always on the left edge of the title bar. The contents of this menu vary, but usually include commands to move, size, maximize, and minimize windows, as well as to close the current window or switch to another application window or the next document window.

Control menu icon    Control menu

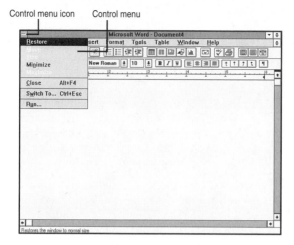

**Fig. C.11.** The control menu.

 To display the control menu of an application window or a dialog box quickly, press Alt–space bar. To open a document window's control menu, press Alt-hyphen.

**control panel**   In Lotus 1-2-3, the top three lines of the display screen. The top line contains the current cell indicator, the mode indicator, and the entry line. The second and third lines contain menus and prompts. In the Macintosh and Windows systems, a utility menu that lists options for hardware devices, such as the mouse, monitor, and keyboard.

**control panel device (CDEV)**   Any Macintosh utility program, placed in the System Folder, that appears as an option in the Control Panel. CDEV is pronounced "see-dev."

**control structure**   A logical organization for an algorithm that governs the sequence in which program statements are executed.

Control statements govern the flow of control in a program. They specify the sequence in which the program's steps are to be carried out. Early programs offered only a few control structures, such as a simple sequence interrupted occasionally by GOTO statements. A major trend in the design of programming languages, however, has been toward the nearly universal adoption of more modern control structures. These control structures include branch structures that cause a special set of instructions to be executed if a specified situation is encountered, loop structures that execute over and over until a condition is fulfilled, and procedure/function structures that set aside distinct program functions or procedures into separate modules, which are invoked from the main program.

The use of sequential, branch, and loop structures to express an algorithm is more than just a good practice; this technique is valid for important scientific reasons. A brilliant mathematical proof demonstrated that these three structures are adequate for the procedural expression of any known algorithm. The use of control structures tends to make a program more readable by humans, and readability is important in organizational settings, where someone other than the original programmer may be called on to maintain or enhance the program. Readability is enhanced, too, by avoiding GOTO statements that tend to produce a jumble of untrackable program interconnections, called *spaghetti code* by the detractors of BASIC (which uses GOTO statements).

In personal computing, you are likely to use control structures even if you do not plan to learn a high-level programming language. Most software command languages, including macro commands, include control structures, such as DO/WHILE loops, case branches, FOR/NEXT loops, IF/THEN/ELSE branches, and repeat loops.

 Take a hint from professional programmers: make your macros more readable (for yourself and others) and avoid spaghetti code by sticking to the three basic control

structures—sequential, branch, and loop—for all program functions. Avoid GOTO statements; instead, use a
named procedure and mark the procedure clearly so
that you can find it if you need to update or debug it.
See *branch control structure*, *case branch*, *DO/WHILE
loop*, *FOR/NEXT loop*, *high-level programming language*, *IF/THEN/ELSE*, *loop control structure*, and *structured programming*.

**control unit**    A component of the central processing unit
(CPU) that obtains program instructions and emits
signals to carry them out. See *arithmetic-logic unit
(ALU)* and *central processing unit (CPU)*.

**conventional memory**    In any personal computer employing an Intel 8086, 8088, 80286, 80386, or 80486
microprocessor, the first 640K of the computer's
random-access memory (RAM) that is accessible to
programs running under DOS.

The Intel 8086 and 8088 microprocessors, which were
available when the IBM Personal Computer (PC) was
designed, can directly use 1M of random-access
memory (RAM). The PC's designers decided to make
640K of RAM accessible to programs, leaving the rest
of the 1M memory space available for internal system
functions.

640K seemed like a great deal of memory in the early
1980s—in fact, the figure was chosen because it was
exactly 10 times the amount of memory available for
the leading microcomputers of the time. 640K has since
proved insufficient, however, because users frequently
want to run more than one program at a time. For this
reason, many users equip their systems with extended
or expanded memory and with the programs (called
*extended memory managers* or *expanded memory
managers*) that are required to access this memory.
See *expanded memory*, *expanded memory manager*,
*extended memory*, *extended memory manager*,
*Microsoft Windows*, *protected mode*, *real mode*, and
*upper memory area*.

**conventional programming** The use of a procedural programming language, such as BASIC, FORTRAN, or assembly language, to code an algorithm in machine-readable form.

In conventional programming, the programmer must be concerned with the sequence in which events occur within the computer. Nonprocedural programming languages enable the programmer to focus on the problem, without worrying about the precise procedure the computer must follow to solve the problem. See *declarative language* and *procedural language*.

**cooperative network** A wide-area computer network, such as BITNET or UUCP, in which the costs of participating are borne by the linked organizations. See *BITNET*, *company network*, *research network*, and *UUCP*.

**coprocessor** A microprocessor support chip optimized for a specific processing operation, such as handling mathematical computations or displaying images on the video display. See *microprocessor* and *numeric coprocessor*.

**copy** The text of a publication, exclusive of all graphics, before the text is formatted and laid out for publication.

**copy editing** A rigorous and exact critique of copy to make sure that it conforms to the publisher's standards for facts, grammar, spelling, clarity, coherence, usage, and punctuation.

**copy fitting** In desktop publishing, a method used to determine the amount of copy (text) that, using a specified font, will fit into a given area on a page or in a publication.

**copy protection** The inclusion in a program of hidden instructions intended to prevent you from making unauthorized copies of software. Because most copy-protection schemes impose penalties on legitimate owners of programs, such as forcing them to insert a specially encoded "key disk" before using a program, most business software publishers have given up using these schemes. Copy protection is still common, however, in recreational and educational software.

**CorelDRAW!**    A sophisticated and elegantly designed illustration program for IBM and IBM-compatible PCs. A Windows application, CorelDRAW! features a variety of special effects, including perspective and highly flexible text-manipulation features. For example, three-dimensional text can be rotated, skewed, stretched, mirrored, or curved. The program weds the capabilities of paint and draw programs to the technical accuracy of professional computer-aided design (CAD) packages. See *computer-aided design (CAD)*, *draw program*, and *paint program.*

**corrupted file**    A file that contains scrambled and unrecoverable data. Files can become corrupted due to bad sectors (surface flaws on the disk), disk drive controller failures, or software errors.

**cost-benefit analysis**    A projection of the costs and benefits of installing a computer system. The analysis compares the costs of operating an enterprise with and without the computer system and calculates the return (if any) on the original investment.

Cost-benefit analyses often involve overly optimistic assumptions about the tangible cost savings of installing a computer system. A word processing program, for example, may enable you to revise a document faster, but the technology invites you to keep working on the document until it is close to perfection, and you may spend more time than you originally would have.

Computerization also may prove more costly than standard methods if the enterprise must carry out its business in an inefficient or unprofitable way. More than a few businesses have failed after installing expensive accounting and inventory systems that proved to be inflexible as the businesses' needs changed.

**counter**   In typography, the space enclosed by the fully or partially enclosed bowl of a letter. See *bowl*.

**Courier**   A monospace typeface, commonly included as a built-in font in laser printers, that simulates the output of office typewriters. For example: `This is Courier type.`

**courseware**   Software developed for computer-assisted instruction (CAI) or computer-based training (CBT) applications. See *computer-assisted instruction (CAI)* and *computer-based training (CBT)*.

**cpi**   See *characters per inch*.

**CP/M**   An operating system for personal computers that uses the 8-bit Intel 8080 and Zilog Z-80 microprocessors.

CP/M (Control Program for Microprocessors) was created in the late 1970s as floppy disk drives became available for early personal computers. Designed for computers with as little as 16K of random-access memory (RAM), CP/M is a command-line operating system that requires users to observe a fussy syntax as they type system commands. CP/M is still widely used, however, on the more than four million 8-bit computers (such as Morrow, Kaypro, and Osborne) still in existence.

CP/M closely resembles MS-DOS; in fact, MS-DOS is a clone of CP/M and was designed to facilitate the translation of 8-bit CP/M business software so that the software would run in the new 16-bit IBM Personal Computer environment. IBM originally approached CP/M's publisher, Digital Research, to write the operating system for its new computer, but Microsoft Corporation got the job instead.

**CPM**   See *critical path method*.

**cps**   See *characters per second*.

**CPU**   See *central processing unit*.

**crash**   An abnormal termination of program execution, usually (but not always) resulting in a frozen keyboard or an unstable state. In most cases, you must reboot the computer to recover from a crash.

**creator type**   In the Macintosh, a four-letter code that identifies the application program used to create a document. The code associates the document with the application so that you can start the application by opening the document. Apple Computer maintains a registry of creator type codes so that no two applications use the same code. See *associated document*.

**criteria range**   In an electronic spreadsheet program that includes data management functions, the range of cells that tells the program how to search or perform aggregate operations on a database. The range contains the conditions, or criteria, you specify to govern how a search is conducted—that is, to control which data records the database commands will locate or affect.

**critical path method (CPM)**   In project management, a technique for planning and timing the execution of tasks that relies on the identification of a critical path— a series of tasks that must be completed in a timely fashion if the entire project is to be completed on time. Project management software helps the project manager identify the critical path.

**cropping**   A graphics editing operation in which you trim the edges from a graphic to make it fit into a given space or to remove unnecessary parts of the image.

**cross-hatching**   The black-and-white patterns added to areas within a pie, bar, or column graph to distinguish one data range from another.

In graphs, the overuse of cross-hatching may create Moiré vibrations, which result from visual interference between cross-hatching patterns. If your graph seems to flicker, reduce the cross-hatching. See *Moiré distortion*.

**cross-linked files**   In DOS, a file-storage error that occurs when two files claim the same disk cluster.

Like lost clusters, cross-linked files occur when the computer is interrupted (by a system crash or a power outage) while it is writing a file.

To repair cross-linked files, run CHKDSK frequently with the /f switch. See *lost cluster*.

**cross-reference** In word processing programs, a code name referring to material previously discussed in a document. When you print the document, the program changes the reference so that the correct page number of the cross-referenced material appears in its place.

Cross-references, such as "See the discussion of burnishing methods on page 19," are helpful to the reader, but they can become a nightmare if you add or delete text. Therefore, the best word processing programs (such as WordPerfect and Microsoft Word) contain cross-reference features. Instead of typing the cross-reference, you mark the original text and assign a code name to the marked text, such as BURNISH. Then you type the code name (not the page number) when you want to cross-reference the original text. When you print your document, the program substitutes the correct page number for the code name. If you discover after printing that you need to add or delete text, the code names are still there, and you can make your changes and print again without worrying about incorrect cross-references.

**crosstalk** The interference generated by cables that are too close to one another.

You sometimes hear crosstalk on the telephone. When speaking long-distance, hearing other voices or entire conversations in the background of your conversation is not uncommon.

**CRT** See *cathode ray tube*.

**CSMA/CD** See *carrier sense multiple access with collision detection*.

**Ctrl**   See *Control (Ctrl) key*.

**Ctrl-Break**   In DOS, a keyboard command that cancels the last command you gave.

**cumulative trauma disorder**   See *repetitive strain injury (RSI)*.

**current cell**   In a spreadsheet program such as Lotus 1-2-3, the cell in which the pointer is positioned. Synonymous with *active cell*.

**current cell indicator**   In Lotus 1-2-3, a message that displays the address of the cell in which the pointer is positioned. If the cell has contents, the program also displays the cell format, its protection status, the column width, and the cell definition.

**current directory**   The directory that DOS or an application uses by default to store and retrieve files.

Within an application, the current directory is usually the one from which you start that application program. Some programs, however, enable you to change the current directory so that you can save data files in a directory other than the one in which the program's files are stored. Synonymous with *default directory*.

**current drive**   The drive the operating system uses for an operation unless you specifically instruct otherwise. Synonymous with *default drive*.

**current graph**   In Lotus 1-2-3, the graph that the program creates when you choose View from the Graph menu and retains in memory until you save the graph or quit the worksheet.

**cursor**   An on-screen blinking character that shows where the next character will appear. See *pointer*.

**cursor-movement keys**   The keys that move the on-screen cursor. Synonymous with *arrow keys*.

The arrow keys on the numeric keypad move the cursor in the directions indicated by the arrows. You can move the cursor one character left or right or one line up or down. Like the keys in the typing area, these keys are autorepeat keys. If you hold down the key, the cursor keeps moving in the direction indicated.

The newest keyboards often include a separate cursor keypad with keys that perform the same function as the arrow keys on the numeric keypad. Some programs configure additional keys so that they move the cursor. These keys include Home, End, Tab, Shift-Tab, PgUp, and PgDn.

Cursor movement is distinguished from scrolling by some programs. The Macintosh version of Microsoft Word, for example, has scrolling commands that display a different portion of the document without moving the cursor. More commonly, however, scrolling commands move the cursor as well as display a different portion of the document. See *scroll*.

**cut and paste**   See *block move*.

**cut-sheet feeder**   A paper-feed mechanism that feeds separate sheets of paper into the printer, where a friction-feed mechanism draws the paper through the printer.

You can purchase cut-sheet feeding mechanisms as optional accessories for dot-matrix and letter-quality printers, but they are standard equipment with laser printers and high-quality inkjet printers. See *friction feed* and *tractor feed*.

**cyberphobia**   An exaggerated and irrational fear of computers. Noted by the psychotherapist Craig Brod and others, cyberphobia stems from the stress individuals encounter as they try to cope with an increasingly computer-driven society.

As personal computing technology diffuses throughout society, cyberphobic acts increasingly find their way into crime and news reports. An unhappy postal inspector, for instance, rushed into the computer room of a main district post office and fired five bullets at the terminal. An employee who believed a new computer system would eliminate her job resisted work assignments at the computer and, when finally forced to sit down in front of it, vomited all over the keyboard.

What is the source of cyberphobia? Often, it develops from an irrational exaggeration of fears that have at least some basis in fact. For example, many people persist in the belief that computers are mathematical devices. Much cyberphobia is therefore a more general form of math anxiety and reflects a deep-set fear of situations that might expose a person's mathematical illiteracy.

Others may fear that computers are about to replace them in their jobs. Such fears may be less easy to dispel, in part because computer professionals have themselves created the myth that computers can replace people. Experience proves, however, that the computer fails as a job-killer. Dianne Feinstein, while serving as mayor of San Francisco, complained that despite the hype of computer salespeople, she had been unable to eliminate a single city job after investing $60 million in new computers. People have lost jobs due to computers, to be sure, but like all forms of cyberphobia, these fears of job loss usually are exaggerated.

Still others feel that computers are dehumanizing and that repeated contact with the computer puts people out of touch with their feelings. Indeed, some computer-oriented people seem unfeeling and mechanical to others. But the belief that computers dehumanize people usually reflects a more general, uncritical notion that logical thinking, scientific activity, mathematical reasoning, or systematic thought are pernicious activities that put people out of contact with their feelings. This notion is as absurd and irrational as claiming that studying the arts or humanities softens your brain to the point that you cannot study calculus. A healthy human mind has room for logic as well as for aesthetic sensibilities and emotion. And today's computers are excellent tools for artistic and literary creativity; most of today's most critically acclaimed novels, for example, were written on personal computers.

**cyclic redundancy check (CRC)**   In DOS, an automatic
error-checking method in which the operating system
performs a computation on the data stored in a disk
sector and writes the result of the computation at the
end of the sector. When the system reads the data from
the file, the computation is performed again, and the
result is compared to the value stored at the end of the
sector. If the two values disagree, the operating system
attempts to read the data again, which usually solves
the problem. If you see an error message such as
CRC ERROR READING DRIVE C, however, it signals
serious problems with the disk. CRC checks are more
commonly used by file compression utilities (such as
PKZIP) and for data communications error detection.

 If DOS can't read a file due to a CRC error,
don't give up hope. A disaster recovery
program such as Diskfix (included with
PC Tools) may be able to recover the file.

**cylinder**   In disk drives, a unit of storage consisting of the
set of tracks that occupy the same position.

On a double-sided disk, a cylinder includes track 1 of
the top and the bottom sides. On hard disks in which
several disks are stacked on top of one another, a cylinder consists of the tracks in a specific location on all
the disks.

# D

**DA**   See *desk accessory*.

**daemon**   Pronounced "demon." In UNIX systems, a utility program that works unobtrusively in the background and comes into play only when needed, performing tasks such as receiving incoming electronic mail. The user is not aware of the daemon's presence.

**daisy chain**   See *chain printing*.

**daisywheel printer**   An impact printer that simulates the typescript produced by an office typewriter.

The term *daisywheel* refers to the mechanism that produces the printout; the characters are mounted in a circular pattern and connected to a hub with spokes, resembling a daisy. To produce a character, the printer spins the wheel until that character is in place. Then the printer strikes the inked ribbon with the character, transferring the image to paper. Because you can remove and replace daisywheels, these printers can print multiple typefaces. However, changing fonts within a document is tedious, because you have to change the daisywheel manually.

Once the ultimate in printing technology, daisywheel printers have all but disappeared from the market, due to the development of inexpensive laser printers. A laser printer can change fonts and typefaces within a document. See *impact printer*.

**DASD**   See *Direct Access Storage Device*.

**data**   Factual information you can use to generate calculations or to make decisions.

**database**   A collection of related information about a subject organized in a useful manner that provides a base or foundation for procedures such as retrieving information, drawing conclusions, and making decisions.

Any collection of information that serves these purposes qualifies as a database, even if the information is not stored on a computer. In fact, important predecessors of today's sophisticated business database systems were files kept on index cards and stored in file cabinets.

Information usually is divided into distinct data records, each with one or more data fields. For example, a video store's record of a children's film may include the following information:

| | |
|---|---|
| TITLE | The Blue Fountain |
| CATEGORY | Children |
| RATING | G |
| RETAIL PRICE | $24.95 |
| RENTED TO | 325-1234 |
| DUE DATE | 12/31/92 |

A data record is a form that includes headings that prompt you to fill in specific information. You can create a database without dividing the record into distinct fields, but headings make accidental omissions more obvious and make retrieval operations function more quickly. See *data field* and *data record*.

**database design**   The choice and arrangement of data fields in a database so that fundamental errors (such as data redundancy and repeating fields) are avoided or minimized. See *data redundancy* and *repeating field*.

**database driver**   In Lotus 1-2-3 Release 3.0, a program that enables 1-2-3 to exchange data with database programs such as dBASE.

**database management**   Tasks related to creating, maintaining, organizing, and retrieving information from a database. See *data manipulation*.

**database management program**   An application program that provides the tools for data retrieval, modification, deletion, and insertion. Such programs also can create a database and produce meaningful output on the printer or on-screen. In personal computing, three kinds of database management programs exist: flat-file, relational, and text-oriented.

Using computers for database management is easier than traditional methods. A computer can sort the records in a few seconds and in several different ways. For example, in a video store's database, you can sort the records by title, category, rating, availability, and so on. Furthermore, a database management program can select just those records that meet the criteria you specify in a query. You can display the results of sorts or selections on-screen or print them in a report. See *flat-file database management program*, *relational database management*, and *text-oriented database management program*.

**database management system (DBMS)**   In mainframe computing, a computer system organized for the systematic management of a large collection of information. In personal computing, a program such as dBASE with similar information storage, organization, and retrieval capacities, sometimes including simultaneous access to multiple databases through a shared field (relational database management). See *flat-file database management program*.

**database structure**   In database management, a definition of the data records in which information is stored, including: the number of data fields; a set of field definitions that for each field specify the type of information, the length, and other characteristics; and a list of field names.

In the following example, the database structure includes six fields:

| | |
|---|---|
| TITLE | The Blue Fountain |
| CATEGORY | Children |
| RATING | G |
| RETAIL PRICE | $24.95 |
| RENTED TO | 325-1234 |
| DUE DATE | 12/31/92 |

The first field is a text field that can accommodate up to 60 characters. The last field is a date field that accepts only eight characters entered in the date format (mm/dd/yy).

Rare is the database structure that does not require alterations after you start entering data. You may not have left enough room for data in a character field, or more likely, you need to add fields to store essential data. Many database management programs, however, do not enable you to redefine the database structure, or if they do, these programs require a cumbersome procedure that may corrupt the data. If you are using such a program, perform exhaustive tests on sample data before typing hundreds of data records. See *data type*.

**data bus**   An internal electronic pathway that allows the microprocessor to exchange data with the random-access memory (RAM). See *bus*, *microprocessor*, and *random-access memory (RAM)*.

**data communication**   The transfer of information from one computer to another.

The transfer can occur via direct cable connections, as in local area networks, or via telecommunications links involving the telephone system and modems. See *local area network (LAN)* and *telecommunications*.

**data deletion**   In a database management program, an operation that deletes records according to specified criteria.

Some database programs do not actually delete the records in such operations; they merely mark the records so that they are not included in data retrieval operations. Therefore, you usually can restore the deleted records if you make a mistake.

**data dictionary**   In a database management program, a listing of all the database files, indexes, views, and other files relevant to a database application. A data dictionary also can include data structures and any information pertinent to the maintenance of a database.

**data-encoding scheme**   The technique a disk drive controller uses to record bits of data on the magnetic surface of a floppy disk or hard disk. See *Advanced Run-Length Limited (ARLL)*, *disk drive controller*, *Modified Frequency Modulation (MFM)*, and *Run-Length Limited (RLL)*.

**data-entry form**   In a database management program, an
on-screen form that makes entering and editing data
easier by displaying only one data record on-screen
at a time. The data fields are listed vertically, as in the
following example:

| TITLE | Barney, the Loyal Puppy |
|-------|-------------------------|
| CATEGORY | Children |
| RATING | G |
| RENTED TO | 325-1234 |
| DUE DATE | 12/31/92 |

dBASE, for example, displays a standard data-entry
form when you add records (see fig. D.1). You also
can create a custom data-entry form (see fig. D.2).

**Fig. D.1.** Standard data-entry form in dBASE.

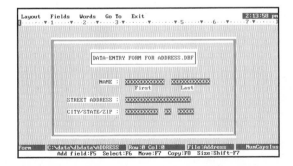

**Fig. D.2.** Custom data-entry form in dBASE.

**data field**   In a database management program, a space for a specified piece of information in a data record. In a table-oriented database management program, in which all retrieval operations produce a table with rows and columns, data fields are displayed as vertical columns.

In the following example, the headings in uppercase letters are the data field titles. The information typed into these fields is to the right of the headings.

| | |
|---|---|
| TITLE | Harold, the Friendly Dinosaur |
| CATEGORY | Children |
| RATING | PG |
| RENTED TO | 325-9178 |
| DUE DATE | 12/31/92 |

See *database*, *field definition*, and *table-oriented database management program*.

**data file**   A disk file containing the work you create with a program; unlike a program file that contains instructions for the computer.

**data independence**   In database management, the storage of data in a way that enables you to access that data without knowing exactly where it is located or how it is stored.

Ideally, you should be able to say to the computer, "Give me information on Acme International." You should not have to say, "Go to record #1142 and match the text string *Acme International*." Many recent database management programs include command languages, called *query languages*, that enable you to phrase questions without worrying about the data's physical location. Even the best query languages require you to know some procedures, such as which database to search, but databases are evolving toward complete data independence. In the future, anyone using a corporate computer will be able to send out a query on a network, searching the company's shared databases and the small, personal ones on some of the computers connected to the network. See *query language* and *Structured Query Language (SQL)*.

**data insertion**   In a database management program, an
operation that adds new records to the database.
Insertion is similar to appending in that new records
are added to the database; however, appending records
adds records only at the end of the database. Insertion
enables you to add records anywhere in the database.
See *append*.

**data integrity**   The accuracy, completeness, and internal
consistency of the information stored in a database.

A good database management program ensures data
integrity by making it difficult (or impossible) to accidentally erase or alter data. Relational database management programs help to ensure data integrity by
eliminating data redundancy. See *data redundancy*.

**data interchange format (DIF) file**   In spreadsheet programs and some database programs, a standard file
format that enables the exchange of data among
different brands or versions of spreadsheet programs.

Originally developed by Software Arts, the creators
of VisiCalc, DIF is supported by Lotus 1-2-3 and other
spreadsheet programs that can read spreadsheets saved
in the DIF format.

**data manipulation**   In database management, the use of
the fundamental database manipulation operations—
data deletion, data insertion, data modification, and
data retrieval—to make changes to data records.

**data mask**   See *field template*.

**data modification**   In database management, an operation
that updates one or more records according to specified criteria.

You use a query language to specify the criteria for the
update. For example, the following statement, written
in a simplified form of Structured Query Language
(SQL), instructs the program to update the inventory
database by finding records in which the supplier field

contains "CC" and then increasing the value in the price data field by 15 percent:

```
UPDATE inventory
    SET price = price * 1.15
    WHERE supplier = "CC"
```

See *query language* and *Structured Query Language (SQL)*.

**data privacy**   In local area networks, the limiting of access to a file so that other participants in the network cannot display the contents of that file. See *encryption*, *field privilege*, *file privilege*, and *password protection*.

**data processing**   Preparing, storing, or manipulating information with a computer. See *word processing program*.

**data record**   In a database management program, a complete unit of related data items expressed in named data fields. In a relational database, *data record* is synonymous with *row*.

A data record contains all the information related to a unit of related information in the database. In a video store's database, for example, the data record lists the following information for each tape the store stocks: title, category (horror, adventure, and so on), rating (such as G, PG, or PG-13), the customer's telephone number, and the due date. Most programs display data records in two ways: as data-entry forms and as data tables.

In a table-oriented relational database management system, which displays the results of all retrieval operations as a table with rows and columns, the data records are displayed as horizontal rows. See *relational database management system (RDBMS)*.

**data redundancy**   In database management, the repetition of the same data in two or more data records.

Generally, you should not enter the same data in two different places within a database—someone may mistype just one character, destroying accurate retrieval. To the computer, *Acme* is not *Acmee*. Suppose that one data record contains the supplier name *Meg Williams*, and another has *Megan Williams*. The program fails to retrieve both data records if you search for all the records with *Megan Williams* in the SUPPLIER field. Integrity is a serious issue for any database management system.

Relational database management programs can reduce the data redundancy problem. Suppose that you are running a retail operation, and you have created a simple inventory database to help you track items in stock. In the SUPPLIER field, you type *USPSI* instead of *Ultra-Sophisticated Products Suppliers Intl*. USPSI appears in several records, such as the following:

| | |
|---|---|
| PRODUCT: | Minoan Pattern Plate |
| STOCKING LEVEL: | 5 |
| CURRENT STOCK: | 4 |
| REORDER AT: | 1 |
| PRICE: | 12.99 |
| SUPPLIER: | USPSI |

| | |
|---|---|
| PRODUCT: | Minoan Pattern Bowl |
| STOCKING LEVEL: | 10 |
| CURRENT STOCK: | 10 |
| REORDER AT: | 3 |
| PRICE: | 9.98 |
| SUPPLIER: | USPSI |

In a second database, you list the suppliers:

| | |
|---|---|
| SUPPLIER | USPSI |
| COMPANY NAME | Ultra-Sophisticated Products Suppliers Intl. |
| ADDRESS | 123 Shady Lane |
| CITY | Merchantville |
| STATE | IL |
| ZIP | 61899 |

Because you type the full name and address of the company just once, in the second database, the address cannot be typed two different ways. Of course, you still can mistype the code *USPSI*; however, a short code is easier to type, and errors are easier to catch.

**data retrieval**   In database management programs, an operation that retrieves information from the database
according to the criteria specified in a query.

A database management program is useless if the program displays all the information at once. You must be
able to access only needed information. The following
query, written in simplified Structured Query Language
(SQL), instructs a program to choose data from the
first_name, last_name, phone_no, and due_date fields
of the Rentals database, when the due_date field contains a date equal to or earlier than May 5, 1993. The
query then instructs the program to sort the displayed
data by the due date, so that the customers whose
tapes are most overdue are at the top of the list.

```
SELECT first_name, last_name, phone_no, due_date
FROM Rentals
WHERE due_date = < 05/05/93
ORDER BY due_date
```

The result of this query is a data table:

| first_name | last_name | phone_no | due_date |
|------------|-----------|----------|----------|
| ANGELINA   | BAKER     | 499-1234 | 03/19/93 |
| TERRENCE   | TARDY     | 499-9876 | 04/30/93 |
| BERMUDA    | JAKE      | 499-5432 | 05/05/93 |

A program that displays data tables as the result
of retrieval operations is a table-oriented database
management program. Record-oriented database management programs are less useful because they display
all the information on all the data records retrieved.

**data series**   In business and presentation graphics, a collection of values that all pertain to a single subject, such as
the third-quarter sales of three products.

**data table**   In a database management program, an
on-screen view of information in a columnar (two-
dimensional) format, with the field names at the top.

Data tables provide a good way to summarize the data
contained in a database for convenient viewing. Most
database management programs display data tables as

the result of sorting or querying operations (see fig. D.3). See *data-entry form*.

```
 Records   Organize   Fields   Go To   Exit
┌──────────┬───────────┬──────────────────┬───────────┬─────┬─────┬─────┬────┐
│LAST_NAME │FIRST_NAME │ADDRESS           │CITY       │STATE│ZIP  │MALE │BIR │
├──────────┼───────────┼──────────────────┼───────────┼─────┼─────┼─────┼────┤
│Harvey    │Jane W.    │9789 Broadway     │Vancouver  │WA   │98665│F    │08/ │
│Bush      │Alfred G.  │13456 N. 95th St  │Seattle    │WA   │98105│T    │08/ │
│Johnson   │Robert J.  │3245 Oak Street   │Portland   │OR   │97203│T    │06/ │
│Morgan    │Albert C.  │1354 S. 78th Ave  │Portland   │OR   │97202│T    │05/ │
│Watson    │James L.   │3891 S.W. Powell  │Portland   │OR   │97201│T    │09/ │
│Ball      │Thomas     │9440 Rockcreek R  │Beaverton  │OR   │97201│T    │12/ │
│Morrow    │Peter T.   │2046 Skyline Dri  │Fremont    │CA   │94538│T    │04/ │
│Peters    │Cathy K.   │3467 First Avenu  │Los Angele │CA   │94321│F    │03/ │
│Swanson   │Linda K.   │1345 Bayview Dri  │San Mateo  │CA   │94105│F    │10/ │
│Peterson  │Janet      │3898 Oceanview R  │San Diego  │CA   │92121│F    │11/ │
│King      │Steven W.  │2771 Plaza Drive  │Pittsburgh │PA   │15238│T    │01/ │
│Taylor    │George F.  │123 Main Street   │New York   │NY   │10021│T    │05/ │
│          │           │                  │           │     │     │     │    │
└──────────┴───────────┴──────────────────┴───────────┴─────┴─────┴─────┴────┘
 Browse    C:\data\dbdata\BYZIP    Rec 1/12    File          NumCaps
```

**Fig. D.3.** A data table (dBASE).

**data type**   In a database management program, a definition that governs the kind of data you can enter in a data field.

In dBASE, for example, you can choose among the following data types:

- *Character field* (or *text field*). Stores any character you can type at the keyboard, including numbers. The program treats numbers as strings (text), however, and cannot perform computations on strings. A character field can contain approximately one line of text.

- *Memo field*. Stores extensive notes about the information contained in a record. A memo field can contain more text than a character field.

- *Numeric field*. Stores numbers in such a way that the program can perform calculations on them.

- *Logical field*. Stores information in a true/false, yes/no format.

- *Date field*. Stores dates so that the program can recognize and compare them.

See *field template*.

**dBASE**   A popular database management system (DBMS) for personal computers.

Database management systems are mainstays in corporate computing systems, but until the development of dBASE II for 8-bit CP/M computers and 16-bit IBM Personal Computers in 1981, these systems were virtually unknown in personal computing. dBASE II, the brainchild of C. Wayne Ratliffe, a Jet Propulsion Laboratory engineer, and marketed by Ashton-Tate, included relational database management capabilities and other sophisticated DBMS features.

Unfortunately, the power of dBASE II came with a price; the program's notorious dot prompt presented the user with a blank screen with no hints about what to do next. However, by learning dBASE's powerful, cryptic software command language, you could build and maintain a database application. System developers often use this full-fledged, high-level programming language to create custom database applications.

dBASE III, introduced in 1984 for IBM Personal Computers, took better advantage of the IBM PC–compatible environment and included many powerful features, such as the capability to work with larger databases. The 1986 release of dBASE III Plus, with a user-friendly, menu-driven user interface, confirmed dBASE's position as the supreme database management product for IBM PC–compatible computers.

dBASE clones soon appeared, however, and took market share away from Ashton-Tate by offering faster program compilation and other features. A court ruled that the much-imitated dBASE command language could not be copyrighted because it was developed with public funds.

Ashton-Tate faltered with the 1988 release of dBASE IV, an ambitious product that was to include Structured Query Language (SQL) for database queries (SQL is the standard dBASE language), an improved menu-driven user interface, and completely redesigned report generation facilities. Version 1.0 of dBASE IV contained bugs that introduced errors into certain calculations, and more than a year passed before the company succeeded in releasing a corrected version (1.1).

In 1992, Borland International bought Ashton-Tate and vowed to improve dBASE and to develop a Microsoft Windows version of the program. Borland's 1992 release of dBASE IV 1.5 featured full mouse support. See *Clipper*, *dot prompt*, *FoxBASE+*, and *software command language*.

**DBMS**   See *database management system*.

**DDE**   See *dynamic data exchange*.

**debugger**   A utility, often included in program compilers or interpreters, that helps programmers find and fix syntax errors and other errors in the source code. See *compiler*, *interpreter*, *source code*, and *syntax error*.

**debugging**   The procedure of locating and correcting errors in a program.

**decimal tab**   In a word processing or page layout program, a tab stop configured so that values align at the decimal point.

**declarative language**   A programming language that frees the programmer from specifying the exact procedure the computer needs to follow to accomplish a task. Programmers use the language to describe a set of facts and relationships so that the user may then query the system to get a specific result.

For example, Structured Query Language (SQL) enables you to perform a search by asking to see a list of records showing specific information rather than by telling the computer to search all records for those with the appropriate entries in specified fields. See *data independence*, *expert system*, and *procedural language*.

**decrement**   To decrease a value. See *increment.*

**decryption**   The process of deciphering data from an encrypted form so that you can read the data. See *encryption*.

**dedicated file server**   In a local area network, a file server dedicated to providing services to the users of the network and running the network operating system.

Some file servers can be used for other purposes. In peer-to-peer networks, for example, all the networked computers are potential file servers, although they are being used for stand-alone applications. See *file server*.

**default button**   In graphical user interfaces such as Microsoft Windows, the highlighted button that is automatically selected as your most likely choice in a dialog box. You can press Enter to choose this button quickly. See *pushbutton*.

**default directory**   See *current directory*.

**default extension**   The three-letter extension an application program uses to save and retrieve files, unless you override the default by specifying another extension.

 If the program you are using supplies a default extension, use the default instead of your own extension. Many programs, such as Lotus 1-2-3 and Microsoft Word, assign extensions if you do not provide one. When saving a file with Microsoft Word, for example, the program assigns the extension DOC. During retrieval operations, such programs display a list of the files with the default extension, making retrieving a file easier. If you give the file an extension that differs from the default extension, however, the file does not appear on the list. You still can retrieve the file, but you must remember the file's name without any help from the program. See *extension* and *file name*.

**default font**   The font that the printer uses unless you instruct otherwise. See *initial base font*.

**default numeric format**   In a spreadsheet program, the numeric format that the program uses for all cells, unless you choose a different one. See *numeric format*.

**default printer**   In Microsoft Windows, the printer that
    Windows applications automatically use when you
    choose Print. See *Microsoft Windows*.

**default setting**   A command option that a program uses
    unless you specify another setting. In Lotus 1-2-3, for
    example, the default column width is nine characters.

 An important step toward the mastery of an
application program is learning the program
defaults. You should learn how to change
the default settings so that the program
works the way you want. Most programs save the
changes you make so that they are in effect for your
next working session, but some options may not be
saved under any circumstances. Microsoft Word, for
example, saves the printer driver you select, but it does
not save settings such as the number of copies you
want to print (the default is always one). If the program
saved the number of copies, you may inadvertently
print unwanted copies of a document the next time
you choose the Print command.

**default value**   A value an application program chooses
    when you do not specify one.

**defragmentation**   A procedure in which all the files on a
    hard disk are rewritten so that all parts of each file are
    written to contiguous sectors. The result is a significant
    improvement—up to 75 percent or more—in the disk's
    speed during retrieval operations. During normal
    operations, the files on a hard disk become fragmented
    so that parts of a file are written all over the disk, slow-
    ing down retrieval operations.

 Equip your system with a utilities package,
such as Norton Utilities or PC Tools, that
includes a defragmentation utility. Run this
utility once per week for maximum system
performance.

**Delete (Del) key**   A key that erases the character at the
    cursor.

Use the Backspace and Delete keys to correct mistakes as you type. If you discover that you have made a typing error, press Backspace to erase the error and then retype. Use the Delete key to erase a character at the cursor.

**delimiter**   A code, such as a space or comma, that marks the end of one section of a command and the beginning of another section.

**demo**   A program designed to emulate some of the functions of an application program for marketing purposes.

**demodulation**   In telecommunications, the process of receiving and transforming an analog signal into its digital equivalent so that a computer can use the information. See *modulation* and *telecommunications*.

**demount**   To remove a disk from a disk drive. See *mount*.

**density**   A measurement of the amount of information (in bits) that can be packed reliably into a square inch of a magnetic secondary storage device, such as a floppy disk. See *double density, high density,* and *single density*.

**dependent worksheet**   In Microsoft Excel, a worksheet that contains a reference formula to another Excel worksheet, called the *source worksheet*, on which it depends for an externally accessed value. More than one worksheet can be dependent on a single source worksheet.

If you include external reference formulas in a dependent worksheet, group the dependent worksheet and the source worksheet as a workgroup to ensure that the changes you make in the source worksheet are always reflected in the dependent worksheet. In Excel, a workgroup is a named collection of worksheets that, after you save it as a workgroup, is treated as if it were a single document. When you open one of the worksheets, you open all the others. When you modify the source worksheet, the changes are automatically reflected in all dependent worksheets. When you save one of the worksheets, you save them all. See *external reference formula* and *source worksheet*.

**derived field**   See *calculated field*.

**descender**   The portion of a lowercase letter that hangs below the baseline. Five letters of the alphabet have descenders: *g, j, p, q,* and *y.*

**descending sort**   A sort that reverses the normal ascending sort order. Instead of sorting *A, B, C, D* and *1, 2, 3, 4,* for example, a descending sort lists *D, C, B, A* and *4, 3, 2, 1.*

**descriptor**   In database management, a term used to classify a data record so that all records sharing a common subject can be retrieved as a group.

In a video store's database, for example, the descriptor *Adventure* appears in the data records of all action-oriented films. See *identifier*.

**desk accessory (DA)**   In a graphical user interface, a set of utility programs that assist with day-to-day tasks such as jotting down notes, performing calculations on an on-screen calculator, maintaining a list of names and phone numbers, and displaying an on-screen calendar (see fig. D.4). See *Font/DA Mover, graphical user interface (GUI),* and *utility program.*

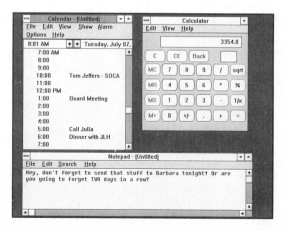

**Fig. D.4.** Desk accessories (Microsoft Windows).

**desktop**   In a graphical user interface, a computer representation of your day-to-day work, as if you were looking at an actual desk littered with folders full of work to do. In Microsoft Windows, this term refers specifically to the background of the screen, on which windows, icons, and dialog boxes appear (see fig. D.5). You can change the desktop color and pattern by choosing Colors in the Control Panel. See *graphical user interface (GUI)*.

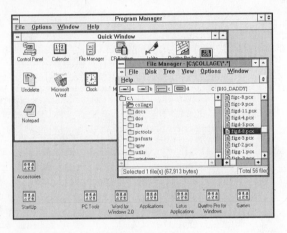

**Fig. D.5.** A Microsoft Windows desktop.

**desktop computer**   A personal computer or professional workstation designed to fit on a standard-sized office desk and equipped with sufficient memory and secondary storage to perform business computing tasks. See *laptop computer*.

**desktop pattern**   In Microsoft Windows, the pattern—called *wallpaper*—assigned to the desktop (the background "beneath" windows, icons, and dialog boxes). To change the desktop pattern, choose Desktop from the Control Panel.

**desktop presentation**   The use of a presentation graphics program's slide show module to create a presentation you can run on a desktop computer. You can tell the program to run the presentation automatically or to give you a menu of options. See *presentation graphics program* and *slide show*.

**desktop publishing (DTP)**   The use of a personal computer as an inexpensive production system for generating typeset-quality text and graphics. Desktop publishers often merge text and graphics on the same page and print pages on a high-resolution laser printer or type-setting machine (see fig. D.6).

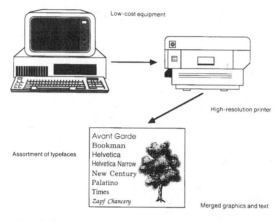

**Fig. D.6.** Elements of desktop publishing.

One of the fastest-growing applications in personal computing, desktop publishing offers cost-saving, productivity, and time-saving advantages that have helped speed the proliferation of desktop computers.

Using traditional methods, a business may find itself paying up to $2,000 per page to prepare camera-ready copy for a technical manual. Such costs may amount to as much as 15 percent of the total manufacturing costs in such industries. A typical document-production project also involves the timely cooperation of layout artists, typesetters, proofreaders, and printers, many of whom are employed by outside firms on a contract basis. But they may not cooperate, and their work may not be completed on time. Traditional methods also make last-minute changes expensive or impossible.

Because one person can produce typeset-quality text and graphics with a personal computer, desktop publishing enables an organization to reduce publication costs by as much as 75 percent, eliminate delays attributable to tardy subcontractors and miscommunication, and make last-minute changes without encountering additional costs or delays.

The capability to make last-minute changes is a key advantage of this technology that should not be underestimated. Several five-star restaurants, for example, use Macintoshes and laser printers to produce daily menus. Freed from dependence on printed menus, these restaurants can experiment with new dishes, adjust the menu to the changing availability of fresh foods, and ensure that every menu looks fresh and clean.

For documents crucial to an organization's public image, however, laser-produced output may not be of high enough quality. For such documents, desktop-published output needs to be produced on professional typesetting machinery.

Desktop publishing's origins are in the early history of word processing software. Some of the earliest word processing programs were devised by computer programmers to assist them in preparing manuals for the programs they had written.

These programs included such features as automatic table-of-contents and index generation, automatic pagination, automatic spelling correction, and other productivity-enhancing features. Printed on low-resolution printers, these manuals were poorly suited to public distribution. Research at Xerox Corporation's Palo Alto Research Laboratories, however, demonstrated the technical feasibility of high-quality document production using WYSIWYG (what-you-see-is-what-you-get) software and laser printers. But with a price tag of $25,000 or more, these early systems could not compete with the traditional document-production process for most firms.

The rapid growth of desktop publishing as a personal
computer application was made possible by four key
innovations: the availability of reasonably inexpensive
personal computers capable of displaying text and
graphics simultaneously, like the Macintosh; the development of page layout programs like PageMaker; the
development of page description languages like
PostScript; and the introduction of moderately priced
laser printers with a variety of typefaces, like the
LaserWriter. Suddenly, you could obtain a high-quality
desktop publishing system for less than $10,000. Be-
cause these innovations originated in the Macintosh
environment, the Macintosh took an early lead in this
area. Desktop publishing technology has since become
available for IBM PC–compatible computers, eroding
the Mac's lead.

 Despite the many advantages of desktop
publishing in organizational settings, desktop
publishing has limitations. Laser printers
produce output with a resolution of 300 or
400 dpi, which appears professionally typeset to the
untrained eye. Type printed at 300 dpi is a major
improvement over the low-resolution output of dot-
matrix printers (about 120 dpi), but 300 dpi still is
considered coarse by typesetting standards (see fig. D.7).

**Fig. D.7.** Characters printed at 120, 300, and 1200 dots per
inch (left to right, respectively).

Professional typesetting equipment has resolutions of
1200 dpi and more. However, page layout programs
can produce output in a form that professional typesetting equipment can read. If you want high-resolution
output for a project, you can engage a professional

typesetting firm to produce high-resolution output from a disk.

A more serious drawback of desktop publishing is that the use of a page layout program does not guarantee that a document meets professional design standards. By observing a few rules, however, virtually anyone can produce a price list, brochure, or report that does not embarrass an organization.

When preparing a brochure or newsletter, for example, you should choose a typeface that sets the tone of the piece effectively, and then stick with the typeface. You should use no more than two typefaces, and you should use white space effectively for emphasis, balance, and proportion. Graphics should be relevant to a key point made in the text, clearly-printed, and tasteful. Use rules and borders conservatively.

Keep the layout simple; for any document that the public will see, engage a professional designer to critique the design before printing. See *dots per inch (dpi)*, *extended memory*, *laser printer*, *page description language (PDL)*, *page layout program*, *PageMaker*, *PostScript*, *resolution*, and *typeface*.

**desktop video**   A multimedia application in which a personal computer, in tandem with a videocassette recorder or laser disk player, is used to control the display of still or motion images.

**DESQview**   A windowing environment developed by Quarterdeck Office Systems for IBM PC–compatible computers.

Comparable to Microsoft Windows, DESQview provides a graphical user interface for MS-DOS and the capability to load more than one program and execute tasks simultaneously. DESQview can take full advantage of the Intel 80386 microprocessor's protected mode and extended memory, even while running under MS-DOS.

DESQview has gained popularity as an alternative to upgrading to OS/2. In response to DESQview's success,

Microsoft Corporation, the publisher of MS-DOS and
OS/2, released Version 3 of Microsoft Windows, which
includes most of DESQview's capabilities. See *context
switching, extended memory, Microsoft Windows,
Operating System/2 (OS/2),* and *protected mode.*

**destination**   The record, file, document, or disk to which
information is taken or moved; as opposed to the
source. See *source.*

**destination document**   In object linking and embedding
(OLE), the document into which you insert or embed
the source data. For example, when you embed a
Microsoft Excel object (such as a range of cells or a
chart) into a Microsoft Word file, the Word document
is the destination document. See *object linking and
embedding (OLE)* and *source document.*

**destination file**   In many DOS commands, the file into
which data or program instructions are copied. See
*source file.*

**device**   Any hardware component or peripheral, such as a
printer, modem, monitor, or mouse, that can receive
and/or send data.

**device contention**   The technique that Microsoft Windows
uses to handle simultaneous requests from multitasked
programs to access peripheral devices.

Device contention is needed in Windows' 386 Enhanced
mode because, in this mode, two or more programs
can run simultaneously. If two programs try to access
the same peripheral device at the same time, Windows
gives one of the programs preference. To control how
Windows gives preference, use the 386 Enhanced option
from the Control Panel group.

**device driver**   A program that extends the operating
system's capabilities by enabling the operating system
to work with a specific hardware device, such as a
printer.

In DOS, device drivers are files with the extension SYS.
To use a device driver, you must enter a configuration

command that identifies the file containing the driver. You place the command in the CONFIG.SYS file. The following command, for example, tells DOS to use a mouse driver:

```
DEVICE = MOUSE.SYS
```

DOS does not need DEVICE commands to work with most keyboards, monitors, and printers. You use DEVICE commands, however, to install a mouse and files that set up RAM disks.

In Microsoft Windows, device drivers have the extension DRV.

After you install a mouse on your system, beware of accidentally erasing the CONFIG.SYS file. If you do, the mouse will not work.

**device independence**   The capability of a computer program, operating system, or programming language to work on a variety of computers or computer peripherals, despite their electronic variation.

Examples of device independence include UNIX and PostScript. UNIX, an operating system for multiuser computer systems, is designed to run on a wide variety of computers, from PCs to mainframes. The portability of UNIX (its capability to run on a variety of hardware platforms) stems from the C language in which it is written. In C, a programmer may embed assembly language instructions that take advantage of a specific computer's electronic capabilities, without sacrificing the overall structure of the program, which can remain the same in its various incarnations. PostScript, a page description language for high-quality printing, relies on a different method: to print PostScript-encoded files, a PostScript-compatible printer must include its own processing circuitry, which includes an interpreter for the PostScript language. See *C*, *portable*, *PostScript*, and *UNIX*.

**device name**   In DOS, the abbreviation that refers to a peripheral device. See *CON* and *LPT*.

**diacritical marks**   Marks added to characters to represent their phonetic value in a foreign language, such as accents. See *accent*.

**diagnostic program**   A utility program that tests computer hardware and software to determine whether they are operating properly.

Most computers initiate a diagnostic check at the start of every operating session. A particular focus of attention is the memory. If any errors are found, you see an error message, and the computer does not proceed. If you run into this problem, start the computer again. If you see the error message again, you may have to replace a memory chip. Because the error message specifies the location of the faulty chip, be sure to write down the number you see on-screen.

**dialog box**   In a graphical user interface, an on-screen message box that conveys or requests information from the user (see fig. D.8). See *graphical user interface (GUI)*.

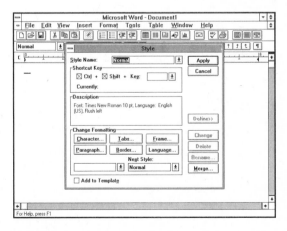

**Fig. D.8.** A typical dialog box (Style).

**dictionary sort**   A sort operation that ignores the case of characters as data is rearranged. See *sort* and *sort order*.

**DIF**   See *data interchange format (DIF) file*.

**digital**   A form of representation in which distinct objects. or *digits*, are used to stand for something in the real world—such as bears, beans, or bikinis—so that counting and other operations can be performed precisely.

Information represented digitally can be manipulated to produce a calculation, a sort, or some other computation. In an abacus, for example, quantities are represented by positioning beads on a wire. A trained abacus operator can perform calculations at high rates of speed by following an algorithm—a recipe for solving the problem. In digital electronic computers, two electrical states correspond to the 1s and 0s of binary numbers, and the algorithm is embodied in a computer program. See *algorithm*, *analog*, *binary numbers*, *computation*, and *program*.

**digital computer**   A computer that uses digits—objects clearly separate and different from each other—to represent information, and then uses at least partly automatic procedures to perform computations on this information. See *analog computer* and *computer*.

**Digital Darkroom**   An image-enhancement program developed by Silicon Beach Software for Macintosh computers. The program uses computer processing techniques to edit and enhance scanned black-and-white photographic images.

**digital monitor**   A cathode-ray-tube (CRT) display that accepts digital output from the display adapter and converts the digital signal to an analog signal.

Digital monitors cannot accept input unless the input conforms to a prearranged standard, such as the IBM Monochrome Display Adapter (MDA), Color Graphics Adapter (CGA), or Enhanced Graphics Adapter (EGA). All these adapters produce digital output.

Digital monitors are fast and produce sharp, clear images. However, they have a major disadvantage: unlike analog monitors, they cannot display continuously variable colors. Simple digital color monitors can display colors in two modes, on and off; more complex color digital monitors recognize more intensity modes. For the Video Graphics Array (VGA) standard, IBM chose to use analog monitors so that you can display continuously variable images on-screen. See *analog monitor, Color Graphics Adapter (CGA), digital, Enhanced Graphics Adapter (EGA), Monochrome Display Adapter (MDA)*, and *Video Graphics Array (VGA)*.

**digital transmission**    A data communications technique that passes information encoded as discrete, on-off pulses. Unlike analog transmission, which uses a continuous wave form to transmit data, digital transmission does not require digital-to-analog converters at each end of the transmission; however, analog transmission is faster and can carry more than one channel at a time. See *analog transmission*.

**digitize**    To transform a continuous-tone image into computer-readable data using a device called a *scanner*. See *scanner*.

**dimmed command**    In a command menu, an option that is not currently available.

**dimmed icon**    In a graphical user interface, a disk, program, or document that isn't accessible at the present time.

**dingbats**    Ornamental characters—such as bullets, stars, and flowers—used to decorate a page. See *Zapf Dingbats*.

**DIP**    See *dual in-line package (DIP)* and *document image processing (DIP)*.

**DIP switch**    One or more rocker or slider switches enclosed in a small plastic case, called a *dual in-line package* (DIP). This plastic housing is designed with downward-facing pins so that you can insert it into a socket on a circuit board or solder it directly to the circuit board. DIP switches are frequently used to provide user-accessible configuration settings for computers, printers, and other electronic devices. Before you can access the DIP switches, however, you must remove the case.

 Always unplug your computer or printer before removing the case to change DIP switch settings. Although your computer's electronic circuits use low-voltage DC, the power supply uses high voltages and may contain a capacitor that stores extremely high voltages for system start-up purposes. Do not touch the power supply, even when the system is unplugged. To change a DIP switch, use a toothpick or another small pointed device. Do not use a pencil; lead shavings can damage the internal workings of a DIP switch. See *dual in-line package (DIP)*.

**Direct Access Storage Device (DASD)** Pronounced "dayz-dee." Any auxiliary storage device, such as a hard disk, that offers random or direct access to the stored data; in contrast to a sequential device (such as a tape unit). See *random access* and *sequential access*.

**direct-connect modem** A modem that makes a direct connection to the telephone line via modular connectors, unlike an acoustic coupler modem designed to cradle a telephone headset. See *acoustic coupler*.

**directory** An index to the files stored on a disk, or on a portion of a disk, that you can display on-screen.

The contents of a disk are not obvious to the eye. A good operating system keeps an up-to-date record of the files stored on a disk, with ample information about the file's content, time of creation, and size.

In DOS, the DIR command displays a disk directory. A typical directory display appears as follows:

```
Volume in Drive A has no label
Directory of A:\
ANSI       SYS     1651    3-21-92      0:01a
DRIVER     SYS     1102    3-21-92      7:47a
RAMDRIVE   SYS     6462    7-07-92     12:00p
CONFIG     SYS       15    1-17-93      3:37p
COMMAND    COM    23612    9-30-92     12:00p
APPEND     COM     1725    3-21-92     11:00p
```

```
ASSIGN    COM     1523    3-21-92     4:50p
CLOCK     COM      505    2-10-92    12:00p
FORMAT    COM    11597    9-30-92     9:00a
SYS       COM     4607    8-01-92    12:00p
ATTRIB    EXE     8234    3-21-92    12:00p
CHKDSK    EXE     9680    3-21-92    12:00p
DEBUG     EXE     5647    3-21-92     8:19p
13 File(s) 12876 bytes free
```

This disk directory contains the following information:

- *Volume label.* When formatting a disk, you can name it; the name is called a *volume label*. You also can name the disk later using the VOL command. If you give the disk a volume label, you see the name at the top of the directory when you use the DIR command.

- *File name.* DOS file names have two parts, the file name and the extension. The first two columns of the directory table show the file name and the extension of each file on the disk.

- *File size.* The third column of the disk directory table shows the size of each file (in bytes).

- *Date last modified.* The fourth column of the disk directory shows the date on which you last modified the file.

- *Time last modified.* The fifth column of the disk directory shows the time when you last modified the file.

- *Space remaining.* The number of bytes of storage space left on the disk is shown at the bottom of the directory. This information is important because you cannot write a file to a disk with insufficient room.

 If your computer is not equipped with a clock/calendar board, be sure to set the system time and system date manually when you start the computer. DOS uses this information to create the date and time listings in disk directories. If the date and time are not set, the dates listed for files are incorrect. See *clock/calendar board* and *subdirectory*.

**directory markers**   In DOS, symbols displayed in a subdirectory's on-screen directory that represent the current directory (.) and the parent directory (..). See *current directory*, *directory*, *parent directory*, and *subdirectory*.

**directory sorting**   The organized display of the files in a disk directory, sorted by name, extension, or date and time of creation. MS-DOS 5.0 introduced directory sorting at the system level; previously, directory sorting was possible only with add-on utility programs.

**directory tree**   A graphical representation of a disk's contents that shows the branching structure of directories and subdirectories. Microsoft Window's File Manager, for example, displays a directory tree (see fig. D.9).

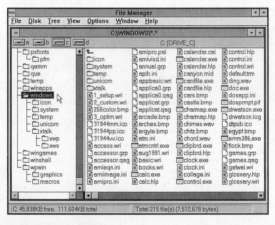

**Fig. D.9.** A directory tree.

**disk**   See *floppy disk* and *hard disk*.

**disk buffer**   See *disk cache*.

**disk cache**   An area of random-access memory (RAM) set aside by the operating system to store frequently accessed data and program instructions. A disk cache (pronounced "cash") can improve the speed of disk-intensive applications such as database management programs. If the central processing unit (CPU) must wait for this information from disk, processing speed slows noticeably.

When the CPU repeatedly accesses the same information, you can obtain modest speed gains by placing the frequently accessed information in a buffer (a temporary storage place in memory). Although using a disk cache does not eliminate disk accesses, the number of accesses is reduced. See *cache controller, central processing unit (CPU), random-access memory (RAM)*, and *RAM cache*.

**disk capacity**   The storage capacity of a floppy disk or hard disk, measured in kilobytes (K) or megabytes (M).

The capacity of a floppy disk depends on the size of the disk, the density of the magnetic particles on its surface, and the capabilities of the drive you use to format the disk. The two most popular disk sizes are 5.25-inch floppy disks and 3.5-inch micro floppy disks. Single-sided disks were once common, but are all but obsolete now; double-sided disks are the norm. Also standard today is the double-density disk; available at a higher cost is the high-density disk. The third variable is the operating system you use to format the disk and the capabilities of the disk drive you are using. The following table shows the relationship of the variables:

| Size | Density | System | Drive | Capacity |
|------|---------|--------|-------|----------|
| 3.5" | DD | MS-DOS | standard | 720K |
| 3.5" | DD | Mac | standard | 800K |
| 3.5" | HD | Mac | SuperDrive | 1.4M |
| 3.5" | HD | MS-DOS | high density | 1.44M |
| 3.5" | HD | MS-DOS 5 | high density | 2.88M |
| 5.25" | DD | MS-DOS | standard | 360K |
| 5.25" | HD | MS-DOS | high density | 1.2M |

If you are shopping for an IBM PC–compatible computer, bear in mind that higher capacity drives aren't much more expensive ($10–30) than their lower capacity counterparts. Don't let a salesperson tell you that a higher capacity drive adds significantly to the cost of your system.

**disk drive**   A secondary storage medium such as a floppy disk drive or a hard disk. This term usually refers to floppy disk drives.

A floppy disk drive is an economical secondary storage medium that uses a removable magnetic disk. Like all magnetic media, a floppy disk can be recorded, erased, and reused over and over. The recording and erasing operations are performed by the read/write head that moves laterally over the surface of the disk—giving the drive its random-access capabilities.

Although floppy disk drives are inexpensive, they are too slow to serve as the main secondary storage medium for today's personal computers; for business applications, a minimum configuration is one hard disk and one floppy disk drive. (The floppy disk drive is needed to copy software and disk-based data onto the system and for backup operations.) See *floppy disk*, *random access*, *read/write head,* and *secondary storage*.

**disk drive controller**   The circuitry that controls the physical operations of the floppy disks and/or hard disks directly connected to the computer.

Until recently, most disk drive controllers were plug-in adapters, but a clear trend toward including this circuitry on the computer's motherboard now exists. With the advent of the Intelligent Drive Electronics (IDE) standard, which transfers much of the controller circuitry to the drive itself, the inclusion of the remaining circuitry on the motherboard has become much more simple.

Wherever it is positioned, the disk drive controller circuitry performs two functions: it employs an interface

standard (such as ST-506/ST-412, ESDI, or SSCI) to
establish communication with the drive's electronics, as
well as a data encoding scheme (such as MFM, RLL, or
ARLL) to encode information on the magnetic surface
of the disk. See *Advanced Run-Length Limited (ARLL),
Enhanced System Device Interface (ESDI), Modified
Frequency Modulation (MFM), Run-Length Limited
(RLL), Small Computer System Interface (SCSI),* and
*ST-506/ST-412.*

**diskless workstation**   In a local area network (LAN), a
workstation that has a CPU and RAM but lacks its own
disk drives.

Do diskless workstations signal the decline of the personal computing ethos? Personal computing, after all, is
about giving computer power to individuals, who are
free to choose their own applications and to develop
their own, unique computing style. In large organizations, data processing managers have typically viewed
the personal computing ethos as if it were tantamount
to anarchy; far better, they believe, to let professionals
choose the software, and impose a single standard on
everyone, so that everyone produces and uses compatible data. An additional argument: personal computers
raise serious security issues for organizations. Anyone
can come into your office and, if you are not around
and have not secured your system, copy a disk containing valuable information.

The rise of local area networks based on personal computers signalled a move away from the decentralism of
personal computing and back toward the sharing of
software and data, but from the data processing
manager's point of view, LANs didn't go far enough. The
diskless work-station returns the personal computer's
control to the hands of system administrators and re-
solves security issues, but at the cost of suppressing
virtually all the distributed computing advantages that
have made personal computing so valuable in modern
organizations.

**disk operating system**   See *operating system*.

**disk optimizer**   See *defragmentation*.

**display**   See *monitor*.

**display adapter**   See *video adapter*.

**display type**   A typeface, usually 14 points or larger and differing in style from the body type, used for headings and subheadings.

 Use a sans serif typeface such as Avant Garde or Helvetica for display type. For body type, use serif fonts such as Times Roman or New Century Schoolbook, because serif fonts are more readable than sans serif fonts. See *body type*.

**distributed processing system**   A computer system designed for multiple users that provides each user with a fully functional computer. Unlike a stand-alone system, however, a distributed system is designed to make communication among the linked computers easier, and to make shared access to central files easier.

In personal computing, distributed processing takes the form of local area networks, in which the personal computers of a department or organization are linked by high-speed cable connections.

Distributed processing offers some advantages over multiuser systems because each user is given a fully functional workstation instead of a remote terminal without processing circuitry. If the network fails, you can still work. You also can select software tailored to your needs. You can start a distributed processing system with a modest initial investment; you need only two or three workstations and, if desired, a central file server. You can add more workstation nodes as needed.

A multiuser system, however, requires a major initial investment in the central computer, which must be

powerful enough to handle system demands as the
system grows. Multiuser systems have legitimate applications—for example, in point-of-sale terminals, in
which you gain by making sure that all information is
posted to a central database. See *file server, local area
network (LAN)*, and *multiuser system*.

**dithering**   In color or gray-scale printing and displays, the
mingling of dots of several colors to produce what
appears to be a new color. With dithering, you can
combine 256 colors to produce what appears to be
a continuously variable color palette, but at the cost
of sacrificing resolution.

**document**   A file containing work you have created, such as
a business report, a memo, or a worksheet.

The meaning of the term *document* has shifted, thanks
to the computer. In librarianship, the term strongly
connotes the authority of an original, fixed text: a document is archived and carefully protected so that it can
serve as the authoritative source for later interpretation
or analysis. In this context, the term *documentation*—
the act of providing footnotes or other references to the
documents used in research—further illustrates this
theme of authoritative reference. Moreover, a document
in the traditional sense has an unambiguous author:
an individual, in most cases, or an organization.

Computers have changed the meaning of the term
*document* in two ways. First, because they make document revision so easy, computers do not preserve
documents in their pristine, unaltered state, and second,
developments in groupware and hypertext are diffusing
authorship. Both points were first noted, with alarm, by
newspaper reporters, who found that, after electronic
editing systems were installed, editors would simply
make changes to their stories without asking their permission. With today's networked computing technology, a document can become a text in flux, constantly
accessed and modified by many people—and, with

dynamic data exchange (DDE), even by the computer itself, as it detects changes in supporting documents and updates dynamic links automatically. See *dynamic data exchange (DDE)*, *groupware*, and *word processing*.

**documentation**  The instructions, tutorials, and reference information that provide you with the information required to use a computer program or computer system effectively. Documentation can appear in printed media or in on-line help systems.

**document base font**  The default font that a word processing program uses, unless you override that font by choosing a different font. Unlike an initial base font that affects all documents, the document base font affects only one document.

You can choose Times Roman as the initial base font for all documents, for example, but for a letter you currently are writing, override that choice by choosing Helvetica as the document base font. You can choose other fonts within this letter, but the program uses Helvetica unless you give an explicit command to the contrary. See *base font* and *initial base font*.

**document comparison utility**  A utility program that compares two documents created with a word processing program. If the two documents are not identical, the program displays the differences between them, line by line.

Document comparison utilities are useful in collaborative writing. Suppose that you create a document, keep a copy, and send one file to the person working with you on the project. This person makes changes and returns an altered version of the file to you.

Using a document comparison utility, you can see the differences between the two documents on-screen. In figure D.10, for example, altered or added passages are shown as highlighted text, and the original version is shown in strike-through text. See *redlining*.

In the old days, writers had to stop editing days before a
document was due and start combing through the main text to
prepare the document references. ~~One of WordPerfect 5's handiest
features is that it speeds up that process. One of WordPerfect
5's handiest features is that it speeds up the process of
assembling document references.~~ With a little foresight and
planning, you can work on a document right down to a few hours
before a deadline, confident that as your main text changes, the
document references will keep right up with it.

This chapter shows you how to create lists, tables of contents,
tables of authorities, and indexes. You also learn to use
automatic cross-referencing, which lets you change the structure
of your document and automatically maintain accurate references
to footnotes, pages and sections. ~~which lets you change the
structure of your document and automatically maintain accurate
references to certain spots in a document.~~ Finally, you learn to
use the Document Compare feature so that you can show someone
else what was omitted from, ~~you learn to use the Document Compare
feature so that you can see what was omitted from,~~ or added to, a
document, without having to mark all those changes yourself.

**Fig. D.10.** Two versions of a document compared by a
document comparison utility.

**document file icon**   In Microsoft Windows, the icon of a
document that has been associated with an application.
You can open the document and launch the application simultaneously just by double-clicking a document
file icon.

When you install Microsoft Windows, the Setup program
scans your disk for applications, such as WordPerfect or
Lotus 1-2-3. When it finds these applications, Setup
places their icons in the Application window. Windows
associates documents with these applications by using
the applications' standard extensions. For example,
Lotus 1-2-3 creates files with the WK1 extension. Windows defines any WK1 file as a Lotus file. If for some
reason you named a non-Lotus file with the WK1 extension, Windows would still associate the file with Lotus
1-2-3. Be sure to use extensions consistently.

 To associate documents with the applications Setup did not detect, use the Associate
command (File menu). If you're using an
application that doesn't automatically assign
extensions, you can take advantage of association by
always saving that application's files using an extension
you make up. For example, WordPerfect 5.1 for DOS is

a popular application that doesn't automatically assign an extension when you save a file. If you save all your WordPerfect files with the extension WP, though, you can use the Associate command to tell Windows to associate all WP files with WordPerfect.

**document format**   In a word processing program, a set of formatting choices that affects the page layout of every page in your current document. Examples of document formats include margins, headers, footers, page numbers, and columns.

**document image processing (DIP)**   A system for the imaging, storage, and retrieval of text-based documents that includes input via optical scanners, storage on optical or magnetic media, and output via monitors, printers, or fax.

The goal of a document image processing system is the much-maligned "paperless office," which is still a worthy goal. Just consider this evidence: According to one recent estimate, it costs about $25,000 to fill a four-drawer file cabinet, and another $2,160 per year to maintain the cabinet. Moreover, 1 out of every 33 documents is lost (usually by incorrect filing), and you'll spend an average of more than $100 per lost document trying to recover the missing information. For that much money, you can buy a pretty nifty document image processing system, scan the documents into a document database, and stick the originals into storage boxes in sequential order.

Alitalia, the Italian airline, implemented a DIP system when its managers realized that they were drowning in paper—an estimated 30,000 repair and purchase orders per year, each of which required 10 supporting documents. Each day, the airline's staff needed about 65 of these 330,000 documents, and they were running themselves ragged storing and retrieving the documents from standard office filing systems. With the DIP system installed, each new document is scanned and date-stamped with a sequential serial number, after which documents can be retrieved through keyword searches. The new system scores high marks for speed, efficiency, low cost, and retrieval effectiveness.

The DIP solution has its detractors, though. Today's optical character recognition (OCR) technology, while vastly improved, is still slow and prone to error. Moreover, the keyword retrieval technology these systems employ has many known shortcomings. A document indexed under the wrong keyword may elude retrieval entirely. Information science research reveals that the retrieval set is almost certain to contain "false drops"— documents that contain one or more of the words you're searching for, but don't really pertain to the subject at hand. Optical scanners, moreover, fall down in performance when text size is smaller than 9 points.

 If you decide to try a DIP system, you can pass the scanned documents through a spelling checker to shorten proofreading time. See *optical character recognition (OCR)*.

**document processing**   The application of computer technology to every stage of the in-house production of documents, such as instruction manuals, handbooks, reports, and proposals.

A complete document processing system includes all the software and hardware needed to create, organize, edit, and print such documents. Because these documents generally are reproduced from camera-ready copy, a document processing system's word processing software should be able to generate indexes and tables of contents. See *word processing program* and *desktop publishing (DTP)*.

**document window**   In Microsoft Windows, a window within an application program's window that displays the document you are creating or altering. You can open more than one document window within an application window. See *Microsoft Windows*.

**DOS**   See *MS-DOS* and *operating system*.

**Doskey**   A utility provided with MS-DOS (5.0 and later) that
enables you to type more than one MS-DOS command
on a line, to store and retrieve previously used MS-DOS
commands, to create stored macros, and to customize
all MS-DOS commands.

**DOS prompt**   In MS-DOS, a letter (representing the current
disk drive) followed by the greater-than symbol (>),
together which inform you when the operating system
is ready to receive a command. You can change the
default DOS prompt (C>). See *prompt*.

**dot-matrix printer**   An impact printer that forms text and
graphic images by pressing the ends of pins against a
ribbon.

A dot-matrix printer forms an image of text or graphics
by hammering the ends of pins against a ribbon. The
ends of these wires form a character made up of a
pattern (a matrix) of dots. Dot-matrix printers are fast,
but the output they produce is generally poor quality
because the character is not fully formed. These printers also can be extremely noisy. Some dot-matrix printers use 24 pins instead of 9, and the quality of their
output is better.

Many of today's dot-matrix printers offer a near–
letter quality (NLQ) mode that sacrifices speed to produce substantially improved output. In NLQ mode, the
printer passes over a line several times, offsetting the
dots to form a solid character.

Better dot-matrix printers can produce printout in
more than one font. Fonts are measured in points
(1/72 inch). A standard type size is 12 points, producing 6 lines per vertical inch on the page, but you usually can choose sizes ranging from 8 to 24 points.

In IBM PC–compatible computing, no
widely accepted standard exists for printer
control commands. De facto standards have
been established by Epson and IBM. Many

dot-matrix printers recognize the Epson or IBM commands, but others do not. If you plan to purchase a dot-matrix printer, make sure that your software includes a printer driver for the model. See *font, impact printer, near–letter quality (NLQ)*, and *nonimpact printer*.

**dot pitch**    The size of the smallest dot that a monitor can display on-screen. Dot pitch determines a monitor's maximum resolution.

To keep the electron beam from activating the wrong part of the screen, color monitors use a shadow mask, a metal sheet with fine perforations. These perforations are arranged so that the beam strikes one hole at a time, corresponding to one dot on-screen. The smaller the hole in the shadow mask, the higher the resolution.

High-resolution monitors use dot pitches of approximately 0.31 mm or less; the best monitors use dot pitches of 0.28 mm or less.

**dot prompt**    In dBASE, the prompt—a lone period on an otherwise empty screen—for the command-driven interface of the program.

**dots per inch (dpi)**    A measure of printer resolution that counts the dots that the device can produce per linear inch.

In describing screen resolutions, the practice is to state the resolution in horizontal pixels (picture elements) by vertical lines, rather than stating a dpi figure. For example, the resolution of a Super VGA monitor is 800 horizontal pixels by 600 vertical lines.

**double-click**    To click the mouse button twice in rapid succession.

In many programs, double-clicking extends the action that results from single-clicking; double-clicking a character in a word, for example, selects the whole word rather than just one character. Double-clicking is used not only to select an item, but also to initiate an action. In a file list, for example, double-clicking a file name selects and opens the file.

**double density**   A widely used recording technique that packs twice as much data on a floppy or hard disk as the earlier, single-density standard. See *high density*, *Modified Frequency Modulation (MFM)*, *Run-Length Limited (RLL)*, and *single density*.

**DO/WHILE loop**   In programming, a loop control structure that continues to carry out its function until a condition is satisfied.

In the following pseudocode example, a database management program's software command language is used to write a short program that prints all the records in the file. In English, the program says, "Open the database called videos. Get ready to route output to the printer. Check to see whether you have reached the end of the file. If you have not reached the end of the file, do the following: print the title, rating, and category, and then skip two lines. Turn off printer output, close the database called videos, and quit."

```
USE videos
SET printer on
DO WHILE end_of_file = false
    PRINT title
    PRINT rating
    PRINT category
    SKIP 2 lines
ENDDO
SET printer off
CLOSE videos
QUIT
```

The external condition is supplied by the variable called end_of_file. When the program reaches the last record, this variable is set to true, so that the

DO/WHILE loop stops. At this point, the sequential control structure takes over again, and the program moves on to the next statement (SET printer off ). See *case branch, loop control structure, sequence control structure, software command language,* and *syntax.*

**Dow Jones News/Retrieval Service**   An on-line information service from Dow Jones, the publishers of the *Wall Street Journal* and *Barron's*, that offers a computer-searchable index to financial and business publications and to up-to-date financial information, such as stock quotes. See *on-line information service.*

**downloadable font**   A printer font that must be transferred from the computer's (or the printer's) hard disk drive to the printer's random-access memory before the printer can print the font.

Often called *soft fonts*, downloadable fonts are the least convenient of the three types of printer fonts you can use. Downloading can consume from 5 to 10 minutes at the start of every operating session.

Purchase a printer with a variety of built-in typefaces or a cartridge that contains several typefaces in a variety of sizes. These fonts are immediately available for printing, because they are resident in the printer's (or cartridge's) ROM.

Downloaded fonts take up room in your printer's memory, leaving less room for page-makeup operations and potentially causing out-of-memory problems. You may have to add one or two additional megabytes of expensive printer memory to avoid such difficulties. However, downloadable fonts are available in hundreds of typefaces, and what they lack in convenience they make up for in versatility.

The hard disk need not be the computer's. High-end PostScript-compatible laser printers such as the Apple LaserWriter NTX come with SCSI ports for hard drives.

Downloadable fonts usually are provided in the form of a font family, with a range of type styles and sizes with the same typeface design. You cannot resize bit-mapped fonts; for example, you cannot print a bit-mapped Helvetica 14-point font at 12 or 16 points. Outline fonts, however, consist of a mathematical font representation (written in a page-description language like PostScript) that the printer can resize. Therefore, you are not limited to a narrow range of font sizes. Only printers with the necessary internal circuitry are capable of decoding and printing outline fonts.

You can download fonts at the start of the operating session by using a downloading utility or while using a word processing or page layout program (such as Microsoft Word, WordPerfect, or PageMaker) capable of downloading fonts as needed.

Some laser printers, such as the Hewlett-Packard LaserJet, categorize fonts as permanent or temporary. Permanent fonts are downloaded at the beginning of the operating session and remain in the printer's memory throughout the session. (They are not really permanent, however, because they are erased—along with everything in the printer's memory—when you shut off the printer.)

Permanent fonts consume memory space. Temporary fonts, in contrast, are downloaded as needed during a printing operation and deleted from memory to make room for other fonts as font changes occur in the document. Temporary fonts do not hold memory, but they interrupt printing with downloads that can make the whole operation tedious.

 After you print a document that requires several downloadable fonts that you no longer need, switch your printer off and on before proceeding, especially if the next document contains graphics. The power interruption clears the printer's memory and makes room for the computations needed to generate the graphic image. See *bit-mapped font, built-in font, cartridge font, downloading utility, font, font family, outline font, page description language (PDL)*, and *PostScript*.

**downloading**   The reception and storage of a program or data file from a distant computer through data communication links. See *file transfer protocol* and *modem*.

**downloading utility**   A utility program that transfers downloadable fonts from your computer's (or printer's) hard disk to the printer's random-access memory (RAM).

Downloading utilities usually are provided free by the publishers of downloadable fonts. You may not need the utility if the word processing or page layout program you are using has downloading capabilities built in, such as WordPerfect, Microsoft Word, Ventura Publisher, and PageMaker.

**downward compatibility**   Hardware or software that runs without modification when used with earlier computer components or software versions. VGA monitors, for example, are downwardly compatible with the original IBM PC, if you use an 8-bit VGA adapter that fits in the PC's 8-bit expansion bus.

**dpi**   See *dots per inch*.

**drag**   To move the mouse pointer while holding down the mouse button.

**drag-and-drop editing**   An editing feature that allows you to perform a block move by highlighting the block and then using the mouse to drag a special pointer to the text's new location. When you release the mouse button, the text appears in the new location. Introduced by Microsoft in its Word and Excel products (Windows and Macintosh versions), drag-and-drop editing is a useful and convenient feature because it requires no commands; you directly manipulate the text on-screen.

 Microsoft Windows 3.1 implements drag-and-drop editing in the File Manager, enabling you to copy and move files quickly and easily. To copy a file from one drive to another, click the file and drag the pointer to the file's destination (see fig. D.11).

Directory tree for drive C          Directory tree for drive D

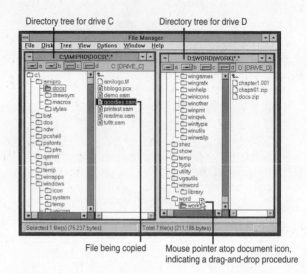

File being copied          Mouse pointer atop document icon,
indicating a drag-and-drop procedure

**Fig. D.11.** Using drag-and-drop editing to copy a file from
drive C to drive D.

**DRAM** See *dynamic random-access memory*.

**draw program** A computer graphics program that uses
object-oriented graphics to produce line art.

A draw program stores the components of a drawing,
such as lines, circles, and curves, as mathematical formulas rather than as a configuration of bits on-screen,
as paint programs do. Unlike images created with paint
programs, line art created with a draw program can be
sized and scaled without introducing distortions.

Draw programs differ from paint programs in another
way: draw programs produce output that prints at a
printer's maximum resolution. Popular draw programs
include MacDraw and SuperPaint for the Macintosh.
See *object-oriented graphic* and *paint program*.

**draw tool** In any program that includes graphics capabilities, a command that transforms the cursor into a "pen"
for creating object-oriented (vector) graphics. Draw
tools typically include options for creating lines, circles,
ovals, polylines, rectangles, and Bézier curves. See
*object-oriented graphics*.

**drive**  See *disk drive*.

**drive bay**  A receptacle or opening into which you can install a hard or floppy disk drive. Common in today's IBM and IBM-compatible personal computers are half-height bays. See *half-height drive*.

**drive designator**  In DOS, an argument that specifies the drive to be affected by the command. For example, the command FORMAT B: instructs DOS to format the disk in drive B. (B: is the drive designator.)

**driver**  A disk file that contains information needed by a program to operate a peripheral such as a monitor or printer. See *device driver*.

**drop cap**  An initial letter of a chapter or paragraph, enlarged and positioned so that the top of the character is even with the top of the first line and the rest of the character descends into the second and subsequent lines (see fig. D.12). See *stickup initial*.

T his is a 24-point Helvetica Big First Char. with Space For Big First: Normal. Ventura automatically aligns the top of the character with the top of the first line of text and calculates the number of lines to indent.

T his is a 24-point Helvetica Big First Char. with Space For Big First: Custom. You set the number of lines to indent and Ventura aligns the baselines of the First Char. and the last indented line of text.

**Fig. D.12.** Drop caps created with Ventura Publisher.

**drop-down list box**  In industry-standard and graphical user interfaces, a list of command options that doesn't appear until you select the command. After you "drop down" the list, you can choose one of its options. The drop-down list box enables a programmer to provide many options without taking up a lot of space on-screen. See *graphical user interface (GUI)* and *industry-standard user interface*.

**drop-out type**  White characters printed on a black background.

**drop shadow**  A shadow placed behind an image, slightly offset horizontally and vertically, that creates the illusion that the topmost image has been lifted off the surface of the page.

**dual in-line package (DIP)**  A standard packaging and mounting device for integrated circuits. The package, made of hard plastic material, encloses the circuit; the circuit's leads are connected to downward-pointing pins that stick in two parallel rows. The pins are designed to fit securely into a socket; you also can solder them directly to a circuit board.

 Don't try to install or remove DIP circuits unless you know what you're doing. You can easily bend or break the pins. See *single in-line package*.

**dual y-axis graph**  In presentation and analytical graphics, a line or column graph that uses two y-axes (values axes) when comparing two data series with different measurement scales (see fig. D.13).

Dual y-axis graphs are useful when you are comparing two different data series that must be measured with two different values axes. In figure D.13, for example, sales are measured in dollars, and temperatures are measured in degrees. See *paired bar graph*.

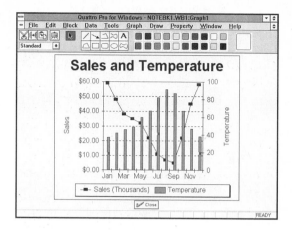

**Fig. D.13.** A dual y-axis graph.

**dumb terminal**   See *terminal*.

**dump**   To transfer the contents of memory to a printing or secondary storage device. Programmers use memory dumps while debugging programs to see exactly what the computer is doing when the dump occurs. See *screen dump*.

**duplex**   See *full duplex* and *half duplex*.

**duplex printing**   Printing or reproducing a document on both sides of the page so that the verso (left) and recto (right) pages face each other after the document is bound.

A document begins on an odd-numbered recto page; verso pages have even numbers. See *binding offset*.

**Dvorak keyboard**   An alternative keyboard layout in which 70 percent of the keystrokes are made on the home row (compared to 32 percent with the standard QWERTY layout).

If you are just learning how to touch-type, consider a Dvorak keyboard; it is easier and faster. Every time you return to a QWERTY keyboard, however, you must go back to the hunt-and-peck method. See *QWERTY*.

**dynamic data exchange (DDE)**   In Microsoft Windows and Macintosh System 7, an interprocess communication (IPC) channel through which correctly prepared programs can actively exchange data and control other applications. To be capable of DDE, the programs must conform to Microsoft Corporation's specifications.

DDE allows simultaneously running programs to exchange data, even as the information changes. For example, with a telecommunications link to a stock-reporting service such as Dow-Jones News/Retrieval Service, a DDE-capable spreadsheet program (such as Microsoft Excel) can receive real-time data from the on-line source, record changes in the price of key stocks, and recalculate the entire worksheet as the change occurs.

Underlying DDE is a client/server model. The application that supplies information is called the *server application*, while the application that receives information is called the *client application*. Most DDE-capable applications can function as both client and server for DDE purposes. Moreover, a single server application can provide data to more than one client. When one DDE application communicates with another, the resulting interaction is called a *conversation*. The DDE exchange begins with one application initiating the conversation, and it continues as the other application acknowledges the conversation and receives the data. Finally, one of the applications terminates the conversation. Every DDE conversation involves a topic and an item. The topic, in most cases, is a file name, and the item is a specific data location, such as a data range or cell in a spreadsheet.

Microsoft's object linking and embedding (OLE) standards have helped to simplify the user's task in setting up dynamic links in Windows and Macintosh systems. In OLE terms, DDE is simply dynamic linking, and you can achieve it in a very easy way: You just paste data from one application to another using the Paste Link or Paste Special command (Edit menu). After you link the server and client applications in this way, DDE updates the destination document if the source document changes. Both programs do not need to be running simultaneously. If the client application isn't running when you update the source document, you see an alert box when you open the destination document, informing you that the source data has changed and asking you whether you want to update it. See *client application, dynamic link, interprocess communication (IPC)*, *object linking and embedding (OLE)*, *server application,* and *System 7*.

**dynamic link**    A method of linking data shared by two programs. When data is changed in one program, the data is likewise changed in the other when you use an update command. See *hot link*.

**dynamic object**    A document or a portion of a document that has been pasted or inserted into a destination document using object linking and embedding (OLE) techniques. A linked object is automatically updated if you make changes to the source document. An embedded object retains all the information that the server application needs to allow you to edit the object. See *object linking and embedding (OLE)*.

**dynamic random-access memory (DRAM)**    A random-access memory (RAM) chip that represents memory states by using capacitors that store electrical charges.

Because the capacitors eventually lose their charges, DRAM chips must refresh continually (hence "dynamic").

Dynamic RAM chips vary in their access times, the speeds with which the central processing unit (CPU) can obtain information encoded within them. These access times are rated in nanoseconds (billionths of a second); a chip marked –12, for example, has an access time of 120 ns. Such access times may seem remarkably fast, but they actually may be insufficient for today's fast microprocessors that must be programmed with wait states so that memory can catch up.

 If you are using an Intel 80286- or 80386-based computer with a fast clock speed (such as 25 or 33 MHz), you need the fastest DRAM chips you can obtain. Chips rated 120 ns are too slow; make sure that your computer is equipped with chips rated at 80 ns or better. See *central processing unit (CPU), nanosecond (ns), static random-access memory (RAM),* and *wait state.*

**EARN**   See *European Academic Research Network*.

**EBCDIC**   See *Extended Binary Coded Decimal Interchange Code*.

**echoplex**   A communications standard for computers in which the receiving station acknowledges and confirms the reception of a message by echoing the message back to the transmitting station. See *full duplex* and *half duplex*.

**edge connector**   The part of an adapter board that plugs into an expansion slot. See *expansion slot* and *adapter*.

**Edit mode**   A program mode that makes correcting text and data easier (see fig. E.1).

**Fig. E.1.** dBASE data record displayed in Edit mode.

In Lotus 1-2-3, for example, you type EDIT to correct a cell definition. After you type EDIT, the program displays the current cell definition on the entry line, and you can use editing keys to correct errors or add characters.

**editor**   See *text editor*.

**EDLIN**   In DOS, the line editor provided with the operating system for light text-creation and editing duties.

A line editor is a primitive word processing program that forces you to work with text line-by-line. Although EDLIN may be suitable for creating a small batch file, EDLIN is cumbersome and difficult to use. For most purposes, a word processing program is better for creating text files.

**EEMS**   See *Enhanced Expanded Memory Specification*.

**EGA**   See *Enhanced Graphics Adapter*.

**EISA**   See *Extended Industry Standard Architecture*.

**Electronic Data Interchange (EDI)**   A standard for the electronic exchange of business documents, such as invoices and purchase orders, that was developed by Data Interchange Standards Association (DISA).

Using field codes, such as BT for "Bill To" or ST for "Ship To," EDI specifies the format in which data is transmitted electronically. By ensuring that all EDI-based communications have the same data in the same place, this protocol enables companies to break the paper habit by exchanging purchase orders and other documents electronically. EDI is currently used by 18,000 organizations worldwide.

**electronic mail**   The use of electronic communications media to send textual messages (such as letters, memos, and reports). Also called *e-mail*.

Electronic mail may involve a one-to-one communication, in which one person sends a private message to another person; or a one-to-many communication, in which one person sends a message to many people connected to the network.

Electronic mail is a store-and-forward technology; unlike a telephone call, the recipient need not be present. The system stores the message and, if the system is a good one, informs the recipients that a message is waiting when they log on to the system.

Electronic mail services are provided privately and publicly. Private electronic mail is possible in local area networks. Mail can be exchanged only among users of the network. Public electronic mail is provided by an on-line information service such as CompuServe or GEnie, or an electronic mail service such as MCI Mail. Users who log on to the information service can exchange mail by using a modem and a communications program. See *communications program*, *local area network (LAN)*, and *modem*.

**elite**   A typeface that prints twelve characters per inch. See *pitch*.

**e-mail**   See *electronic mail*.

**embedded chart**   In Microsoft Excel, a chart created within a worksheet rather than as a separate chart document.

**embedded formatting command**   A text formatting command placed directly in the text to be formatted. The command does not affect the appearance of the text on-screen.

Considered by many to be an undesirable formatting technique in word processing programs, embedded commands cannot be seen until the document is previewed on-screen or printed. Studies in work environments show that using word processors with embedded commands may take longer to produce documents than using typewriters. Synonymous with *off-screen formatting*. See *hidden codes, on-screen formatting,* and *what-you-see-is-what-you-get (WYSIWYG)*.

**embedded object**   In object linking and embedding (OLE), a document or a portion of a document created with one application that has been wholly inserted into a destination document created by another application (see fig. E.2). The result is a compound document that contains all the information needed by all the contributing applications to edit the data. Object linking and embedding is possible only when you're using OLE-compatible applications on a Windows system or on a Macintosh system running System 7.

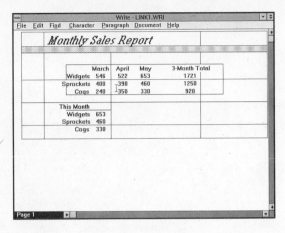

**Fig. E.2.** An Excel worksheet embedded in a Write document.

An embedded object differs from a linked file in that no dynamic link is created between the source document and the destination document. For this reason, changes to the source document are not automatically updated in the destination document. But embedding offers much more than the standard Clipboard technique of copying and pasting. When you embed an object, the object is fully editable. You have embedded all the information the server application needs in order to edit the embedded object. (Linking places only a static representation of the data in the destination document.) Double-clicking the object starts the server application (the application that created the object). Using the server application, you edit the file and then choose Update from the File menu to update the embedded object. The source document is not affected by this change. In sum, embedding allows you to place a fully editable document or a portion of a document into a document created by another application. See *linked object* and *object linking and embedding (OLE)*.

**em dash**   A continuous dash equal in width to one em, the width of the capital letter *M* in a given typeface.

Em dashes often are used to introduce parenthetical remarks. The following sentence contains em dashes: The butler—or someone who knows what the butler knows—must have done it. See *en dash*.

**em fraction**   A single-character fraction that occupies one em of space and uses a diagonal stroke (¼).

Em fractions are used when fractions appear occasionally within body text, but em fractions are not available in some fonts. A true em fraction is one character and should be distinguished from a piece fraction made from three or more characters (1/4). See *en fraction*.

**EMM386.EXE**   An expanded memory emulator that simulates expanded memory on an 80386 or higher computer equipped with extended memory. EMM386.EXE also enables the user to load device drivers and programs into the upper memory area. See *device driver*, *expanded memory, expanded memory emulator, extended memory,* and *upper memory area.*

**emphasis**   The use of a non-Roman type style, such as underlining, italic or bold typefaces, and small caps, to highlight a word or phrase.

Word processing and page layout programs provide many more ways to emphasize text than typewriters do. Use these options judiciously, however. Emphasis is often overdone by inexperienced writers.

Effective page layout design calls for restraint in the use of emphasis. Because underlining is a signal to the typesetter to set the text in italic, underlining is redundant in documents prepared using desktop publishing techniques. Many programs include outline and shadow characters that should be used only rarely. See *type style*.

**EMS**   See *Lotus-Intel-Microsoft Expanded Memory Specification (LIM EMS)*.

**emulation**   The duplication of the functional capability of one device in another device.

In telecommunications, for example, a personal computer emulates a dumb terminal for on-line communication with a distant computer. See *dumb terminal*.

**en**   A unit of measurement in typesetting that equals half the width of an em space, the width of the capital letter *M* in the current typeface.

**Encapsulated PostScript (EPS) file**   A high-resolution graphic image stored in PostScript page description language. You use this language to write instructions for storing the graphic image.

The EPS standard enables the device-independent transfer of high-resolution graphic images between applications. EPS graphics are of outstanding quality and can contain subtle gradations in shading, high-resolution text with special effects, and graceful curves generated by mathematical equations.

The printout resolution is determined by the printing device's maximum capabilities; on laser printers, EPS graphics print at 300 dpi, but on Linotronic typesetters, resolutions of up to 2,540 dpi are possible. EPS images can be sized without sacrificing image quality (see fig. E.3).

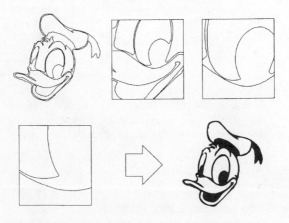

**Fig. E.3.** An EPS graphic image scaled to various sizes without distortion.

The major drawback of EPS graphics is that a PostScript-compatible laser printer is required to print them—and with most application programs, the image is not visible on-screen unless a PICT- or TIFF-format screen image has been attached to the EPS file.

Programs capable of creating, displaying, and editing EPS graphics include Adobe Illustrator (Adobe Systems) and Aldus Freehand (Aldus Corporation). You create the image using on-screen graphics tools, and the program saves the image as a text file containing PostScript instructions.

As an alternative to expensive PostScript printers, developers have created programs that interpret and print EPS files on standard dot-matrix printers or non-PostScript laser printers. One such program is GoScript (LaserGo, Inc.). See *PostScript*.

**encryption**   The process of enciphering, or encoding, data so that users who do not possess the necessary password cannot read the data. See *decryption*.

**en dash**   A continuous dash equal in width to one half em, the width of the capital letter *M* in the current typeface.

En dashes are used in place of the English words *to* or *through*, as in January 9–14 or pp. 63–68. See *em dash*.

**End key**   A key on IBM PC–compatible keyboards with varying functions from program to program.

Frequently, the End key is used to move the cursor to the end of the line or the bottom of the screen, but the assignment of this key is up to the programmer.

**endnote**   A footnote positioned at the end of the document rather than the bottom of the page.

Many word processing programs enable the user to choose between footnotes and endnotes.

**end user**   The person who benefits, directly or indirectly, from the capabilities of a computer system and uses these capabilities to perform a professional,

managerial, or technical task, such as analyzing a
company's finances, preparing a publication-quality
report, or maintaining an inventory of items in stock.

In corporate data processing during the 1950s and
1960s, people typically had little or no data processing
or computer expertise and were kept at arm's length
from computer resources. One significant outcome of
the personal computer has been the distribution of
computer tools to people who previously could not
gain access to such tools.

With the distribution of tools has come the distribution
of computer expertise. Today's end user possesses
sufficient expertise to carry out routine system maintenance tasks and to run application programs. Increasing numbers of end users modify application programs
by writing macros and using software command
languages.

**en fraction**   A single-character fraction that occupies one en
of space and uses a horizontal stroke. See *en* and *em
fraction*.

**Enhanced Expanded Memory Specification (EEMS)**   An
enhanced version of the original Lotus-Intel-Microsoft
Expanded Memory Specification (LIM EMS) that enables DOS applications to use more than 640K of
memory. Version 4.0 of EMS supports both the original
version of EMS and the enhanced version (EEMS). See
*expanded memory* and *Lotus-Intel-Microsoft Expanded
Memory Specification (LIM EMS)*.

**Enhanced Graphics Adapter (EGA)**   A color, bit-mapped,
graphics display adapter for IBM PC–compatible computers. The EGA adapter displays up to 16 colors simultaneously with a resolution of 640 pixels horizontally
by 350 lines vertically.

 For slightly more than the cost of a good
EGA adapter and monitor, you can buy the
superior VGA technology that preserves the
correct aspect ratio of on-screen graphics.
See *Color Graphics Adapter (CGA)* and *Video Graphics
Array (VGA)*.

**Enhanced Graphics Display**   A color digital monitor
designed to work with the IBM Enhanced Graphics
Adapter (EGA).

**Enhanced System Device Interface (ESDI)**   An interface
standard for hard disk drives. Drives using the ESDI
standard transfer data at 10 megabits per second, twice
as fast as the earlier ST-506/ST-412 interface standard.

 ESDI drives are substantially more expensive
than drives conforming to other interface
standards. If your system uses an 80286,
80386, or 80486 microprocessor, and if the
system's clock speed is approximately 12 MHz or
higher, an ST-506 drive may slow down your system's performance. See *interface standard* and
*ST-506/ST-412*.

**Enter/Return**   A key that confirms a command, sending the
command to the central processing unit (CPU). In
word processing, the Enter/Return key starts a new
paragraph.

 On early IBM PC keyboards, this key is
labeled with a hooked left arrow. On more
recent IBM keyboards and the keyboards of
most IBM PC compatibles, *Enter* or *Return* is
printed on the key.

 Most IBM PC–compatible keyboards have
two Enter/Return keys. The first is located to
the right of the typing area, and the second
is located at the lower right of the numeric
keypad. These two keys have identical functions in
most but not all programs. Synonymous with *carriage
return*.

**entry-level system**   A computer system considered to be
the minimal system for undertaking serious applications with the computer, such as using electronic
spreadsheets or word processing software.

The definition of *entry-level system* changes rapidly. Ten years ago, an entry-level system had at least one 160K floppy disk drive, a monochrome text monitor, and 64K of RAM. Today, an entry-level system is, minimally, an IBM or IBM-compatible system that includes an 80386SX microprocessor, 2M (preferably 4M) of RAM, at least a 40M (preferably 80M) hard disk, and a VGA monitor. In the Macintosh world, an entry-level system includes a 68030 microprocessor, 4M of RAM, a 40M or 80M hard disk, and a 12-inch monochrome or color monitor. But by the time you read this, industry pundits may well be insisting that 80486SX or 68040 technology is the bare minimum.

Contributing to the steady increase in "minimum" system requirements are two trends. First, the computer industry is noteworthy for a very unusual fact, one that is related to its impressive technological progress: computers get cheaper even as they become more powerful. Second, programmers keep creating ever more complex programs to run on these more powerful computers. Yesterday's 80286 is still a useful machine—as long as you run yesterday's software.

**entry line**   In a spreadsheet program, the line in which the characters you type appear. The program does not insert the characters into the current cell until you press Enter.

If the cell has contents, the entry line displays the current cell definition.

**envelope printer**   A printer designed specifically to print names, addresses, and USPS Postnet bar codes on business envelopes.

Most envelope printers can print USPS Postnet bar codes. Businesses that use the bar codes receive an attractive discount on postal rates. The use of Postnet bar codes, which are printed on envelopes and automatically read by Postal Service computer equipment, means faster and more accurate delivery of your business correspondence.

If you have a laser printer, you may not need an envelope printer because laser printers are capable of printing Postnet codes. Envelope printers, however, do a better job of handling high-volume printing jobs.

**environment**   The hardware and/or operating system for application programs, such as the Macintosh environment.

**environment variable**   A character string stored in a special, reserved memory space that provides crucial configuration information for certain applications. In DOS, the SET command defines environment variables.

 After you have installed Microsoft Windows, be careful not to erase the AUTOEXEC.BAT file that Windows created or modified during installation. This file contains a SET command that tells Windows where to store the many temporary files it creates.

**EOF**   Abbreviation for *end of file*.

**EOL**   Abbreviation for *end of line*.

**EPS**   See *Encapsulated PostScript file*.

**equation typesetting**   Embedded codes within a word processing document that cause the program to print multiline equations, including mathematical symbols such as integrals and summation signs.

The best word processing programs, such as WordPerfect and Microsoft Word, provide commands and symbols that enable technical writers to create multiline equations. You write the equation by embedding special codes for symbols such as radicals and integrals. You then use a command that displays the equation on-screen as it will print.

**erasable optical disk drive**   A read/write secondary storage medium that uses a laser and reflected light to store and retrieve data on an optical disk.

Unlike CD-ROM and write-once, read-many (WORM) drives, erasable optical disk drives can be used like hard disks are used: you can write and erase data repeatedly. Storage capacities are enormous; current drives store up to 650 megabytes of information.

However, erasable optical disk drives are expensive and much slower than hard disks and are not expected to displace magnetic secondary storage media soon. Like CD-ROM, erasable optical disk drives are used in organizations that need on-line access to huge amounts of supplementary information, such as engineering drawings or technical documentation. See *CD-ROM disk drive*, *optical disk*, *secondary storage*, and *write-once, read-many (WORM)*.

**erasable programmable read-only memory (EPROM)**
A read-only memory (ROM) chip that can be programmed and reprogrammed.

The erasability of EPROM chips matters to computer manufacturers, who often find that they need to reprogram ROM chips containing bugs. PROM chips, which cannot be reprogrammed, must be discarded when a programming error is discovered.

EPROM chips are packaged in a clear plastic case so that the contents can be erased using ultraviolet light. To reprogram the EPROM chip, a PROM programmer is necessary. See *programmable read-only memory (PROM)* and *read-only memory (ROM)*.

 Because of the slight possibility that EPROM chips may be damaged by ultraviolet light, you should avoid exposing your computer's innards to bright sunlight.

**ergonomics**   The science of designing machines, tools, and computers so that people find them easy and healthful to use.

**error handling**   The way a program copes with errors, such as the failure to access data on a disk or a user's failure to press the appropriate key.

A poorly written program may fail to handle errors at all, leading to a system lockup. The best programmers anticipate possible errors and provide information that helps the user solve the problem. See *error trapping*.

**error message**   In interactive computing, an on-screen message informing you that the program is unable to carry out a requested operation.

Early computing systems assumed users to be technically sophisticated, and frequently presented cryptic error messages such as

```
EXECUTION TERMINATE-ERROR 19869087
```

Applications for general use should display more helpful error messages that include suggestions about how to solve the problem, such as

```
You are about to lose work you have
not saved. Click OK if you want to
abandon this work. Click Cancel to
return to your document.
```

**error trapping**   A program or application's capability to recognize an error and perform a predetermined action in response to that error.

**Esc**   A key that can be implemented differently by application programs. Esc usually is used to cancel a command or an operation.

**escape code**   A combination of the Esc code and an ASCII character that, when transmitted to a printer, causes the printer to perform a special function, such as printing characters in boldface type. Synonymous with *escape sequence*.

**ESDI**   See *Enhanced System Device Interface*.

**EtherNet**   A local area network hardware standard, originally developed by Xerox Corporation, capable of linking up to 1,024 nodes in a bus network.

A high-speed standard using a baseband (single-channel) communication technique, EtherNet provides for a raw data transfer rate of 10 megabits per second, with actual throughputs in the range of 2 to 3 megabits per second. EtherNet uses carrier sense multiple access with collision detection (CSMA/CD) techniques to prevent network failures when two devices attempt to access the network at the same time. See *AppleTalk*, *bus network*, *carrier sense multiple access with collision detection (CSMA/CD)*, and *local area network (LAN)*.

 Several firms, such as 3Com and Novell, manufacture local area network hardware that uses EtherNet protocols, but the products of one firm often are incompatible with the products of another.

**EtherTalk**   An implementation of EtherNet local area network hardware, jointly developed by Apple and 3Com, designed to work with the AppleShare network operating system. A network with a bus topology, EtherTalk transmits data via coaxial cables at the EtherNet rate of 10 megabits per second, in contrast to AppleTalk's much slower rate of only 230 kilobits per second. An EtherTalk network requires that each networked Macintosh be equipped with a compatible network interface card.

**ETX/ACK handshaking**   See *handshaking*.

**European Academic Research Network (EARN)**   A European wide-area network fully integrated with BITNET. See *BITNET*.

**even parity**   In asynchronous communications, an error-checking technique that sets an extra bit (called a *parity bit*) to 1 if the number of 1 bits in a 1-byte data item adds up to an even number. The parity bit is set to 0 if the number of 1 bits adds up to an odd number. See *asynchronous communication*, *odd parity*, and *parity checking*.

**event**   In an event-driven environment, an action—such as moving or clicking the mouse—that results in the generation of a message. See *event handler* and *event-driven program*.

**event-driven environment**   A program or operating system that normally functions in an idle loop, waiting for events to occur, such as a mouse click, keyboard input, or messages from peripheral devices. When an event occurs, the program exits the idle loop and executes the program code designed to handle the specific event. This code is called an *event handler*. After the event is handled, the program returns to the idle loop. Microsoft Windows and Macintosh system software exemplify event-driven environments.

**event-driven language**   A programming language that creates programs responsive to events such as input, incoming data, or signals received from other applications. Such programs keep the computer in an idle loop until event occurs, at which time they execute code that is relevant to the event. HyperTalk, the language included with the HyperCard application packaged with every Macintosh, is an event-driven language. See *object-oriented programming language.*

**event-driven program**   A program designed to react to user-initiated events, such as clicking a mouse, rather than forcing the user to go through a series of prompts and menus in a predetermined way.

Macintosh application programs are event-driven. Unlike conventional programs that have an algorithm for solving a problem, the central feature of a Mac program is the main event loop that forces the program to run in circles while waiting for the user to do something such as clicking the mouse.

**event handler**   In an event-driven environment, a block of program code designed to handle the messages generated when a specific kind of event occurs, such as a mouse click.

**Excel**   A graphics-based spreadsheet program developed by Microsoft Corporation that incorporates some of the features of page layout programs.

Available for the Macintosh and IBM PC compatibles running Windows, Excel combines an excellent spreadsheet program and presentation graphics package with user-selectable typefaces, color, and shading. Excel provides the tools to create and analyze spreadsheets and to desktop publish the results. See *character-based program* and *Lotus 1-2-3*.

**EXE**   In DOS, an extension that indicates that a file is an executable program. To run the program with DOS, you simply type the file name (but not the extension) and press Enter.

**executable file**   See *executable program.*

**executable program**   A computer program that is ready to run on a given computer. To be executable, the program must have been translated, usually by a compiler, into the machine language appropriate for the computer. A program written for a Macintosh computer (and its Motorola 680x0 microprocessors) will not run on an IBM PC unless the program has been specifically modified for this purpose.

 In DOS, you can tell whether a file is an executable program by looking at the extension: EXE and COM files are executable programs.

**execute**   To carry out the instructions in an algorithm or program.

**expand**   In an outlining utility or a graphical disk directory (such as Microsoft Window's File Manager), to reveal all the subordinate entries below the selected outline heading or directory.

 In Windows' File Manager, you can expand a directory quickly by double-clicking the directory icon.

**expandability**   The ability of a computer system to accommodate more memory, additional disk drives, or adapters.

Computers vary in their expandability. The Macintosh IIsi, for instance, offers much of the functionality of the more expensive IIci, but it has only one expansion slot. Inexpensive 80386 computers may offer only two or three expansion slots and room for only one or two megabytes of RAM on the motherboard; with a little comparison shopping, you can get a machine with more slots available and room for 8M of RAM.

 Consider expandability when you're shopping for a computer. What accessories are you likely to add to your system? A modem? A fax adapter? Additional disk drives? As for memory, remember that what seems adequate now will prove woefully insufficient in the future. If you're planning to use Windows, and particularly if you're planning to run more than one application, you may need as much as 4M or more RAM.

**expanded memory**    In IBM PC–compatible computers, a method of getting beyond the 640K DOS memory barrier by swapping programs and data in and out of the main memory at high speeds.

When the IBM Personal Computer was designed, many people thought that 640K was more than enough memory for any application. (The first IBM PCs were available with as little as 16K of RAM.) The IBM PC architecture and DOS, the PC's operating system, were designed to use a maximum of 640K of RAM.

By the mid-1980s, however, people realized that the 640K RAM barrier was imposing severe limitations on many new programs. Spreadsheets, for example, reserve all available memory space for the active worksheet, and the computer can run out of memory after filling in even a small fraction of the available cells. Many users also want to load several programs into RAM simultaneously and switch from one to the other in a keystroke.

Expanded memory uses a programming trick to get beyond the 640K RAM barrier. A peephole of 64K of RAM is set aside so that program instructions and data can be paged in and out in 64K chunks. When the computer requires a 64K chunk not currently paged in, expanded memory software finds and inserts the chunk into the peephole. Such swapping (bank switching) occurs so quickly that the computer seems to have more than 640K of RAM.

If your computer uses the 8088, 8086, or 80286 microprocessor and you want to take advantage of expanded memory, equip your computer with an expanded memory board conforming to the Lotus-Intel-Microsoft Expanded Memory System. If you are using an 80386 or 80486 computer with more than one megabyte of extended RAM, you can take advantage of this additional RAM under DOS by using a memory management program such as Quarterdeck's Expanded Memory Manager (QEMM/386). But by far the most popular solution is to run Microsoft Windows with MS-DOS 5.0, which together can make available all memory installed in your system. See *extended memory* and *Lotus-Intel-Microsoft Expanded Memory System (LIM EMS)*.

**expanded memory board**   An adapter that adds expanded memory to an IBM-compatible computer. See *expanded memory*.

**expanded memory emulator**   A utility program for 80386 and 80486 IBM-compatible computers that uses extended memory to simulate expanded memory.

Expanded memory provided a means to prolong the useful life of 8086- and 8088-based personal computers. When IBM-compatible computers based on the 80286 and later microprocessors became available, it became possible to equip these computers with 16 megabytes (80286) or more (80386) of extended memory, which is superior to expanded memory. But DOS still couldn't use this memory; DOS runs these microprocessors in real mode, which restricts programs to the same old 640K conventional memory space. Expanded memory emulators address this problem by

configuring extended memory as if it were expanded
memory. With an expanded memory emulator, there's
no need for an expensive expanded memory adapter
board. See *EMM386.EXE, expanded memory*, and
*extended memory*.

**expanded memory manager**   A utility program that manages expanded memory in an IBM-compatible computer equipped with an expanded memory board. See
*expanded memory* and *expanded memory board*.

**Expanded Memory Specification (EMS)**   See *Lotus-Intel-
Microsoft Expanded Memory Specification (LIM EMS)*.

**expanded type**   Type that has been increased laterally so
that fewer characters are contained per linear inch.

**expansion board**   See *adapter*.

**expansion bus**   An extension of the computer's data bus
and address bus that includes a number of receptacles
(slots) for adapter boards.

Because each generation of microprocessors has a
wider data bus, the expansion bus of IBM PC–compatible computers has changed. The original IBM Personal
Computer and XT, based on the 8/16-bit 8088 chip,
used an expansion bus with 62-pin expansion slots; the
IBM Personal Computer AT, based on the 16-bit 80286,
uses the same 62-pin expansion slot plus a supplemen-
tal 36-pin expansion slot.

Non–IBM PC compatibles based on the 32-bit Intel
80386 microprocessor require a 32-bit data bus structure to connect with primary storage. Because even
these computers use 16-bit peripherals such as disk
drives and video displays, however, some of them set
aside adequate room for memory expansion on the
motherboard and use the standard, AT-style expansion
bus for peripherals. Some machines have expansion
slots for full 32-bit memory boards.

If you are buying an 80386 computer and plan to run OS/2, you need as much as eight megabytes of memory, if you plan to run several applications at once. Make sure that the motherboard of your computer has adequate room for expansion if the computer does not offer 32-bit memory expansion slots.

With the advent of true 32-bit microprocessors such as the Intel 80386, the 32-bit data bus is extended throughout the machine, and the full performance benefits of 32-bit chips are realized. However, two competing standards have emerged for 32-bit expansion buses. See *address bus*, *bus*, *Extended Industry Standard Architecture (EISA)*, *Micro Channel Bus*, *microprocessor*, and *motherboard*.

**expansion card**    See *adapter*.

**expansion slot**    A receptacle connected to the computer's expansion bus, designed to accept adapters. See *adapter*.

**expert system**    A computer program that contains much of the knowledge used by an expert in a specific field and that assists nonexperts as they attempt to cope with problems.

Expert systems contain a knowledge base that expresses an expert's knowledge in a series of IF/THEN rules and an inference engine capable of drawing inferences from the knowledge base. The system engages you in a dialogue, prompting you to supply information needed to assess the situation.

After the information is provided, the system's inference engine consults the rules and attempts to come to a conclusion. Most expert systems express such conclusions with a confidence factor, ranging from speculation to educated guess to firm conclusion.

Creating an expert system is more difficult than it appears. A surprisingly high proportion of expertise is based on experientially learned rules of thumb, such as cleaning the video board contacts with an ink eraser if the computer does not start.

Some of these rules are little more than hunches or guesses. In knowledge acquisition, interviewers attempt to glean such knowledge from experts so that the knowledge can be placed into an expert system. Research efforts now are focused on creating expert systems capable of acquiring the necessary knowledge without so much assistance.

Expert systems that rely on IF/THEN rules are severely limited in their performance capabilities. Like the BASIC programming language, the formulation of knowledge in the form of IF/THEN rules results in chaos because the total number of interrelationships among program statements quickly grows beyond the programmer's comprehension. An expert system containing 10,000 or more IF/THEN rules, therefore, is likely to perform in an erratic and unstable manner. Yet, most significant areas of human expertise involve far more than 10,000 rules.

Owing to their performance limitations, rule-based expert systems are not likely to displace human professionals such as physicians or attorneys. However, expert systems have proven commercially viable for limited applications, in which the number of rules falls within the technology's capabilities. A major life insurance firm, for example, uses an expert system to perform a preliminary analysis on life insurance applications. The system's judgments then are subject to review by an expert. See *PROLOG*.

**exploded pie graph**   A pie graph in which one or more of the slices has been offset slightly from the others (see fig. E.4). See *pie graph*.

**export**   To output data in a form that another program can read.

Most word processing programs can export a document in ASCII format, which almost any program can read and use. See *import*.

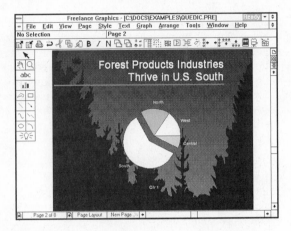

**Fig. E.4.** An exploded pie graph.

**Express Publisher**   An entry-level desktop publishing program marketed by Power Up Software. This popular program includes many of the features of more expensive programs, such as PageMaker, at significantly less cost.

**Extended Binary Coded Decimal Interchange Code (EBCDIC)**   A standard computer character set coding scheme used to represent 256 standard characters.

IBM mainframes use EBCDIC coding, and personal computers use American Standard Code for Information Interchange (ASCII) coding. Communications networks that link personal computers to IBM mainframes must include a translating device to mediate between the two systems.

**extended character set**   In IBM PC–compatible computing, a 254-character set based in the computer's read-only memory (ROM) that includes, in addition to the 128 ASCII character codes, a collection of foreign language, technical, and block graphics characters. The characters

with numbers above ASCII code 128 sometimes are
referred to as higher-order characters.

**Extended Graphics Array (XGA)**   An IBM video display
standard intended to replace its older, 8514/A standard
and to bring 1,024 by 768 resolution to IBM and IBM-
compatible video displays. XGA boards equipped with
sufficient memory (1M) can display 65,536 colors at its
low-resolution mode (640 by 480) and 256 colors at its
high-resolution mode (1,024 by 768). For downward
compatibility with software that supports earlier standards, XGA boards also support the VGA standard. The
XGA standard faces stiff competition from makers of
extended VGA (high-resolution Super VGA) video
adapters. See *Super VGA, video adapter,* and *video
standard.*

**Extended Industry Standard Architecture (EISA)**   A 32-bit
expansion bus design introduced by a consortium of
IBM PC–compatible computer makers to counter IBM's
proprietary Micro Channel Bus.

Unlike the Micro Channel Bus, the EISA bus is downwardly compatible with existing 16-bit peripherals such
as disk drives and display adapters. See *Micro Channel
Bus* and *expansion bus.*

**extended-level synthesizer**   In Microsoft Windows'
Multimedia Personal Computer (MPC) specification, a
synthesizer capable of playing a minimum of 16 simultaneous notes on nine melodic instruments, and 16
simultaneous notes on eight percussive instruments.
See *Multimedia Personal Computer (MPC).*

**extended memory**   In 80286 or later IBM-compatible computers, the random-access memory (RAM), if any, above
1M (megabyte).

Personal computers based on the Intel 8088 and 8086
microprocessors are limited to 1M of random-access
memory (RAM), of which DOS is able to access 640K.
PCs based on the 80286, 80386, and 80486 microprocessors can directly address more than 1M of RAM. An
80286-based computer can address up to 16M of main
memory directly, whereas an 80386-based computer
can address a whopping 4 gigabytes.

The term *extended memory* often is confused with *expanded memory*, but the distinction is important. Extended memory is RAM above 1M that usually is installed directly on the motherboard of 80286 and later computers and is all directly accessible to the microprocessor. Expanded memory, in contrast, is a tricky way of getting beyond MS-DOS's 640K RAM barrier by using a technique called *bank switching*. A bank of conventional memory is set aside to be swapped in and out as needed, providing up to 8M of apparent RAM. But the bank switching technique results in memory access times that are slower than true, extended memory. With expanded memory, a program must wait until the memory circuits swap the correct bank of memory into conventional memory.

With 8088 and 8086 machines, your only option for memory expansion is expanded memory. With 80286 and later machines, you can add extended memory. That's the good news. The bad news is that your MS-DOS applications probably can't use this memory without help. Even if you have 5M of RAM installed in your computer, MS-DOS can use only the first 640K, called *conventional memory*.

What personal computing has needed, ever since the introduction of 80286-based computers, is a set of standards and an operating environment that enable all programs to access extended memory. Microsoft Windows 3.0, coupled with the eXtended Memory Specification (XMS), provides a much-needed solution to this problem. An MS-DOS application designed in accordance with XMS guidelines can, with the assistance of a utility program known as an *extended memory manager*, use the extended memories (if any) of 80286 and later machines. An extended memory manager (HIMEM.SYS) is provided with MS-DOS 5.0 and Microsoft Windows 3.0, currently the most popular operating platform for extended memory access. In Windows' standard and 386 Enhanced modes, Windows allows MS-DOS applications to use all the extended memory available, provided that these applications are written in conformity to the XMS guidelines. Most popular applications now observe the XMS guidelines.

Sometimes you see *extended memory* defined as "the memory above 640K." For example, many 80386 computers sold with 1M of RAM are said to contain 640K of conventional memory and 384K of extended memory. (Microsoft Windows' documentation defines extended memory this way.) Technically, this definition is incorrect; extended memory begins at 1,024K (1M). However, many extended memory managers can configure the upper memory area, the memory between 640K and 1M, as if it were extended memory and allow programs to access a portion of this memory. From the user's viewpoint, this upper memory area is an important extended memory resource. See *conventional memory, expanded memory, extended memory manager, eXtended Memory Specification (XMS), Microsoft Windows,* and *upper memory area.*

 If you have an 80286 or later personal computer and you are contemplating additional memory, skip expanded memory. The expanded memory option is, at best, an option of last recourse for owners of 8088 and 8086 systems who prefer not to upgrade. With an 80286 or later machine, the extended memory option costs less, provides better performance, and prepares your system for Microsoft Windows and Windows applications.

**extended memory manager**   A utility program that enables certain DOS programs to access extended memory. The programs must be written to conform to the XMS memory standard. See *conventional memory, extended memory,* and *eXtended Memory Specification (XMS).*

**eXtended Memory Specification (XMS)**   A set of rules for programmers to follow so that DOS programs can access extended memory in an orderly way. The device driver HIMEM.SYS, or an equivalent memory management program, must be present in your computer's CONFIG.SYS file before programs can access XMS

memory. The specification was jointly developed by
Lotus Development Corporation, Intel Corporation,
Microsoft Corporation, and AST. See *CONFIG.SYS,
extended memory, HIMEM.SYS,* and *memory-
management program.*

**extended VGA**   See *Super VGA.*

**extensible**   Able to accept new, user-defined commands.

**extension**   A three-letter suffix added to a DOS file name
that describes the file's contents. The extension is
optional. It must be preceded by a period.

 Use extensions to categorize files, not to
name them. Because DOS gives you only
eight characters for file names, you may be
tempted to use the extension as part of the
name (LETTER3.JOE). Doing so, however, makes
grouping files more difficult for backup and other
operations. If you're using Microsoft Windows, bear in
mind that Windows uses a program's default extension
(such as WB1) to associate files with that program, so
you should let your programs assign their default extensions to their files. See *file name.*

**external command**   In DOS, a command that cannot be
used unless the program file is present in the current
drive, directory, or path.

If you try to use the BACKUP command and see the
message Bad command or file name, for example,
you must switch to the directory or disk containing
your DOS files. See *internal command.*

**external command (XCMD)**   In HyperTalk programming,
a user-defined command (written in a language like
Pascal or C) that uses built-in Macintosh routines to
perform tasks not normally available within HyperCard.

A popular XCMD is ResCopy, written by Steve Maller of
Apple Computer and widely available in public domain
or shareware stack-writing utilities. ResCopy enables a
HyperTalk programmer to copy external commands
and external resources from one program or stack to

another. Using ResCopy, even a novice HyperTalk programmer can add resources to a HyperCard stack by copying resources from another stack. See *external function (XCFN)* and *ResEdit*.

**external function (XCFN)**   In HyperTalk programming, a program function (written in a language like Pascal or C) that is external to HyperTalk but returns values to the program that can be used within the HyperTalk program.

For example, Resources, an XCFN written by Steve Maller of Apple Computer and widely available in public domain or shareware stack-writing utilities, returns a list of all named resources in a file of a specified type. See *external command (XCMD)*.

**external hard disk**   A hard disk equipped with its own case, cables, and power supply. External hard disks generally cost more than internal hard disks of comparable speed and capacity.

**external modem**   A modem equipped with its own case, cables, and power supply. External modems are designed to plug into the serial port of a computer. See *internal modem*.

**external reference formula**   In Microsoft Excel and other DDE-capable spreadsheet programs, a formula placed in a cell that retrieves a value from a cell in another spreadsheet. See *dynamic data exchange (DDE)*.

**external table**   In Lotus 1-2-3 Release 3, a database created with a database management program (such as dBASE III) that Lotus 1-2-3 can access directly with the Data External command.

**extremely low-frequency (ELF) emission**   The magnetic field generated by commonly used electrical appliances such as electric blankets, hair dryers, food mixers, and computer display monitors, and extending one to two meters from the source. ELF fields are known to cause tissue changes and fetal abnormalities in laboratory test animals and may be related to reproductive anomalies and cancers among frequent users of computer displays.

The debate over the health implications posed by computer displays illustrates the challenges citizens face as they try to sort out the conflicting claims made by scientists, government regulators, Congressional committee reports, employers, and equipment manufacturers. In the mid-1970s, two *New York Times* copy editors were found to have developed ocular opacities (the predecessor of cataracts) after intensively using computer displays. After a newspaper union charged that the displays posed a health threat to workers, the National Institute of Occupational Safety and Health (NIOSH) conducted a study of the emissions produced by these and other displays. NIOSH concluded that these and other emissions fell below the measurement threshold of the equipment used and could not be distinguished from background radiation, thereby posing no hazards to public health. Subsequent charges state that the equipment used to perform these tests was not appropriate and that the data confirming strong magnetic fields was dismissed inappropriately as an experimental anomaly.

Despite repeated assurances by employers, computer manufacturers, federal officials, and scientific researchers that computer displays were safe, evidence continued to accumulate of reproductive disorders among pregnant computer workers. A 1981 congressional inquiry, however, concluded that the preponderance of evidence suggested no cause for linking the use of computer displays to reproductive disorders or other health issues. During the hearings, computer manufacturers were unanimous in insisting that their products posed no hazards to users.

Subsequently, scientific researchers worldwide were beginning to document serious tissue changes and abnormalities in laboratory animals after exposure to ELF fields, but very few of these results appeared in North American newspapers. The dearth of coverage continued well into the late 1980s, despite additional reports of reproductive anomalies and additional scientific studies affirming a link between ELF fields and tissue abnormalities. These studies suggested that computer display use in excess of 20 hours per week brought about a significant increase in the miscarriage rate among pregnant women, and that the risk of cancer increased by 30 percent among children who used electric blankets. When such evidence was brought before government regulators or industry spokesmen, the position was taken that these studies had serious methodological flaws or that they failed to provide a theoretical explanation that could draw a link between ELF and living cell abnormalities.

A study conducted by the U.S. Environmental Protection Agency, originally scheduled for release in November of 1990, concluded that the overall weight of the evidence suggested "modestly elevated" risks of cancer (especially leukemia, lymphoma, and cancer of the nervous system) after prolonged exposure to ELF fields. However, the release of the study was held up on the insistence of administration officials who added qualifiers to the study's claims. In the meantime, a study jointly conducted by Columbia University and Hunter College demonstrated a link between ELF fields and a dramatically increased rate of DNA transcription in living cells, thus suggesting the missing theoretical link between ELF emissions and cancer.

 Although a link between computer display usage and cancer has not been proven beyond doubt, sufficient evidence suggests that computer users should take steps to reduce their exposure to ELF fields. Contrary to what you might suppose, a computer display's ELF emissions are weakest in front of the screens; emissions from the back and sides are stronger. If your desk is positioned back to back with another, so that you are close to the side or back of another computer display, you should move your desk away. To reduce exposure to the emissions coming from the display's screen, remain an arm's length away from the screen.

Here's an excellent argument for investing in a Windows or Macintosh system, preferably with a large, full-page or two-page display. Because these systems can display font sizes on-screen, you can define a 14- or 18-point font size as the normal font for writing and editing purposes. You can easily read such a font from a distance of two or three feet. When it's time to print the document, switch to 12-point or 10-point type. Another strategy: Sweden has instituted tough new emissions standards for computer displays, and displays are now available on the U.S. market that meet or exceed these standards. You may be able to replace your current display with a low-emissions model that meets the Swedish standards. Another alternative is to use a laptop or notebook computer with an LCD or gas-plasma display; neither emit an ELF field.

**facing pages**   The two pages of a bound document that face each other when the document is open.

The even-numbered page (verso) is on the left, and the odd-numbered page (recto) is on the right. See *recto* and *verso*.

**facsimile machine**   See *fax machine.*

**family**   In a windowing system such as X Windows or an outlining utility such as ThinkTank, a unit (such as a window or outline heading) that includes all the units subordinate to it at lower levels of the hierarchy. In the following outline, the heading *ABUNDANT BIRDS OF WEST VIRGINIA*—the parent—and its three children make up a family.

> ABUNDANT BIRDS OF WEST VIRGINIA [parent]
>> Bluejay [child]
>> Cardinal [child]
>> Goldfinch [child]

See *child* and *parent*.

**Fastback Plus**   A popular hard disk backup utility developed by Fifth Generation Systems for IBM PC–compatible computers.

**FAT**   See *file allocation table.*

**fatal error**   A processing error from which the program cannot recover. Exiting the program without having to restart the computer may be possible, but you will probably lose any unsaved data.

**fault tolerance**   The capability of a computer system to cope with internal hardware problems without interrupting the system's performance. Fault tolerant designs typically use backup systems automatically brought on-line when a failure is detected.

The need for fault tolerance is indispensable whenever computers are assigned critical functions, such as guiding an aircraft to a safe landing or ensuring a steady flow of medicines to a patient. Fault tolerance also is beneficial for noncritical, everyday applications.

**fax**   The transmission and reception of a printed page between two locations connected via telecommunications.

Fax, short for *facsimile*, has taken the business world by storm. A fax machine scans a sheet of paper and converts its image into a coded form that can be transmitted via the telephone system. A fax machine on the other end receives and translates the transmitted code and prints a replica of the original page.

**fax board**   An adapter that fits into the expansion slot of a personal computer, providing much of the functionality of a fax machine at a significantly lower cost.

Compared to fax machines, fax boards have advantages and disadvantages. The advantages include lower cost, crisper output, and convenience, but the disadvantages are significant, too. What's so convenient about a fax machine is that it accepts as input anything that can be represented on paper, including handwriting, graphics, and text. To send a fax through a fax board, you must first get the material to be faxed into the computer; unless your system is equipped with a scanner, this restriction rules out sending handwriting and graphics. For the most part, you will send text files. Some fax boards are send-only. Other machines, however, receive anything anyone can send to you via a fax machine.

 Don't settle for a fax board that supports 4,800-bps transmission speeds; 9,600-bps boards aren't much more expensive and provide twice the transmission speed.

**fax machine**   A device that can send (and receive) images of pages, including graphics and text, to another fax machine—or to a computer equipped with a fax board—via the telephone system.

Fax machines, the new mainstay of office technology, represent the latest chapter in paper's victory over the once-vaunted "paperless office." Rather than making use of the paperless communication media made possible by computer technology, such as electronic mail and voice mail, people prefer technologies that allow them to continue dealing with paper—despite the increasingly onerous task of keeping it all filed neatly. But there's a ready reason for fax's popularity: unlike electronic mail, which in most systems forces you to express everything in ASCII text, fax machines allow you to send pictures, scribbles, hieroglyphics, newspaper clippings, copies of photographs—in short, anything you can put onto a piece of paper. Fax technology is now invading computers; a fax board gives your computer much of the functionality of a fax machine (except the capability to scan pages of graphics or text, unless you equip your computer with a scanner).

The current fax rage stems from the mid-1980s, when a European standards organization (CCITT) formulated specifications for the transmission of fax information at 9600 baud. See *Comité Consultatif International Téléphonique et Télégraphique (CCITT)*.

**fax modem**   See *fax board.*

**fax server**   In a local area network, a personal computer or a self-contained unit that provides fax capabilities to all the workstations in the network. See *fax board* and *local area network (LAN)*.

**FCC certification**   An attestation, formerly made by the U.S. Federal Communications Commission, that a given brand and model of a computer meets the FCC's limits for radio frequency emissions.

There are two certification levels: Class A, for computers to be used in industrial and commercial locations, and Class B, for computers to be used in home locations, including home offices. The Class B requirements are more stringent, because home computers often are used in proximity to radios and televisions. Excessive radio frequency interference (RFI) generated by computers can severely degrade the quality of radio and television reception. See *Class A certification, Class B certification,* and *radio frequency interference (RFI)*.

**FDHD** See *SuperDrive*.

**feathering** Adding an even amount of space between each line on a page or column to force vertical justification. See *vertical justification*.

**female connector** A computer cable terminator and connection device with receptacles designed to accept the pins of a male connector. See *male connector*.

**femto-** Prefix indicating one quadrillionth, or a millionth of a billionth ($10^{-15}$).

**field** See *data field*.

**field definition** In a database management program, a list of the attributes that define the type of information you can enter into a data field. The field definition also determines how the field's contents appear on-screen.

In dBASE, the field definition includes the following:

- *Field name.* A ten-character, one-word field name that appears as a heading in data tables and as a prompt on data-entry forms.

- *Data type.* A definition that governs the type of data you can enter into a field.

- *Field width.* The maximum number of characters the field accommodates.

- *Number of decimal places.* The number of decimal places to appear if the field is a numeric field.

- *Index attribute.* The field that appears when you turn on the index attribute to construct an index to the database.

See *data type* and *field template*.

**field name**  In a database management program, a name
given to a data field that helps you identify the field's
contents.

 Field names are important from the user's
standpoint, because they describe the data
contained in each data field. You see the
field names on data-entry forms and data
tables. Ideally, the field names you choose are descriptive. If you name a field MX388SMRPS, nobody else will
know what the name means.

In dBASE, field names are restricted to one word consisting of a continuous series of characters. You can
write two- or three-word field names by separating the
words with underscore characters, as in the following
example:

```
FIRST_NAME
LAST_NAME
PHONE_NO
```

In dBASE, field names are limited to 10 characters.
Some programs do not impose such stringent limitations. Even so, you should keep field names short.
When you display data in a columnar format, therefore,
you see more columns of data on-screen. However, do
not make the names so short that they become cryptic.

**field privilege**  In a database management program, a database definition that establishes what you can do with
the contents of a data field in a protected database.
See *data field*.

**field template**  In database management programs, a field
definition that specifies which kind of data you can type
in the data field. If you try to type data into a field that
does not match the field template, the program displays an error message. Synonymous with *data mask*.

 You should use field templates as often as
possible. They help to prevent users from
adding inappropriate information to the
database.

In dBASE, you can specify the following field templates for each character field in the database structure:

X       Accepts any character

A       Accepts alphabetic letters (a–z, A–Z)

#       Accepts numbers (0–9)

N       Accepts alphabetic letters, numbers, or an underscore character

Y       Accepts Y (for Yes) or N (for No)

L       Accepts T (for True) or F (for False)

!       Converts all inputted characters to uppercase

For numeric fields, you can specify the following templates:

9       Accepts numbers and + or – signs, and requires you to type the number of characters specified (for example, 99999 requires you to type five numbers)

#       Accepts numbers, spaces, and + or – signs

*       Displays leading zeros as asterisks

$       Displays leading zeros as dollar signs

,       Displays numbers larger than 999 with commas

.       Displays a decimal point

See *data type*.

**file**   A named collection of information stored as an apparent unit on a secondary storage medium such as a disk drive.

Although a file appears to be whole, the operating system may distribute the file among dozens or even hundreds of noncontiguous sectors on the disk, storing the links (chains) among these sectors in a file allocation table. To the user, however, files appear as units on disk directories and are retrieved and copied as units. See *file allocation table (FAT)* and *secondary storage*.

**file allocation table (FAT)**   A hidden table on a floppy disk
  or hard disk that stores information about how files are
  stored in distinct (and not necessarily contiguous)
  sectors. See *file fragmentation*.

**file attribute**   A hidden code stored with a file's directory
  that contains its read-only or archive status and other
  information about the file. See *archive attribute, hidden file, locked file,* and *read-only attribute.*

**file compression utility**   A utility program that compresses
  and decompresses infrequently used files so that they
  take up 40 to 50 percent less room on a hard disk. The
  utility decompresses these files when they are needed.
  File compression utilities commonly are used for two
  purposes: to decompress files that have been downloaded from a bulletin board system (BBS) and to make
  room on a hard disk by compressing all files opened
  for a specified period, such as one week. See *archive,
  bulletin board system (BBS),* and *compressed file.*

**file conversion utility**   A utility program that converts files
  created with one program so that the files can be read
  by a program that employs an incompatible file format.
  One popular word processing conversion utility is
  Word for Word, which can convert files among 30 file
  formats. File conversion utilities are available for graphics as well as word processing file conversion. Increasingly, applications include conversion utilities that can
  handle as many as a dozen or more file formats.

**file defragmentation**   See *defragmentation.*

**file deletion**   The removal of a file name from a directory
  without actually removing the contents of the file from
  the disk.

  You should understand how personal computers erase
  files for two reasons: security and the recovery of accidentally deleted files.

  When you erase a file with a DEL or ERASE statement,
  the operating system does not actually destroy the
  data or program instructions stored on the disk; the

operating system merely deletes the name of the file from the disk directory so that the space the file occupies is made available for future storage operations.

This procedure brings up the security angle: others can recover sensitive data from your system, even if you think you have erased the information. To prevent the recovery of such data, you can use a shareware program such as Complete Delete (Macintosh) that totally erases the information on disk.

The fact that file deletions do not actually erase the data on disk can be helpful if the deletion was accidental. An undelete utility, widely available as shareware and in utility program packages such as Symantec Utilities (Macintosh environment) and Norton Utilities (IBM PC–compatible environment), can restore a deleted file if no other information has been written over the file.

 If you accidentally delete a file, stop working. Do not perform any additional operations that write information to the disk. Use an undelete utility immediately. See *shareware*, *undelete utility*, and *utility program*.

**file extension**   See *extension*.

**file format**   The patterns and standards a program uses to store data on disk.

Few programs store data in ASCII format; most use a proprietary file format that other programs cannot read. For example, Microsoft Word cannot read files created with WordPerfect, and WordPerfect cannot read files created with Microsoft Word. The use of proprietary file formats stems from marketing strategy—ensuring that customers continue to use the company's program. Proprietary file formats also enable programmers to include special features that standard formats may not allow.

 If you are stuck with some documents your program cannot read, you can use a data conversion service or a file conversion utility. To locate a data conversion service, look in the Yellow Pages or in the back advertising sections of popular personal computer magazines. See *file conversion utility*, *native file format*, and *proprietary file format*.

**file fragmentation**   The inefficient allocation of files in noncontiguous sectors on a floppy disk or hard disk. Fragmentation occurs because of multiple file deletions and write operations.

When MS-DOS writes a file to disk, the operating system looks for available clusters. If you have created and erased many files on the disk, few files are stored in contiguous clusters; the disk drive's read/write head must travel longer distances to retrieve the scattered data. A process known as *defragmentation* can improve disk efficiency by as much as 50 percent by rewriting files so that they are placed in contiguous clusters. See *defragmentation*.

**file locking**   In a local area network, a method of concurrency control that ensures the integrity of data. File locking prevents more than one user from accessing and altering a file at a time. See *concurrency control* and *local area network (LAN)*.

**FileMaker Pro**   A popular flat-file database management program created by Claris Corporation for the Macintosh. See *flat-file database management program*.

**file management program**   See *flat-file database management program*.

**file name**   A name assigned to a file so that the operating system can find the file. You assign file names when you create the files. Every file on a disk must have a unique name.

In DOS and early versions of OS/2, file names have two parts: the file name and the extension. These names must conform to the following rules.

• *Length.* You may use up to eight characters for the file name and up to three characters for the extension. The extension is optional.

- *Delimiter.* If you use the extension, you must separate the file name and extension by typing a period (no spaces).

- *Legal characters.* You may use any letter or number on the keyboard for file names and extensions. You also may use the following punctuation symbols:

    ' ~ ! @ # $ ^ & ( ) _ - { }

 One of the shortcomings of DOS and the early versions of OS/2 is the eight-character restriction on file names. (OS/2 Versions 1.2 and 2.0 enable you to use longer file names.) You are given little room to express the contents of a file, yet the file name must express the file's contents well enough so that you recognize the file in a disk directory. Obviously, a file name such as @12AX97.TBT is not going to mean much to you a few months later. Good file-naming practice restricts the use of extensions to describe the type of file, not its contents. Files labeled with the extensions COM and EXE are program files. Files labeled DOC and TXT are word processing or text files. Files labeled WK1 or WKS are spreadsheet (worksheet) files, and so on.

In the Macintosh environment, you can use up to 32 characters for file names, and file names can contain any character (including spaces) with the exception of the colon (:). The colon is restricted because the Mac's Hierarchical File System (HFS) uses the colon to construct path names. For example, the path name *Proposals:Foundations:Proposal No. 1* describes the location of the file *Proposal No. 1*. This file is in the Foundations folder within the Proposals folder.

 The Mac's Open and Save dialog boxes can display only 22 characters; the last 10 characters of longer file names are truncated. Because seeing the entire file name when retrieving or saving files is convenient, knowledgeable Mac users restrict file names to 22 characters.

**file privilege**   In dBASE, an attribute that determines what you can do with a protected database on a network. The options are DELETE, EXTEND, READ, and UPDATE. See *field privilege*.

**file recovery**   The restoration of an erased disk file. See *undelete utility*.

**file server**   In a local area network, a personal computer that provides access to files for all the workstations in the network.

In a peer-to-peer network, all workstations also are file servers, because each workstation can provide files to other workstations. In the more common client/server network architecture, a single, high-powered machine with a huge hard disk is set aside to function as the file server for all the workstations (clients) in the network.

Crucial to the file server's functions is the network operation system (NOS), which accepts incoming requests from client workstations and responds with the requested files or data. From the user's point of view at each workstation, the file server's resources appear as if they were just another hard disk that is directly connected to the workstation itself. See *network operating system (NOS)*.

**filespec**   In MS-DOS, a complete specification of a file's location, including a drive letter, path name, file name, and extension, such as C:\REPORTS\REPORT1.WK1.

**file transfer protocol**   In asynchronous communications, a standard that ensures the error-free transmission of program and data files via the telephone system. See *asynchronous communication, Kermit,* and *XMODEM*.

**file transfer utility**   A utility program that transfers files between different hardware platforms, such as the IBM Personal Computer and the Macintosh, or between a desktop and a laptop computer.

Popular file transfer utilities include MacLink Plus, which links PCs and Macs via their serial ports, and Brooklyn Bridge, which links desktop IBM computers with IBM PC–compatible laptops.

**fill** In spreadsheet programs, an operation that enters a sequence of values (numbers, dates, times, or formulas) in a worksheet.

In Lotus 1-2-3, for example, you use the Fill command from the Data menu to fill a range with values, beginning with the start value (the number Lotus 1-2-3 uses to start filling the range), the step value (the number Lotus 1-2-3 uses to increment each number placed in the range), and the stop value (the highest number placed in the range).

 You can use the Fill command from the Data menu to enter a column or row of dates automatically. If you enter *@DATE(91,11,1)* as the start value, *14(days)* as the step value, and *@DATE(92,10,1)* as the stop value, 1-2-3 enters dates at two-week intervals between November 1, 1991, and October 1, 1992, in the column or row.

**filter** In DOS and UNIX, an operating system command that processes data that is directed to pass through the command.

The DOS filters are MORE (scrolls long output screen by screen), FIND (searches for text), and SORT (sorts in order of ASCII characters). To send a file through a filter on its way to the screen, you use the less-than symbol (<). For example, the following command sorts the lines in a file called LIST.TXT:

```
SORT < list.txt
```

To route another command's output through a filter, you use a pipe (¦). The following command, for example, sends the output of the TREE command through the MORE filter:

```
TREE C:\ ¦ MORE
```

 Use MORE whenever you're using a DOS command that will produce more than one screen of output (such as MEM, DIR, or TREE). Here's a sample:

```
MEM /c ¦ MORE            Display memory map
TYPE report.txt ¦ MORE  Display long file
DIR C: /s ¦ MORE         Display long directory
```

**filter command**   In DOS, a type of command that takes input from a device or file, changes or reduces the input, and sends the result to an output device or printer.

**Finder**   A file and memory management utility provided by Apple for Macintosh computers. This utility enables you to run one application at a time.

Often mistakenly referred to as the Macintosh's operating system, the Finder is nothing more than a shell that can be replaced by other shell programs such as XTreeMac. Although the Finder's intuitive and easy-to-use icons and menus have contributed to the Mac's success, the program's limitations quickly become apparent on systems equipped with large hard disks. An improved Finder shipped with System 7 addresses many of the program's shortcomings. See *Multifinder*.

**firmware**   Broadly, the system software permanently stored in a computer's read-only memory (ROM) or elsewhere in the computer's circuitry. You cannot modify the firmware.

**fixed disk**   See *hard disk*.

**fixed-frequency monitor**   An analog monitor designed to receive input signals at only one frequency, as contrasted with a multisynch monitor, which automatically adjusts to match the incoming signal. Most of the VGA monitors sold with inexpensive entry-level 80386SX systems are fixed frequency monitors. See *analog monitor* and *multisynch monitor*.

**fixed length**   In a database management program, a field whose length cannot vary, as opposed to a variable-length field, which can grow to accommodate lengthy entries.

**fixed numeric format**   In spreadsheet programs, a numeric format in which values are rounded to the number of decimal places you specify. See *numeric format*.

**Fkey**   A Macintosh utility program executed by pressing the Command (⌘) and Shift keys with a number key from 0 to 9—the keys that simulate the function keys on IBM PC keyboards.

Four Fkey utilities are included with the Macintosh system software:

| | |
|---|---|
| ⌘-Shift-1 | Ejects the disk from the internal drive |
| ⌘-Shift-2 | Ejects the disk from the external drive |
| ⌘-Shift-3 | Saves the current screen as a MacPaint file |
| ⌘-Shift-4 | Prints the current screen |
| ⌘-Shift-0 | Ejects the disk from the third drive, if any |

Additional Fkey utilities (and software to manage them) are available through shareware and commercial sources.

**flame**   In electronic mail, to lose one's self-control and write a message that uses derogatory, obscene, or inappropriate language. (Slang term.)

**flatbed scanner**   An optical graphics digitizer that can transform a full-page (8 1/2-by-11-inch) graphic into a digitized file. See *digitize* and *scanner*.

**flat-file database management program**   A database management program that stores, organizes, and retrieves information from one file at a time. Such programs lack relational database management features. See *data integrity* and *relational database management*.

**flat-panel display**   A thin display screen used in notebook and laptop computers that uses one of several display technologies, such as electroluminescence, gas plasma displays, liquid crystal displays, or thin film transistors (TFT). A backlit display makes the display easier to read. See *laptop computer* and *notebook computer*.

**flicker**   A visible distortion that occurs when you scroll the screen of a video monitor that employs a low refresh rate—the rate at which the monitor refreshes the illumination of individual pixels on-screen.

**floating graphic**   A graph or picture that has not been fixed in an absolute position on the page, so that it moves up or down on the page as you delete or insert text above the graphic.

**floating-point calculation**   A method for storing and calculating numbers so that the location of the decimal is not fixed but floating (the decimal moves around as needed so that significant digits are taken into account in the calculation). Floating-point calculation can be implemented in numeric coprocessors or in software, improving the accuracy of computer calculations.

Floating-point notation helps computers perform calculations more accurately. But an inherent limitation to any computer's capability to deal with large and small numbers still exists. Some programs set aside more memory than others for number storage; any program has a range of numbers that it can handle accurately. One program can handle any number from $10^{-20}$ to $10^{20}$, but smaller or larger numbers produce erroneous results.

A good program states the range of acceptable numbers in the manual. Some programs do not inform you what the range is and enable you to enter truncated numbers without your knowledge. These programs can produce erroneous results when used for any calculation involving very large or small numbers. See *numeric coprocessor*.

**floppy disk**   A removable and widely used secondary storage medium that uses a magnetically sensitive flexible disk enclosed in a plastic envelope or case.

Software publishers provide their applications on floppy disks. At one time, they also were the only medium for secondary storage for personal computers, but the availability of inexpensive hard disks has relegated floppy disks to the sidelines.

Hard disks are preferred for many reasons: floppy disk drives are slower, and the disks are damaged more easily and offer less storage. However, floppy disks are essential for getting programs and data into your computer and for backup purposes.

A floppy disk is a magnetically coated, flexible disk of plastic. The disk rotates within a flexible or firm plastic envelope (see fig. F.1). The access hole (head slot) provides an opening so that the drive's read/write head can perform recording and playback operations on the disk's surface, within the magnetically-encoded tracks and sectors created when disks are formatted. You can use the write-protect notch to keep the drive from erasing the data on the disk; when the notch is covered, the drive cannot perform erase or write operations.

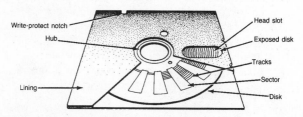

**Fig. F.1.** A floppy disk.

Most floppy disks used in personal computing come in two sizes: 5 1/4 and 3 1/2 inches. Floppy disks are available in single-sided or double-sided and standard double-density or high-density. Single-sided disks are rarely used, and high-density disks are becoming more popular than double-density disks. 5 1/4-inch disks, with flimsy sleeves and open access holes, are more susceptible to damage; 3 1/2-inch disks come in rigid plastic cases and have a sliding door that covers the access hole. (The drive opens the door after you insert the disk.)

5 1/4-inch and 3 1/2-inch disks are used in IBM PC–compatible computing. The single-sided disks used in the original IBM Personal Computer held only 160K; the drives introduced soon after accommodated 320K on a double-sided disk. In 1983, changes in the formatting procedure introduced with PC DOS Version 2.0 increased the figure to 360K for double-sided disks. With the IBM Personal Computer AT came MS-DOS 3.0 and the capability to store 1.2M on a high-density 5 1/4-inch disk. Later IBM PC–compatible computers came with 3 1/2-inch drives capable of storing 720K or 1.44M with high-density disks.

Macintoshes use 3 1/2-inch disks. The original Macintosh stored 400K on single-sided disks; this figure was doubled to 800K when double-sided disk drives were introduced. A floppy drive high density (FDHD) drive capable of storing 1.4M on high-density floppies was introduced in 1988; this technically sophisticated drive can read and write DOS disks, giving Mac users an easy way to exchange data with users of IBM PC–compatible computers.

 5 1/4-inch disks are more susceptible to damage than 3 1/2-inch disks; avoid pressing down hard with a ball-point pen as you label the disk, and be wary of fingerprints on the actual surface of the disk, which is easy to touch through the open access hole. Always keep 5 1/4-inch disks in protective envelopes when you are not using them, and do not leave the disk in the drive when the computer is turned off; the disk may accumulate dust. Although less susceptible than 5 1/4-inch disks, 3 1/2-inch disks can be damaged. Keep both types of disks away from moisture, dust, and strong magnetic fields. See *access hole*, *double density*, *hard disk*, *high density*, *read/write head*, *single-sided disk*, and *write-protect notch*.

**flow**   To import text into a specific text area on a page lay-out so that the text wraps around graphics and fills in specified columns. Page layout programs can import text in this way. See *page layout program*.

**flow chart**   A chart that contains symbols referring to computer operations, describing how the program performs.

**flush left**   In word processing, the alignment of text along the left margin, leaving a ragged right margin. Flush left alignment is easier to read than right-justified text.

**flush right**   In word processing, the alignment of text along the right margin, leaving a ragged left margin. Flush right alignment is seldom used except for decorative effects or epigrams.

**folder**   In the Macintosh Finder, an on-screen representa-tion of a file folder on the desktop and into which you can place files so that the display is not overly cluttered with files.

Folders are analogous to subdirectories in the DOS world, but with an unfortunate difference: with the exception of HyperCard, you cannot define default paths for the system to follow as it attempts to locate program and data files. A DOS user can set up a hard disk using PATH statements in the AUTOEXEC.BAT file, and if done correctly, you only rarely need to explore the disk manually in search of a file. Macintosh users, in contrast, must frequently open and scroll through folders in search of a file.

 If you're a Mac user, you can equip your system with an outstanding shareware pro-gram called Boomerang (Zeta Soft). The creation of H. Yamamoto, Boomerang is a CDEV program that automatically modifies the Open dialog box of all Mac applications. Boomerang automatically highlights the name of the file you last accessed. It also places within the Open dialog box a pull-down menu of the files and folders you have ac-cessed in recent operating sessions. See *control panel device (CDEV)*.

**font**   One complete collection of letters, punctuation marks, numbers, and special characters with a consistent and identifiable typeface, weight (Roman or bold), posture (upright or italic), and font size.

Technically, *font* still refers to one complete set of characters in a given typeface, weight, and size, such as Helvetica italic 12. But the term often is used to refer to typefaces or font families.

Two kinds of fonts exist: bit-mapped fonts and outline fonts. Each comes in two versions: screen fonts and printer fonts. See *bit-mapped font, font family, outline font, posture, printer font, screen font, typeface, type size,* and *weight.*

**font cartridge**   A plug-in ROM cartridge—designed to fit into a receptacle on a printer—that contains one or more fonts and expands the printer's font capabilities. See *cartridge font.*

**Font/DA Mover**   A utility program provided with Macintosh system software that adds fonts and desk accessories to the System file of the computer's startup disk. See *desk accessory (DA)* and *startup disk.*

**font downloader**   See *downloading utility.*

**font family**   A set of fonts in several sizes and weights that share the same typeface.

The following list illustrates a font family in the Helvetica typeface:

Helvetica Roman 10
**Helvetica bold 10**
*Helvetica italic 10*
Helvetica Roman 12
**Helvetica bold 12**
*Helvetica italic 12*
***Helvetica bold italic 12***

**font ID conflict**   In the Macintosh environment, a system error caused by conflicts between the identification numbers assigned to the screen fonts stored in the System Folder.

The Macintosh System and many Macintosh applications recognize and retrieve fonts by the identification number assigned to them, not by name. The original Macintosh operating system, however, enabled you to assign only 128 unique numbers to fonts, so that you inadvertently could assemble a repertoire of screen fonts with conflicting numbers, causing printing errors. Beginning with System 6, a New Font Numbering Table (NFNT) scheme was introduced that enables you to assign 16,000 unique numbers, reducing—but not ruling out—the potential for font ID conflicts.

**font metric**   The width and height information for each character in a font. The font metric is stored in a width table.

**Fontographer**   A computer typography program developed for Macintosh computers.

Using Fontographer, a graphics artist can create custom-designed screen fonts and printer fonts that use outline font technology and print at the maximum resolution possible. See *outline font*, *printer font*, and *screen font*.

**font smoothing**   In high-resolution laser printers, the reduction of aliasing and other distortions when text or graphics are printed. See *aliasing*.

**font substitution**   Substituting an outline font in place of a bit-mapped screen font for printing purposes.

In the Macintosh environment, the LaserWriter printer driver substitutes the outline fonts Helvetica, Times Roman, and Courier for the screen fonts Geneva, New York, and Monaco. However, spacing may be unsatisfactory. Better results are obtained by using the screen font equivalent to the printer font.

**footer**   In a word processing or page layout program, a short version of a document's title or other text positioned at the bottom of every page of the document. See *header*.

**footnote**   In a word processing or page layout program, a note positioned at the bottom of the page.

Most word processing programs with footnoting capabilities number the notes automatically and renumber them if you insert or delete a note. The best programs can float lengthy footnotes to the next page so that no more than half the page is taken up by footnotes.

 If you are writing business reports or scholarly work that requires excellent footnoting capabilities, make sure that you can format the footnotes properly. For example, many publishers require double-spacing of all text, even footnotes, but some word processors cannot perform this task. See *endnote*.

**footprint**   The space occupied by a computer's case on a desk.

**forced page break**   A page break inserted by the user; the page always breaks at this location.

**forecasting**   Using a spreadsheet program, a method of financial analysis that involves the projection of past trends into the future.

 Implementing a forecast with a spreadsheet program is easy, but beware that a forecast is only a model of reality: any model is only as good as the assumptions it is based on. Your forecast may project stable or slightly declining revenues into the next three months, but you may have failed to take into account a seasonal variable that could stimulate sales. Your forecast may lead you to underestimate the inventory you actually need.

**foreground task**   In a computer capable of multitasking, a job done in priority status before subordinate, or background, tasks are executed. The foreground task generally is the one you see executing.

**format**   Any method of arranging information for storage, printing, or displaying.

The format of floppy disks and hard disks is the magnetic pattern laid down by the formatting utility. Programs often use proprietary file formats for storing data on disk. Because of these special formats, some programs cannot read files saved by other programs. WordPerfect, for example, cannot read files prepared with Microsoft Word.

In a spreadsheet program, the format is the style and physical arrangement of labels, values, and constants in a cell. Numeric formats include the display of decimal places and currency symbols. Alignment formats for labels include flush left, centered, and flush right.

In a database management program, the format is the physical arrangement of field names and data fields in a data-entry form displayed on-screen. In a word processing program, document formats include the style and physical arrangement of all document elements, including characters (typeface, type size, weight, posture, and emphasis), lines and paragraphs (alignment and leading), and page design elements (folios, margins, headers, and footers).

In a graphics program, the format is the way in which text and numbers are displayed within charts and graphs and the way in which graphics are stored on disk. See *Browse mode*, *Edit mode*, and *graphics mode*.

**format file**   In dBASE, a file that stores the formats you have chosen for a custom data-entry form.

**formatting**   An operation that establishes a pattern for the display, storage, or printing of data.

In operating systems, an operation that prepares a floppy disk for use in a particular computer system by laying down a magnetic pattern. See *format*, *high-level format*, and *low-level format*.

**form feed**   A command that forces the printer to eject the current page and load a new page.

**formula**   In a spreadsheet program, a cell definition that defines the relationship between two or more values. In a database management program, an expression that instructs the program to perform calculations on numeric data contained in one or more data fields.

To enter values in a spreadsheet formula, you enter constants, cell references, or a combination. For example, +2+2 is a valid formula, as is +A2+A4 and +A4+38.9.

To express the formula in a way that most spreadsheets can recognize, you must convert the formula to spreadsheet notation. Spreadsheet notation differs from mathematical formulas. One key difference between the usual way you write formulas and spreadsheet notation lies in the operators, the symbols that indicate the arithmetic operation, such as addition, subtraction, multiplication, and division. The operators for addition and subtraction are the same: plus (+) and minus (–). However, you indicate multiplication by using an asterisk (*) and division by using a slash ( / ). You type a caret ( ^ ) before an exponent. See *calculated field*, *cell definition*, *precedence*, and *value*.

**formula bar**   In Microsoft Excel, the bar at the top of the screen where you enter or edit formulas.

**FOR/NEXT loop**   A loop control structure that carries out a procedure a specified number of times.

The following pseudocode example shows how you can use a page layout program's macro command language to locate and kern (adjust the spacing of) two troublesome letter pairs, *av* and *aw*. The letters in these pairs look awkward if not moved closer together.

```
FOR count = 1 to 10
   FIND av OR aw
   KERN selection
   NEXT count
END
```

Suppose that the two letter pairs occur 10 times in a document. In English, the macro reads, "Set the count to 1, and find *av* or *aw*. After a match has been found and the characters have been selected (highlighted in reverse video), kern the selection. Then set the count to the previous count plus 1. Keep doing this until the count is equal to 10." See *loop control structure*, *macro*, and *pseudocode*.

**FORTH** A high-level programming language that offers direct control over hardware devices.

Developed in 1970 by an astronomer named Charles Moore to help him control the equipment at the Kitt Peak National Radio Observatory, FORTH—short for FOuRTH-generation programming language—quickly spread to other observatories but has been slow to gain acceptance as a general-purpose programming language. The language is highly extensible: one FORTH programmer's code may be unintelligible to another FORTH programmer. FORTH sometimes is preferred for laboratory data acquisition, robotics, machine control, arcade games, automation, patient monitoring, and interfaces with musical devices. See *high-level programming language*.

**FORTRAN** A high-level programming language well suited to scientific, mathematical, and engineering applications.

Developed by IBM in the mid-1950s and released in 1957, FORTRAN—short for FORmula TRANslator—was the first compiled high-level programming language. The nature of FORTRAN shows the predominance of scientific applications in the early history of computing; the language enables you to describe and solve mathematical calculations. Still highly suited to such applications, FORTRAN is widely used in scientific, academic, and technical settings. For anyone familiar with BASIC, FORTRAN is immediately recognizable. Indeed, FORTRAN was BASIC's progenitor. FORTRAN shares BASIC's unfortunate limitations as a general-purpose programming language, such as the tendency to produce spaghetti code; however, recent versions of FORTRAN are more structured and have fewer limitations. See *BASIC*, *high-level programming language*, *modular programming*, *Pascal*, and *structured programming*.

**forward chaining**   In expert systems, an inference technique that requires the user to state all the relevant data before processing begins.

A forward chaining system starts with the data and works forward through its rules to determine whether additional data is required and how to draw the inference. See *backward chaining*, *expert system*, and *knowledge base*.

**FoxPro**   A dBASE-compatible database management system, offered by Microsoft Corporation, for Macintosh and IBM PC–compatible computers.

FoxPro improves on dBASE by offering a highly regarded compiler for the dBASE software command language. With this compiler, FoxPro users can create custom, stand-alone database applications. The Macintosh version of the program is compatible with dBASE files.

**fragmentation**   See *file fragmentation*.

**frame**   In desktop publishing and word processing, a rectangular area absolutely positioned on the page. The frame can contain text, graphics, or both.

**free-form text chart**   In presentation graphics, a text chart used to handle information difficult to express in lists, such as lengthy explanations, directions, invitations, and certificates (see fig. F.2). See *text chart*.

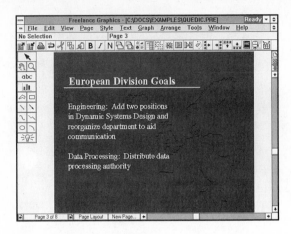

**Fig. F.2.** A free-form text chart.

**Freehand**   A professional illustration program for Macintosh computers that produces object-oriented images.

Freehand shares many of Adobe Illustrator's features, such as Bézier curves, an autotrace tool, precision coding for color printing, and many other features for professional illustration. Freehand does not require a PostScript printer. See *Adobe Illustrator*, *autotrace*, *Bézier curve*, *object-oriented graphic*, and *PostScript*.

**freeware**   Copyrighted programs that have been made available without charge for public use. The programs may not be resold for profit. See *public domain software* and *shareware*.

**frequency division multiplexing**   In local area networks, a technique for transmitting two or more signals over one cable by assigning each to its own frequency. This technique is used in broadband (analog) networks. See *broadband*, *local area network (LAN)*, and *multiplexing*.

**frequency modulation (FM) recording**   An early, low-density method of recording digital signals on computer media such as tape and disks. Synonymous with *single-density recording*. See *Modified Frequency Modulation (MFM)* and *single density*.

**friction feed**   A printer paper-feed mechanism that draws individual sheets of paper through the printer by using pressure exerted on the paper by the platen.

Friction-feed mechanisms usually require you to position the paper manually. For a document of more than one or two pages in length, however, manual feeding can be tedious. See *cut-sheet feeder* and *tractor feed*.

**front end**   The portion of a program that interacts directly with the user. In a local area network, this portion of the program may be distributed to each workstation so that the user can interact with the back end application on the file server. See *back end* and *client/server architecture*.

**full backup**   A hard disk backup that backs up every file on the entire hard disk. The procedure is extremely tedious if you're backing up to floppy disks, but it's necessary for secure computing; if it takes too long, consider adding a tape drive to your system. See *backup procedure*, *differential backup*, and *incremental backup*.

**full duplex**   An asynchronous communications protocol in which the communications channel can send and receive signals at the same time. See *asynchronous communication*, *communications protocol*, *echoplex*, and *half duplex*.

**full justification**   The alignment of multiple lines of text along the left and the right margins.

 Word processing programs justify both margins by placing extra spaces between words. Because such spacing irregularities destroy the color of a block of text, full justification is rarely advisable. Also, research has shown that text formatted with a ragged right margin is more readable than fully justified text. See *color* and *justification*.

**full-motion video adapter**   A video adapter capable of displaying moving TV images, both prerecorded and live, in a window that appears on the computer's screen.

To display TV images, the adapter is connected to
a videocassette recorder, laser disk player, or a
camcorder (for live images). Most full-motion video
adapters come with software that enables the development of a multimedia presentation, complete with
wipes, washes, fades, animation, and sound. Full-
motion video applications are expected to play a growing role in corporate and professional presentations
and training applications.

**full-page display**   A computer video monitor that is capable
of displaying a full page of text at a time.

Some computer users believe that a full-page display
should be considered a minimal system configuration.
With a full-page display, you can view and edit an entire
page of text, figures, or graphics at a time. For this
reason, you can get a better grasp of the overall structure and organization of your document.

If you're thinking about equipping your
DOS system with a full-page display, be
aware that not all the programs you're using
can take advantage of it. Check your programs' documentation.

If you're still planning your system and you
want to use a full-page display, consider a
Macintosh or Windows system. The Mac's
Finder supports a full-page display for most
Macintosh applications; Windows supports a full-page
display for most Windows applications.

**full-screen application**   In Microsoft Windows, a non-
Windows application that takes up the entire screen
after you launch it from Windows.

With Windows' 386 Enhanced mode, you
can run a DOS application in a window—
and when you do, you can switch to other
applications without halting the DOS
application's execution. If you plan to initiate a lengthy
processing operation, such as compressing or printing

several files, open the DOS application in a window
instead of running it as a full-screen application. You
can then perform work with other applications while
the DOS program runs in the background.

**full-screen editor**   A word processing utility designed for
application program development, which is often included in programming environments and application
development systems.

The term *full screen* refers to the utility's ability to
enable cursor movement and editing within text that
has already been created. Unlike a word processing
program, which is designed for creating and printing
documents such as letters and reports, a typical full-
screen editor lacks most of the formatting and printing
capabilities of word processing software. A full-screen
editor is designed specifically for creating and editing
computer programs. It therefore includes special features for indenting lines of program code, searching for
nonstandard characters, and interfacing with program
interpreters or compilers.

Full-screen editing is no big deal to any user of a word
processing program, but it's a major improvement over
the line editors (such as the notorious EDLIN of MS-
DOS) that usually are provided as part of an operating
system's programming environment. With Version 5.0
of MS-DOS, a good full-screen editor (MS-DOS Editor)
has finally become part of the operating system's standard equipment. See *application development system,
line editor,* and *programming environment.*

**function**   In programming languages and electronic spreadsheet programs, a named and stored procedure that
returns a value. Typically, a spreadsheet program includes hundreds of functions, in categories such as
finance date and time, mathematics and trigonometry,
statistics, lookup and reference, database manipulation,
text processing, logical comparison, and engineering.
In Microsoft Excel, for example, the NPV function returns the net present value of an investment, after you
supply the data about periodic cash flow and the discount rate. Synonymous with *built-in function.*

**function key** A programmable key—conventionally numbered F1, F2, and so on—that provides special functions, depending on the software you are using.
See *Fkey*.

**G**   Abbreviation for *gigabyte*.

**gamut**   In computer graphics, the range of colors that can be displayed on a color monitor.

**gas plasma display**   See *plasma display*.

**gateway**   In distributed computing, a device that connects two dissimilar local area networks or that connects a local area network to a wide-area network, a minicomputer, or a mainframe. A gateway has its own processor and memory and may perform protocol conversion and bandwidth conversion.

Gateways typically are found in large organizations in which more than one local area network protocol is installed. For example, a gateway called FastPath (Kinetics) provides a link between AppleTalk and EtherNet networks. See *bridge* and *local area network (LAN)*.

**general format**   In most spreadsheet programs, the default numeric format in which values are displayed with all significant (nonzero) decimal places, but without commas or currency signs.

**General MIDI (GM)**   In multimedia, a standard controlled by the MIDI Manufacturers' Association (MMA) that defines a set of 96 standard voices corresponding to traditional musical instruments, and an additional set of voices corresponding to non-melodic percussion instruments. When you use the standard code numbers from these sets to create a MIDI file, any GM-compatible synthesizer will reproduce the sounds in the file the way you intended them. See *Musical Instrument Digital Interface (MIDI)*.

**general-purpose computer**   A computer that contains a sufficiently simple and general instruction set so that a wide variety of algorithms can be devised for the computer.

**GEnie**   Developed by General Electric, an on-line information service that, like CompuServe, offers many of the attractions of a bulletin board system (BBS) and up-to-date stock quotes, home shopping services, and news updates. See *on-line information service*.

**GIF**   A bit-mapped color graphics file format for IBM and IBM-compatible computers. GIF is commonly used to exchange graphics on bulletin board systems because it employs an efficient compression technique for high-resolution graphics, such as scanned pictures.

**giga-**   A prefix indicating one billion ($10^9$).

**gigabyte**   A unit of memory measurement approximately equal to one billion bytes (1,073,741,824). One gigabyte equals 1,000 megabytes.

**global backup**   A hard disk backup procedure. Everything on the hard disk, including all program files, is backed up onto a medium such as floppy disks. See *incremental backup*.

**global format**   In a spreadsheet program, a numeric format or label alignment choice that applies to all cells in the worksheet. With most programs, you can override the global format by defining a range format for certain cells.

 If you are working on a financial spreadsheet, the values in your worksheet may require dollar signs and two decimal places. You should choose this global format, therefore, when you begin the worksheet. You can override the global format in sections of the worksheet in which dollar signs are not required by creating a range format. See *label alignment*, *numeric format*, and *range format*.

**glossary**   In a word processing program, a storage utility that stores frequently used phrases and boilerplate text and inserts them into the document when needed. See *boilerplate*.

**GM**   See *General MIDI*.

**grabber hand**   In graphics programs and HyperCard, an on-screen image of a hand that you can position with the mouse to move selected units of text or graphics from place to place on-screen.

**Grammatik**   A style and grammar checker for IBM and Macintosh computers (Reference Software International).

Grammatik employs a user-modifiable database to flag common errors of usage and style, such as archaic expressions, clichés, jargon, legalese, sexist phrases, and deadwood phrases. The program also checks for common punctuation errors, as well as spelling errors that spelling checkers cannot identify.

**graphical user interface (GUI)**   A design for the part of the program that interacts with the user and takes full advantage of the bit-mapped graphics displays of personal computers. Like the industry-standard interface increasingly common in DOS applications, a GUI employs pull-down menus and dialog boxes. But on-screen graphics are required to display a GUI's icons (pictorial representations of computer resources and functions) as well as a variety of visually attractive on-screen typefaces.

The graphical user interface (GUI) has its origins in ground-breaking research at Xerox Corporation's Palo Alto Research Center (PARC) in the early 1970s. At PARC, a team of some of the brightest researchers in computer science devoted themselves to the task of making computers easier to use. Having found that people recognize graphic representations faster than they read words or phrases, the PARC team designed a user interface that represents computer processes and entities as on-screen graphic images called *icons*. An icon is a picture that closely resembles or reminds the viewer of the concept it represents. Examples of icons are a picture of a disk to represent a floppy disk inserted in a drive, a trash can or a black hole to represent the place to discard unwanted files, or a file folder to represent a subdirectory.

The use of a graphical user interface requires a computer with sufficient speed, power, and memory to display a high-resolution, bit-mapped display. In the 1970s, before very large scale integration (VLSI) and microprocessors were in common use, such machines were by necessity quite expensive. Xerox Corporation estimated that a GUI could not be implemented on a machine costing less than $15,000. For this reason, Xerox's management refused to market the PARC team's prototype computer, called the Alto, and in consequence many PARC researchers left Xerox to found a variety of start-up firms. In 1979, Steve Jobs of Apple Computer visited PARC and instantly perceived the significance of the GUI interface; he lured some top PARC researchers to Apple, where they assisted in the development of the Lisa computer. A market failure, the Lisa was nevertheless an important commercial implementation of GUI technology and served to link Apple, not Xerox, with this important technological innovation. With the Macintosh, Apple succeeded in bringing to market a significant portion of the Lisa's functionality at a reasonable cost.

The ideas that came out of PARC have traveled many roads, and lawsuits have followed. Xerox Corporation sued Apple Computer in 1989, alleging that Apple had unlawfully infringed on the "look and feel" of copyrighted Xerox software, but the case was thrown out of court because the suit was brought too late. For its part, Apple Computer sued Microsoft Corporation, charging that Microsoft Windows illegally infringes on the GUI technology that Apple developed.

A graphical user interface is usually associated with additional PARC innovations, such as the use of a mousable interface with pull-down menus, dialog boxes, check boxes, radio buttons, and the like. However, these features can be implemented quite easily on a character-based display, and many DOS programs that run PCs in the character mode (as opposed to the graphics mode) employ these features. Strictly speaking, a GUI requires a bit-mapped graphics display and portrays computer operations and entities as on-screen icons. See *check box, dialog box, drop-down list box, Macintosh, Microsoft Windows, mousable interface, pull-down menu, radio button,* and *scroll bar/scroll box.*

**graphics**   In personal computing, the creation, modification, and printing of computer-generated graphic images.

The two basic types of computer-produced graphics are object-oriented graphics, also called *vector graphics*, and bit-mapped graphics, often called *raster graphics*.

Object-oriented graphics programs, often called *draw programs*, store graphic images in the form of mathematical representations that can be sized and scaled without distortion. Object-oriented graphics programs are well suited for architecture, computer-aided design, interior design, and other applications in which precision and scaling capability are more important than artistic effects.

Bit-mapped graphics programs, often called *paint programs*, store graphic images in the form of patterns of screen pixels. Unlike draw programs, paint programs can create delicate patterns of shading that convey an artistic touch, but any attempt to resize or scale the graphic may result in unacceptable distortion. See *bit-mapped graphic, draw program, object-oriented graphic,* and *paint program.*

**graphics accelerator board**   An expansion board that includes a graphics coprocessor and all the other circuitry normally found on a video adapter. By taking graphics processing tasks away from the central processing unit (CPU) and placing them in the hands of the coprocessor, which is specially designed for fast graphics processing, a graphics accelerator board can dramatically improve your system's capability to display Windows and Windows applications. See *central processing unit (CPU), graphics coprocessor, Microsoft Windows,* and *video adapter.*

**graphics character**   In a computer's built-in character set, a character composed of lines, rectangles, or other shapes. Graphics characters can be combined to form block graphics: simple images, illustrations, and borders. See *block graphics* and *character-based program*.

**graphics coprocessor**   A microprocessor specially designed to speed the processing and display of high-resolution video images. A graphics accelerator board that includes a graphics coprocessor can speed the display of graphical user interfaces such as Windows. Popular graphics coprocessors include the Weitek W5086 and W5186, as well as S3 Inc.'s 86C911. See *graphics accelerator board*.

**graphics file format**   In a graphics program, the way in which the information needed to display a graphic is arranged and stored on disk.

Little standardization exists for graphics file formats. Your graphics program may be unable to read the files created by another graphics program. The situation is in many ways similar to the profusion of file formats among word processing programs. Many popular programs such as AutoCAD, GEM Draw, Lotus 1-2-3, Windows Paint, and PC Paintbrush generate files in proprietary file formats that other programs can read only if they have been specially equipped to do so.

The Macintosh environment has a standard file format called *PICT* that uses routines drawn from the Mac's QuickDraw toolbox, a set of image-producing programs stored in the Mac's read-only memory (ROM). This format, however, is not satisfactory for many applications. Additional formats include the MacPaint file format for 72-dpi bit-mapped graphics, tagged image file format (TIFF) files for scanned images stored at up to 300 dpi, and Encapsulated PostScript (EPS) graphics that produce high-resolution graphics on PostScript laser printers.

In the IBM PC environment, many programs can recognize TIFF and EPS files. The graphics file format of Lotus 1-2-3 charts and graphs, stored in files with the extension PIC, is widely recognized by presentation graphics packages; many of these programs are designed to read and enhance charts created with Lotus 1-2-3.

Also widely recognized is the Hewlett-Packard Graphics Language (HPGL), a graphics format created for HP plotters, and some programs recognize the Computer Graphics Metafile (CGM) format. Microsoft Windows, unlike DOS, establishes graphics file format conventions, and programs designed to run under Windows must adhere to this format. See *Encapsulated PostScript (EPS) file*, *file format*, *QuickDraw*, and *Tagged Image File Format (TIFF)*.

**graphics mode**    In video adapters, a display mode in which everything displayed on-screen—including both text and graphics—is created by the adapter's selectively illuminating, tiny, on-screen dots, called *pixels*. Many adapters also offer a character mode, which runs more quickly because it draws on the computer's built-in, ready-made characters instead of composing them individually.

 Windows users who frequently run graphics-intensive applications, such as desktop publishing programs, should consider purchasing a video adapter that includes a graphics accelerator. If Windows runs sluggishly, chances are that the processing bottleneck lies in the video circuitry. Adding a graphics accelerator board will result in impressive performance gains. See *character mode* and *graphics view*.

**graphics primitive**    In an object-oriented (vector) graphics program, the most basic unit of graphic expression, such as a line, arc, circle, rectangle, or oval.

**graphics scanner**    A graphics input device that transforms a picture into an image displayed on-screen.

**graphics spreadsheet**    A spreadsheet program that displays the worksheet on-screen by using bit-mapped graphics instead of relying on the computer's built-in character set.

Graphics spreadsheets such as Lotus 1-2-3 for Windows and Microsoft Excel for Windows make available desktop publishing tools such as multiple typefaces, type sizes, rules, and screens (grayed areas). Also, printouts can combine spreadsheets and business graphs on one page. See *Lotus 1-2-3* and *Microsoft Excel*.

**graphics tablet**   A graphics input device that enables you to draw with an electronic pen on an electronically sensitive table. The pen's movements are relayed to the screen.

**graphics view**   In some non-Windows DOS applications, a mode in which the program switches the display circuitry to its graphics mode. In graphics mode, the computer is capable of displaying bit-mapped graphics.

 On all except the fastest computers, graphics mode is significantly slower than character mode. See *character view*.

**gray scale**   In computer graphics, a series of shades from white to black.

**gray-scale monitor**   A monitor (and compatible display adapter) capable of displaying a full range of shades from white to black on-screen.

 True gray-scale monitors are expensive and, in comparison to color monitors, offer few benefits to most users. They're essential, however, for a few applications, such as photographic image processing and retouching. A VGA monitor may suffice; it can display a minimum of 64 gray-scale levels.

**greeking**   Displaying a simulated version of a page on-screen, showing lines or bars instead of text so that the overall page layout design is apparent.

**Greek text**   A block of simulated text or lines used to represent the positioning and point size of text in a designer's composition of a page.

Greek text is used to simulate the appearance of the
document so that the aesthetics of the page design can
be assessed. Standard Greek text used by typesetters
actually looks more like Latin:

*Lorem ipsum dolor sit amet . . .*

Some word processing and page layout programs use a
print preview feature analogous to greeking.

**group**   In Microsoft Windows, a collection of program item
icons that are stored together under a group icon.
When you open the group icon, you see a window
showing the program item icons in the group. Examples of groups include the Accessories, Main, and
Games groups.

**group icon**   In Microsoft Windows, an icon that represents
a group—a collection of program item icons. When you
open the group icon, you see a group window, which
contains the program item icons (see fig. G.1).

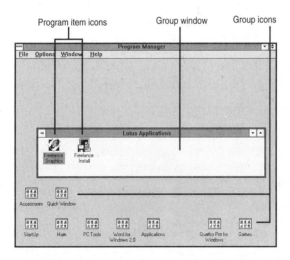

**Fig. G.1.** Group icons in the Program Manager (Microsoft
Windows).

**groupware**   Application programs that increase the coop-
eration and joint productivity of small groups of coworkers.

An example of groupware is ForComment (Broderbund Software), designed to make collaborative writing easier. The program enables each member of the group to insert comments and make changes to the text, subject to the other members' approval.

Is groupware just a marketing gimmick? Some industry observers thought so after it was reported that Broderbund did not employ its own product, ForComment, for internal collaborative writing. The success of Lotus Notes, a groupware program designed for minicomputer and mainframe computer systems, suggests otherwise. Notes provides tools for creating a database of shared documents, document retrieval using sophisticated filtering techniques, and multi-media electronic mail.

**guest**   In a local area network, an access privilege that allows you to access another computer on the network without having to provide a password. See *local area network (LAN)*.

**GUI**   Acronym for graphical user interface, and pronounced—yes, you guessed it—"gooey." See *graphical user interface (GUI)*.

**guide**   In a page layout program, a nonprinting line that appears as a dotted line on-screen, showing the current location of margins, gutters, and other page layout design elements.

**gutter**   In word processing and desktop publishing, an additional margin added to allow room for the binding in duplex printing. An extra margin is added to the left side of odd-numbered (recto) pages and to the right side of even-numbered (verso) pages. See *duplex printing*.

**GW-BASIC**   A version of the BASIC programming language often licensed to PC-compatible computers.

GW-BASIC is nearly identical to the BASIC interpreter distributed with IBM PCs, but each manufacturer is free to customize the language.

**hacker** A technically sophisticated computer enthusiast who enjoys making modifications to programs or computer systems and breaking a system's security simply for the challenge of doing so.

Hackers can be seen at virtually any college or university computer lab, where they spend inordinate amounts of time trying to master a computer system. Often described as "addicted to computers," hackers nevertheless learn skills that prove valuable to organizations.

**half duplex** An asynchronous communications protocol in which the communications channel can handle only one signal at a time. The two stations alternate their transmissions. Synonymous with *local echo*. See *asynchronous communication*, *communications protocol*, *echoplex*, and *full duplex*.

**half-height drive** A drive bay half the size of the 3-inch-high drive bays in the original IBM Personal Computer. Half-height drive bays and drives are standard in today's PCs.

If you're shopping for a computer, make sure that it has plenty of drive bays. You may want to add an extra floppy disk drive or a second hard disk drive.

**halftone** A copy of a photograph prepared for printing by breaking down the continuous gradations of tones into a series of discontinuous dots. Dark shades are produced by dense patterns of thick dots, and lighter shades are produced by less dense patterns of smaller dots.

A black-and-white photograph is a continuous-tone image of varying shades of gray. Photographs do not photocopy well; the fine gradations of gray tones are lost. To print a photograph in a newspaper or magazine, the photograph is copied using a halftone screen in front of the film. The screen breaks up the image into patterns of dots of varying size, depending on the intensity of the light coming from the photograph.

Halftones are usually superior to digitized photographs for professional-quality reproduction. Even professionals who use the latest desktop publishing technology may prefer to leave space for halftones and paste them in after printing the document. See *scanner* and *Tagged Image File Format (TIFF)*.

**handle** In an object-oriented graphics program, the small black squares that surround a selected object, enabling you to drag, size, or scale the object. See *draw program* and *object-oriented graphic*.

**handler** In object-oriented programming, the program instructions (called a *script*) embedded within an object. The instructions are designed to trap messages that begin within the object.

In HyperTalk, for example, one such object is a button you place on a card in a HyperCard stack. Within the button is a set of programming instructions (the script) designed to intercept certain user-initiated actions, such as the click of a mouse. After a click is trapped, the code carries out a procedure, such as displaying another card. See *event-driven program* and *object-oriented programming language*.

**handshaking** A method for controlling the flow of serial communication between two devices, so that one device transmits only when the other device is ready.

In hardware handshaking, a control wire is used as a signal line to indicate when the receiving device is ready to receive a transmission; software handshaking uses a special control code.

Hardware handshaking is used for devices such as serial printers, because the device is nearby and a special cable can be used. For long-distance serial communication, software handshaking must be used when the telephone system is involved. (Because the telephone system uses only two wires, hardware handshaking is impossible.) The two software handshaking techniques are ETX/ACK, which uses the ASCII character Ctrl-C to pause in data transmission, and XON/XOFF, which uses Ctrl-S to pause and Ctrl-Q to resume transmission.

**hanging indent**   A paragraph indentation in which the first line is flush with the left margin, but subsequent lines (called *turnover lines*) are indented. The entries in this book use hanging indents.

**hard**   Permanent, physically defined, permanently wired, or fixed, as opposed to soft (changeable or subject to redefinition). For example, the printed version of a document is hard, because changing the printed document is difficult. A document still in the computer's memory, in contrast, is soft, because you can still make changes to it. See *hard copy, hard hyphen, hard return, hard space*, and *hard wired*.

**hard card**   A hard disk and disk drive controller that are contained on a single plug-in adapter.

You easily can add a hard disk to a system using a hard card: you just press the adapter into the expansion slot, as you would any other adapter.

**hard copy**   Printed output, distinguished from data stored on disk or in memory.

**hard disk**   A secondary storage medium that uses several nonflexible disks coated with a magnetically sensitive material and housed, together with the recording heads, in a hermetically sealed mechanism. Typical storage capacities range from 10M to 140M.

Developed by IBM in 1973, the hard disk often is called a *Winchester disk* after the code name assigned to the development project. Early hard disks were extremely expensive. With the rise of a mass personal computer aftermarket in the early 1980s, however, hard disks have been manufactured in huge quantities and now are available for as little as $200. Because hard drives are almost a necessity for efficient use of personal computers today, they have become a standard element in computer systems.

A hard disk is a complex storage subsystem that includes the disks, the read/write head assembly, and the electronic interface that governs the connection between the drive and the computer (see fig. H.1).

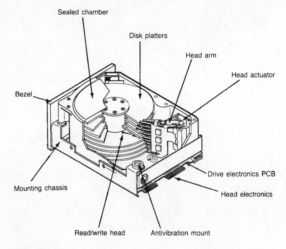

**Fig. H.1.** The components of a hard disk drive.

The disks, numbering from three to five, revolve 60 times per second (3,600 rpm); the read/write head floats on a thin pocket of air just above the magnetically encoded surface of the disk, so that no wear occurs on the disk itself. Less expensive hard drives use 5 1/4-inch disks, but the trend is toward 3 1/2-inch disks, because the read/write heads have shorter distances to move. The technology used to position the read/write heads in the least expensive hard disks uses stepper motors that move the heads one step at a time over the disk. However, stepper motors gradually lose their alignment, necessitating an annual reformatting procedure to make sure that the disk remains aligned with the read/write heads. More expensive drives use voice coil motors that are more reliable and less likely to go out of alignment.

Hard drive interface standards include ST506, IDE, ESDI, and SCSI. With typical storage spaces of 20M to 40M, hard disks have ample room for storing several major application programs, system software, and data files. Because most hard disks are not removable, however, you should develop a regular backup procedure. Hard disks occasionally fail, and they may take the data with them.

Some hard drives use removable cartridges, a significant advantage over normal hard drives. See *access time*, *backup*, *backup utility*, *Bernoulli box*, *Enhanced System Device Interface (ESDI)*, *Intelligent Drive Electronics (IDE)*, *Run-Length Limited (RLL)*, *secondary storage*, and *Small Computer System Interface (SCSI)*.

**hard disk backup program**   A utility program that backs up hard disk data and programs onto floppy disks.

 The best backup programs are capable of performing incremental backups, in which the program backs up only those files that have changed since the last backup procedure. See *backup utility* and *utility program*.

**hard disk interface**   An electronic standard for the connection of a hard disk to the computer. See *Enhanced System Device Interface (ESDI)*, *hard disk*, *Intelligent Drive Electronics (IDE)*, and *Small Computer System Interface (SCSI)*.

**hard drive**   See *hard disk*.

**hard hyphen**   In word processing programs, a hyphen specially formatted so that a program does not introduce a line break between the hyphenated words.

Hyphenated proper nouns, such as Radcliffe-Brown and Evans-Pritchard, should not be interrupted with line breaks. A hard hyphen prevents the insertion of a line break between the two hyphenated words. Synonymous with *nonbreaking hyphen*. See *soft hyphen*.

Use a hard hyphen for hyphenated names, even if the names are not positioned near the end of a line. Remember, you may add or delete text in the paragraph later, and these changes are likely to push the name to the end of a line.

**hard return** A manually inserted page break that remains in effect even after you later add or delete text above the break. In contrast, a soft return, which the program automatically inserts, may move after you change the text. Synonymous with *forced page break*.

**hard space** In word processing programs, a space specially formatted so that the program does not introduce a line break at the space's location. Hard spaces often are used to keep two-word proper nouns together, such as Key Biscayne or West Point.

**hardware** The electronic components, boards, peripherals, and equipment that make up your computer system—distinguished from the programs (software) that tell these components what to do.

**hardware platform** A computer hardware standard, such as IBM PC–compatible or Macintosh personal computers. Devices or programs created for one platform will not run on others. See *device independence* and *platform independence*.

**hardware reset** A system restart you perform by pushing the computer's reset button. A hardware reset may be necessary after a system crash so severe that you cannot use the keyboard restart command (in DOS, Ctrl-Alt-Del) to restart the computer. See *programmer's switch* and *warm boot*.

**hard wired** A processing function built into the computer's electronic circuits rather than facilitated by program instructions.

Computer science theorists regard the ideal computer as one containing only general-purpose logic circuits that can perform no specific task without program instructions. To improve computer performance, computer designers depart from this philosophy and include circuits designed to perform specific functions, such as multiplication or division, at higher speeds. These functions are hard wired.

The term *hard wired* also refers to the program instructions contained in the computer's read-only memory (ROM) or firmware. See *read-only memory (ROM)*.

**Harvard Graphics**   A full-featured presentation graphics program (Software Publishing Corp.) for IBM PC–compatible computers.

With the capability to produce a wide variety of text charts (including organization charts), column charts, bar graphs, line graphs, area graphs, pie graphs, and combination charts, Harvard Graphics is an exceptionally versatile and easy-to-use program.

You can type data into the program or import data from a Lotus 1-2-3 spreadsheet. After a chart or graph is created, it can be enhanced with the program's built-in clip art or vector graphics drawing program. You can produce output in the form of on-screen slide shows or route the output to a film recorder or printer.

The program requires little knowledge of graphics presentation principles because it guides the user through each step of the process and produces output that meets high standards of aesthetics and professional graphics.

**Hayes command set**   A standardized set of instructions used to control modems.

Common Hayes commands include the following:

| | |
|---|---|
| AT | Attention (used to start all commands) |
| ATDT 322-1234 | Dial the number with touch tones |
| +++ | Enter command mode during communication session |
| ATH | Hang up |

See *modem*.

**Hayes-compatible modem**   A modem that recognizes the Hayes command set. See *Hayes command set* and *modem*.

**head**   See *read/write head*.

**head crash**   The collision of a hard disk drive's read/write head with the surface of the disk, resulting in damage to the disk surface and possibly to the head.

 Most disk drives can withstand some jostling, but you should avoid moving your computer or bumping its case while the drive is running.

**header**   Repeated text, such as a page number and a short version of a document's title, that appears at the top of each page in a document.

Some programs include odd headers and even headers, enabling you to define mirror image headers for documents printed with duplex printing (both sides of the page). For example, you may want to place the page number on the outside corner of facing pages.

Word processing programs vary significantly in the flexibility of header commands. The best programs, such as WordPerfect and Microsoft Word, enable you to suppress the printing of a header on the first page of a document or a section of a document and to change headers within the document. Synonymous with *running head*. See *footer*.

**head seek time**   See *access time*.

**Helvetica**   A sans serif typeface frequently used for display type applications and occasionally for body type. The following example shows Helvetica type:

ABCDEFGHIJKLMNOPQRSTUVWXYZ
abcdefghijklmnopqrstuvwxyz 1234567890

One of the most widely used fonts in the world, Helvetica is included as a built-in font with many laser printers.

**Hercules Graphics Adapter**   A single-color display adapter
for IBM PC–compatible computers. The Hercules
Graphics Adapter displays text and graphics on an IBM
monochrome monitor with a resolution of 720 pixels
horizontally and 320 lines vertically.

The Hercules (and Hercules-compatible)
display adapter works only with graphics
software that includes drivers for its non-
IBM display format. Software designed to
work with the Color Graphics Adapter (CGA), for example, does not display graphics on systems equipped
with Hercules cards unless the software specifically
includes a Hercules driver. Many shareware, public
domain, and low-priced graphics programs do not
include the necessary driver and do not work with
Hercules-equipped systems; however, Hercules display
adapters work with all programs that display monochrome text. See *monochrome display adapter (MDA)*.

**hertz (Hz)**   A unit of measurement of electrical vibrations;
one Hz is equal to one cycle per second. See *megahertz
(MHz)*.

**heterogeneous network**   A local area network that includes
computers and devices from several manufacturers.
Many firms create heterogeneous networks that successfully link Macintosh and Windows systems. See
*local area network (LAN)*.

**heuristic**   A method of solving a problem by using rules of
thumb acquired from experience. Heuristics rarely are
stated formally in textbooks, but they are part of the
knowledge that human experts use in problem solving.
See *expert system* and *knowledge base*.

**Hewlett-Packard Co. (HP)**   A major manufacturer of minicomputers, personal computers, plotters, laser printers, and scientific and technical instruments.

The company's headquarters are located in Palo Alto,
California. See *LaserJet* and *Vectra*.

**Hewlett-Packard Graphics Language** A page description
language (PDL) and file format for graphics printing
with the HP LaserJet line of printers, and now widely
emulated by HP-compatible laser printers. See *Hewlett-
Packard Printer Control Language (HPPCL)*.

**Hewlett-Packard Printer Control Language (HPPCL)** The
proprietary printer control language introduced by
Hewlett-Packard in 1984 with the company's first
LaserJet printer. Like the Hayes command set in the
modem world, HPPCL has become a standard. See
*LaserJet* and *printer control language*.

**hexadecimal** A numbering system that uses a base (radix)
of 16.

Unlike decimal numbers (base 10), hexadecimal numbers require 16 digits: 0, 1, 2, 3, 4, 5, 6, 7, 8, 9, A, B, C,
D, E, and F. When counting in hexadecimal, you don't
carry over to the next place until you reach the first
number past F (in decimal, you carry over when you
reach the number past 9).

Programmers use hexadecimal numbers as a convenient way of representing binary numbers. Using binary
numbers is inconvenient because they use a base or
radix of 2, and you must carry over to the next place
when you reach the first number past one. Binary numbers, therefore, grow in length quickly. In binary, for
example, the decimal number 16 requires four places
(1111).

Binary numbers are ideally suited to the devices used
in computers, but these numbers are hard to read.

For any four-digit set of binary numbers, you have 16
possible combinations of 1s and 0s. Hexadecimal numbers, therefore, provide a convenient way for programmers to represent four-digit clumps of binary numbers,
as shown in the following table.

| Binary | Hex | | Binary | Hex |
|--------|-----|--|--------|-----|
| 0000 | 0 | | 1000 | 8 |
| 0001 | 1 | | 1001 | 9 |
| 0010 | 2 | | 1010 | A |
| 0011 | 3 | | 1011 | B |
| 0100 | 4 | | 1100 | C |
| 0101 | 5 | | 1101 | D |
| 0110 | 6 | | 1110 | E |
| 0111 | 7 | | 1111 | F |

**hidden codes**   The hidden text formatting codes embedded in a document by an on-screen formatting program.

Even a what-you-see-is-what-you-get (WYSIWYG) word processing program, in which formatting commands directly affect the appearance of the text on-screen, generates and embeds codes in your text as a result of formatting commands. The codes are necessary because the screen imaging technique may have no connection to the technique used to generate output to the printer. Most word processing programs hide these codes, making formatting operations completely transparent to the user. In WordPerfect, however, you can view and edit the codes.

**hidden file**   A file with file attributes set so that the file name does not appear on the disk directory. You cannot display, erase, or copy hidden files.

**Hierarchical File System (HFS)**   A Macintosh disk storage system, designed for use with hard disks, that enables you to store files within folders so that only a short list of files appears in the dialog boxes.

The previous Macintosh Filing System (MFS) enabled you to organize files into folders in the Finder. In Open and Save dialog boxes, the names of all the files on the disk appeared without any hierarchical organization.

HFS is analogous to the directory/subdirectory organization of DOS disks but with one important exception: with DOS, you can define default paths that applications follow to locate data files and program files. In HFS, no such path definition facilities exist, with the exception of the System Folder consulted when an application searches for a data or program file. Mac users, therefore, must guide applications manually through the structure of nested folders when a program cannot find a file.

 Macintosh users, who often have to assist an application manually as it tries to find a program or data file, should avoid the temptation of nesting too many levels of folders. Using two or three nested levels reduces the amount of pointing or clicking when searching for a file; using five or six, however, increases the tedium. To automate the process, consider purchasing a file-location utility such as Findswell (Working Software) or Boomerang (ZetaSoft).

**high density**   A storage technique for secondary storage media such as floppy disks. This technique requires the use of extremely fine-grained magnetic particles. High-density disks are more expensive to manufacture than double-density disks. High-density disks, however, can store one megabyte or more of information on one 5 1/4- or 3 1/2-inch disk. Synonymous with *quad density*.

**high-density disk**   See *floppy disk*.

**high end**   An expensive product at the top of a firm's offerings; includes features or capabilities likely to be needed only by the most discriminating users or professionals. See *low end*.

**high-level format**   A formatting operation that creates housekeeping sections on a disk. These sections, including the boot record and file allocation table, track free and in-use areas of the disk.

When you use the DOS FORMAT command to format a
floppy disk, the computer performs a low-level format
in addition to the high-level format. When you use a
hard disk, however, DOS performs just the high-level
format.

If a low-level format has not been performed at the
factory, you must run a program (probably provided on
a floppy disk that comes with the hard disk) that performs the absolute format. See *boot record*, *file allocation table (FAT)*, and *low-level format*.

**high-level programming language**   A programming language such as BASIC or Pascal that crudely resembles
human language. A high-level language enables the
programmer to concentrate on the problem that the
program is designed to solve, instead of concentrating
on how the computer will carry out the program.

Each statement in a high-level language corresponds to
several machine language instructions. Therefore, a
programmer can write programs more quickly in a
high-level language than in a low-level language. However, programs written in a high-level language run
slower. See *assembly language*, *low-level programming language*, and *machine language*.

**highlight**   A character, word, text block, or command displayed in reverse video on-screen. This term sometimes
is used synonymously with *cursor*.

**highlighting**   The process of marking characters or command names in reverse video on-screen.

**high/low/close/open graph**   In presentation graphics, a line
graph in which a stock's high value, low value, closing
price, and average value are displayed (see fig. H.2).
The x-axis (categories axis) is aligned horizontally, and
the y-axis (values axis) is aligned vertically.

Another application for a high/low/open/close graph
is a record of daily minimum, maximum, and average
temperatures. Synonymous with *HLCO chart*. See
*column graph* and *line graph*.

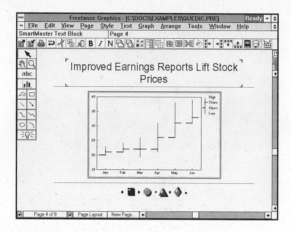

**Fig. H.2.** A high/low/close/open graph.

**high memory**   See *upper memory area.*

**high memory area (HMA)**   In a DOS computer, the first 64 kilobytes of extended memory above 1 megabyte. Programs that conform to the eXtended Memory Specification (XMS) can use HMA as a direct extension of conventional memory. See *conventional memory, extended memory,* and *eXtended Memory Specification (XMS).*

**high resolution**   In computer monitors and printers, a visual definition that is sufficient to produce well-defined characters, even at large type sizes, as well as smoothly defined curves in graphic images. A high-resolution video adapter and monitor can display 1,024 pixels horizontally by 768 lines vertically; a high-resolution printer can print at least 300 dots per inch (dpi). See *low resolution.*

**HIMEM.SYS**   A DOS device driver, supplied with Microsoft Windows and DOS, that configures the upper memory area, extended memory, and the high memory area so that properly written programs can access it. The programs must conform to the eXtended Memory Standard (XMS). See *CONFIG.SYS, device driver, eXtended Memory Standard (XMS), high memory area (HMA),* and *upper memory area.*

If you use Microsoft Windows, the Windows Setup program automatically installed HIMEM.SYS in the CONFIG.SYS file of your computer's hard disk.

**hinting**   In digital typography, the reduction of the weight of a typeface so that small-sized fonts print without blurring or losing detail on 300-dpi printers.

**histogram**   A stacked column graph in which the columns are brought together to emphasize variations in the distribution of data items within each stack (see fig. H.3).

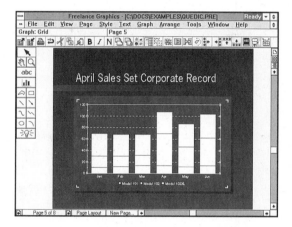

**Fig. H.3.** A histogram.

By stacking the data items in a column, you emphasize the contribution each data item makes to the whole (as in a pie graph). By placing the columns adjacent to one another, the eye is led to compare the relative proportions of one data item as the item varies from column to column.

**home computer**   A personal computer specifically designed and marketed for home applications, such as educating children, playing games, balancing a checkbook, paying bills, and controlling lights or appliances.

A home computer usually has less memory, less secondary storage, and a slower microprocessor than a business computer.

In the late 1970s, people predicted that home computers would improve the quality of family life by providing convenient and sophisticated tools for education, finance management, and other household chores, but the low-powered machines marketed for such purposes typically lacked the software and memory required to carry out tasks effectively.

In 1978, a *Wall Street Journal* reporter was given a home computer for six months and assigned to use the machine for recipes, taxes, education, and so on. He concluded that the machine was most adept at gathering dust in the closet.

Millions of home computers, however, were sold—including the Commodore 64, an 8-bit home computer based on the same MOS Technology 6502 chip used in the Apple II. (The Commodore 64, however, does not run Apple II programs.) Most of these computers were used infrequently, and did not materially alter the patterns of American family life.

By 1984, the market for home computers had collapsed, and most of the personal computers that found their way into homes were more powerful business computers, such as the IBM Personal Computer. Most of these machines were used as a means of extending the workday by enabling users to accomplish tasks such as word processing and financial analysis at home.

Home computing applications today actually require as much processing power and memory as business applications do—and perhaps more. Easy-to-use home computing applications are best implemented with a graphical user interface that requires a powerful microprocessor and as much as one or more megabytes of internal memory.

Now that such machines are in homes, home computing applications may become a reality. For example, the idea that people would balance their checkbooks by using their computer remained something of a joke until Intuit Software successfully marketed a best-selling checkbook-management program called Quicken. Compared to early home computing programs, Quicken is in a different league in every possible sense: programming sophistication, the quality of the user interface, the capacity for virtually unlimited numbers of transactions, the features you actually need in order to carry out home financial tasks, speed, and ease of use. Quicken requires a business computer such as an IBM PC–compatible or Macintosh computer.

American companies may have failed to place useful home computers in every American home, but a Japanese firm may have succeeded at precisely this task. Unknown to most video-game addicts, the Nintendo game system is based on a general-purpose, 8-bit computer specifically designed to serve as the platform for other computer applications besides playing video games. Among the possible applications are home education, telecommunications, and home financial management. Whether the firm can market such applications, however, remains to be seen.

**Home key**    A key on IBM PC–compatible keyboards that has varying functions from program to program.

Frequently, the Home key is used to move the cursor to the beginning of the line or the top of the screen, but the assignment of this key is up to the programmer.

**hook**    In programming, a feature of an operating system or application programming interface (API) that allows programmers to access operating system features quickly and easily. For example, Microsoft Windows provides over 500 functions that programmers can access directly to perform tasks such as opening and closing windows, reading keyboard input, and interpreting mouse activity.

**horizontal scroll bar**   See *scroll bar/scroll box.*

**host**   In a computer network, the computer that performs centralized functions such as making program or data files available to workstations in the network.

**hot key**   A keyboard shortcut that accesses a menu command.

In Microsoft Windows, you can use keyboard shortcuts for many menu commands. If you see an underlined character in a command or option name, you can access that command or option by holding down the Alt key and pressing that letter.

**hot link**   A method of copying information from one document (the source document) to another (the target document) so that the link remains active; if you change the information in the source document, the change is automatically reflected in the target document.

In Microsoft Windows, you can create a hot link between an Excel source document and a Word target document by using the Paste/Link command. After the hot link has been established, Windows will automatically update the Word document if you make a change in the Excel spreadsheet.

In Macintosh System 7, the metaphor used to describe hot links is drawn from publishing rather than editing: you select the data you want to copy and then choose Publish from the Edit menu. In a second application, you choose Subscribe to establish the hot link. See *dynamic data exchange (DDE)* and *object linking and embedding (OLE).*

**HP-compatible printer**   A printer that responds to the Hewlett-Packard printer control language (PCL), which has become a de facto standard for laser printing in the IBM and IBM-compatible computing world.

**HPGL**   See *Hewlett-Packard Graphics Language.*

**HP LaserJet**   See *LaserJet*.

**hung system**   A computer that has experienced a system
failure sufficiently grave to prevent further processing,
even though the cursor may still be blinking on-screen;
the only option in most cases is to restart the system,
which entails loss of any unsaved work.

 If you are experiencing computer crashes
frequently, eliminate any terminate-and-stay-
resident (TSR) programs you're using. These
programs, called *INITs* in the Mac world,
sometimes conflict with one another or with application programs, producing hung systems. Add the programs again, one by one, to determine which one of
them (if any) is causing the problem. In addition, check
the documentation provided with TSRs or INITs to
determine whether a given program must be loaded
last. Some TSRs and INITs operate in an unstable fashion unless they are the last program to be loaded at the
time of system startup. See *INIT* and *terminate-and-
stay resident (TSR) program*.

**HyperCard**   An authoring language bundled with the
Macintosh that facilitates storing and interactively retrieving on-screen cards containing text, bit-mapped
graphics, sound, and animation. HyperCard was developed in 1984 by Bill Atkinson at Apple Computer.

In HyperCard, a stack is a collection of one to several
thousand cards. On each card, you find a background
layer—consisting of buttons, graphics, and fields that
several or all cards in the stack share—and the card
layer, which contains the buttons, graphics, and fields
unique to the card.

You interact with the stack by clicking the buttons.
Each button has an associated script, written in
HyperTalk, that specifies the procedure to follow
when a button is clicked. Clicking a button may display
another card in the stack or initiate an animation
sequence that may include sound.

HyperCard comes with several prewritten stacks, but the program's significance is that it provides you with a way to create your own HyperCard applications.

The Macintosh is a formidable machine even for accomplished programmers, and the Mac received a great deal of criticism from hobbyists and users who wanted to develop their own applications without spending inordinate amounts of time. HyperCard answers these criticisms by providing a complete application development environment for nonprogrammers.

The range of applications is limited to those that can be displayed as HyperCard stacks. However, what many people would like to do with computers is related to the storage and retrieval of textual and graphic information, and HyperCard provides excellent tools for such applications.

The result is not a database management system in the traditional sense, but what Apple calls *hypermedia*, a way of displaying information by embedding links within the system and giving people the tools to explore these links interactively.

Because HyperCard is so well suited to the creation of instructional software, one could call HyperCard an authoring language. A major area of application development lies in the use of HyperCard as a front end for huge external information resources encoded on CD-ROM and interactive laser disks.

HyperCard also is serving as the platform for the development of multimedia applications, many with an educational emphasis. However, HyperCard can be used to create stand-alone applications. Commercial applications include a musical composition program, an appointment/calendar system, an employee payroll and check-writing program, and a game that enables you to explore a huge labyrinth of interconnected rooms. See *authoring language*, *front end*, *hypermedia*, *HyperTalk*, *script*, and *stack*.

**hypermedia**   A computer-assisted instructional application such as HyperCard that is capable of adding graphics, sound, video, and synthesized voice to the capabilities of a hypertext system.

In a hypertext system, you select a word or phrase and give a command to see related text. In a hypermedia system, such a command reveals related graphic images, sounds, and even snippets of animation or video. See *hypertext*.

**HyperScript**   The software command language provided with Wingz, an innovative Macintosh spreadsheet program developed by Informix, Inc. Using HyperScript, even a novice programmer can develop spreadsheets by using on-screen buttons containing scripts for specific, customized spreadsheet functions. These scripts are the equivalent of macros in programs such as Lotus 1-2-3, but they are much easier to develop and use.

HyperScript resembles HyperTalk, the object-oriented programming language supplied with HyperCard. See *HyperCard*, *HyperTalk*, and *object-oriented programming language*.

**HyperTalk**   The scripting language provided with HyperCard, an accessory program shipped with every Macintosh. HyperTalk is an event-oriented language. To create a HyperTalk program, you begin by using HyperCard to create screen objects (cards with text fields, buttons, and other features), and then you write short, English-like programs, called *scripts*, that tell HyperCard what to do when one of these objects is manipulated. HyperScript programming is fun and introduces a programming novice to the fundamental principles of object-oriented programming. The language is too slow, however, for professional program development, for which it was never intended. See *object-oriented programming language* and *SmallTalk*.

**hypertext**   The nonsequential retrieval of a document's text. The reader is free to pursue associative trails through the document by means of predefined or user-created links.

A hypertext application seeks to break away from a sequentially oriented text presentation of information and to provide the reader with tools to construct his own connections among the component texts of the document. A hypertext application is a form of nonsequential writing.

In a true hypertext application, you can highlight virtually any word in a document and immediately jump to other documents containing related text. Commands also are available that enable you to create your own associative trails through the document.

Computer technology helps when constructing a hypertext application. If this book were presented in hypertext format, for example, you could click your mouse on one of the cross-references, and a window would pop up displaying the cross-referenced entries.

**hyphenation**   In word processing and page layout programs, an automatic operation that hyphenates words on certain lines to improve word spacing.

When used with caution and manual confirmation of each inserted hyphen, a hyphenation utility can improve the appearance of a printed work by improving the line spacing. Automatic hyphenation is especially helpful with newspaper columns or narrow margins. An unhyphenated, lengthy word such as *collectivization* can introduce ugly word-spacing irregularities into your document.

Do not count on automatic hyphenation utilities to do the job perfectly; you should confirm each hyphen. Some programs break fundamental hyphenation rules, such as leaving fewer than two characters on one side of the hyphen or hyphenating a one-syllable word. No automatic hyphenation utility can cope effectively with homographs, two words spelled the same but that have different meanings and pronunciations, as in the following examples:

| in-val-id | in-va-lid |
|-----------|-----------|
| min-ute   | mi-nute   |
| put-ting  | putt-ing  |

Watch out for hyphen ladders, an unsightly formatting error that occurs when three or more sentences in a row are hyphenated. You may need to use additional, manual hyphenation to finish the job. The automatic hyphenation utility consults an on-disk hyphenation database, but this file probably contains only a fraction of the words in your manuscript. See *hard hyphen*, *hyphen ladder*, and *soft hyphen*.

**hyphen ladder**    A formatting flaw caused by the repetition of hyphens at the end of two or more lines in a row.

Hyphen ladders attract the eye and disrupt the text's readability.

 If you insert hyphens throughout a document, proofread the results carefully. Hyphenation utilities cannot prevent hyphen ladders. If hyphen ladders occur, adjust word spacing and hyphenation manually.

**Hz**    See *hertz (Hz)*.

**IAC** See *inter-application communication.*

**I-beam pointer** In Macintosh and Windows applications, a mouse pointer that appears when you're editing text.

In Macintosh and Windows applications, the cursor does not appear *on* a character, as it does in DOS applications; it appears *between* characters at all times. The I-beam pointer is thin enough to enable you to position the pointer between characters with precision.

**IBM 8514/A display adapter** A video adapter for IBM Personal System/2 computers that, with the on-board video graphics array (VGA) circuitry, produces a resolution of 1,024 pixels horizontally and 768 lines vertically. The adapter also contains its own processing circuitry that reduces demand on the computer's central processing unit (CPU).

For IBM PC–compatibles using the 16-bit AT bus rather than IBM's proprietary Micro Channel Bus, VGA adapters are available with the 1,024 by 768 high-resolution mode. See *Super VGA* and *video adapter.*

**IBM PC–compatible computer** A personal computer— dubbed a clone by industry analysts—that runs all or almost all of the software developed for the IBM Personal Computer (whether in PC, XT, or AT form) and accepts the IBM computer's cards, adapters, and peripheral devices. See *clone.*

**IBM Personal Computer** A personal computer based on the Intel 8088 microprocessor.

Personal computers existed before the IBM Personal Computer, but the release of the IBM PC in 1981 legitimized the fledgling personal computer industry and ensured the technology's acceptance in the business community. No longer a plaything for hobbyists, the personal computer became a serious business tool—or so many people concluded because those magic three letters, *IBM*, appeared on the nameplate.

The story of the PC's development is an interesting chapter in technological innovation. IBM had been burned in the past by failing to recognize the market potential of small computers. The company thought that no market existed for minicomputers, leaving the market open for start-up firms such as Digital Equipment Corporation (DEC) and Hewlett-Packard (HP). Both companies cashed in under the umbrella created by IBM's disinterest in small-scale computer technologies.

IBM was not about to permit this setback to occur again and made an early decision to move into the personal computer market (then dominated by Apple Computer, Radio Shack, and 8-bit CP/M computers). Recognizing that a bureaucracy can frustrate an innovation effort, the team assigned to develop the PC was given substantial autonomy. Looking at the success of the Apple II, the team decided to emulate Apple's example by creating an open bus, open architecture system that would attract droves of third-party suppliers.

The computer developed by this team (at the Entry Level Systems Division in Boca Raton, Florida) was by no means a state-of-the-art device. The machine used the Intel 8088 microprocessor instead of the faster Intel 8086, largely because the 8088 can take advantage of the numerous and inexpensive 8-bit peripherals and microprocessor support chips that worked with the 8088 (but not with the 8086).

IBM also did not attempt to develop an operating system for the new computer. Instead, the firm hired Microsoft Corporation to develop an operating system that would enable CP/M programs to be quickly and easily modified to run on the new PC, because hundreds of business programs were available for CP/M computers. Microsoft bought an operating system under development by a small Seattle firm and dubbed the system *MS-DOS* (Microsoft Disk Operating System). Few people realized that MS-DOS is little more than a clone of CP/M. Therefore, the IBM PC fairly may be said to represent the technology of the late 1970s, not the early 1980s.

The 1981 machine is almost laughable by today's standards. It was released with a total of 16K of random-access memory (RAM), expandable to 64K on the motherboard. The monochrome display adapter (MDA) and monochrome monitor are incapable of displaying bit-mapped graphics—only the 254 characters (including block graphics characters) in the extended character set can be displayed. The disk drive held 160K of data—much more than the 50K to 90K drives in widespread use at the time.

Recognizing the limitations of the original IBM PC, the company introduced the PC-2 in 1983. This model came with 64K of RAM expandable to 256K on the motherboard without additional memory cards. Its disk drives used both sides of disks (they stored 320K). Also introduced was the Color Graphics Adapter (CGA) and an RGB color monitor.

IBM's choice of an open architecture and open bus for the PC quickly engendered a huge support industry as third-party vendors created memory cards, video adapters, and other accessories for the system. A major step forward was the Hercules Graphics Adapter that displayed bit-mapped graphics on the monochrome monitor.

By 1984, clones (non-IBM computers that claimed compatibility with the IBM PC) had appeared on the market and, because of their lower price, quickly gained market share. IBM countered with enhanced versions of the PC—the IBM Personal Computer XT in 1983 and the IBM Personal Computer AT in 1984.

These models were not successful in stemming the tide of clones, however. In 1987, IBM introduced the IBM PS/2 line, partly abandoning the open bus architecture of the PC in favor of the proprietary Micro Channel Bus.

Because few clone manufacturers have decided to obtain the necessary license to create Micro Channel machines, the world of IBM PC–compatible computing has split into two camps: on one side is IBM, with its proprietary technology, and on the other is a consortium of clone manufacturers (led by Compaq Corp.) that continues to advocate the open architecture and open bus principles of the original IBM PC. This consortium has developed its own high-speed bus standard: Extended Industry Standard Architecture (EISA). Facing increasing competition in the early 1990s from mail-order firms selling high-quality clones, IBM itself began directly marketing its PCs through mail-order channels. See *Apple II, clone, CP/M, Extended Industry Standard Architecture (EISA), Micro Channel Bus, open architecture,* and *open bus*.

**IBM Personal Computer AT**   A personal computer, based on the Intel 80286 microprocessor, that was introduced in 1984.

The AT (short for *Advanced Technology*) significantly improved on the performance of PCs and XTs. Using the 80286 microprocessor and a 16-bit data bus, the computer's throughput was approximately 50 to 75 percent better than the fastest XTs.

Widely emulated by clones, the AT standard lives on in the form of AT compatibles, now available at bargain prices. See *Intel 80286*.

**IBM Personal Computer XT**   A personal computer, based on the Intel 8088 microprocessor and including a hard disk, that was introduced in 1983.

In addition to its hard disk, the XT (short for *eXtended Technology*) added a heftier power supply, additional expansion slots, and room for up to 640K of random-access memory (RAM) on the motherboard.

The XT standard lives on in 8088-based compatible machines, called *Turbo XTs,* because they offer a clock speed of approximately 10 MHz, twice that of the original XT. See *Intel 8088*.

**IBM Personal System/2**   A series of personal computers
introduced in 1987 and based on the Intel 8086,
80286, and 80386 microprocessors. Most PS/2s contain
a proprietary expansion bus format, called the *Micro
Channel Bus*. In 1992, IBM began shipping high-end
PS/2s with OS/2 2.0, which can run and multitask
MS-DOS, Windows, and OS/2 applications. See *Micro
Channel Bus* and *Operating System/2 (OS/2)*.

**icon**   In a graphical user interface, an on-screen symbol that
represents a program file, data file, or some other computer entity or function (see fig. I.1).

**Fig. I.1.** On-screen icons representing program and data
files.

**IDE**   See *Intelligent Drive Electronics (IDE)*.

**IDE drive**   A hard disk for 80286, 80386, and 80486 computers, that contains most of the controller circuitry
within the drive itself. Designed to connect to computers containing an IDE interface on their motherboards,
IDE drives combine the speed of ESDI drives with the
intelligence of the SCSI hard drive interface. This performance is offered at a price lower than most ESDI
and SCSI drives. Moreover, IDE drives present themselves to the computer electronically as if they were
standard ST506 drives, for which the 80286 and 80386
were originally designed.

If you are shopping for an 80286 or 80386
computer and value is uppermost in your
mind, look for a machine that includes an
IDE interface and IDE drive. You need an
ESDI or SCSI drive only if you run applications that

demand the highest possible performance from your computer. See *Intelligent Drive Electronics (IDE)*.

**identifier**   In database management, an identifier is used to specify the uniqueness of the information contained in the data record.

For example, the descriptor *Norway* appears in the data record of the only travel film that depicts scenery from that country.

**IF/THEN/ELSE**   A branch control structure that tests a variable or data to see whether a condition is true. If the condition is true, the program branches to option A, but if the condition is false, the program branches to option B.

The following example tests to see whether a file exists. If the file exists, the program instructs the computer to open the file. If the file does not exist, the program instructs the computer to create a file.

```
IF file_exists = true
        THEN open_file
        ELSE create_new_file
ENDIF
```

**illegal character**   A character that cannot be used according to the syntax rules of command-driven programs and programming languages. Such characters usually are reserved for a specific program function.

For example, with DOS, you cannot assign a file name to a file if the name includes an asterisk (*). The asterisk is reserved for use as a wild-card symbol. Commas also are illegal characters for file names. DOS uses commas as an argument separator in commands requiring two or more arguments.

**image compression**   The use of a compression technique to reduce the size of a graphics file, which consumes inordinate amounts of disk space.

A single gray-scale TIFF file, for instance, can consume more than 100K of disk space, but the file can be reduced by as much as 96 percent for storage or telecommunications purposes. Some graphics programs compress images automatically. File compression programs such as PKZIP (PKWARE, Inc.) also can do the job.

**image processing**  In computer graphics, the use of a computer to enhance, embellish, or refine a graphic image. Typical processing operations include enhancing or reducing contrast, outlining shapes, altering colors so that the image is more easily analyzed, correcting underexposure or overexposure, and outlining objects so that they can be identified.

**imagesetter**  A professional typesetting machine that generates very high-resolution output on photographic paper or film.

Popular imagesetters include the Agfa Compugraphic, Linotronic, and Varityper models that recognize PostScript commands. All are capable of resolutions of 1,200 or more dots per inch (dpi), unlike the 300-dpi resolution of laser printers. They also are quite expensive, selling for $30,000 and up.

If you have a PostScript-compatible word processor or page layout program, you can take a disk to a service bureau that owns one of these machines to obtain high-resolution output. See *PostScript* and *service bureau*.

**imaging model**  The method of representing output on-screen.

In character-based programs, a connection may not exist between the screen and printer fonts. The screen font appears to be a monospaced typewriter font, but the printer font may be a proportionally spaced font with a different typeface.

In a graphical user interface, the goal is to use a unified imaging model, so that the text displayed on-screen closely resembles the text printed. See *graphical user interface (GUI)* and *screen font*.

**impact printer**  A printer that forms an image by pressing a physical representation of a character against an inked ribbon, forming an impression on the page.

Impact printers are noisy, but they can produce
multiple copies of business forms using carbons.
See *dot-matrix printer*, *letter-quality printer*, and
*nonimpact printer*.

**import**    To load a file created by one program into a different program. Harvard Graphics, for example, can
import the PIC files created by Lotus 1-2-3.

**increment**    To increase a value. See *decrement*.

**incremental backup**    A backup procedure in which a hard
disk backup program backs up only the files changed
since the last backup procedure. See *archival backup*.

**incremental update**    See *maintenance release*.

**indentation**    The alignment of a paragraph to the right or
left of the margins set for the entire document.

Do not use the space bar or Tab key to
indent text. If a printer uses proportional
typefaces, the text will not align properly.
You also cannot change the indentation of
all the lines with just one command; you must change
each line individually.

Most word processing programs include commands
that indent text from the left, right, or both margins
(see fig. I.2). You also can create a hanging indent.

**index**    In database management programs, a compact file
containing information (called *pointers*) about the
physical location of records in a database file. When
searching or sorting the database, the program uses the
index rather than the full database. Such operations are
faster than sorts or searches performed on the actual
database.

In word processing programs, an index is an appendix
that lists important words, names, and concepts in
alphabetical order, with the page numbers where the
terms appear. With most word processing programs,
you must mark terms to be included in the index the
program constructs. See *active index*, *concordance
file*, *sort*, and *sort order*.

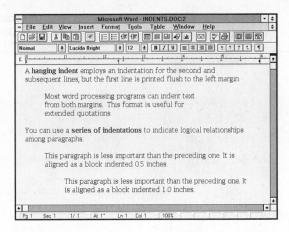

**Fig. I.2.** Text indented from the left margin and from both margins.

**index hole**   In a floppy disk, a hole that is electro-optically detected by the drive to locate the beginning of the first sector on the disk. See *floppy disk* and *sector*.

**industry-standard architecture (ISA)**   The bus design of IBM's AT (Advanced Technology) computer, which employs a 16-bit bus with some 9-bit slots for downward compatibility. See *bus, Extended Industry Standard Architecture (EISA),* and *Micro Channel Architecture (MCA).*

**industry-standard user interface**   An IBM standard for the organization of on-screen computer displays and part of the company's Systems Application Architecture (SAA). The standard, called *Common User Access* (CUA), calls for the use throughout a computing system of many of the user interface features found in graphical user interfaces: pull-down menus, dialog boxes with check boxes and option buttons, and highlighted accelerator keys for rapid keyboard selection of commands.

The CUA standard is now widely found in character-based MS-DOS applications, and it's bringing a new uniformity to the previously chaotic world of MS-DOS

user interfaces, typified by WordPerfect's idiosyncratic
function-key assignments and menus. Strictly speaking,
the CUA interface isn't a graphical user interface (GUI),
because it runs in the character mode and doesn't use
the on-screen pictorial representation of computer
resources in the form of icons. But the CUA interface
has just about every other GUI benefit, including a
refreshing commonality of key assignments and procedures across applications: F1 brings up Help, F3 cancels or exits, F10 displays the menu, and so on.

 To avoid the big investment necessary to run
Windows and Windows applications, you
can set up a very nice, near-GUI system by
choosing a library of CUA-compliant MS-DOS
applications and running a CUA-compliant MS-DOS
shell (such as the new MS-DOS shell provided with
MS-DOS 5.0). See *application program interface (API)*,
*graphical user interface (GUI)*, *Microsoft Windows*,
and *mousable interface*.

**infection**    The presence of a virus or Trojan Horse within a
computer system. The infection may not be obvious to
the user; many viruses, for example, remain in the
background until a specific time and date, when they
display prank messages or erase data. See *Trojan Horse*
and *virus*.

**information service**    See *bibliographic retrieval service*,
*bulletin board system (BBS)*, and *on-line information
service*.

**inheritance**    In object-oriented programming, the passing
of a message up through the levels of objects until an
object is reached that traps the message.

In HyperTalk, for example, the lowest-level object is a
button. If the user produces a message by clicking the
button, and the button contains no programming code
(called a *handler*) that traps this message, the message
is passed up to the next level of the hierarchy, the card.
If the card contains no handler, the message is passed

to the next level, the stack. If the stack contains no handler, the message is passed to the highest level, HyperCard. See *object-oriented programming language*.

**INIT** In the Macintosh environment, a utility program that executes during a system start or restart.

Examples of INITs are SuperClock, which displays the current system date and time in the menu bar, and Adobe Type Manager, which uses outline-font technology to display Adobe screen fonts.

 Like terminate-and-stay resident (TSR) programs in the IBM environment, INITs can conflict with each other and cause system crashes. If your system is behaving erratically, try removing INITs one at a time from the System Folder and restarting your system; you may be able to determine whether an INIT is the culprit.

**initial** In typography, an enlarged letter at the beginning of a chapter or paragraph.

Initials set down within the copy are drop caps, and initials raised above the top line of the text are stickup caps (see fig. I.3).

**Fig. I.3.** Examples of drop caps (*S* and *Y*) and stickup caps (*T* and *L*).

You can create initials with many word processing and page layout programs, but to avoid a common formatting error, make sure that the letter aligns precisely at the base of a line of text.

**initial base font**   The default printer font used by word processing programs to print all documents unless you instruct otherwise.

You can override the initial base font for a particular document by choosing a document base font, and you can override this choice by formatting individual characters or blocks of characters within the document. See *document base font*.

**initialization**   The process of formatting a disk so that it is ready for use. See *format*.

**initialize**   See *format*.

**inkjet printer**   A nonimpact printer that forms an image by spraying ink from a matrix of tiny jets.

Inkjet printers are quiet and can produce excellent results. Hewlett-Packard's DeskJet and DeskWriter printers can produce text and graphics at resolutions of 300 dpi, rivaling the output of laser printers to the untrained eye.

 The ink used by most inkjet printers is water-soluble and smears easily. See *nonimpact printer*.

**input**   The information entered into the computer for processing purposes.

**input device**   Any peripheral that assists you in getting data into the computer: a keyboard, mouse, trackball, voice recognition system, graphics tablet, or modem.

**input/output (I/O) redirection**   In DOS and UNIX, the routing of a program's output to a file or device, or the routing of a program's input from a file rather than the keyboard.

Most DOS commands (such as DIR) send output to the screen, but you can easily redirect a command's output by using the greater-than sign (>). For example, to redirect the output of DIR to the LPT1 (printer) port, you type *DIR > lpt1* and press Enter. To redirect the command's output to a file, you type *DIR > dir.txt* and press Enter.

In DOS, input redirection is frequently used with filters. See *filter, input/output redirection, MS-DOS,* and *UNIX.*

**input/output (I/O) system**   One of the chief components of a computer system's architecture, the channels and interfaces that make data and program instructions smoothly flow into and out of the central processing unit (CPU).

**insertion point**   In Macintosh and Windows applications, the vertical bar that shows the point at which text will appear when you start typing. The insertion point is analogous to the cursor in DOS applications. See *cursor.*

**Insert mode**   In word processing programs, a program mode (usually toggled with the Ins key) in which inserted text pushes existing text to the right and down. See *Overtype mode.*

**Ins key**   In IBM PC–compatible keyboards, a programmable key frequently (but not always) used to toggle between the Insert mode and Overtype mode in applications with text entry. See *Insert mode* and *Overtype mode.*

**installation program**   A utility program provided with an application program that assists you in installing the program on a hard disk and configuring the program so that you can use it.

In IBM PC–compatible computing, installation programs sometimes must change the CONFIG.SYS configuration file or the AUTOEXEC.BAT startup file on your hard disk. Some programs execute this procedure in a well-mannered way: they append instructions to the existing files. Other installation programs, however, are ill-mannered, and actually delete files without asking you and write new ones in their place. If an old program stops working just after you install a program, the newly installed program may be the offender. You may have to reinstall the old program.

**instruction**   In computer programming, a program statement interpreted or compiled into machine language that the computer can understand and execute.

**instruction cycle**   The time it takes a central processing unit (CPU) to carry out one instruction and move on to the next.

**instruction set**   A list of keywords describing all the actions or operations that a central processing unit (CPU) can perform. See *complex instruction set computer (CISC)* and *reduced instruction set computer (RISC)*.

**integer**   A whole number without any decimal places.

**integrated accounting package**   An accounting program that includes all the major accounting functions: general ledger, accounts payable, accounts receivable, payroll, and inventory.

Unlike modular accounting packages, integrated programs update the general ledger every time an accounts payable or accounts receivable transaction occurs. You do not need to periodically batch update the general ledger. One such integrated accounting program is Plains and Simple (Great Plains Software). This program is designed to emulate the way small-business users keep the books in their businesses, rather than forcing them to think like accountants.

**integrated circuit**   A semiconductor circuit that contains more than one transistor and other electronic components.

**integrated program**   A program that combines two or more software functions, such as word processing and database management.

When Symphony (Lotus Development Corp.) and Framework (Ashton-Tate) were released in 1984, many thought these programs had ushered in a new era in personal computing. Both programs contained a spreadsheet, a database management program, a word processing program, a telecommunications program, and an analytical graphics program.

Every program within each package had a consistent user interface, so that you could switch from one program to the next without having to learn a new set of commands and menus. These programs facilitated the movement of data from one program to another.

For most users, however, the gains achieved by the consistent user interface were not worth the sacrifice involved—neither package's set of programs measured up to the standards of the best stand-alone programs. Most users preferred to assemble their own repertoire of programs.

Apple Computer's Lisa and Macintosh computers introduced the idea of using an application programming interface (API) that any program can access, with built-in routines for generating screen menus, scroll bars, dialog boxes, alert boxes, and other user interface amenities. The use of an API creates an environment in which programs share a common core of identical commands and menus, departing from the core only to implement unique program functions.

Along with a copy-and-paste buffer called the *Clipboard*, the API approach offers the advantages of software integration plus an attractive addition: you can assemble precisely the repertoire of programs you want, and they all function together effectively and effortlessly.

With the introduction of a multiple-loading operating system called *MultiFinder* (for the Macintosh), Macintosh users achieved precisely the level of context-switching functionality that Symphony and Framework users possessed.

The Macintosh example shows that the goal of software integration is correct, but the way to implement software integration is at the level of the operating system. The success of Microsoft Windows confirms this point. IBM PC–compatible computing is moving in the same direction. See *application programming interface (API)*, *Clipboard*, *Macintosh*, and *Microsoft Windows*.

**Intel 8086**   A microprocessor introduced in 1978 with a full 16-bit data bus structure.

Although the 8086 communicates with the rest of the computer more quickly than the 8088, the 8086 was not chosen for the first IBM Personal Computer because of the high cost of 16-bit peripherals and microprocessor support chips.

By the time such peripherals became available at low prices, however, Intel had developed the Intel 80286 microprocessor, which addresses 16 megabytes of memory (in contrast to the 8086's one megabyte).

Few personal computers, therefore, have used the 8086 chip. One exception is the use of the 8086 for the unsuccessful lower-end models of the PS/2 line, such as the Model 25. See *IBM Personal System/2*, *Intel 8088*, and *Intel 80286*.

**Intel 8088**   A microprocessor introduced in 1978 with an 8-bit external data bus and an internal 16-bit data bus structure and used in the original IBM Personal Computer.

Although the Intel 8088 can process 16 bits at a time internally, the 8088 communicates with the rest of the computer 8 bits (1 byte) at a time. This design compromise was deliberate. Intel designers wanted to introduce 16-bit microprocessor technology and take advantage of the inexpensive 8-bit peripherals (such as disk drives) and 8-bit microprocessor support chips.

Capable of addressing up to 1 megabyte of random-access memory, the original 8088 operated at 4.77 MHz, a speed now considered too slow for business and professional applications. Later versions of the chip have pushed its clock speed to approximately 10 MHz; such chips power IBM PC–compatible computers known as Turbo XTs. See *Intel 8086*.

**Intel 80286**   A microprocessor introduced in 1984 with a 16-bit data bus structure and the capability to address up to 16 megabytes of random-access memory (RAM).

The Intel 80286 powered the high-performance IBM Personal Computer AT. The chip requires 16-bit peripherals that are more expensive than the 8-bit peripherals used in machines such as the original IBM PC, but by the time of the AT's introduction, such peripherals were available.

The 80286 has a split personality: in real mode, the chip runs DOS programs in an 8086 emulation mode and cannot use more than 1M (megabyte) of RAM (under DOS, the limit is 640K), but in protected mode, the 80286 can use up to 16M. However, DOS cannot take advantage of this mode without the assistance of a memory-management program.

 If you are planning to run OS/2 or Microsoft Windows, avoid the 80286 in favor of the 80386 or 80486 microprocessors, which have superior memory-management capabilities. The 80286 runs Microsoft Windows, but not as well as the newer microprocessors. If you are using an 80386-based system, Windows becomes capable of true multitasking, allowing you, for example, to print a document in the background while you continue to work with another application. See *Microsoft Windows*.

**Intel 80287/Intel 80387**   Numeric coprocessors designed to work (respectively) with the Intel 80286 and 80386. See *numeric coprocessor* and *Weitek coprocessor*.

**Intel 80386DX**   A microprocessor introduced in 1986 with a 32-bit data bus structure and the capability to address up to four gigabytes of main memory directly.

The Intel 80386 represented a revolutionary advance
over its predecessors. Not only did the chip introduce a
full 32-bit data bus structure to IBM PC–compatible
computing, the 80386 also brought technical advances
such as a much-improved memory architecture.

Because this full 32-bit chip requires 32-bit microprocessor support chips, computers using the 80386
are more expensive than their 16-bit predecessors.

The 80386 includes a mode that enables the operating
system to divide memory into separate blocks of 640K
so that DOS applications can run concurrently. You
can, for example, run Lotus 1-2-3 and WordPerfect
at the same time. To use this mode, however,
requires special software such as DESQview/386 or
Windows/386. See *Microsoft Windows*.

**Intel 80386SX**   A microprocessor introduced in 1988 with
all the electronic characteristics of the Intel 80386,
except that the chip has a 16-bit external data bus structure that enables it to use the inexpensive peripherals
developed for the Intel 80286.

The 80386SX is like the Intel 8088 because it processes
data internally twice as fast as it communicates with the
rest of the computer. However, this compromise enables the computer to use the significantly less expensive 16-bit peripherals and microprocessor support
chips.

 If you are thinking about purchasing an
80286 computer, consider an 80386SX
computer instead. The prices are comparable, and the 80386SX is equipped to
handle 80386 software.

**Intel 80486DX**   A microprocessor introduced in 1989 with
a full 32-bit data bus structure and the capability to
address 64 gigabytes of main memory directly.

Packing more than one million transistors into one tiny
silicon chip, the 80486 incorporates the formerly separate numeric coprocessor. The 80486 microprocessor

can execute some instructions in just one clock cycle.
For this reason, it is significantly faster than the 80386,
which requires two or more clock cycles to execute
instructions.

 The clock speeds of 80386 and 80486 microprocessors are not directly comparable.
Because the 80486 can execute the same
instructions in fewer clock cycles, an 80486
running at 20 MHz will outperform an 80386 running
at 25 MHz. See *clock speed*.

**Intel 80486SX**   A version of the 80486DX microprocessor,
introduced in 1990, that omits the numeric coprocessor circuitry.

The 80486SX retains the full 32-bit data bus structure
of the 80486DX; the only difference lies in the omis-
sion of the numeric coprocessor circuitry. For this
reason, the 80486SX is not comparable to the 80386SX,
which has a 16-bit external data bus structure—a significant design compromise. You should choose the
80486DX, however, if your work commonly involves
extensive spreadsheet recalculations or statistical
analysis.

**Intel 82385**   A cache controller chip that governs cache
memory in fast personal computers using the Intel
80386 and 80486 microprocessors. See *cache memory*.

**Intelligent Drive Electronics (IDE)**   A hard disk interface
standard for 80286, 80386, and 80486 computers that
offers high performance at low cost. The IDE standard
transfers most of the controller electronics to the hard
disk mechanism. For this reason, the IDE interface can
be contained on the computer's motherboard; no
controller card is necessary, and no expansion slot is
necessary. See *controller card, hard disk interface,* and
*IDE drive*

**interactive processing**   A method of using the computer in
which the computer's processing operations are moni-
tored directly on a video display so that the user can

catch and correct errors before the processing operation is completed.

Interactive processing is so characteristic of personal computing that it's easy to forget the old days, when batch processing was the only way you could use the computer. Certain features of today's programs, however, hearken back to the early days. Word processing programs, for example, sometimes require you to embed formatting commands into the text, rather than showing you their effects directly on-screen. See *batch processing*.

**interactive videodisk**   A computer-assisted instruction (CAI) technology that uses a computer to provide access to up to two hours of video information stored on a videodisk.

Like CD-ROM, videodisks are read-only optical storage media, but they are designed specifically for the storage and random-access retrieval of images, including stills and continuous video.

An interactive videodisk application includes a computer program that serves as a front end to the information stored on the videodisk, a cable that links the computer to the videodisk player, and a videodisk that contains the appropriate images.

Using the front end program, the user explores the contents of the videodisk. For example, with a videodisk of paintings in the National Gallery of Art, the user can demand, "Show me all the renaissance paintings that depict flowers or gardens." A well-designed front end program can lead the viewer through a series of vivid instructional experiences under the viewer's complete control.

With interactive videodisk technology, television viewing promises to become a less passive activity. See *computer-assisted instruction (CAI)* and *videodisk*.

**inter-application communication (IAC)**   In the Macintosh System 7, a specification for creating hot links and cold links between applications. See *cold link, hot link,* and *System 7*.

**interface**  An electronic circuit that governs the connection between two hardware devices and helps them exchange data reliably. Synonymous with *port*.

**interface standard**  In hard disk drives, a set of specifications for the connection between the drive controller and the drive electronics. Common interface standards in personal computing include ST506, ESDI, and SCSI. See *Enhanced Small Device Interface (ESDI)*, *Small Computer System Interface (SCSI)*, and *ST-506/ST-412*.

**interlacing**  A video monitor display technology that enables a display device to display higher resolution, but at the cost of increased screen flickering. In an interlaced monitor, the monitor's electron gun—the device that creates the image by shooting electrons at a phosphorescent screen—paints only half the screen with each pass; the other half is painted on the second pass. This technique provides higher resolution, but because screen images may not be immediately refreshed, rapidly moving images may appear to streak or flicker.

 When you buy a monitor, make sure that it's a non-interlaced monitor. See *non-interlaced monitor*.

**interleaved memory**  A method of speeding access to dynamic random-access memory (DRAM) chips by dividing RAM into two large banks or pages and storing bit pairs in alternate banks; the microprocessor accesses one bank while the other is being refreshed. See *random-access memory (RAM)*.

**interleave factor**  The ratio of physical disk sectors on a hard disk that are skipped for every sector actually used for write operations.

If the interleave factor is 6:1, the disk writes to a sector, skips six sectors, writes to a sector, skips six sectors, and so on. The interleave factor is set by the hard disk manufacturer, but the factor can be changed by system software capable of performing a low-level format.

An interleave factor greater than 1:1 slows down the transfer rate so that the computer can keep up with the disk drive. Synonymous with *sector interleave*.

 Do not attempt to change the interleave factor of your hard disk unless you know what you are doing. In almost all cases, the interleave factor set by the disk manufacturer is optimal for your disk drive and computer.

**internal command**   In DOS, a command such as DIR or COPY that remains in memory and is always available when the DOS prompt is visible on-screen. See *external command*.

**internal font**   See *printer font*.

**internal hard disk**   A hard disk designed to fit within a computer's case and use the computer's power supply.

 Because internal hard disks do not require their own power supply, case, or cables, they generally cost less than external hard disks of comparable quality.

**internal modem**   A modem designed to fit into the expansion bus of a personal computer. See *expansion bus, external modem,* and *modem.*

**interpreter**   A translator for a high-level programming language that does not create an executable version of a program; instead, an interpreter translates and runs the program at the same time.

Interpreters run a program more slowly than compilers, because a compiler does all the translating before the program is run.

However, interpreters are excellent for learning how to program, because if an error occurs, the interpreter shows you the likely place (and sometimes even the cause) of the error. You can correct the problem immediately and execute the program again. In this way, you learn interactively how to create a successful program.

If a compiler is available for the programming language you are using, you can compile the program to make it run faster. See *compiler*.

**interprocess communication (IPC)**   In a multitasking computing environment such as Microsoft Windows running in the 386 Enhanced mode, the communication of data or commands from one program to another while both are running.

Interprocess communication is possible in the Windows and Macintosh environments thanks to Microsoft's Dynamic Data Exchange (DDE) specifications, which are supported by some applications. In Microsoft Excel, for instance, you can write a DDE command that accesses dynamically changing data, such as stock prices, being received on-line in a communications program. See *dynamic data exchange (DDE)*.

**interrupt**   A microprocessor instruction that halts processing momentarily so that input/output or other operations can take place. When the operation is finished, processing resumes.

In a hardware interrupt, the instruction is generated within the computer as the control unit manages the flow of signals within the machine. In a software interrupt, a program generates an instruction that halts processing so that a specific operation can take place.

**interrupt request (IRQ) lines**   In DOS and Windows systems, the hardware lines over which peripherals (such as printers or modems) can get the attention of the microprocessor when the device is ready to send or receive data.

**invisible file**   See *hidden file*.

**I/O**   See *input/output (I/O) system*.

**italic**   A posture of a serif typeface that slants to the right and commonly is used for emphasis. See *oblique* and *Roman*.

**iteration**   The repetition of a command or program statement. See *loop control structure*.

**jaggies**  See *aliasing*.

**job**  A unit of work to be performed by the computer, especially one that does not require human intervention (such as printing a file or a group of files).

This term originates from the world of mainframe data processing, in which an end user does not directly use the computer but submits a request that the data processing staff will carry out, much as one requests a print job from the printing department.

The term *job*, however, is not unknown in personal computing. In WordPerfect, for example, you can define a print job in which one or more documents are printed in the background.

**job control language (JCL)**  In mainframe computing, a programming language that enables programmers to specify batch processing instructions, which the computer then carries out.

The abbeviation JCL refers to the job control language used in IBM mainframes. See *batch processing*.

**job queue**  Pronounced "cue." A series of tasks automatically executed, one after the other, by the computer.

In mainframe data processing during the 1950s and 1960s, the job queue was literally a queue, or waiting line. You brought your stack of keypunch cards to the computer room, where technicians told you how many jobs were ahead of yours and how long you had to wait. When you went back, you saw reams of spurious printout full of error messages, and you had to go through the queue all over again.

With the rise of interactive, multiuser computing and personal computing, you do not need to line up to get your work done. The term is still used, however, to describe the assignment of a specific order in which tasks are executed (usually in the background, while

you are performing other tasks). In WordPerfect, for
example, you can assign a job number to several files
you want to print, and the program prints the files in
the order you assign.

**join**   In a relational database management program, a data
retrieval operation in which a new data table is constructed from data in two or more existing data tables.

To illustrate how a join works (and why join operations
are desirable in database applications), consider a
database design that minimizes data redundancy. Suppose, for example, that for your video store, you create
a database table called RENTALS. The database table
lists the rented tapes with the phone number of the
person renting the tape and the due date:

```
TITLE            PHONE_NO       DUE_DATE
Alien Beings     499-1234       05/07/92
Almost Home      499-7890       05/08/92
```

You also create another database table, called
CUSTOMERS, in which you list the telephone number,
name, and credit card number of all your customers:

```
PHONE_NO    F_NAME     L_NAME    CARD_NO
499-1234    Terrence   Jones     1234-4321-098
499-1234    Jake       Smith     9876-1234-980
```

Suppose that you want to find out whether any of your
customers are more than two weeks late returning a
tape. You want to know the title and due date of the
movie and the phone number, name, and credit card
number of the customer. You need to join information
from the two databases.

The following Structured Query Language (SQL) command retrieves the information you need:

```
SELECT TITLE, DUE_DATE, PHONE_NO, L_NAME,
F_NAME, CARD_NO
FROM RENTALS, CUSTOMERS
WHERE DUE_DATE=<05/07/92
```

This command tells the program to display the information contained in the data fields called TITLE, DUE_DATE, PHONE_NO, L_NAME, F_NAME, and CARD_NO, but only for those records in which the data field DUE_DATE contains a date equal to or earlier than May 7, 1992. The result is the following display:

| TITLE        | DUE_DATE | PHONE_NO | L_NAME | F_NAME   | CARD_NO        |
|--------------|----------|----------|--------|----------|----------------|
| Alien Beings | 05/07/92 | 499-1234 | Jones  | Terrence | 1234-4321-098  |
| Almost Home  | 05/05/92 | 499-7890 | Smith  | Jake     | 9876-1234-980  |

**joystick**   A cursor-control device widely used for computer games and some professional applications, such as computer-aided design.

**jumper**   An electrical connector that enables an end user to customize a circuit board. The jumper is a small rectangle of plastic with two or three receptacles. You install a jumper by pushing it down on two- or three-prong pins sticking up from the circuit board's surface.

**jump line**   A message at the end of part of an article in a newsletter, magazine, or newspaper, indicating the page on which the article is continued.

Page layout programs include features that make using jump lines for newsletters easier.

**justification**   The alignment of multiple lines of text along the left margin, the right margin, or both margins.

The term *justification* often is used to refer to full justification, or the alignment of text along both margins.

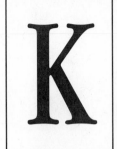

**K**   Abbreviation for *kilobyte* (1,024 bytes).

**KB**   Abbreviation for *kilobyte* (1,024 bytes).

**Kermit**   An asynchronous communications protocol that makes the error-free transmission of program files via the telephone system easier.

Developed by Columbia University and placed in the public domain, Kermit is used by academic institutions because, unlike XMODEM, Kermit can be implemented on mainframe systems that transmit seven bits per byte. See *asynchronous communication*, *communications protocol*, and *XMODEM*.

**kernel**   In an operating system, the core portions of the program that perform the most essential operating system tasks, such as handling disk input and output operations and managing the internal memory.

The kernel can be used with a variety of external shells that vary in their user-friendliness. The shell handles the task of communicating with the user.

**kerning**   The reduction of space between certain pairs of characters in display type, so that the characters print in an aesthetically pleasing manner.

Kerning is rarely necessary for body type, but may be required for headlines and titles. Some page layout programs include an automatic kerning feature, relying on a built-in database of letter pairs that require kerning (such as AV, VA, WA, YA, and so on). Manual kerning is possible with most page layout and some word processing programs (see fig. K.1).

**key assignments**   The functions given to specific keys by a computer program.

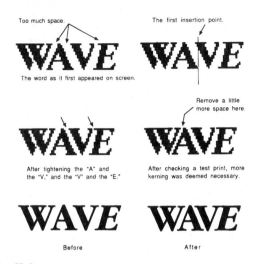

Too much space.

The word as it first appeared on screen.

The first insertion point.

Remove a little more space here.

After tightening the "A" and the "V," and the "V" and the "E."

After checking a test print, more kerning was deemed necessary.

Before

After

**Fig. K.1.** Manual kerning steps with PageMaker.

Most of the keys on a personal computer keyboard are fully programmable, meaning that an application programmer can use them in different ways. The best programs, however, stick to standards in key assignments.

One such standard is the use of the F1 key on IBM PC–compatible keyboards for initiating on-screen help. A program that violates these standards raises the cost of training users and restricts their ability to export their skills to other application programs.

**keyboard** The most frequently used input device for all computers.

The keyboard provides a set of alphabetic, numeric, punctuation, symbol, and control keys. When an alphanumeric or punctuation key is pressed, the keyboard sends a coded input signal to the computer, which echoes the signal by displaying a character on-screen. See *autorepeat key, keyboard layout,* and *toggle key*.

**keyboard buffer**    A small area of primary storage set aside to hold the codes of the last keystrokes you pressed on the keyboard so that the computer can continue to accept your typing even if the computer is busy.

**keyboard layout**    A personal computer's keyboard provides an excellent example of how computer technology has had to adapt to people (rather than people adapting to computers). A PC's keyboard layout uses the standard QWERTY layout that typewriters have used for a century. Another keyboard layout is the Dvorak keyboard, designed in the 1930s by August Dvorak, a professor of education at the University of Washington. The Dvorak keyboard is designed so that more than two-thirds of the words you type require only the home-row keys. (For QWERTY keyboards, the figure is 32 percent.)

Early IBM Personal Computers used a standard 83-key layout that attracted a good deal of criticism because of the odd key layout, such as placing the backslash key between the Z and the Shift keys (see fig. K.2). Many people also considered the Enter key too small. Toggle keys such as Scroll Lock, Num Lock, and Caps Lock lacked lights, and you could not tell whether one was active.

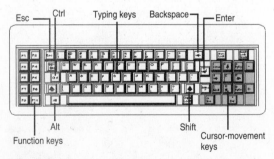

**Fig. K.2.** The original PC keyboard.

In response to this criticism, IBM introduced a new 84-key layout with the release of the IBM Personal Computer AT (see fig. K.3). The AT keyboard uses the standard Selectric typewriter key layout for the typing area, with three indicators that light up when you press Scroll Lock, Num Lock, or Caps Lock. The new 84th key, called Sys Req, is used only when you are running an operating system other than MS-DOS.

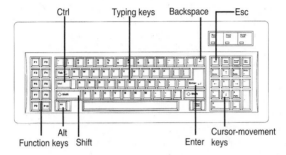

**Fig. K.3.** The AT keyboard.

The latest standard is an enhanced, 101-key layout (see fig. K.4). The 12 function keys (instead of 10) are lined up above the number keys. The 101-key layout also has a separate cursor-control keypad.

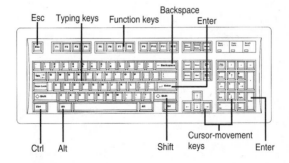

**Fig. K.4.** The enhanced keyboard.

The 101-key standard includes a relocated Ctrl key that touch typists dislike. The Ctrl key is used with other keys to give commands. In the earlier keyboard, Ctrl was situated left of the A key, within easy reach of your left pinky. In the 101-key layout, however, Ctrl is at the lower left, requiring a contorted movement to reach it. Many IBM PC–compatible computers use a corrected 101-key layout that places the Ctrl key back beside the A key.

The original Macintosh keyboard contained only 58 keys. This keyboard lacked a numeric keypad and arrow keys, which the Apple engineers thought were unnecessary because of the Mac's extensive use of the mouse.

Widely criticized, this keyboard was replaced by a 78-key keyboard for the Macintosh Plus. This keyboard included a numeric keypad and arrow keys. With the release of the Macintosh SE and Macintosh II computers, Apple created a new interface standard for input peripherals called the *Apple Desktop Bus* (ADB). Today's ADB keyboards include the 81-key Apple keyboard with Ctrl and Esc keys, and the 105-key Apple Extended Keyboard, which includes function keys.

Increasingly, you may choose among several keyboard alternatives when you purchase a personal computer system. Some keyboards require extremely awkward fingerings for certain operations, such as holding down the Ctrl key and pressing another key to give a keyboard command. Before buying a keyboard, try holding down the Ctrl, Alt, or Command keys and pressing various alphanumeric keys.

Fast typists should make sure that the keyboard has N-key rollover, enabling you to strike an additional key even while the previous key is still engaged at the end of a stroke. To find out whether a keyboard has N-key rollover, hold down the A key and press *S D F* in rapid succession. Due to the keyboard's autorepeat feature, you probably will see several *a* characters, but you also should see the *s*, *d*, and *f*.

**keyboard template**   A plastic card with adhesive that can be pressed onto the keyboard to explain the way a program configures the keyboard.

Many applications provide keyboard templates, which are helpful when you are learning the program.

**key status indicator**   An on-screen status message displayed by many application programs that informs you which, if any, toggle keys are active on the keyboard.

The earliest IBM PC keyboards lacked indicator lights that informed you when you had pressed a toggle key such as Num Lock or Caps Lock. If you inadvertently press Num Lock, for example, the arrow keys on the numeric keypad do not control the cursor; they enter numbers instead. To make up for this oversight, many application programs provide on-screen indicators that flash when you press Num Lock, Scroll Lock, or Caps Lock.

**keystroke**   The physical action of pressing down a key on the keyboard so that a character is entered or a command is initiated.

Programs vary in the number of keystrokes they require to perform basic and often-repeated operations, such as highlighting text for a block move. Other things being equal, a program that requires fewer keystrokes for such tasks probably is more convenient to use.

**key variable**   In a spreadsheet program, a constant placed in a cell at the upper left corner of the spreadsheet and referenced throughout the spreadsheet using absolute cell references.

The use of key variables is essential to good spreadsheet design. If you place a key variable, such as a tax or commission rate, in one cell and reference this rate by using absolute cell references throughout the spreadsheet, you need make only one change if the rate changes. If you place the constant in all the formulas, you have to change every cell to update your spreadsheet.

**keyword**   In programming languages (including software command languages), a word describing an action or operation that the computer can recognize and execute.

**kilo-**   A prefix indicating one thousand ($10^3$).

**kilobit**   1,024 bits of information. See *kilobyte (K)*.

**kilobyte (K)**   The basic unit of measurement for computer memory, equal to 1,024 bytes.

The prefix *kilo-* suggests 1,000, but the computer world contains twos, not tens: $2^{10} = 1,024$. Because one byte is the same as one character in personal computing, a memory of 1K can contain 1,024 characters (letters, numbers, or punctuation marks).

Early personal computers (mid-1970s) offered as little as 16K or 32K of random-access memory (RAM); memory chips were expensive. In IBM PC–compatible computing, 640K is considered a standard figure (the maximum under MS-DOS); today, Macintosh computers are equipped with at least 1M of RAM.

**kludge**   An improvised, technically inelegant solution to a problem.

**knowledge acquisition**   In expert system programming, the process of acquiring and systematizing knowledge from experts.

A major limitation of current expert system technology is that knowledge cannot be acquired by the systems directly; the knowledge must be acquired by engineers and, in a slow and painstaking process, systematized so that the knowledge can be expressed in the form of computer-readable rules. See *expert system* and *knowledge engineer*.

**knowledge base**   In an expert system, the portion of the program that expresses an expert's knowledge, often in IF/THEN rules (such as "If the tank pressure exceeds 600 pounds per square inch, then sound a warning").

**knowledge domain**   In artificial intelligence, an area of problem-solving expertise.

Current artificial intelligence technology works well only in sharply limited knowledge domains, such as the configuration of one manufacturer's computer systems, the repair of a specific robotic system, or investment analysis for a limited range of securities. See *artificial intelligence (AI)*.

**knowledge engineer**   In expert system programming, a specialist who elicits the knowledge possessed by experts in a knowledge domain and expresses this knowledge in a form that an expert system can use. See *expert system* and *knowledge domain*.

**knowledge representation**   In expert system programming, the method used to encode and store the knowledge in a knowledge base.

Although several alternative knowledge representation schemes have been proposed and implemented in systems currently under development, most commercially available expert system environments use the production system approach. In this approach, knowledge is represented in the form of production rules, which have the following form:

> IF {condition} THEN {action}

A given rule may have multiple conditions as in the following example:

IF {a person's intraocular pressure is raised}
AND {the person has pain in the left quadratic region}
THEN {immediate hospitalization is indicated}

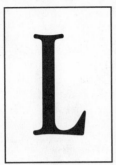

**label**   In a spreadsheet program, text or a heading placed in a cell. In DOS batch files, a string of characters preceded by a colon that marks the destination of a GOTO command. See *value*.

**label alignment**   In a spreadsheet program, the way labels are aligned in a cell (flush left, centered, flush right, or repeating across the cell).

In Lotus 1-2-3, you can control the alignment of a label as you type it by beginning the label with a prefix. Usually optional, the label prefix specifies how 1-2-3 aligns the label within the cell:

| Label Prefix | Alignment |
| --- | --- |
| ' | Flush left |
| ^ | Centered |
| " | Flush right |
| \ | Repeating across the cell |

See *label* and *label prefix*.

**label prefix**   In a spreadsheet program, a punctuation mark at the beginning of a cell entry that tells the program that the entry is a label and specifies how the program should align the label within the cell.

Most programs enter the label prefix—often an apostrophe—when you begin the cell entry with an alphabetical character.

If you begin a cell entry with a number, the program interprets the number as a value rather than a label; however, you can make a number into a label by starting the entry with a label prefix. In Lotus 1-2-3, for example, if you type '*1991*, the program interprets the entry as a label and formats the label flush left. See *label alignment*.

**label printer**   A printer designed specifically to print names and addresses on continuous labels.

**LAN**   See *local area network*.

**LAN-aware program**   A version of an application program specifically modified so that the program can function in a network environment.

In a local area network, you cannot place an application program on a file server and expect the application to function when several people try to use it at once. The licensing agreements of most applications prohibit placing the application on a file server. Network versions of programs, however, are designed for concurrent access. Network versions of transactional application programs—such as database management programs—create and maintain shared files. For example, an invoice-processing program has access to a database of accounts receivable.

The network versions of nontransactional programs—such as word processing programs—include file security features. For example, the word processor can lock files to prevent unauthorized users from gaining access to your documents. See *concurrency control, file locking, file server, LAN-ignorant program, local area network (LAN), nontransactional application*, and *transactional application*.

**LAN backup program**   A program designed specifically to back up the programs and data stored on a local area network's file server. The best LAN backup programs automatically back up the file server at scheduled times, without user intervention.

**landscape orientation**   The rotation of a page design to print text and/or graphics horizontally across the longer axis of the page. See *portrait orientation*.

**LAN-ignorant program**   An application program designed for use only as a stand-alone program and that contains no provisions for use on a network (such as file locking and concurrency control). See *concurrency control*.

**LAN memory management program**   A utility program
designed specifically to free conventional memory so
that you can run applications on a network workstation. Every workstation in a local area network must
run network software, which can consume as much as
100K of conventional memory. The result is "RAM
cram," the reduction of conventional memory to the
point that the workstation may not be able to run
certain memory-hungry applications. LAN memory
managers address this problem by moving the network software, as well as device drivers, terminate-
and-stay-resident (TSR) programs, and other utilities
into the upper memory area, extended memory, or
expanded memory.

A popular and well-rated LAN management program is
NetRoom (Helix Software). See *conventional memory*,
*device driver*, *expanded memory*, *extended memory*,
*local area network (LAN)*, *network operating system
(NOS)*, and *terminate-and-stay-resident (TSR)
program*.

**LAN server**   See *file server* and *printer server*.

**laptop computer**   A small portable computer that is light
enough to hold on your lap. The smallest laptop computers, which weigh less than six pounds and can fit in
a briefcase, are called *notebook computers*.

Laptop computers vary widely in quality. Many offer
specifications that make them appear comparable to
powerful desktop computers, but the small case ensures that you cannot readily expand or modify such
systems should your computing needs change. In addition, the display device will almost certainly prove
inferior to standard VGA displays, and in general, the
better the display, the less time the battery lasts. Be
sure to inspect a laptop before you buy it—you might
not be happy with its screen display. The limitations of
laptop computers argue against buying one as a main
system, especially when you consider that laptops are
generally more expensive than desktop computers. But
many people have legitimate needs for a second, portable computer.

**large-scale integration (LSI)**   In integrated circuit technology, the fabrication on one chip of up to 100,000
discrete transistor devices. See *very large scale
integration (VLSI)*.

**laser font**   See *outline font*.

**LaserJet**   A series of laser printers manufactured by Hewlett-
Packard and widely used in IBM PC–compatible computing.

Introduced in 1984, the LaserJet offered only one built-
in font (the monospace Courier), but its 300-dpi resolution and capability to accept font cartridges helped to
launch desktop publishing. The LaserJet Plus, introduced in 1985, offered sufficient internal random-
access memory (RAM) so that the printer could accept
downloadable fonts, further increasing its versatility as
a desktop typesetter.

The LaserJet Series II was introduced in 1987 with
additional built-in fonts, a larger paper tray, and additional memory. The LaserJet IIP Personal Laser Printer
was added in 1989 and brought the street cost of laser
printing technology below $1,000 for the first time. A
new version of Hewlett-Packard's proprietary printer
control language has brought scalable (outline) font
technology to middle- and high-end LaserJet printers.
LaserJet printers also can be equipped with PostScript
cartridges, although such cartridges operate more
slowly than true PostScript printers. See *laser printer,
outline font,* and *PostScript laser printer*.

**laser printer**   A high-resolution printer that uses a version
of the electrostatic reproduction technology of copying
machines to fuse text and graphic images to the page.

Although laser printers are complex machines, understanding how they work is not difficult. The printer's
controller circuitry receives the printing instructions
from the computer and, for each page, constructs a bit
map of every dot on the page (about 1M of memory is
required to ensure adequate storage space for graphic
images). The controller ensures that the print engine's

laser transfers a precise replica of this bit map to a photostatically sensitive drum or belt. Switching on and off rapidly, the beam travels across the drum, and as the beam moves, the drum charges the areas exposed to the beam. The charged areas attract toner (electrically charged ink) as the drum rotates past the toner cartridge.

In a write-black engine, the beam charges the areas that print and does so with a positive charge that attracts toner. In a write-white engine, the beam charges the areas not printed, giving the areas a negative charge that repels toner. Because of this technique, write-black engines show details of images better than write-white engines, but write-white engines print denser images. An electrically charged wire pulls the toner from the drum onto the paper, and heat rollers fuse the toner to the paper. A second electrically charged wire neutralizes the drum's electrical charge.

Alternative technologies include light-emitting diode (LED) imaging printers that use a dense array of LEDs instead of a laser to generate the light that exposes the drum, and liquid crystal shutter (LCS) printers that use a lattice-like array of liquid crystal gateways to block or transmit light as necessary. See *print engine* and *resolution*.

**LaserWriter**   A series of PostScript laser printers manufactured by Apple Computer and used with Macintosh and IBM PC–compatible computers.

Introduced in 1985 with a list price of nearly $8,000, the Apple LaserWriter was the first commercial laser printer to offer a built-in interpreter for the PostScript page description language. Capable of using the sophisticated and scalable outline fonts created by Adobe Systems, Inc., and other firms, the LaserWriter is well-integrated with the Macintosh family of computers because a standard PostScript-compatible printer driver is available for any application to use. (For an IBM PC compatible running DOS, an application cannot produce PostScript-compatible output unless the application includes a PostScript-compatible driver.)

Coupled with the Mac's capability to display screen fonts that suggest the typeface and type size changes, the LaserWriter gave the Macintosh an early lead in desktop publishing.

Designed to be connected to the Macintosh through inexpensive AppleTalk network connections, Apple envisioned the LaserWriter as a shared peripheral, designed for use by a small workgroup of four to seven individuals. A standard serial port is included, however, for direct connection to IBM PC–compatible computers.

The LaserWriter II series, introduced in 1987, featured a better print engine, more memory, and faster output. At the top of the line is the LaserWriter II NTX, which includes 11 Adobe typefaces (a total of 35 fonts), a 68020 microprocessor running at 16.7 MHz, and a SCSI output port for a dedicated hard disk. The LaserWriter II SC is not a PostScript printer and therefore relies on Apple's built-in QuickDraw technology to generate fonts. Macintoshes equipped with System 7 can print TrueType outline (scalable) fonts on the LaserWriter IISC, and also on Apple's newest and cheapest laser printer, the Apple Personal LaserWriter.

The LaserWriter has been imitated—many PostScript laser printers are functionally identical. Although LaserWriter printers are much cheaper now than they were originally, they can cost as much as or more than a well-equipped personal computer. LaserWriters will never be as inexpensive as LaserJets, because unlike LaserJets, PostScript-compatible printers must have their own microprocessing circuitry and require large amounts of RAM. Non-PostScript outline font technologies, however, promise to lower prices by circumventing Adobe Systems' licensing fees. See *AppleTalk*, *laser printer*, *PostScript laser printer,* and *System 7.*

**latency**   In disk drives, the delay caused by the disk rotating so that the desired data is positioned under the read/write head.

**launch**   To start a program.

**layer**   In some illustration and page-layout applications, an on-screen sheet on which you can place text or graphics so that they are independent of any text or graphics on other sheets. The layer can be opaque or transparent.

In SuperPaint, for example, you can create illustrations on two layers: a paint layer for bit-mapped graphics and a draw layer for object-oriented graphics. In FreeHand, you can draw or paint on up to 200 transparent layers. Commands typically named *Bring to Front* or *Send to Back* enable you to bring a background layer forward so that you can edit that layer.

**layout**   In desktop publishing and word processing, the process of arranging text and graphics on a page. In database management systems, the arrangement of report elements, such as headers and fields, on a printed page.

**LCD**   See *liquid crystal display*.

**LCD printer**   See *liquid crystal display printer*.

**leader**   In word processing, a row of dots or dashes that provides a path for the eye to follow across the page.

Leaders often are used in tables of contents to lead the reader's eye from the entry to the page number. Most word processing programs enable you to define tab stops that insert leaders when you press the Tab key.

**leading**   Pronounced "ledding." The space between lines of type, measured from baseline to baseline. Synonymous with *line spacing*.

The term originated from letterpress-printing technology, in which thin lead strips were inserted between lines of type to control the spacing between lines.

**leading zero**   The zeros added in front of numeric values so that a number fills up all required spaces in a data field. For example, three leading zeros are in the number 00098.54.

Most of today's database management programs do not require leading zeros; they are symbolic of previous generations of software, which often forced you to enter data to conform to the program's limitations.

**LED**   See *light emitting diode.*

**LED printer**   See *light emitting diode printer.*

**left justification**   The alignment of text along only the left margin. Synonymous with *ragged-right alignment.*

**legend**   In presentation graphics, an area of a chart or graph that explains the meaning of the patterns or colors used in the presentation.

**letter-quality printer**   An impact printer that simulates the fully formed text characters produced by a high-quality office typewriter.

The print technology used is a spin-off of office typewriter technology. Many letter-quality printers use daisywheels or printing mechanisms in which the character images are positioned on the ends of spokes of a plastic or metal hub that rotates quickly as printing occurs. You change fonts by changing the daisywheel.

A major drawback of letter-quality printers is that they cannot print graphics. This fact ensures a brisk market for dot-matrix printers that, despite their poorer quality for text output, can print charts and graphs. With the arrival of laser printers, the market for letter-quality printers has all but disappeared.

 If you plan to purchase a letter-quality printer, make sure that your software includes a printer driver for the specific brand and model you are buying. In IBM PC–compatible computing, no single, widely accepted standard for printer control commands exists. De facto standards are established by Diablo and Qume letter-quality printers. Many letter-quality printers recognize the Epson or IBM commands, but others do not. See *impact printer.*

**library** A collection of programs kept with a computer system and made available for processing purposes. The term often refers to a collection of library routines written in a given programming language such as C or Pascal. See *library routine*.

**library routine** In programming, a well-tested subroutine, procedure, or function in a given programming language.

The library routine handles tasks that all or most programs need, such as reading data from disks. The programmer can draw on this library to develop programs quickly.

**ligature** In typography, two or more characters designed and cast as a distinct unit for aesthetic reasons, such as *æ*.

Five letter combinations beginning with *f* ( *fi*, *ff*, *fl*, *ffi*, and *ffl* ) and two dipthongs (*ae* and *oe*) commonly are printed as ligatures. Some outline fonts available for PostScript laser printers include ligatures for professional typesetting applications. See *outline font* and *PostScript laser printer*.

**light emitting diode (LED)** A small electronic device made from semiconductor materials. An LED emits light when current flows through it.

LEDs are used for small indicator lights, but because they draw more power than liquid crystal displays (LCD), they rarely are used for computer displays.

**light emitting diode (LED) printer** A high-quality printer that closely resembles the laser printer in that it electrostatically fuses toner to paper; however, the light source is a matrix of light emitting diodes. To create the image, the diodes flash on and off over the rotating print drum. See *laser printer* and *liquid crystal display (LCD) printer*.

**light pen** An input device that uses a light-sensitive stylus to enable you to draw on-screen, draw on a graphics tablet, or select items from menus.

**LIM EMS**  See *Lotus-Intel-Microsoft Expanded Memory System*.

**line**  In programming, one program statement. In data communications, a circuit that directly connects two or more electronic devices.

**line adapter**  In data communications, an electronic device that converts signals from one form to another so that you can transmit the signals.

A modem is a line adapter that converts the computer's digital signals to analog equivalents so that you can transmit these signals via the telephone system.

**line art**  In computer graphics, a drawing that does not contain halftones so that low- to medium-resolution printers can accurately reproduce the drawing. See *halftone*.

**line chart**  See *line graph*.

**line editor**  A primitive word processing utility often is provided with an operating system as part of its programming environment. Line editors are notoriously difficult to use. Unlike a full-screen editor, you can write or edit only one line of program code at a time.

Even if you're programming just for fun or for hobby purposes, obtain and use a full-screen editor. See *full-screen editor* and *programming environment*.

**line feed**  A signal that tells the printer when to start a new line.

**line graph**  In presentation and analytical graphics, a graph that uses lines to show the variations of data over time or to show the relationship between two numeric variables (see fig. L.1). In general, the x-axis (categories axis) is aligned horizontally, and the y-axis (values axis) is aligned vertically. A line graph, however, may have two y-axes. See *bar graph*, *presentation graphics*, *x-axis*, and *y-axis*.

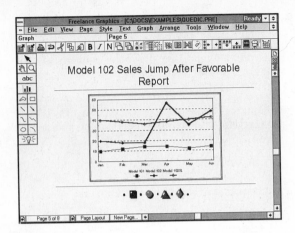

**Fig. L.1.** A line graph.

line spacing   See *leading*.

link   To establish a connection between two files or data
items so that a change in one is reflected by a change in
the second.

A cold link requires user intervention and action, such
as opening both files and using an updating command,
to make sure that the change has occurred; a warm link
occurs automatically. See *cold link* and *hot link*.

linked list   See *list*.

linked object   In object linking and embedding (OLE), a
source document or portion of a document created
with one application and inserted into a destination
document, created with another application.

Unlike embedding, which places a live, independent,
and editable object into the destination document,
linking places a static copy of the source document into
the destination document. Unlike Clipboard copying
and pasting, however, this copy contains a hidden
reference to the source document's location. The
source document still exists separately. When you
change the source document, Windows automatically
updates the copy that is in the destination document.

Object linking and embedding is possible only when you're using OLE-compatible applications on a Windows system or on a Macintosh system running System 7.

 To edit a linked object quickly, double-click the object. Your computer will start the application that created the object and allow you to edit it. When you choose Update from the File menu, you return to the destination application and see the edited object. See *destination document, embedded object, object linking and embedding (OLE),* and *source document.*

**linked pie/column chart**   See *linked pie/column graph.*

**linked pie/column graph**   In presentation graphics, a pie graph paired with a column graph so that the column graph displays the internal distribution of data items in one of the pie's slices (see fig. L.2).

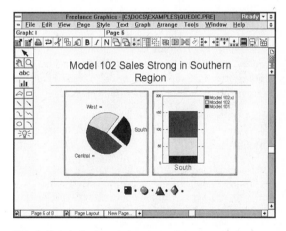

**Fig. L.2.** A linked pie/column graph.

Use linked pie/column graphs to show the internal breakdown of the values that make up one slice of a pie graph. For example, in an exploded pie graph emphasizing total sales for a region, the linked column graph could display a breakdown of the products sold.

**liquid crystal display (LCD)**   A low-power display technology used in laptop computers and small, battery-
powered electronic devices such as meters, testing
equipment, and digital watches. The display device
uses rod-shaped crystal molecules that change their
orientation when an electrical current flows through
them. When no current exists, the crystals seem to
disappear. When energized, they direct light to a polar-
izing screen, producing a darkened area.

LCD displays are flat and draw little power, but they are
not bright enough for sustained use without causing
eyestrain. A compromise design uses a backlit screen.
This design improves the LCD screen's readability but
draws more power.

**liquid crystal display (LCD) printer**   A high-quality printer
that closely resembles the laser printer in that it electrostatically fuses toner to paper; however, the light
source is a matrix of liquid crystal shutters. The shutters open and close to create the pattern of light that
falls on the print drum. See *laser printer* and *light
emitting diode (LED) printer*.

**LISP**   A high-level programming language, often used for
artificial intelligence research, that makes no distinction between the program and the data. This language
is considered ideal for manipulating text.

One of the oldest programming languages still in use,
LISP (short for *list processing*) was developed by John
McCarthy and his colleagues at the Massachusetts
Institute of Technology in the early 1960s.

LISP is a declarative language; the programmer does
not write a series of instructions that tells the computer
what to do; instead, the programmer composes lists
that declare the relationships among symbolic values.
Lists are the fundamental data structure of LISP, and
the program performs computations on the symbolic
values expressed in those lists. A variable is declared in
the following way:

```
(SETQMAP(NATION(STATE(COUNTY(CITY
(ZONE(STREET(HOUSE))))))))
```

Because LISP is a symbolic processing language, this expression is evaluated by the LISP interpreter, which returns a value—in this case, the variable map is bound to the following hierarchical list:

```
(NATION(STATE(COUNTY(CITY(ZONE
(STREET(HOUSE)))))))
```

Because each LISP statement produces a value that can be passed to other statements, no inherent distinction exists between data and program instructions; on the contrary, each LISP statement is potentially an item of data that another LISP statement can consider. Writing LISP programs that modify themselves or writing new programs is easy. By using recursion, moreover, you can build complex applications.

Not all of these applications lie in the field of artificial intelligence research. LISP was used to write EMACS— a respected mainframe text editor that has influenced the design and implementation of personal computer word processing packages such as WordPerfect and Sprint.

A distinctive feature of LISP, as the preceding example suggests, is the use of parentheses to express the logical structure of the program. Critics of LISP say the use of parentheses makes the language difficult to read.

Like other public domain programming languages, LISP has appeared in a number of mutually unintelligible versions. A standardization effort, however, resulted in Common LISP, which defines a fully configured, current version of the language that is widely accepted. See *declarative language* and *interpreter*.

**list**    In programming, a data structure that lists and links each data item with a pointer showing the item's physical location in a database.

Using a list, a programmer can organize data in various ways without changing the physical location of the data. For example, a database can be displayed on-screen so that it appears to be sorted in alphabetical order, even though the actual physical data records still are stored in the order in which they were entered.

**live copy/paste**   See *hot link*.

**load**   To transfer program instructions or data from a disk into the computer's random-access memory (RAM).

**local area network (LAN)**   The linkage of personal and other computers within a limited area by high-performance cables so that users can exchange information, share expensive peripherals, and draw on the resources of a massive secondary storage unit, called a *file server*.

Local area networks offer the advantages of a distributed computing system in which computational power is distributed to users without sacrificing their ability to communicate (see fig. L.3).

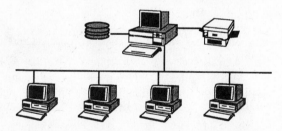

**Fig. L.3.** An illustration of a personal computer local area network.

Ranging tremendously in size and complexity, LANs may link only a few personal computers to an expensive, shared peripheral, such as a laser printer. More complex systems use central computers (file servers) and enable users to communicate with each other via electronic mail to share multiuser programs and to access shared databases.

Some of the largest and most complex LANs are found on university campuses and in large corporations. Such networks may be composed of several smaller networks interconnected by electronic bridges. Unlike a multiuser system, in which each user is equipped with a dumb terminal that may lack processing capabilities, each user in a LAN possesses a workstation containing its own processing circuitry. High-speed cable communication links connect these workstations.

LANs are not without their disadvantages when compared to multiuser systems, however. Multiuser systems may be highly appropriate for vertical applications such as point-of-sale systems, in which it is unnecessary to provide each node with its own processing circuitry and software.

In addition, much of the software developed for multiuser systems has its origins in vertical application development—such as the creation of software for hospital management—and as such, it represents the accumulation of years of experience in managing specific organizations with computers.

A set of standards (network protocols) governs the flow of information within the network. These standards determine when and how a node may initiate a message. Network protocols also handle conflicts that occur when two nodes begin transmitting at the same time. Common network protocols for personal computers include AppleTalk and EtherNet.

The basic components of a LAN are cables, a network interface card, a file server (which includes the central mass storage), a network operating system (NOS), and personal computers or workstations linked by the system.

Three alternative network topologies (methods for interconnecting the network's workstations) exist: bus networks, ring networks, and star networks. In addition, two methods for communicating information via the network's cables exist: baseband and broadband. See *AppleTalk, baseband, broadband, bus network, EtherNet, file server, multiuser system, network operating system (NOS), Novell Netware, ring network,* and *star network.*

**local drive**   In a local area network, a disk drive that's part of the workstation you currently are using, as distinguished from a network drive (a drive made available to you through the network).

**local echo**   See *half duplex*.

**local printer**   In a local area network, a printer directly connected to the workstation you are using, as distinguished from a network printer (a printer made available to you through the network).

**LocalTalk**   The physical connectors and cables manufactured by Apple Computer for use in AppleTalk networks.

**locked file**   In a local area network, a file attribute that prevents applications or the user from updating or deleting the file.

**logarithmic chart**   See *logarithmic graph*.

**logarithmic graph**   In analytical and presentation graphics, a graph displayed with a y-axis (values axis) that increases exponentially in powers of 10.

On an ordinary y-axis, the 10 is followed by 20, 30, 40, and so on. On a logarithmic scale, however, 10 is followed by 100, 1,000, 10,000, and so on.

Use a logarithmic scale when one of the data series has very small values, and others have large values. In an ordinary graph, you can hardly see a data series with small values (see fig. L.4); on a logarithmic chart, however, the small values show up much better (see fig. L.5). See *analytical graphics* and *presentation graphics*.

**logical drives**   The disk drives of a computer system presented to the user as if they were identical, even though physically they are very different. The computer's operating system masks these differences. For this reason, you can use the same file-management commands, such as COPY or DELETE, on any logical drive, despite the fact that each drive may have its own, unique way of storing, retrieving, and deleting data. See *physical drive*.

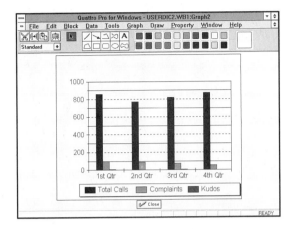

**Fig. L.4.** A column graph with an ordinary y-axis.

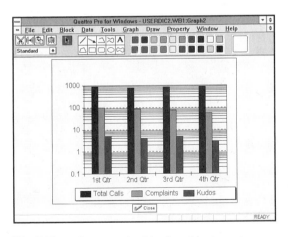

**Fig. L.5.** A column graph with a logarithmic y-axis.

**logical format**   See *high-level format*.

**logical operator**   A symbol used to specify the logical relationship of inclusion or exclusion between two quantities or concepts.

In query languages, the inclusive operator (OR) broadens the number of data records retrieved, and the exclusive operators (AND and NOT) restrict the number retrieved.

Suppose that you specify a query that asks "Show me the titles of all the videotapes in which the field RATING contains PG *or* PG-13." You see a list of the titles with either rating; the program retrieves records that meet either of the criteria you specify.

To illustrate the restrictive effect of the AND operator, consider the following example: you ask, "Show me the titles of all the videotapes in which the field CATEGORY contains Adventure *and* the field RATING includes PG." Only those records that meet both of the criteria you specify in your query appear on-screen.

The NOT operator also is restrictive, as in the following example: "Show me the titles of all the videotapes in which the field CATEGORY contains Adventure, but *not* the ones in which the field RATING includes R." Synonymous with *Boolean operator*.

**logic board**   See *motherboard*.

**log-in security**   In local area and mainframe networks, a validation process that requires you to type a password before gaining access to the system. See *local area network (LAN)* and *password protection*.

**Logo**   A high-level programming language well suited to teaching fundamental programming concepts to children.

Developed at the Massachusetts Institute of Technology in the 1960s with the assistance of the National Science Foundation, Logo is the creation of computer scientist Seymour Papert. A special version of LISP, Logo was designed as an educational language to illustrate the concepts of recursion, extensibility, and other fundamental concepts of computing; however, it doesn't require math skills. The language also provides an environment in which children can develop their reasoning and problem-solving skills.

A key feature of Logo is turtle graphics, in which a graphic representation of a turtle creates graphic images under program control. Program instructions tell the turtle to put down the pen and move forward, backward, left, or right. After the child succeeds in writing a program that defines a shape such as a rectangle, he or she can save the program as a new command; this teaches the concept of extensibility. Through recursion, children can create and print beautiful geometric diagrams. See *LISP*.

**log off**   The process of terminating a connection with a computer system or peripheral device in an orderly way.

**log on**   The process of establishing a connection with, or gaining access to, a computer system or peripheral device.

In MS-DOS, *logging on* refers to the process of activating a drive by typing the drive letter and a colon, and then pressing Enter. In computer networks, you may be required to type a security password to log on.

**log-on file**   In a local area network, a batch file or configuration file that starts the network software and establishes the connection with the network when you turn on the workstation.

**lookup function**   A procedure in which the program consults stored data listed in a table or file.

**lookup table**   In a spreadsheet program, a range of cells set apart from the rest of the worksheet and dedicated to a lookup function, such as determining the correct tax rate based on annual income.

**loop**   In programming, a set of program instructions that executes repeatedly until a condition is satisfied. See *loop control structure*.

**loop control structure**   In computer programming, a control structure in which a block of instructions repeats until a condition is fulfilled. See *control structure, DO/WHILE loop,* and *FOR/NEXT loop*.

**lost chain** In MS-DOS, a section of a file once connected with other sections, but the file allocation table (FAT) no longer contains the information needed to reconstruct the links between those sections.

**lost cluster** A section of a file that remains on the disk, even though the file allocation table (FAT) contains no record of its links to the rest of the file.

Lost clusters occur when the computer is turned off (or the power fails) while a file is being written. They do not pose a problem other than consuming disk space.

**Lotus 1-2-3** A spreadsheet program for IBM PC–compatible computers that integrates database management and analytical graphics capabilities.

Introduced in 1982 by Lotus Development Corporation, Lotus 1-2-3 supplanted VisiCalc, the original spreadsheet program, by offering all of VisiCalc's functions and adding database and graphics functions.

Developed by Mitchell D. Kapor, Lotus 1-2-3 is sometimes credited with being responsible for the success of the IBM Personal Computer. Many people bought IBM PCs (equipped with Hercules Graphics Adapters) so that they could run 1-2-3 and transform spreadsheet data into vivid, on-screen charts and graphs.

Like dBASE, the popular database management system for IBM PC–compatible computers, many clones have imitated Lotus 1-2-3. Lotus countered this competition by successful product introductions in 1989.

Release 3.0, designed for computers with the Intel 80286 and Intel 80386 microprocessors, requires at least 1M of RAM under MS-DOS (640K of conventional memory and 384K of expanded memory). This release of the program features three-dimensional worksheets and other advanced features.

To address the much larger market of users still running computers with the Intel 8088 microprocessor, Lotus also released Release 2.2, which was followed by Release 2.3 in 1992. Lotus 1-2-3 for Windows extends to the Windows environment the familiar 1-2-3 way of building a spreadsheet, but the product faces stiff competition from programs that take more explicit advantage of the Windows environment.

**Lotus-Intel-Microsoft Expanded Memory Specification (LIM EMS)**   An expanded memory standard that enables the programs that recognize the standard to work with more than 640K RAM under DOS.

The LIM Version 4.0 standard, introduced in 1987, supports up to 32M of expanded memory and enables programs to run in expanded memory.

 Software cannot work with expanded memory unless specifically designed to do so. Most popular application packages—such as WordPerfect, Lotus 1-2-3, and dBASE—work with LIM 4.0 expanded memory, but less popular programs and shareware may not function in EMS unless you use a windowing environment such as Quarterdeck's DESQview or Microsoft Windows. See *expanded memory* and *extended memory*.

**low end**   An inexpensive product at the bottom or near the bottom of a firm's offerings; includes only a subset of the features available in more expensive products and may rely on obsolete or near-obsolete technology to keep costs down.

 You can get PC-compatible computers based on the Intel 8086, 8088, and 80286 microprocessors quite cheaply, but these computers cannot take full advantage of the 386 Enhanced mode of Microsoft Windows, in which Window's technical advantages are fully available. See *386 Enhanced mode* and *Microsoft Windows*.

**low-level format**   The physical pattern of magnetic tracks and sectors created on a disk during formatting. This operation, sometimes called a *physical format*, is different from the high-level format that establishes the housekeeping sections that track free and in-use areas of the disk. See *high-level format*.

**low-level programming language** In computer programming, a language, such as machine language or assembly language, in which the programmer must pay strict
attention to the exact procedures occurring in the
computer's central processing unit (CPU). See *assembly language, high-level programming language*, and
*machine language*.

**low resolution** In computer monitors and printers, a visual
definition that isn't sufficient to produce well-defined
characters or smoothly defined curves in graphic images, resulting in characters and graphics with jagged
edges.

The IBM Color Graphics Adapter (CGA) and monitor,
for example, can display 640 pixels horizontally, but
only 200 lines vertically, resulting in poor visual definition. See *high resolution*.

**LPT** In DOS, a device name that refers to one of the parallel
ports to which you can connect parallel printers.

**LSI** See *large-scale integration*.

**M**    Abbreviation for *megabyte*.

**MacBinary**    A file transfer protocol for Macintosh computers that enables you to store Macintosh files on non-Macintosh computers without losing icons, graphics, and information about the file (such as the creation date). Most Macintosh communication programs send and receive files in MacBinary.

**machine language**    The language recognized and executed by the computer's central processing unit (CPU). The language is symbolized by 0s and 1s and is extremely difficult to use and read. See *assembly language* and *high-level programming language*.

**Macintosh**    A family of personal computers introduced by Apple Computer in 1984 that features a graphical user interface.

The Macintosh has its origins in one of the country's most inventive research laboratories: Xerox Palo Alto Research Center (PARC). During the 1970s, PARC attracted what were unquestionably some of the greatest minds in computer design. In an organizational context well suited to technical innovation, the PARC scientists generated an astonishing series of innovations: a WYSIWYG word processor called Bravo that inspired Microsoft Word, desktop publishing with laser printers, local area networks for workgroups, and a graphical user interface with pull-down menus and a mouse.

Visiting PARC in 1979, Steve Jobs of Apple Computer was so impressed that he hired several PARC scientists. At Apple, they joined a team that created the Lisa—a $10,000 computer released in 1983. The Lisa, however, was a commercial flop. Well received and considered a milestone in computer design, the Lisa was too expensive for its market.

In the meantime, IBM was running away with Apple's market share in personal computing with the phenomenal success of the IBM Personal Computer. In response, a team at Apple wanted to bring PARC-like technology to the masses, in the form of a computer named Macintosh (after the apple of the same name). The people at Apple developed the Mac with a utopian idealism and a near-religious fervor for changing the world; this computer was to be the "computer for the rest of us." The machine the team produced, however, departed significantly from the open-architecture and open-bus philosophy that had done so much to ensure the popularity of Apple's previous product, the Apple II. With a sealed case that users could not open without a special tool, the Mac seemed to be designed to bring user-friendly technology to people, but also to keep the market for expensive peripherals and accessories in Apple's hands.

With the release of the open-bus Macintosh II in 1987, Apple tacitly admitted that the closed-bus architecture of the early Mac was a mistake. By 1989, a healthy support industry had grown up around the Macintosh, with many suppliers providing adapters, monitors, and printers for Macintosh computers.

The earliest Mac had other problems besides the sealed case. Jobs is said to have stated that the average personal computer user did not want a fast computer or a lot of memory—and given that the original Mac was equipped with only 128K of RAM and only one 400K disk drive, the computer reflected this philosophy.

In other ways, however, the Macintosh was technologically advanced. The Mac was the first computer to offer a 32-bit microprocessor: the Motorola 68000, running at a clock speed of 7.8 MHz, a modest improvement over the Intel 8088's 4.77 MHz. A striking innovation was the original Mac's medium-resolution monitor that displayed 512 by 312 black pixels on a paper-white background. Perhaps most importantly, the Mac's application program interface (API) and mouse gave programmers a standard that reduced the learning time for programs.

Although the Macintosh sold well at first, the original Mac never found a mass market, especially in the business context. Pressures inside Apple led to Jobs' departure, and under the leadership of Apple's CEO, John Sculley, Apple made the necessary changes: the Macintosh received more memory (1M in the Macintosh Plus), hard disks, facilities for communication with corporate mainframes, and a library of business software.

What ensured the Mac's entrance into the business world, however, was the 1986 release of the LaserWriter printer, coupled with the PageMaker page-layout program and high-resolution outline fonts. This technology made desktop publishing possible, and with a major technological advantage over IBM PC–compatible computers, the Macintosh made significant inroads into the world of corporate computing in the closing years of the 1980s.

Because of the brisk market for inexpensive clones, however, twelve IBM PC–compatible computers existed for every Mac in use. A series of successful product innovations in 1989, including high-performance Macintosh II computers based on the Motorola 68030 microprocessor, ensured the computer's continuing place in organizational and home computing.

In 1990, however, it became clear that the concentration on the high end of the market had potentially disastrous implications. Inexpensive IBM PC clones were invading Apple's traditional market niches—home and school computing—and the company had not made sufficient progress in readying an inexpensive Mac for this market. In 1990, the company released Macintoshes that cost less than $1,000: the Macintosh Classic, which has sold well, and the Macintosh LC, Apple's least expensive color Macintosh. The 1991 release of System 7 continued Apple's technological lead, which is steadily narrowing as Microsoft Windows gains momentum. Microsoft's release of Windows 3.0 and 3.1 gave inexpensive 80386SX machines much of the Mac's functionality and ease of use at a lower price.

1992 upgrades, the Macintosh Classic II and LC II, came equipped with 68030 processors and 4M of RAM, thus defining the new, minimal Mac configuration. A new line of portable Macs, called *PowerBooks*, gave Apple a much-needed entrance into the laptop market, and the high-end Quadras, also introduced in 1992, made Apple a contender in the professional workstation market. See *graphical user interface (GUI)*, *Microsoft Windows*, *Macintosh Classic*, *Motorola 68000*, *Motorola 68030*, *PowerBook*, *Quadra*, and *System* 7.

**Macintosh II** An open-bus, high-performance personal computer introduced by Apple Computer in 1987.

The earliest Macintosh II featured a Motorola 68020 microprocessor, but Macintosh IIs using the Motorola 68030 running at 15.67 MHz soon replaced the 68020. Current Macintosh II computers include the popular Macintosh IIci, the high-performance Macintosh IIfx, and the lowest-cost color Mac, the Macintosh LC II.

The Macintosh II was a significant departure from the Mac's previous closed-bus architecture. For the first time, users could assemble a system using video cards, monitors (including color monitors), and even keyboards derived from non-Apple suppliers. See *Motorola 68030*.

**Macintosh Classic** The successor to the popular Macintosh Plus and Macintosh SE, an entry-level Macintosh that employs the 68000 microprocessor running at 8 MHz.

The 1990 introduction of the Classic followed a period of management turmoil and firings within Apple as the company realized that its preoccupation with high-end products had left the market wide open to penetration by inexpensive IBM PC clones. The Classic, retailing for less than $1,000, sluggishly runs today's complex Mac software. The 1992 Classic II, equipped with a 68030 microprocessor, provides excellent performance.

**MacPaint** The first (and now widely imitated) paint program created for the original Macintosh computer. See *paint program*.

**macro**   A stored list of two or more application program
commands that, when retrieved, replays the commands
to accomplish a task. Macros automate tedious and
often-repeated tasks (such as saving and backing up a
file to a floppy) that otherwise would require you to
press several command keys or choose several options
from menus.

Some programs provide a macro-recording mode, in
which the program records your keystrokes; you then
save the recording and play it back when you want.
Other programs provide a built-in macro editor that
enables you to type and edit macro commands instead
of recording them. Such facilities often amount to a
full-fledged software command language, including
a full set of modern control structures such as
DO/WHILE loops, IF/THEN/ELSE branches, and other
advanced features.

Full-featured application programs such as Microsoft
Word, WordPerfect, and Lotus 1-2-3 include macro
capabilities. Commercially available macro programs
such as SuperKey or AutoMac III provide macro capabilities for programs that lack them. See *IF/THEN/ELSE*
and *DO/WHILE loop*.

**MacroMind Director**   An animation-development program,
developed by MacroMind, Inc. for Macintosh computers, that creates animated sequences, including graphics, text, and sound.

**MacWrite**   The first Macintosh word processing program—
an easy-to-use and fast program designed for beginning
users.

The new version, MacWrite II (from Claris Corporation,
an Apple spin-off), is substantially slower, but includes
many new features.

**magnetic disk**   In secondary storage, a random-access storage medium that is the most popular method for storing and retrieving computer programs and data files. In
personal computing, common magnetic disks include
5 1/4-inch floppy disks, 3 1/2-inch floppy disks, and
hard disks of various sizes.

The disk is coated with a magnetically sensitive material. Like a record player's arm, the magnetic read/write head moves laterally across the surface of the spinning disk, accessing locations of the disk under the disk drive's automatic control. Unlike a record, however, the information stored on a magnetic disk can be repeatedly erased and rewritten, like any other magnetic storage medium. See *3 1/2-inch disk*, *5 1/4-inch disk*, *floppy disk*, *hard disk*, and *random access*.

**magnetic media**   In secondary storage, the use of magnetic techniques to store and retrieve data on disks or tapes coated with magnetically sensitive materials.

Like iron filings on a sheet of waxed paper, these materials are reoriented when a magnetic field passes over them. During write operations, the read/write head emits a magnetic field that reorients the magnetic materials on the disk or tape so that they are positively or negatively charged, corresponding to a bit of data. During read operations, the read/write head senses the magnetic polarities encoded on the tape.

**magnetic tape**   In secondary storage, a high-capacity mass storage and backup medium.

Although magnetic tape drives must use slow sequential access techniques, magnetic tape is inexpensive and offers a cost-effective way to store massive amounts of data; one roll of tape can store as much as 100M of data. Magnetic tape drives are available for IBM Personal Computers and compatibles. A 1991 price break placed tape cartridge drives within the reach of many PC users; drives became available for as little as $250. Most tape drives are used for hard disk backup purposes. See *sequential access*.

**mailbox**   In electronic mail, a storage location that holds messages addressed to an individual until he or she accesses the system. An on-screen message informs the user that mail is waiting.

**mail merge**   A utility common in full-featured word processing programs that draws information from a database—usually a mailing list—to print multiple copies of a document. Each copy contains one or part of one of the database records and text that does not vary from copy to copy.

The most common application of the mail merge utility is the generation of personalized form letters. A personalized form letter contains text that you send to all recipients, but mail merge has personalized the letter with the correspondent's name and address. You also may insert personalized information anywhere within the letter, as in this example, "In all honesty, *Dr. Richards*, we have never received a complaint about this product before your letter of *October 3*."

In a mail-merge application, you use the word processing program to create the database, called the *secondary file* or *data document*, and you create a primary file (sometimes called a *main document*) that contains the text you want to send. In place of the correspondent's name and address, however, you type codes that refer to fields in the name-and-address database. Finally, you give a command that prints one copy of the primary file for each record in the database.

 Most programs enable you to perform conditional merging that prints an optional passage of text if a database record meets a specified condition.

**mainframe**   A multiuser computer designed to meet the computing needs of a large organization.

Originally, the term *mainframe* referred to the metal cabinet that housed the central processing unit (CPU) of early computers. The term came to be used generally to refer to the large, central computers developed in the late 1950s and 1960s to meet the accounting and information-management needs of large organizations. The largest mainframes can handle thousands of dumb terminals and use gigabytes of secondary storage.

Rather than differentiating such machines by size alone, experts increasingly differentiate them by function: a mainframe meets the computing needs of an entire organization, and a minicomputer meets the needs of a department within an organization. By accepting this definition, one must concede that a minicomputer should be termed a mainframe if a small business uses it as its sole computing resource. The boundaries between the two types of computers are blurring. See *minicomputer*, *personal computer*, and *workstation*.

**main memory**   See *random-access memory (RAM)*.

**main program**   In programming, the part of the program containing the master sequence of instructions, unlike the subroutines, procedures, and functions that the main program calls.

**main storage**   See *random-access memory (RAM)*.

**maintenance release**   A program revision that corrects a minor bug or makes a minor new feature available, such as a new printer driver. Maintenance releases are usually numbered in tenths (3.2) or hundredths (2.01), to distinguish them from major program revisions. Synonymous with *incremental update*.

**male connector**   In computer cables, a cable terminator and connection device in which the pins protrude from the connector's surface. See *female connector*.

**management information system (MIS)**   A computer system, usually based on a mainframe or minicomputer, designed to provide management personnel with up-to-date information on the organization's performance.

**manual recalculation**   In a spreadsheet program, a recalculation method that suspends the recalculation of values until you press a key that forces recalculation to take place.

Most spreadsheet programs recalculate all values within the spreadsheet after you change the contents of an individual cell. If you are using a slow computer and creating a large spreadsheet, you may want to choose the manual recalculation mode as you enter data.

After you enter data or labels in the manual recalculation mode, be sure to recalculate the spreadsheet and turn automatic recalculation on again. If you do not, you may forget that you chose manual recalculation, and the spreadsheet may display an incorrect result after you make additional changes.

The latest generation of spreadsheet software offers background recalculation, in which the keyboard does not lock up as recalculation occurs. With these spreadsheet programs, such as Lotus 1-2-3 Release 3, you do not need to use manual recalculation. See *automatic recalculation*.

**map**    A representation of data stored in memory. See *bit map*.

**mapping**    The process of converting data encoded in one format or device to another format or device.

In database management, for example, the database index provides a way of mapping the actual records (which are stored on disk in a fixed order) to the display screen in useful ways.

**marquee**    In Microsoft Excel, a moving dotted line that surrounds a cell or a range of cells that you have cut or copied.

**mask**    A pattern of symbols or characters that, when imposed on a data field, limits the kinds of characters that you can type into the field.

In a database management program, for example, the mask *Az* enables you to type any alphabetical character, uppercase or lowercase, but not numbers or other symbols.

**mass storage**    See *secondary storage*.

**master boot record**    See *boot record*.

**master document**    In word processing, a document that contains commands that tell the program to print additional documents at the commands' locations. The program prints all the documents as though they were one. See *chain printing*.

**masthead**   In desktop publishing, the section of a newsletter or magazine that gives the details of its staff, ownership, advertising, subscription prices, and so on.

**math coprocessor**   See *numeric coprocessor*.

**maximize**   To zoom or enlarge a window so that it fills the screen.

In Microsoft Windows, you maximize a window by clicking the maximize button (the top arrow in the upper right corner) or by choosing Maximize from the Control menu. See *Microsoft Windows* and *minimize*.

**MB**   Abbreviation for *megabyte* (1,048,576 bytes).

**MCA**   See *Micro Channel Architecture*.

**MCGA**   See *MultiColor Graphics Array (MCGA)*.

**MCI**   See *Media Control Interface (MCI)*.

**MDA**   See *Monochrome Display Adapter (MDA)*.

**mean time between failures (MTBF)**   The statistical average operating time between the start of a component's life and the time of its first electronic or mechanical failure.

 You should not take MTBF figures too seriously when comparison shopping. The figures stem from laboratory tests performed under extreme conditions; the results are then statistically extrapolated to determine the MTBF. Little pressure exists for manufacturers to use an extrapolation procedure that revises the MTBF figure downward.

**mechanicals**   In desktop publishing, the final pages or boards with pasted-up galleys of type and line art, sometimes with acetate or tissue overlays for color separations and notes, which you send to the offset printer. See *camera-ready copy* and *desktop publishing (DTP)*.

**media**   The plural of medium. See *secondary storage medium*.

**Media Control Interface (MCI)**   In Microsoft Windows, the multimedia extensions that greatly simplify the task of programming multimedia device functions such as Stop, Play, and Record. See *multimedia extensions*.

**Media Player**   An accessory provided with Microsoft Windows 3.1 that provides a control center for multimedia devices, such as CD-ROM drives. The buttons resemble the familiar controls of a tape player (see fig. M.1).

**Fig. M.1.** Microsoft Windows' Media Player.

**meg**   Common abbreviation for *megabyte*.

**mega-**   Prefix indicating one million.

**megabyte (M)**   A unit of memory measurement equal to approximately one million bytes (1,048,576 bytes).

**megaflop**   A benchmark used to rate professional workstations and scientific mainframe or minicomputers; a megaflop is equal to one million floating point operations per second.

**megahertz (MHz)**   A unit of measurement equal to one million electrical vibrations or cycles per second; commonly used to compare the clock speeds of computers.

One million cycles per second sounds impressive, but microprocessors actually take three or four clock cycles to execute one instruction. A 1 MHz computer, in fact, is too slow by today's standards; even the 4.77 MHz clock speed of the original IBM Personal Computer is considered sluggish. Clock speeds of 16 MHz, 20 MHz, 25 MHz, and even 33 MHz are increasingly common in personal computing. See *clock speed* and *hertz (Hz)*.

**membrane keyboard**   A flat and inexpensive keyboard covered with a dust- and dirt-proof plastic sheet on which only the two-dimensional outline of computer keys appears.

The user presses the plastic sheet and engages a switch hidden beneath. Accurately typing on a membrane keyboard is more difficult, but such keyboards are needed in restaurants or other locations where users may not have clean hands.

**memory**   The computer's primary storage, such as random-access memory (RAM), as distinguished from its secondary storage, such as disk drives. See *primary storage* and *secondary storage*.

**memory address**   A code number that specifies a specific location in a computer's random-access memory. See *random-access memory (RAM)*.

**memory cache**   See *cache memory*.

**memory controller gate array**   Synonymous with *MultiColor Graphics Array (MCGA)*, a video display standard of the low-end models of IBM's Personal System/2 computers.

**memory-management program**   A utility program that increases the apparent size of random-access memory (RAM) by making expanded memory, extended memory, or virtual memory available for the execution of programs.

Memory-management programs include utilities provided with expanded memory boards, windowing environments such as Microsoft Windows, and virtual memory programs that set aside a portion of a hard disk and treat it as a RAM extension. See *EMM386.EXE*, *expanded memory*, *expanded memory emulator*, *extended memory*, and *HIMEM.SYS*.

**memory map**   An arbitrary allocation of segments of a
computer's primary storage that defines which areas
the computer can use for specific purposes.

Although the Intel 8088 microprocessor can use 1M
of RAM, a portion of this potential memory space is
reserved for the system's use of such functions as the
keyboard buffer and display adapters. User programs
may use the remaining 640K of base memory.

This decision, although arbitrary, is irrevocable if
MS-DOS is involved, because MS-DOS and its application programs cannot operate unless the memory map
remains exactly the way it was laid out when IBM
designed the Personal Computer.

**memory-resident program**   See *terminate-and-stay-
resident (TSR) program*.

**memory word**   See *word*.

**menu**   An on-screen display that lists available command
choices. See *pull-down menu*.

**menu bar**   In industry-standard and graphical user interfaces, a bar stretching across the top of the screen (or
the top of a window) that contains the names of pull-
down menus. See *graphical user interface (GUI)*, *industry-standard user interface*, and *pull-down menu*.

**menu-driven program**   A program that provides you with
menus for choosing program options so that you do
not need to memorize commands. See *command-
driven program*.

**merge printing**   See *mail merge*.

**MFM**   See *Modified Frequency Modulation*.

**MHz**   Abbreviation for *megahertz*.

**micro-**   Prefix indicating one millionth, and an abbreviation
(increasingly rare) for *microcomputer*.

**Micro Channel Architecture (MCA)** The design specifications of IBM's proprietary Micro Channel Bus. An MCA-compatible peripheral is designed to plug directly into a Micro Channel Bus, but will not work with other bus architectures. See *Micro Channel Bus.*

**Micro Channel Bus** A proprietary 32-bit expansion-bus architecture introduced by IBM for its high-end PS/2 computers. The Micro Channel Bus is not downwardly compatible with previous bus architectures.

Given the achievement of 32-bit microprocessors such as the Intel 80386 and 80486, the AT expansion bus, with its 16-bit data bus structure, was destined to receive competition from a true, 32-bit expansion bus.

Almost all non-IBM 80386 computers use a 32-bit bus structure only on the motherboard, where the RAM is linked to the microprocessor. Outside the motherboard, these computers use the 16-bit AT expansion bus, for which a huge supply of cheap peripherals is available. But the improvement of PCs clearly calls for a 32-bit expansion bus. In an attempt to define a 32-bit bus standard, IBM introduced Micro Channel Architecture (MCA) in 1987 and used the Micro Channel Bus on its high-end PS/2 models.

The MCA standard is not downwardly compatible with existing peripherals and adapters designed for the AT expansion bus; therefore, some industry analysts believe that MCA was designed primarily to recapture for IBM part of the lucrative market for peripherals and adapters. But the MCA bus has many technical advantages, including the capability to use 32-bit peripherals, higher speed, greater reliability, and even the capability to use more than one central processing unit (CPU) in one computer.

IBM has offered the technology to clone-makers under a licensing scheme, but few have taken up IBM on the offer. Instead, the major manufacturers of IBM compatibles have offered their own 32-bit bus design, called *Extended Industry Standard Architecture* (EISA), which has most of MCA's benefits but also is compatible with peripherals and adapters designed for the AT expansion bus. See *Extended Industry Standard Architecture (EISA)*.

**microcomputer**　Any computer with its arithmetic-logic unit (ALU) and control unit contained on one integrated circuit, called a *microprocessor*.

When personal computers first appeared in the mid-to-late 1970s, people often referred to them as microcomputers, because their central processing units (CPUs) were microprocessors. Microcomputers were designed as single-user machines. For the first time, microcomputers placed the processing circuitry entirely under the end user's control. Many computing professionals, however, did not take microcomputers seriously at first. For them, "microcomputer" had the connotation of an amusing toy.

Since the mid-1980s, the distinction between minicomputers (as multiuser computers) and microcomputers (as single-user computers) has become blurry. Many microcomputers are substantially more powerful than the mainframes of just ten years ago. You can transform some of today's more powerful microcomputers into minicomputers by equipping them with remote terminals. Also, many of today's minicomputers use microprocessors.

An attempt was made recently to put a mainframe on one large chip, but it failed. Theoretically, however, it is possible, and someday, someone will succeed. Technological change has made the distinction between microcomputers and minicomputers all but meaningless.

Differentiating among these machines by the function they are designed to perform makes the most sense.

- *Centralized Computing Systems.* Designed for use by several users simultaneously, most mainframe and minicomputer systems meet the needs of an organization or a department within an organization. The emphasis in such computer systems is on keeping programs, data, and processing capabilities under central control, so that end users gain access to these systems through remote terminals.

- *Stand-Alone Computers.* Designed for single-user applications, a stand-alone computer such as a personal computer is a self-contained, stand-alone microcomputer that does not rely on external resources such as a central database. A PC is ideal for personal, home, or private use by an individual who does not need to share computing resources with other people.

- *Distributed Computing Systems.* In a distributed system, the object is to get computing power to the user without giving up the means to share external computing resources, such as access to a central database. An example of a distributed computing system is a network of professional workstations.

- *Professional Workstation.* A professional workstation is an advanced microcomputer that contains the advanced display and processing circuitry needed by professionals such as engineers, financial planners, and architects. Because their computers are linked in a computer communications network, these professionals can send messages to each other via their computers, share expensive printers, and create a common pool of data and programs.

Today's advanced personal computers are powerful enough to migrate around these categories with ease. You can use most powerful PCs, for example, as centralized systems with remote terminals. These machines are as powerful as the professional workstations of five years ago and can work smoothly in a distributed computing system.

**microdisk**   See *3 1/2-inch disk*.

**microfloppy**   See *3 1/2 inch disk*.

**micro manager**   The person responsible for managing the acquisition, modification, and maintenance of an organization's personal computers. The micro manager also trains individuals to use application programs.

**microprocessor**  An integrated circuit that contains the arithmetic-logic unit (ALU) and control unit of a computer's central processing unit (CPU). See *Intel 8086*, *Intel 8088*, *Intel 80286*, *Intel 80386DX*, *Intel 80386SX*, *Intel 80486DX*, *Intel 80486SX*, *Motorola 68000*, *Motorola 68020*, and *Motorola 68030*.

**Microsoft Corporation**  A major personal computer software firm, located in Redmond, Washington, that markets MS-DOS, Microsoft Windows, and several market-leading application programs, including Microsoft Word and Microsoft Excel. The firm also offers compilers for a variety of programming languages.

Founded in 1975 by two ex-college students, Bill Gates and Paul Allen, Microsoft's first product was a BASIC interpreter for the Altair 8080 microcomputer. The firm did well with BASIC, but its early success was only a prelude to the rapid growth that followed IBM's selection of Microsoft to develop the operating system for the IBM Personal Computer.

This system, called PC DOS when sold directly to IBM and called MS-DOS when separately marketed by Microsoft, is now the most popular computer operating system in the world, despite its technical shortcomings. Microsoft's future as the key player in personal computing has been assured by the phenomenal success of Microsoft Windows 3.0, which sold more than eight million copies in the year following its 1990 release. A significant 1991 revision of MS-DOS, Version 5.0, remedied many of the operating system's limitations and breathed new life into MS-DOS computing. Microsoft Windows 3.1, released in 1992, addressed significant performance shortcomings of the previous Windows release and solidified Microsoft's claim that Windows represents the future of personal computing. As a measure of Microsoft's success, a 1992 estimate identified Bill Gates as one of the world's wealthiest business leaders.

Microsoft has met with market success in other areas, too. Microsoft Word is second only to WordPerfect in the world of IBM and IBM PC–compatible word processing programs, and Excel, Microsoft's graphics spreadsheet program, dominates the Macintosh and Windows software markets. The firm's 1992 acquisition of Fox Software, Inc., a technologically innovative publisher of dBASE-compatible database management software, remedies the firm's previous deficiencies in database software. See *compiler*, *Microsoft Excel*, *Microsoft Word*, and *MS-DOS*.

**Microsoft Excel**    A graphics-oriented spreadsheet program developed by Microsoft Corporation for IBM PC–compatible computers (running Microsoft Windows) and the Macintosh computer.

Unlike character-based spreadsheets, Excel enables you to use multiple typefaces, type sizes, object-oriented graphics, shading, and even color; you can include business charts and graphs in the output. A significant Excel innovation is the program's toolbar, which places buttons on-screen that initiate automated command sequences. For example, clicking the Chart tool starts ChartWizard, which guides you through the process of creating a chart.

**Microsoft Mouse**    A mouse and associated software for IBM and IBM-compatible personal computers, including IBM's PS/1 and PS/2 computers.

By far the best selling mouse for the IBM environment, the Microsoft Mouse has established a standard that third-party mice must emulate to compete effectively. Available in both serial and bus versions, the Microsoft Mouse employs the optical-mechanical technology that most mouse users favor.

**Microsoft Windows**    A windowing environment and application user interface (API) for DOS that brings to IBM-format computing some of the graphical user interface features of the Macintosh, such as pull-down menus, multiple typefaces, desk accessories (a clock, calculator, calendar, and notepad, for example), and the capability to move text and graphics from one program to another via the Clipboard. Because Windows provides all the functions needed to implement user-interface features such as command menus, windows, and dialog boxes, all Windows applications have a consistent interface (see fig. M.2).

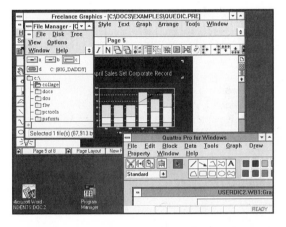

**Fig. M.2**. The Microsoft Windows desktop with several open applications.

The history of Windows shows the reluctance of users and software developers to move to OS/2, the operating system that was supposed to replace MS-DOS. Originally, Windows was to be little more than a preview of OS/2's Presentation Manager. Windows ran the few applications specifically developed for it in a graphical user interface environment, but like MS-DOS, Windows was tied to the 640K random-access memory limit.

Windows used expanded memory schemes such as the Lotus-Intel-Microsoft Specification 4.0, but the new generation of IBM-format programs needed the technically superior protected mode of the Intel 80286 and

80386 microprocessors, with their 16M of undifferentiated memory space. Microsoft had taken the position that protected-mode programs must be developed for OS/2 and Presentation Manager.

As windowing systems such as DESQview (QuarterDeck Systems) appeared, however, with the capability to run MS-DOS programs in protected mode, Microsoft released a new version of Windows, Version 3.0, that runs MS-DOS applications in protected mode. Windows 3.0 was phenomenally successful, exceeding Microsoft's own optimistic forecasts by a wide margin. Within months, Microsoft sold millions of copies of Windows, forcing software publishers to reconsider their plans to develop Windows applications. In the meantime, Microsoft's Windows-compatible applications, Excel and Word for Windows, were poised to grab a commanding share of the lucrative spreadsheet and word processing markets. Many Windows purchasers, however, bought the program to run more than one program at a time and to transfer data between MS-DOS applications via Windows' Clipboard. The leading MS-DOS spreadsheet (Lotus 1-2-3) and word processing program (WordPerfect) were released in Windows versions considerably later, and have not managed to displace the Microsoft applications in software best-seller lists.

The 1992 release of Windows 3.1 consolidated Windows' claim to represent the standard computing platform of the future. It offered major speed improvements, Program Manager enhancements, an expanded an improved File Manager, TrueType font technology, mouse control of MS-DOS applications, improved Help screens, improved multitasking, built-in screen savers, object linking and embedding (OLE) capabilities, and multimedia extensions.

MS-DOS users continue to carp about Windows' performance and the way it insulates the user from the internal workings of the computer, but millions of computer users agree that Microsoft Windows is a joy to use. Many Windows applications are full-featured, beautifully implemented, and consistent with one another, so that learning a new application is easy after mastering the Windows basics. Because the standard Windows hardware platform includes a color VGA monitor, these applications typically implement color in a way that pleases the eye.

The success of Microsoft Windows raises serious questions about the Macintosh's future. Windows has virtually eradicated Apple Computer's once formidable technological edge, with just a few exceptions. For example, the Mac—unlike the run-of-the-mill 80386SX Windows machine—comes equipped with much of its windowing functions encoded in ROM, from which the operating system can retrieve them very rapidly. In addition, all Macs come equipped with digital sound capabilities, and Apple has purchased a revolutionary new voice recognition technology that may make it more possible for users to command their computers by voice. But these advantages are thin in comparison to the huge technological lead the Macintosh once possessed, now withered away by Windows' advance. Windows systems, moreover, are making inroads into vertical market niches once dominated by Macintoshes, such as desktop publishing and multimedia.

 To run Windows, you need much more computing horsepower than you need to run comparable MS-DOS applications. Experienced Windows users agree that a minimal Windows platform includes an 80386SX running at 16 MHz (but preferably 20 or 25 MHz), at least 4M of RAM, an 80M hard disk (yes, a 40M hard disk is too small!), a 16-bit VGA video adapter and VGA monitor, and an inkjet or laser printer capable of printing Window's TrueType fonts. An ideal system? Get an 80486 running at 25 MHz, 8M of RAM, a 200M hard disk, a Super VGA adapter and monitor, and a fast laser printer.

**Microsoft Word**   A full-featured word processing program for MS-DOS, Microsoft Windows, and the Macintosh computer.

Inspired by an on-screen formatting program called Bravo, developed during the 1970s at Xerox's Palo Alto Research Center (PARC), Microsoft Word brings the what-you-see-is-what-you-get philosophy of word processing to the IBM PC–compatible and Macintosh environments.

With its natural affinities to the Macintosh graphical user interface, Microsoft Word for the Mac has assumed a position of dominance. WordPerfect still leads in the PC market, however.

Version 5.5 of Word for the PC offers a list of features competitive with WordPerfect and many features normally associated with page-layout programs, such as the capability to position text or a graphic image on the page so that text flows around it. The program also offers an industry-standard user interface, making it significantly easier to use. Word for Windows, a new Windows version similar to the Macintosh version, rose quickly to dominance in the market for Windows word processing programs. See *what-you-see-is-what-you-get (WYSIWYG)*.

**Microsoft Works**   An easy-to-use integrated program for Macintosh computers and IBM PC compatibles. Works offers a word processing module with a spelling checker, a spreadsheet with business charts, a flat-file database manager, a macro-recording utility, and a telecommunications utility. An object-oriented drawing program is available in the word processing and spreadsheet modules.

Although each of its modules is no match for a full-featured, stand-alone program (such as WordPerfect, Lotus 1-2-3, or dBASE), Works packs an amazing amount of functionality into one package. Each module includes the most frequently used features, omitting the complexity of advanced program functions.

You also can move data around with ease within the program, and the object-oriented drawing program makes it easier to print attractive-looking output. Applications that can be challenging with full-featured programs, such as printing form letters and mailing labels or including a chart in a business report, are easy to accomplish in Works. See *flat-file database integrated program*, *management program*, *module*, and *object-oriented graphic*.

**micro-to-mainframe**   The linkage of personal computer to mainframe or minicomputer networks.

**MIDI**   See *Musical Instrument Digital Interface*.

**MIDI cuing**   In multimedia, a set of MIDI messages that determines the occurrence of events other than musical notes (such as recording, playing back, or turning on lighting devices). See *Musical Instrument Digital Interface (MIDI)*.

**MIDI file**   A file containing musical data encoded according to MIDI specifications. In Microsoft Windows, MIDI files employ the extension MID. See *Musical Instrument Digital Interface (MIDI)*.

**MIDI port**   A port that enables you to connect a personal computer directly to a musical synthesizer.

**migration**   A change from an older computer hardware platform, operating system, or software version to a newer one. For example, industry observers expect corporations to *migrate* from MS-DOS to Microsoft Windows.

**milli-**   Prefix indicating one thousandth.

**million instructions per second (MIPS)**   A benchmark method for measuring the rate at which a computer executes microprocessor instructions. A computer capable of 0.5 MIPS, for example, can execute 500,000 instructions per second.

MIPS ratings are associated with sophisticated mainframes and supercomputers; only recently has the performance of personal computers improved to the point that their processing speed can be described in MIPS. However, MIPS measurements inadequately state a computer system's throughput—a performance measurement that takes into account the speed of internal data transfer to and from the memory and the speed of important peripherals such as disk drives. See *benchmark*, *Norton SI*, *supercomputer*, and *throughput*.

**millisecond (ms)** A unit of measurement, equal to one-thousandth of a second, commonly used to specify the access time of hard disk drives. See *access time*.

**minicomputer** A multiuser computer designed to meet the needs of a small company or a department. A minicomputer is more powerful than a personal computer but not as powerful as a mainframe. Typically, about 4 to 100 people use a minicomputer simultaneously.

**minifloppy** See *5 1/4-inch disk*.

**minimize** In Microsoft Windows, to shrink a window so that it collapses to an icon on the desktop. You minimize a window by clicking the minimize button (the down arrow in the upper right corner) or by choosing Minimize from the Control menu.

 When you minimize a window in Microsoft Windows, the window appears at the bottom of the screen as an icon. If you minimize a lot of windows, the icons may overlap or appear untidy. To tidy up the row of icons, choose Arrange Icons from the Window menu.

**MIPS** See *million instructions per second*.

**MIS** See *management information system*.

**mixed cell reference** In a spreadsheet program, a cell reference in which the column reference is absolute but the row reference is relative ($A9) or in which the row reference is absolute but the column reference is relative (A$9). See *absolute cell reference*, *cell reference*, and *relative cell reference*.

**mixed column/line chart** See *mixed column/line graph*.

**mixed column/line graph** In presentation and analytical graphics, a graph that displays one data series using columns and another data series using lines (see fig. M.3).

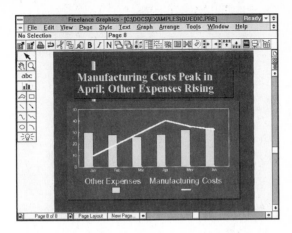

**Fig. M.3.** A mixed column/line graph.

You use a line graph to suggest a trend over time; a
column graph groups data items so that you can compare one to another. In this illustration, for example,
the trends in manufacturing costs, represented by a
line, are compared to expenses, shown as columns.

**mode** The operating state in which you place a program by
choosing among a set of exclusive operating options.
Within a given mode, certain commands and operations are available, but you may need to change modes
to use other commands or operations.

Most programs can function in alternative modes.
For example, Microsoft Word functions in Edit and
Command modes. In Edit mode, you can enter and
edit text. In Command mode, you choose and carry
out commands.

Lotus 1-2-3 always operates in one of the following
modes:

| Mode | Description |
|------|-------------|
| READY | 1-2-3 is waiting for you to enter a command or make a cell entry. |
| VALUE | You are entering a number or formula. |
| LABEL | You are entering a label. |
| EDIT | You can edit the cell entry currently displayed on the control panel. |
| POINT | You can use the arrow keys to expand the highlight and define a range. |
| FILES | 1-2-3 is waiting for you to choose a file name from the list that appears on-screen. |
| NAMES | 1-2-3 is waiting for you to choose a range name from the list that appears on-screen. |
| MENU | You are choosing an item from the command menu. |
| HELP | 1-2-3 is displaying a help screen. |
| ERROR | 1-2-3 could not carry out the command or operation you requested; you must press Esc or Enter to confirm the message and continue. |
| WAIT | 1-2-3 is carrying out an operation and cannot respond to additional commands or keyboard input. |
| FIND | 1-2-3 is carrying out a data retrieval operation and cannot respond to additional commands or keyboard input. |
| STAT | 1-2-3 is displaying the status of your worksheet. |

A key step in learning a program is to understand its modes and how to switch from one mode to another. Beginners may reach a frustrating roadblock when they inadvertently choose an unfamiliar mode and do not know how to exit that mode. Find out where the mode indicator is located on-screen and learn what the messages mean. See *mode indicator*.

**mode indicator**   An on-screen message that displays the program's current operating mode.

In Lotus 1-2-3, for example, the mode indicator appears in reverse video at the upper right corner of the screen.

**model**   A mathematical or pictorial representation of an object or system that exists in the real world, such as an aircraft fuselage or a business's cash flow.

The purpose of constructing a model is to gain a better understanding of the prototype in a cost-effective way. By examining or changing the characteristics of the model, you can draw inferences about the prototype's behavior. In a spreadsheet model of a business enterprise, for example, you can explore the impact of increasing advertising expenditures on market share.

Use a model with caution. A model is only as good as its underlying assumptions. If these assumptions are incorrect, or if important information is missing from the model, it may not reflect the prototype's behavior accurately. Many spreadsheet programs enable you to use a linear regression analysis to predict future values based on data from the past; however, the prediction won't be accurate unless you include in the analysis all possible factors   an impossible task, in many situations. For example, you could predict future sales based on past sales data for your five-and-dime store, but the prediction won't be accurate if Wal-Mart opens a store next door to yours.

**modem**   A device that converts the digital signals generated by the computer's serial port to the modulated, analog signals required for transmission over a telephone line and, likewise, transforms incoming analog signals to their digital equivalents. In personal computing, people frequently use modems to exchange programs and data with other computers, and to access on-line information services such as the Dow Jones News/Retrieval Service.

Modem stands for *modulator/demodulator*. The modulation is necessary because telephone lines are designed to handle the human voice, which warbles between 300 and 3,000 Hz in ordinary telephone conversations (from a growl to a shriek). The speed at which a modem transmits data is measured in units called *bits per second* (technically not the same as bauds, although the terms are often used interchangeably). See *acoustic coupler*, *auto-dial/auto-answer modem*, *direct-connect modem*, *echoplex*, *external modem*, *full duplex*, *half duplex*, *Hayes command set*, *Hayes-compatible modem*, *internal modem*, and *Universal Asynchronous Receiver/Transmitter (UART)*.

**Modified Frequency Modulation (MFM)**   A method of recording digital information on magnetic media such as tapes and disks by eliminating redundant or blank areas. Because the MFM data-encoding scheme doubles the storage attained under the earlier frequency-modulation (FM) recording technique, MFM recording usually is referred to as *double density*.

MFM often is used erroneously to describe ordinary hard disk controllers, those conforming to the ST-506/ST-412 standard. MFM refers to the method used to pack data on the disk and is not synonymous with disk drive interface standards such as ST506, SCSI, or ESDI. See *data-encoding scheme*, *double density*, *interface standard*, and *Run-Length Limited (RLL)*.

**Modula-2**   A high-level programming language that extends Pascal so that the language can execute program modules independently.

Developed in 1980 by the European computer wizard Niklaus Wirth, the creator of Pascal, Modula-2 is an enhanced version of Pascal that supports the separate compilation of program modules and overcomes many other shortcomings of Pascal. A programmer working on a team can write and compile the module he or she has been assigned, testing the module extensively to make sure that it functions correctly.

Although Modula-2 is increasingly popular as a teaching language at colleges and universities, the C language dominates professional software development. See *C, modular programming, Pascal*, and *structured programming*.

**modular accounting package**   A collection of accounting programs—one for each of the chief accounting functions (general ledger, accounts payable, accounts receivable, payroll, and inventory, for example)— designed to work together, even though they are not integrated into one program.

Modular accounting programs are computerized versions of traditional accounting practices, in which a firm keeps several ledgers: one for accounts receivable, another for accounts payable, and a general ledger. You update the general ledger in batches at period intervals after carefully proofing the hard copy for errors. Modular packages generally are sold with several separate programs for each of these functions, and you must follow special procedures to make sure that all the transactions are correctly updated.

These programs have not found a large market in personal computing for two reasons. First, because people with professional accounting experience designed them, these programs often do not reflect the way people in small businesses keep their books. Second, most of these programs are far from easy to use.

Some of these packages, however, are available with automatic links to point-of-sale terminals—for example,

Flexware (Microfinancial Corporation) for Macintosh computers and Excalibur (Armour Systems, Inc.) for IBM PC–compatible computers.

**modular programming**   A programming style that breaks down program functions into modules, each of which accomplishes one function and contains all the codes and variables needed to accomplish that function.

Modular programming is a solution to the problem of very large programs that are difficult to debug and maintain. By segmenting the program into modules that perform clearly defined functions, you can determine the source of program errors more easily.

Modula-2 and some other languages can compile modules separately. A member of a team working on a program, therefore, can write and compile his or her module independent of the whole program and of other team members, making sure that the module works properly before adding it to the larger program.

Modular programming principles have clearly influenced the design of object-oriented programming languages such as SmallTalk and HyperTalk, both of which enable you to create fully functional program objects (such as the buttons in HyperCard) which function so independently that you can copy them from one program to another.

**modulation**   The conversion of a digital signal to its analog equivalent, especially for the purposes of transmitting signals via telecommunications. See *demodulation* and *modem*.

**module**   In a computer program, a unit or section capable of functioning on its own. In an integrated program, for instance, you can use the word processing module as if it were a separate, stand-alone program.

**Moiré distortion**   Pronounced "mwah-ray'." An optical illusion, perceived as flickering, that sometimes occurs when you place high-contrast line patterns (such as cross-hatching in pie graphs) too close to one another.

Many business graphics programs produce charts and graphs with undesirable Moiré distortions. You can avoid this problem by choosing no more than two or three cross-hatching patterns and separating them with solid white, gray, or black colors. See *cross-hatching*.

**monitor**   The complete device that produces an on-screen display, including all necessary internal support circuitry. A monitor also is called a *video display unit* (VDU) or *cathode-ray tube* (CRT). See *analog monitor*, *digital monitor*, *Enhanced Graphics Display*, *monochrome monitor*, and *multisync monitor*.

**monochrome display adapter (MDA)**   A single-color display adapter for IBM PC–compatible computers that displays text (but not graphics) with a resolution of 720 pixels horizontally and 350 lines vertically, placing characters in a matrix of 7 by 9. See *Hercules Graphics Adapter*.

**monochrome monitor**   A monitor that displays one color against a black or white background.

Examples include the IBM monochrome monitor that displays green text against a black background, and paper-white VGA monitors that display black text on a white background.

**monospace**   A typeface such as Courier in which the width of each character is the same, producing output that looks like typed characters. See *proportional spacing*.

**motherboard**   A large computer circuit board that contains the computer's central processing unit (CPU), microprocessor support chips, random-access memory, and expansion slots. Synonymous with *logic board*.

**Motorola 68000**   A microprocessor that processes 32 bits internally, although it uses a 16-bit data bus to communicate with the rest of the computer.

The 68000, with its 32-bit address bus, can address up to 32 gigabytes of random-access memory (RAM). Running at 8 MHz, the 68000 powers the entry-level Macintosh Classic.

Avoid purchasing Macs powered by 68000 chips. Today's software designers assume that you're using a peppier machine.

**Motorola 68020**   A microprocessor electronically similar to the Motorola 68000, except that this microprocessor uses a full 32-bit architecture and runs at a clock speed of 16 MHz.

The 68020 powers the original Macintosh II, displaced by newer models using the Motorola 68030 chip. Macintosh system software limits the amount of usable RAM to 8M (Apple's System 7 boosts this amount to 4 gigabytes).

**Motorola 68030**   A full 32-bit microprocessor capable of running at substantially higher clock speeds (16 to 50 MHz) than its predecessors, the Motorola 68000 and 68020. The 68030 includes special features for virtual memory management.

The 68030 incorporates a chip that controls page-mode RAM, so that any 68030-equipped Macintosh can implement the advanced memory management features of System.

If you are buying a Mac, purchase a machine based on the 68030. The chip includes circuits that you need to take full advantage of System 7. See *clock speed*, *page-mode RAM*, and *System* 7.

**Motorola 68040**   A 32-bit microprocessor in Motorola's 680x0 family that represents an evolutionary advance over its immediate predecessor, the 68030. Analogous to the Intel 80486DX microprocessor, the 68040 packs more circuitry into its tiny confines, reducing the need for support chips and improving performance. For example, the 68040 includes a numeric (floating-point) coprocessor, eliminating the need for a coprocessor chip. The 68040 powers the high-end Quadra models of Apple's Macintosh computers.

**Motorola 68881**   The numeric coprocessor used with the Motorola 68000 and 68020 microprocessors. See *numeric coprocessor*.

**mount**   To insert a disk into a disk drive.

**mousable interface**   A program's user interface that responds to mouse input for such functions as selecting text, choosing commands from menus, and scrolling the screen.

**mouse**   An input device, equipped with one or more control buttons, that is housed in a palm-sized case and designed so that you can roll it about on the table, next to your keyboard. As the mouse moves, its circuits relay signals that correspondingly move a pointer on-screen.

The simplest of all mouse functions is repositioning the cursor: you point to the cursor's new location and click the mouse button. You also can use the mouse to choose commands from menus, select text for editing purposes, move objects, and draw pictures on-screen.

The mouse was developed by researchers to make computers easier to use. Instead of forcing users to memorize long lists of keyboard commands, they reasoned, displaying a menu or list of commands on-screen would be easier. The user then could point the cursor at the desired command and click the mouse button.

Most people who have used a mouse agree that it makes the computer easier to use. Others, however, do not like to take their fingers away from the keyboard. Programs that use the mouse often include keyboard equivalents.

Mice are distinguished by the internal mechanism they use to generate their signal and by their means of connection with the computer. Two types of internal mechanisms are popular:

- *Mechanical mouse.* This mouse has a rubber-coated ball on the underside of the case. As you move the mouse, the ball rotates and optical sensors detect the motion. (Many companies, therefore, advertise their mice as "optomechanical.") You can use a mechanical mouse on virtually any surface, although a mouse pad made of special fabric usually gives the best results.

- *Optical mouse.* This mouse registers its position by detecting reflections from a light-emitting diode that directs a beam downward. You must have a special metal pad to reflect the beam properly, and you cannot move the mouse beyond the pad.

Mice are connected to the computer in the following three ways:

- *Bus mouse.* You connect a bus mouse to the computer with an adapter that you press into one of the computer's expansion slots.

- *Serial mouse.* You connect a serial mouse to the computer via the standard serial port.

- *Regular mouse.* You connect most mice to a special mouse port on the computer.

 Mechanical mice are prone to collect dirt within their internal mechanisms. If too much debris accumulates, the pointer may behave erratically. You usually can clean a mechanical mouse. Turn the mouse over and rotate the ball-retainer ring so that it pops out, freeing the ball. Clean the ball and the ball rollers with a cotton swab moistened in rubbing alcohol. Blow dust out of the ball chamber and reassemble the mouse.

**MPC**   See *Multimedia Personal Computer.*

**ms**   See *millisecond.*

**MS-DOS**   The standard, single-user operating system of IBM and IBM-compatible computers.

Introduced in 1981, MS-DOS (Microsoft Disk Operating System) is marketed by IBM as PC DOS; the two systems are almost indistinguishable.

MS-DOS's origins lie in CP/M—the operating system for 8-bit computers popular in the late 1970s. The original version of what was to become MS-DOS was created for experimental purposes by a small Seattle firm. Because Microsoft had landed an IBM contract to create an operating system for the IBM Personal Computer, Microsoft purchased and developed the program.

The similarity between MS-DOS and CP/M is no accident—MS-DOS was designed to enable an inexpensive and fast conversion of popular CP/M business programs to the new IBM Personal Computer. IBM analysts thought that their new computer would not succeed unless software publishers could rewrite their programs with a minimum of expense. The chief advantages of MS-DOS over CP/M are that some commands were improved and that you couldn't crash the computer by removing a disk before rebooting the system. In addition, Version 2.0 of MS-DOS added UNIX-like directories and subdirectories to the system, enhancing its usefulness with hard disks. Even the most recent versions of MS-DOS are still compatible with Version 2.0.

Although the IBM Personal Computer architecture supports up to 640K of RAM, the earliest IBM PCs were sold with 64K (a standard figure in 1981). MS-DOS was designed as an extremely compact operating system that could operate under severely limited memory conditions. MS-DOS, therefore, provides little in the way of an application program interface (API) or a set of standard routines that applications can use to handle the display of information on-screen. Individual applications are free to configure the screen and keyboard as they like, and the result is a jumble of confusing and mutually incompatible user interfaces.

MS-DOS is a command-line operating system with an interface that requires you to memorize a limited set of commands, arguments, and syntax to use MS-DOS computers successfully. After mastering MS-DOS commands, however, you can achieve a high degree of control over the operating system's capabilities—including setting file attributes, creating automatically executed batch files, and developing semi-automated backup procedures.

The most severe limitation of MS-DOS is the 640K RAM barrier that the operating system imposes on IBM PC–compatible computing. When the system was devised, 640K seemed like a copious amount of memory; however, the creation of applications such as Lotus 1-2-3 and the advent of terminate-and-stay resident (TSR) programs soon demonstrated that 640K was barely adequate even for a stand-alone workstation.

Operating systems that offer an API—the Macintosh System, for example—encourage the development of programs that use the same user actions and interface procedures for common operations such as selecting and deleting text, using menus, opening and closing applications, and printing. Recognizing the advantages of an API, Microsoft developed Windows, an optional API for MS-DOS. Windows solves almost all of MS-DOS's problems: Windows breaks the 640K RAM barrier, enables you to run more than one program at a time, provides an easy-to-use graphical user interface, and greatly simplifies program installation and configuration. To use Windows efficiently, however, you must understand MS-DOS file name restrictions and subdirectories. This limitation is expected to disappear in the next version of Windows, Windows NT, which will replace MS-DOS entirely.

Although many users are migrating to Windows, millions of older IBM PC and compatible computers exist that are not capable of running Windows well. MS-DOS is unquestionably the world's most widely used operating system and is likely to remain so for years to come.

## *MS-DOS Features*

| Version Number | Features |
|---|---|
| 1.25 | 320K floppy disk support |
| 2.0 | 360K floppy disk support |
| | ANSI display driver |
| | CONFIG.SYS file |
| | Device drivers |
| | File handles |
| | Filters |
| | Hard disk support |
| | Hierarchical file systems |
| | Improved batch program language |
| | Input/output redirection |
| | International features |
| | More file attributes |
| | Pipes |
| | Print spooling |
| | Volume labels |
| 3.0 | 1.2M floppy disk support |
| | Clock/calendar board support |
| | File locking |
| | Multiple hard disk partitions |
| | Network support |
| | RAM disk |
| 3.1 | Network drives |
| | Network file sharing |
| 3.2 | 3 1/2-inch 720K floppy disk support |
| | XCOPY command |
| 3.3 | 3 1/2-inch 1.44M floppy disk support |
| | Multiple 32M hard disk partitions |
| 4.0 | Hard disk partitions to 2 gigabytes |
| | Memory drivers |
| | MS-DOS Shell |

| Version Number | Features |
| --- | --- |
| 5.0 | 2.88M floppy disk support |
| | Accesses more than two hard disks |
| | Device drivers in upper memory |
| | Directory sorting with DIR |
| | DOS in high memory area (HMA) |
| | Doskey macros |
| | Improved hard disk partition |
| | MS-DOS Editor (full-screen editor) |
| | MS-DOS QBasic (improved BASIC) |
| | MS-DOS Shell improved |
| | On-line help for MS-DOS commands |
| | Undelete command |
| | Unformat command |

 For maximum performance with Microsoft Windows, upgrade to MS-DOS 5.0, which takes full advantage of all your system's memory. See *application program interface (API)*, *CP/M*, *Microsoft Windows*, *MS-DOS QBasic*, *MS-DOS Shell*, *Operating System/2 (OS/2)*, *Presentation Manager*, *protected mode*, *real mode*, *terminate-and-stay-resident (TSR) program*, and *UNIX*.

**MS-DOS QBasic**   An improved BASIC programming environment, supplied with MS-DOS 5.0 and later, that includes extensive on-line help.

**MS-DOS Shell**   An improved, menu-driven user interface for the MS-DOS operating system, supplied with MS-DOS 5.0 and later, that conforms to the industry-standard user interface.

MS-DOS Shell provides menu-driven access to most DOS commands. Using Shell, you can copy, delete, move, and rename files; back up and restore a hard disk; format disks and recover from an accidental format of the wrong disk; undelete files that were deleted accidentally; create and remove directories; and even view and edit file attributes. In other words, MS-DOS Shell finally provides much of the functionality that has long been missing from MS-DOS. Users may find less need for utility packages such as PC Tools.

**MTBF**   See *Mean Time Between Failures*.

**MultiColor Graphics Array (MCGA)**   A video display standard of IBM's Personal System/2. MCGA adds 64 grayscale shades to the CGA standard and provides the EGA standard resolution of 640 pixels by 350 lines with 16 possible colors.

**MultiFinder**   A utility program, supplied by Apple Computer, that extends the Finder's capabilities so that the Macintosh can run more than one application at a time. System 7 incorporates MultiFinder, which no longer is a separate utility.

The Finder—the Macintosh operating system's shell—is the program that handles communication with the user. The Finder can handle only one program at a time.

With MultiFinder, the Macintosh becomes a multiloading operating system with some limited capabilities to perform tasks in the background, such as downloading information via telecommunications and carrying out background printing.

Contrary to common belief, MultiFinder is not a true multitasking operating system; when you activate one application, the other application freezes. See *context switching*, *multiple program loading*, *multitasking*, *shell*, and *System 7*.

**multilaunching**   In a local area network, the opening of an application program by more than one user at a time.

**multilevel sort**   In database management, a sort operation that uses two or more data fields to determine the order in which data records are arranged.

To perform a multilevel sort, you identify two or more fields as sort keys—fields used for ordering record.

In a library's bibliographic database, for example, the primary sort key is LAST_NAME. All records are alphabetized by the author's last name. The second sort key, FIRST_NAME, comes into play when two or more records have the same last name. A third sort key, PUB_DATE (publication date), is used when two or more records have the the the same last name and the same first name. The following sample is the properly sorted output:

```
Smith, Bill
        1990   101 Fonts for Desktop
               Publishing
Smith, Fern
        1986   Organic Gardening
Smith, Jack
        1987   The American Space Program
        1989   The Soviet Space Program
        1991   Private Ventures into Space
```

 Use a multilevel sort when one sort key cannot resolve the order of two or more records in your database.

**MultiMate**    A word processing program marketed by Ashton-Tate that emulates the Wang dedicated word processing machines.

**multimedia**    A computer-based method of presenting information by employing more than one medium of communication and emphasizing interactivity. In general, multimedia combines text, graphics, and sound.

In an auditorium, a 35mm slide show with background music employs multiple media, but it's not *multimedia*: the term strongly implies interactivity and user involvement. The computer makes interactivity possible. In a multimedia presentation called Beethoven's World, for example, you can see portraits of the composer, hear his music, and even print scores (see fig. M.4). Advances in sound and video synchronization enable you to display moving video images within on-screen windows (see fig. M.5).

**Fig. M.4.** A multimedia application.

**Fig. M.5.** A segment of a full-motion video image in a multimedia application.

Because graphics and sound require so much storage space, a minimal configuration for a multimedia system includes a CD-ROM drive.

 Windows users should look for multimedia products (including CD-ROM drives and software) that have the MPC label. This label is your assurance that the product fully conforms to the MPC standards and will function correctly with Microsoft Windows. See *Multimedia Personal Computer (MPC)*.

**multimedia extensions** Additions to an operating system that enable multimedia software to synchronize graphics and sound. These extensions—called "hooks" in programmers' slang—allow multimedia software designers to access sound and video capabilities without extensive, nonstandard programming. Apple's Quick-Time is a multimedia extension to its System 7 software. Windows 3.1 includes the multimedia extensions (called Media Control Interface, or MCI) that were formerly available separately.

Multimedia extensions provide an application program interface (API) for multimedia software developers, who can make use of the multimedia hooks for such tasks as accessing a CD-ROM drive or playing a sound. Using the hooks is much easier than writing all the code needed to access the multimedia hardware directly. Early multimedia programs were tied to specific brands and models of CD-ROM drives because no such hooks existed and, in consequence, the programmers had to write code that accesses the drive directly. With multimedia extensions, however, you can use any CD-ROM player (or any other compatible multimedia device) supported by the system software. See *application program interface (API), Microsoft Windows, multimedia, QuickTime,* and *Media Control Interface (MCI)*.

**Multimedia Personal Computer (MPC)** A standard for multimedia hardware and software jointly developed by the MPC Consortium, which includes Microsoft, Philips, Tandy, and Zenith Data Systems. Microsoft Windows 3.1, which incorporates multimedia extensions that used to be packaged separately, provides the foundation for MPC. The MPC standard assumes an IBM PS/2 or IBM-compatible hardware platform; Apple Computer, not surprisingly, has offered a competing standard (QuickTime) for its Macintosh computer.

An MPC-capable IBM-compatible system includes, minimally, an 80386SX computer running at 20 MHz, 2M of RAM, a VGA graphics display adapter and monitor, a hard disk, a joystick, Microsoft Windows 3.1, a mouse, and an MPC-compatible CD-ROM drive. For high-quality sound, you need a sound adapter. See *CD-ROM, multimedia,* and *QuickTime.*

**multiple program loading** An operating system that enables you to start more than one program at a time; only one of the programs is active at any one time, however. You press a key to switch from one program to another. See *context switching* and *MultiFinder.*

**multiple selection** In an electronic spreadsheet program, a selection of two or more noncontiguous ranges. In figure M.6, for example, you see three ranges selected. Multiple selection is a very desirable feature in spreadsheet programs because it allows you to apply formats and perform other operations on more than one range at a time.

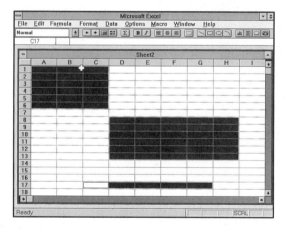

**Fig. M.6.** Multiple selection of ranges.

**multiplex**  To combine or interleave messages in a communications channel.

**multiplexing**  In local area networks, the simultaneous transmission of multiple messages in one channel.

A network capable of multiplexing can enable more than one computer to access the network simultaneously. Multiplexing increases the cost of a network, however, because multiplexing devices must be included that can mix the signals into a single channel for transmission. See *frequency division multiplexing*, *local area network (LAN)*, and *time division multiplexing*.

**multisync monitor**  A color monitor capable of adjusting to a range of input frequencies so that it can work with a variety of display adapters.

**multitasking**  The execution of more than one program at a time on a computer system. Multitasking should not be confused with multiple program loading, in which two or more programs are present in RAM but only one program executes at a time.

The active, or foreground, task responds to the keyboard while the background task continues to run (but without your active control).

In a multitasking operating system, terminate-and-stay-resident (TSR) programs are unnecessary, because you simultaneously can run any programs you want to, as long as the computer has enough memory.

Critics of multitasking operating systems say that users of stand-alone workstations have little need for multiprogramming operations. Programs that can print or download files in the background, however, hint at the power of multitasking. Imagine being able to write with your word processing program at the same time that your spreadsheet program prints a lengthy report.

Among the operating systems or shells that provide multitasking are OS/2 and Microsoft Windows. See *Microsoft Windows*, *multiple program loading*, and *Operating System/2 (OS/2)*.

**multiuser system**   A computer system that enables more than one person to access programs and data at the same time.

Each user is equipped with a terminal. If the system has just one central processing unit, a technique called *time-sharing* provides multiple access. A time-sharing system cycles access to the processing unit among users.

Personal computers equipped with advanced microprocessors such as the Intel 80486 are sufficiently powerful to serve as the nucleus of a multiuser system. Such systems typically are equipped with the UNIX operating system, designed for multiuser systems.

Such technical advances have helped blur the distinction between personal computers and minicomputers. If a minicomputer is a multiuser system designed to meet the needs of 4 to 100 people, multiuser computers based on 80386 and 80486 chips are legitimate minicomputers. Given such advances, the term *personal computer* usually is reserved for computers dedicated to stand-alone applications.

 If you are considering installing a system that more than one person will use, familiarize yourself with the pros and cons of the two alternatives: multiuser systems and local area networks. See *local area network (LAN)* and *time-sharing*.

**Musical Instrument Digital Interface (MIDI)**   A standard communications protocol for the exchange of information between computers and musical synthesizers.

MIDI provides tools that many composers and musicians say are becoming almost indispensable. With a synthesizer and a computer equipped with the necessary software and a MIDI port, a musician can transcribe a composition into musical notation by playing the composition at the keyboard. After being placed into computer-represented form, virtually every aspect of the digitized sound—pitch, attack, delay time, tempo, and more—can be edited and altered.

**nano-**   A prefix indicating one-billionth.

**nanosecond (ns)**   A unit of time equal to one billionth of a second.

Far beyond the range of human perception, nanoseconds are relevant to computers. For example, an advertisement for 120 ns RAM chips means that the RAM chips respond within 120 nanoseconds. Macintosh computers with the 68030 microprocessor need faster RAM chips, 80 ns or better. See *millisecond (ms)*.

**National Television Standards Committee (NTSC)**   A standards organization that governs standards for television broadcasting in the United States and most of Central and South America (but not Europe or Asia). NTSC television uses 525-line frames and displays full frames at 30 frames per second, employing two interlaced fields at about 60 frames per second to correspond to the U.S. alternating-current frequency of 60 Hz. NTSC video connections employ standard RCA phonograph plugs and jacks.

Television engineers joke that NTSC really stands for "Never Twice the Same Color," because the NTSC standard provides poor color control. Most European and Asian countries use the PAL standard based on their 50-Hz power-line frequencies.

**native code**   See *machine language*.

**native file format**   The default file format an application program uses to store data on disk.

The format is often a proprietary file format that cannot be read by other programs; however, many programs can save data in several formats. See *ASCII*, *file format*, and *proprietary file format*.

**natural language**   A naturally occurring language such as Spanish, French, German, or Tamil, unlike an artificial language such as a computer programming language.

Computer scientists are working to improve computers so that they can respond to natural language. Human language systems are so complex that no single theoretical model of a natural language grammar system has yet to gain widespread acceptance among linguists. The complexity of human languages, coupled with the lack of understanding about precisely what information is needed to decode naturally occurring human sentences, makes it difficult to devise programs that recognize speech. The recognition of human speech patterns also poses substantial problems in pattern recognition, and progress in solving these problems has been slow.

Computer programs such as Lotus HAL occasionally are marketed with the claim that they can accept natural language input, but your input must be phrased so that it conforms to fairly strict syntax guidelines. Because no computer program yet devised can understand the meaning of spoken words, natural-language programs must use relatively crude pattern-matching techniques to accept such input.

**natural recalculation**   In a spreadsheet program, a recalculation order that performs worksheet computations in the manner logically dictated by the formulas you place in cells. If the value of a formula depends on references to other cells that contain formulas, the program calculates the other cells first. See *column-wise recalculation*, *optimal recalculation*, and *row-wise recalculation*.

**near–letter quality (NLQ)**   A dot-matrix printing mode that prints typewriter-quality characters. As a result, printers using this mode print slower than other dot-matrix printers.

**needle drop**   In multimedia, the use of a short excerpt from a recorded musical piece instead of creating an original composition. The term stems from days of vinyl and phonograph needles.

Do not use recorded music in your multimedia presentations without first seeking permission and paying the required needle-drop fee.

**nested structure**   A structure in which one control structure is positioned within another. See *control structure* and *DO/WHILE loop*.

**NetBIOS**   See *Network Basic Input/Output System*.

**NETNORTH**   A Canadian wide-area network fully integrated with BITNET and that performs the same functions as BITNET. See *BITNET*.

**NetWare**   A network operating system, manufactured by Novell, for local area networks.

NetWare links hardware and accommodates more than 90 types of network interface cards, 30 network architectures, and several communications protocols. Versions are available for IBM PC compatibles and Macintosh computers. See *network operating system (NOS)*.

**network**   A computer-based communications and data exchange system created by physically connecting two or more computers.

Personal computer networks differ in their scope. The smallest networks, called *local area networks* (LANs), may connect just two or three computers so that they can share an expensive peripheral, such as a laser printer. Some LANs connect as many as 75 or more computers. Larger networks, called *wide area networks* (WANs), employ telephone lines or other long-distance communications media to link the computers together.

Personal computer networks also differ in their topology, the geometry of their connections. Common personal computer network topologies include the star topology, in which machines are linked to a central file server, and the bus topology, in which machines are linked to a single backbone cable.

Several competing standards govern the communications standard by which data is exchanged in networks.

Built into all Macintosh computers is AppleTalk, a low-bandwidth network protocol suitable for small networks. Larger networks can employ EtherNet or IBM's token-ring network. See *bus network, local area network (LAN), network architecture, network operating system (NOS), network protocol, network topology, star network,* and *token-ring network.*

**network administrator**   In local area networks, the person responsible for maintaining the network and assisting its users.

**network architecture**   The complete set of hardware, software, and cabling standards that specifies the design of a local area network. See *network topology.*

**Network Basic Input/Output System (NetBIOS)**   A system program included in MS-DOS (Version 3.1 and later) that establishes standard methods for linking personal computers to local area networks.

**network drive**   In a local area network, a disk drive made available to you through the network, as distinguished from a drive connected directly to the workstation you're using.

 In a DOS network, local drives are labeled *A, B, C, D,* or *E;* network drives have a letter chosen from the rest of the alphabet.

**network interface card**   An adapter that enables you to hook a network cable directly to a microcomputer.

Rather than forcing network communications to occur through the serial port, a network interface card takes advantage of a microcomputer's internal bus to make network communications easier.

The board includes encoding and decoding circuitry and a receptacle for a network cable connection. Because data is transmitted more rapidly within the computer's internal bus, a network interface card enables the network to operate at higher speeds than it would if delayed by the serial port.

Networks such as EtherNet and ARCnet, which use interface cards, can transmit information much faster than networks such as AppleTalk, which uses serial ports.

**network operating system (NOS)**   The system software of a local area network that integrates the network's hardware components. Network operating systems for personal computers usually provide facilities adequate for connecting up to approximately 50 workstations. Included, typically, are such features as a menu-driven administration interface, tape backup of file server software, security restrictions, facilities for sharing printers, central storage of network-capable applications and databases, remote log-in via modem, and support for diskless workstations.

Crucial to the network's operation, a network operating system establishes and maintains the connection between the workstations and the file server; the physical connections alone are not sufficient to support networking. A network operating system consists of two parts: the file server software and workstation software.

 The workstation software can consume enough base memory to prevent you from running MS-DOS applications. When considering a network, find out how much workstation memory is required, and whether it's possible to store some or all of it in extended or expanded memory. See *file server, local area network (LAN), Microsoft LAN Manager, Novell NetWare,* and *workstation*.

**network printer**   In a local area network, a printer made available to you through the network, as distinguished from a local printer (a printer connected directly to the workstation you're using).

**network protocol**   The method by which a workstation's access to a computer network is governed to prevent data collisions. Examples include carrier sense multiple access with collision detection (CSMA/CD) and token passing. See *carrier sense multiple access with collision detection (CSMA/CD)* and *token passing*.

**network server**   See *file server*.

**network topology**   The geometric arrangement of nodes and cable links in a local area network.

Network topologies fall into two categories: centralized and decentralized. In a centralized topology such as a star network, a central computer controls access to the network. This design ensures data security and central management control over the network's contents and activities.

In a decentralized topology such as a bus network or ring network, no central computer controls the network's activities; rather, each workstation can access the network independently and establish its own connections with other workstations. See *bus network*, *ring network*, and *star network*.

**newspaper columns**   A page format in which two or more columns of text are printed vertically on the page so that the text flows down one column and continues at the top of the next (see fig. N.1).

**Fig. N.1.** Newspaper columns.

Sometimes called *snaking columns* to suggest the flow of text, newspaper columns differ from side-by-side columns, in which paragraphs are printed in linked pairs—one to the left and one to the right.

Many word processing programs and all page-layout programs can print multiple-column text, but only the best programs can display multiple columns on-screen while you edit the text. High-end word processing programs such as Microsoft Word and WordPerfect do a good job of producing newspaper columns, but you need a page-layout program such as Ventura Publisher to justify the columns vertically so that all columns align precisely with the bottom margin.

Vertical justification is by no means necessary, but newspapers and magazines often use vertical justification to create a professional-looking effect. You can accomplish vertical justification manually with a word processing program, but the operation is tedious, and the columns may fall out of alignment if you add or delete text.

 Research on legibility demonstrates that a line should have approximately 55 to 60 characters (about nine or ten words) for optimum readability. If line lengths exceed this amount, break up the text into two or more columns.

**NeXT**   An innovative, UNIX-based professional workstation developed by NeXT, Inc.

The NeXT series of professional workstations is the brainchild of Steve Jobs, the cofounder of Apple Computer and a guiding figure in the development of the Macintosh. A disappointing product release in 1988 was followed by the 1990 release of four competitively priced workstations, all based on the Motorola 68040 microprocessor. All four NeXT workstations drive the 68040 at 25 MHz and optionally can be equipped with high-resolution color displays. NeXT products are earning an enviable reputation for engineering innovation, excellence, and value.

Originally aimed at the higher education market, NeXT's goals have changed: the company now targets the lower end of the professional workstation market, currently dominated by Sun and other workstation makers. Compared to comparable products from workstation makers, and to high-end Macintosh systems, NeXT's offerings are competitively priced.

A significant advantage of the NeXT environment is NeXTStep, an integrated windowing environment and application development system. NeXT computers run Berkeley 4.3 UNIX, normally an impediment to user-friendly operation, but NeXT's programmers have created a graphical user interface for UNIX that makes it unnecessary to enter UNIX commands directly. On-screen, you see precisely the same fonts that print on the system's 400-dpi laser printer, thanks to the computer's use of Display PostScript. Programmers can draw from NeXT's Application Kit, which includes preprogrammed buttons, scrollers, font panels, window managers, and memory management modules. The result is an application development environment that can cut program development time by as much as 75 percent, compared to the time required to develop Macintosh or Windows applications.

A barrier to the business acceptance of NeXT computers has been a dearth of application software, but the recent release of two full-featured spreadsheet packages for NeXT computers—Lotus Improv and Ashton-Tate's PowerStep—has improved the outlook for this hardware platform.

**NLQ**   See *near–letter quality*.

**node**   In a local area network, a connection point that can create, receive, or repeat a message.

In personal computer networks, nodes include repeaters, file servers, and shared peripherals. In common usage, however, the term *node* is synonymous with *workstation*. See *network topology* and *workstation*.

**noise**   The extraneous or random electrical content of a communications channel, unlike the signal, which carries information. All communications channels have noise, and if the noise is excessive, data loss can occur.

Telephone lines are particularly noisy. The error-free transmission of data via telecommunications, therefore, requires communications programs that can perform error-checking operations to make sure that the data being received is not corrupted.

**nonimpact printer**   A printer that forms a text or graphic image by spraying or fusing ink to the page.

Nonimpact printers include inkjet printers, laser printers, and thermal printers. All nonimpact printers are considerably quieter than impact printers, but non-impact printers cannot print multiple copies by using carbon paper. See *impact printer*, *inkjet printer*, *laser printer*, and *thermal printer*.

**non-interlaced monitor**   A computer monitor that does not employ the screen refresh technique called *interlacing* and, in consequence, is able to display high-resolution images without flickering or streaking. See *interlacing*.

**nonprocedural language**   See *declarative language*.

**nontransactional application**   In a local area network, an application program that produces data that you do not need to record and keep in one, commonly shared database so that all network participants have access. Most of the work done with word processing programs, for example, is nontransactional.

**nonvolatile memory**   The memory specially designed to hold information even when the power is switched off. Read-only memory (ROM) is nonvolatile, as are all secondary storage units such as disk drives. See *random-access memory (RAM)* and *volatile*.

**non-Windows application**   An MS-DOS application program that wasn't designed to take full advantage of Microsoft Windows' application program interface, including Windows' on-screen display of fonts and user interface conventions. Microsoft Windows can run non-Windows applications just as MS-DOS would run them. In Windows' Standard or 386 Enhanced modes, you can switch from one non-Windows application to another without quitting a program. In 386 Enhanced mode, you can multitask two or more MS-DOS applications, each in its own window. Industry experts believe that many copies of Microsoft Windows have been purchased to run MS-DOS applications in this way. See *386 Enhanced mode*, *application program interface (API)*, *Microsoft Windows,* and *Standard mode*.

**no parity**   In asynchronous communications, a communications protocol that disables parity checking and leaves no space for the parity bit. See *asynchronous communication, communications protocol, parity bit*, and *parity checking*.

**Norton SI**   In IBM PC–compatible computing, a widely used benchmark measurement of a computer's throughput.

Short for *Norton System Information*, Norton SI is a program included in the Norton Utilities. The program's composite performance index provides a balanced picture of a computer system's throughput, including its internal processing speed and the speed of peripherals such as disk drives.

The original IBM XT provides the base reference of Norton SI 1.0. 80386-based machines operating at clock speeds of 33 MHz can achieve Norton SI ratings of 40 and higher, which means that the machines run 40 times faster than the original XT. See *benchmark, million instructions per second (MIPS)*, and *throughput*.

**Norton Utilities**   A best-selling package (from Peter Norton Computing) of utility programs for IBM PC–compatible computers, including a benchmark program that measures a computer's throughput, an undelete program that restores files accidentally deleted from the disk, and management utilities for directories and subdirectories.

**NOS**   See *network operating system*.

**notebook computer**   A portable or laptop computer that weighs approximately six pounds.

**Novell NetWare**   A network operating system for 80286- and 80386-based DOS computers.

> With an excellent reputation for reliability, software compatibility, and system features, Novell's NetWare 286 and NetWare 386 have established a commanding lead in the local area network market for IBM PCs and PC compatibles: an estimated 70 percent of PC-based LANS use NetWare. See *local area network (LAN)* and *network operating system (NOS)*.

**NSFNET**   A wide-area network developed by the Office of Advanced Scientific Computing at the National Science Foundation (NSF). NSFNET was developed to take over the civilian functions of the U.S. Defense Department's ARPANET, which, for security reasons, has been closed to public access. See *ARPANET*.

**NTSC**   See *National Television Standards Committee*.

**NuBus**   The high-speed expansion bus of Macintosh II computers. NuBus requires adapters specifically designed for its 96-pin receptacles. See *expansion bus*.

**null modem cable**   A specially configured serial cable that enables you to connect two computers directly, without the mediation of a modem.

**null value**   In an accounting or database management program, a blank field in which you have never typed a value, as distinguished from a value of zero that you enter deliberately.

In some applications, you need to distinguish between a null value and a deliberately entered zero; a null value doesn't affect computations, but a zero does.

**number crunching**   Calculation, especially of large
amounts of data. (Slang term.)

**numeric coprocessor**   A microprocessor support chip that
performs mathematical computations—specifically
those using binary-coded decimal (BCD) and floating-
point calculations—at speeds of up to 100 times faster
than a microprocessor alone.

The Intel numeric coprocessors—8087, 80287, and
80387—are designed to work with their microprocessor counterparts: the 8087 is designed to work the
8088 and 8086, and the 80287 and 80387 are designed
to work with the 80286 and 80386, respectively. Otherwise, all three Intel numeric coprocessors are similar;
they are designed to work with 80 bits at a time so that
a programmer can express a number of sufficient
length to ensure accurate calculations. An innovative
feature of the Intel 80486DX chip is the inclusion of the
numeric coprocessor circuitry on the microprocessor
chip.

If you work with spreadsheets or any other
application that performs calculations intensively, add a numeric coprocessor to your
system. You will see substantial gains in the
apparent speed of your system without any modification to your software. See *binary coded decimal
(BCD)*, *floating-point calculation*, and *microprocessor*.

**numeric coprocessor socket**   A push-down socket on the
motherboard of many personal computers into which
you or a dealer can mount a numeric coprocessor,
such as the Intel 80287. The coprocessor improves the
performance of the computer system when running
calculation-intensive applications such as a
spreadsheet.

**numeric format**   In a spreadsheet program, the way in
which the program displays numbers in a cell.

With Lotus 1-2-3, for example, you may choose among
the following numeric formatting options:

- *Fixed*. Displays values with the number of decimal places you specify, ranging from 0 to 15. Lotus 1-2-3 rounds numbers that have more decimal places than you specified. If the number of digits exceeds the column width, you see a row of asterisks across the cell.

- *Scientific*. Displays very large or small numbers using scientific notation; for example, 12,460,000,000 appears as 1.25E+11.

- *Currency*. Displays values with commas and dollar signs. You specify the number of decimal places (0 to 15). If the number of digits exceeds the column width, you see a row of asterisks across the cell.

- *Comma*. Displays numbers larger than 999 with commas separating thousands; 1-2-3 inserts the commas automatically.

- *General*. Displays numbers without commas. Does not display trailing zeroes to the right of the decimal point. If the number of digits to the left of the decimal point exceeds the column width, 1-2-3 uses scientific notation. If the number of digits to the right of the decimal point exceeds the column width, 1-2-3 rounds the number.

- *+/–*. Converts the number to a simple bar graph appearing in the cell, with the number of plus or minus signs equaling the whole-value number of the entry; for example, 5 appears as +++++. Plus signs indicate a positive value; minus signs indicate a negative value.

- *Percent*. Multiplies the value by 100 and adds a percent sign; for example, 0.485 appears as 48.5%. You specify the number of decimal places (0 to 15). If the number of digits exceeds the column width, you see a row of asterisks across the cell.

- *Date*. Converts a number to a date. The number 32734, for example, converts to the date August 14, 1989.

- *Text*. Displays the formula instead of the value computed by the formula.

- *Hidden*. Makes the cell entry invisible on-screen. You can see the entry by placing the pointer in the cell and looking at the cell contents indicator.

See *cell*.

**numeric keypad**   A group of keys, usually to the right of the typing area on a keyboard. The keypad is designed for the rapid, touch-typing entry of numerical data.

**Num Lock key**   A toggle key that locks the numeric keypad into a mode in which you can enter numbers. When the Num Lock key is on, the cursor-movement keys are disabled.

On IBM PC–compatible keyboards, the keys on the numeric keypad are labeled with arrows and numbers. You can use these keys to move the cursor or to enter numbers. The Num Lock key toggles the keypad back and forth between these two modes.

 If you are trying to move the cursor with the cursor-movement keys and instead are typing numbers on-screen, you have pressed Num Lock accidentally. To use the cursor-movement keys, press Num Lock again.

**object** In object linking and embedding (OLE), a document or portion of a document that has been pasted into another document. Using the Clipboard, you can paste a static object, such as an Excel chart, into a document. But this object is only a static, noneditable representation of the source data. With OLE-capable applications, you can use two techniques—linking and embedding—to insert dynamic objects. With either technique, the object isn't static; you can choose a command that displays the object in the application in which you created it, where it is fully editable. See *dynamic object, object linking and embedding (OLE),* and *static object.*

**object code** In computer programming, the machine-readable instructions created by a compiler or interpreter from source code.

**object linking and embedding (OLE)** A set of standards, developed by Microsoft Corporation and incorporated into Microsoft Windows and Apple's Macintosh system software, that allows you to create dynamic, automatically updated links between documents, and also to embed a document created by one application into a document created by another.

To understand linking and embedding, start by considering the limitations of standard Clipboard techniques for copying information. When you use the Clipboard to copy a Microsoft Excel chart into a Microsoft Word document, there is no link between the source document (the Excel chart) and the destination document (the Word document). If you later change the Excel chart, your changes are not reflected in the copy you placed in the Word document. You must remember to update this copy, and you must do so manually by repeating the entire copy procedure.

With OLE, you can create a *dynamic* link between the source document and the destination document, so that the changes you make to the source document are automatically reflected in the destination document. With linking, you use the Clipboard to copy the source document, as before, but you choose a command called Paste Link or Paste Special, instead of the usual Paste command, to insert the copy in the destination document. Pasting the copy this way creates a dynamic link between the source document and the destination document. If you make a change to the source document, these changes are automatically reflected in the destination document; you don't have to do anything. What is more, you can easily edit the linked object just by double-clicking it; this action starts the object's server application—the one that created the object— enabling you to edit the source document and to update the copy.

OLE also supports embedding, which differs from linking. When you embed an object, you actually place the source document (or a portion of the source document) physically into the destination file, resulting in a compound file—a file that contains information needed by both applications: the server application (the one that created the embedded object) and the client application (the one that received the embedded object). With embedding, no link is created between the source document and the embedded object. If no link is created, then why bother with embedding? The answer is that embedding places a *fully editable* copy of the source document into the destination document. You can modify this copy as much as you like without worrying about affecting the source document.

To sum up the difference between linking and embedding, linking is useful when you want to maintain one authoritative version of a file, which you may want to copy many times. For example, suppose that you keep your firm's price list in one authoritative Excel worksheet. You often copy all or part of this document to Word documents, such as reports or proposals. You always want any changes in the Excel document to be reflected automatically in all the copies you have made. You choose linking.

Embedding is useful when you want to place just one copy of an object in a file, and you don't want the changes you make to this object to be reflected in the original or any other copies. For example, suppose that you embed your firm's price list in a proposal in which you want to cut all your prices by 10 percent for just one client. You don't want this change to be reflected in the original Excel worksheet. You choose embedding. After embedding the object, you double-click it to start Excel and make the price changes. The changes you make don't affect the original worksheet. Here, embedding is the better choice.

To use OLE, you must be running applications that are capable of serving as client and server applications for OLE purposes.

 You can tell quickly whether an application has linking or embedding capabilities, or both. Just pull down the Edit menu and look for a command such as Paste Link or Paste Special; if you find one, the application can function as a client application for linking. Look in the Edit menu or other menus for an Insert Object command, which indicates that the program can function as a client application for embedding purposes. Most programs that can function as OLE clients also can function as servers. See *client application, embedded object, linked object,* and *server application.*

**object-oriented graphic**  A graphic image composed of discrete objects—such as lines, circles, ellipses, and boxes—that you can move independently.

Object-oriented graphics often are called *vector graphics* because the program stores them as mathematical formulas for the vectors, or directional lines, that compose the image. Unlike bit-mapped graphics, you can resize object-oriented graphics without introducing distortions.

Increasing the size of a bit-mapped rectangle introduces distortions, because you thicken the lines as you increase the overall size (see O.1). Moreover, the image prints using the printer's highest resolution (up to 300 dpi with laser printers). See *bit-mapped graphic*.

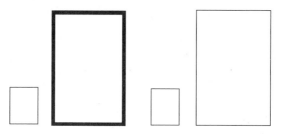

**Fig. O.1.** A rectangle magnified by a bit-mapped graphics program (left) and by an object-oriented graphics program (right).

**object-oriented programming language**    A nonprocedural programming language in which program elements are conceptualized as objects that can pass messages to each other.

In an object-oriented program, each object has its own data and programming code and is internally self-reliant; the program makes the object part of a larger whole by incorporating it into a hierarchy of layers. Object-oriented programming, therefore, is the ultimate extension of the concept of modular programming.

In object-oriented programming, the modules are independent enough to stand on their own so that you can copy the modules into other programs. This capability raises the possibility of inheritance; you can copy and add some new features to an old object and then move that object to a new program. You do not have to re-create the object.

The objects created in object-oriented programming are excellent tools for program construction because they hide their internal complexity. The objects are self-sufficient and susceptible to copying; you can move the objects around in chunks to compose new programs.

Any object-oriented programming language, then, is highly extensible. Object-oriented programming languages also have natural affinities with graphical user interfaces. You can display a completed object on-screen as an icon—effectively hiding its complexity—and drag the icon around with a mouse to reposition or copy the object. In HyperCard, for example, when you select and copy a button and paste it on another card, you also copy the script. This technique is extremely powerful and is easy to learn.

Whether or not object-oriented programming will ever replace conventional programming techniques is far from clear. Object-oriented programming languages require a great deal of memory and execute slowly, compared to languages such as assembly language and C.

The popularity of a language such as C stems from the primitivity of current computing equipment; most people still are working with machines based on Intel 8088 and Motorola 68000 microprocessors, which run so sluggishly that a programmer must find the fastest way of executing an algorithm. In the future, however, a programming language's speed will be less of an issue, and object-oriented programming may find professional applications. See *extensible*, *modular programming*, *nonprocedural language*, and *script*.

**Object Packager**   In Microsoft Windows, an accessory that transforms a document into an icon, which you can then insert within another document (even one created by another compatible application) as a linked or embedded object. (To package documents this way, both applications must be compatible with Microsoft's object linking and embedding, or OLE, specifications.) When the reader of this document double-clicks the icon, Windows starts the application that created the embedded document and displays the document in a new window. Using Object Packager, you can embed a spreadsheet as an icon in a word processing document, with a note such as, "Jan, just double-click this icon to see our Excel worksheet showing the Fall Quarter figures I told you about."

Windows 3.1 users can make use of Object Packager for many purposes, such as to include information of a variety of types. In figure O.2, you see five packaged objects created by a variety of applications. This dynamic and interactive document plays a recording, displays text, runs through a worksheet "what if" scenario, displays a chart, and displays a bit-mapped graphic image. See *object linking and embedding (OLE)*, and *voice annotation*.

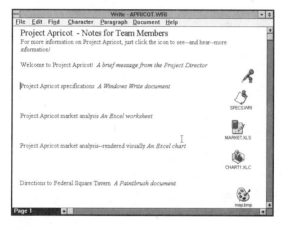

**Fig. O.2.** An interactive document combining packages created by several server applications.

**oblique**   The italic form of a sans serif typeface. See *sans serif*.

**odd parity**   In asynchronous communications, an error-checking protocol in which the parity bit is set to 1 if the number of 1 digits in a one-byte data item adds up to an odd number. The parity bit is set to 0 if the number of 1 digits adds up to an even number. For example, the following byte has four 1s: 01001011. The parity bit therefore would be set to 0 in an odd parity-checking scheme. If the parity bit indicates *even* but the data transmitted actually contains an odd number of 1s, the system will report that a transmission error has occurred. See *asynchronous communication*, *communications parameter*, *communications protocol*, *even parity*, and *parity checking*.

**OEM**   See *original equipment manufacturer*.

**office automation**   The use of computers and local area networks to integrate traditional office activities such as conferencing, writing, filing, and sending and receiving messages.

Because many tasks such as filing or word processing can be performed much faster on a computer than with manual techniques, many firms hoped to reap huge productivity gains from office automation systems. With some exceptions, these gains have not materialized.

Training employees to use the systems often is expensive and time-consuming, and after the systems are installed, perfectionists may use the technology to do a better job rather than to do more work. In the days of typewriters, a letter may have been sent out with some imperfections, such as a minor misspelling, because too much work was required to retype the letter, but with today's technology, you may spend more time correcting mistakes until the letter is perfect.

Businesses that have met with success in office automation begin by identifying a specific activity that can be done more cheaply or more rapidly on the computer, and then they develop a system—hardware and software included—for that specific application. For example, an insurance company has realized a major productivity gain by having agents fill out application data directly on portable computers. The software then uploads the applications to the company's main offices via telecommunications.

Another strategy that has produced productivity gains is called *reengineering*. In reengineering, a firm identifies ways to reorganize work so that people can do it more efficiently. Then computers are used to support the

altered work roles. In reengineering, the productivity
gains really stem from the redesigned work roles, not
from the computer.

 If you automate a mess, you get an automated mess. Develop ways of working
more effeciently, and *then* automate. See
*reengineering*.

**off-line**   Not directly connected with a computer; for example, a device that is not hooked up to your PC is off-
line. In data communications, not connected with
another, distant computer; for example, a workstation
you have temporarily or permanently disconnected
from a local area network is off-line. In a BBS, a file is
off-line if the system operator (SYSOP) has moved the
file from main storage (the area that callers may access)
to secondary storage. Most SYSOPs will activate an off-
line file for downloading purposes if specifically requested to do so.

**off-screen formatting**   In a word processing program, a
formatting technique in which formatting commands
are embedded in the text so that they affect printing,
but the formatting is not visible on-screen. See *embedded formatting command*, *on-screen formatting*, and
*what-you-see-is-what-you-get (WYSIWYG)*.

**offset**   In word processing, the amount of space added to
leave space for binding. Synonymous with *gutter*.

**OK button**   A pushbutton you can activate in a dialog box to
confirm the current dialog box settings and execute the
command.

 If the OK button is highlighted or surround-
ed by double angle brackets, you can press
Enter to choose OK.

**OLE client**   In object linking and embedding, an application
capable of serving as the recipient of a linked or embedded object created by a client application. See *object linking and embedding (OLE)*.

**OLE server** In object linking and embedding, an application capable of providing an object to be linked or embedded into a destination document. See *object linking and embedding (OLE)*.

**one hundred percent (100%) column graph** A column graph that resembles a pie graph in that each "slice" of the column displays the relative percentage of that data item compared to the total (see fig. O.3). See *stacked column graph*.

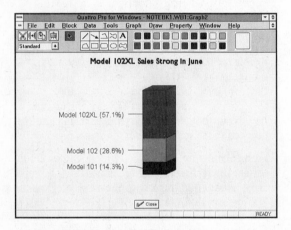

**Fig. O.3.** A 100% column graph.

**on-line** Directly connected with a computer; for example, a device is on-line after you successfully hook it up to your PC. In data communications, connected with another, distant computer; for example, *on-line* refers to the successful connection with a host computer in a client-server network. In a BBS, a file or application is on-line if it is available to the users.

**on-line help** A help utility available on-screen while you are using a network or an application program.

**on-line information service** A for-profit firm that makes current news, stock quotes, and other information available to its subscribers via telecommunications links. See *bibliographic retrieval service*, *CompuServe*, *Dow Jones News/Retrieval Service*, *GEnie*, and *Prodigy*.

**on-screen formatting**   In a word processing program, a formatting technique in which formatting commands directly affect the text that is visible on-screen. See *embedded formatting command*, *off-screen formatting*, and *what-you-see-is-what-you-get (WYSIWYG)*.

**OOPS**   Acronym for *object-oriented programming system*. See *object-oriented programming language*.

**open architecture**   A computer system in which all the system specifications are made public so that other companies will develop add-on products such as adapters for the system.

**open bus system**   A computer design in which the computer's expansion bus contains receptacles that readily accept adapters.

An open-architecture system generally has an open bus, but not all systems with open buses have open architectures; the Macintosh is an example of the latter. See *expansion bus*.

**Open System Interconnection (OSI) reference model**
An international standard for the organization of local area networks (LANs) established by the International Standards Organization (ISO) and the Institute of Electrical and Electronic Engineers (IEEE).

The OSI reference model is an important contribution to the conceptual design of local area networks because this model establishes hardware independence. The model separates the communication process into distinct layers: the physical hardware (such as the cabling), the transport layer (the method by which data is communicated via the physical hardware), the presentation layer (the method by which the transmitted data interacts with application programs in each computer), and the application layer (the programs available to all users of the network). Figure O.4 shows the OSI reference model divided into layers.

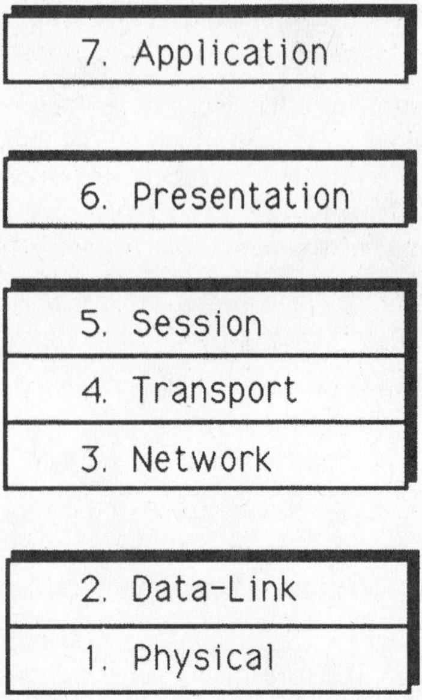

**Fig. O.4.** The OSI reference model.

Because each layer is to some extent independent of the others, you can, in theory, change the cabling (from twisted-pair cable to coaxial cable, for example) without making changes at the other layers. Of course, not all local area networks live up to this level of independence.

From the user's perspective, however, the most important point about the OSI reference model is that you can distinguish between the network hardware and the network software. For example, TOPS, a local area network system, runs on systems physically wired with AppleTalk hardware and twisted-pair cables as well as EtherNet hardware and coaxial cables. See *local area network (LAN)*.

**operating system**   A master control program for a computer that manages the computer's internal functions and provides you with a means to control the computer's operations.

The most popular operating systems for personal computers include MS-DOS, OS/2, and the Macintosh System. See *MS-DOS*, *Operating System/2 (OS/2)*, and *System 7*.

**Operating System/2 (OS/2)**   A multitasking operating system for IBM PC–compatible computers that breaks the 640K RAM barrier, provides protection for programs running simultaneously, and enables the dynamic exchange of data between applications.

The history of OS/2 has all the drama of nineteenth-century, cutthroat industrial competition. Originally, the operating system was jointly developed by IBM and Microsoft and was positioned as the heir apparent to MS-DOS. At the time of OS/2's release, there were plenty of good reasons to regard OS/2 as the operating system of the future. OS/2, unlike MS-DOS, could take advantage of the protected mode of 80286 and 80386 microprocessors, meaning that the system could break MS-DOS's 640K RAM barrier and prevent programs from invading each other's memory space. Yet very few users upgraded to OS/2, in part because very few software publishers developed OS/2 applications, and the early versions of OS/2 ran MS-DOS programs poorly.

When OS/2 was first released, Microsoft Corporation also was busily developing Microsoft Windows, a graphical user interface for MS-DOS. Even as it became plain that OS/2 wasn't doing well in the marketplace, Microsoft continued to insist that Windows was a stopgap measure until the marketplace accepted OS/2. The early versions of Windows were little more than fancy shells for MS-DOS systems and offered few technical advantages. But by 1989, QuarterDeck Office Systems had amply confirmed that its windowing environment, DESQview, running under MS-DOS, could switch the 80286 and 80386 machines to protected mode without sacrificing full MS-DOS compatibility. Windows 3.0 stunned the industry by incorporating full protected-mode processing; suddenly the rationale for upgrading to OS/2 disappeared almost entirely, and Windows 3.0 sold millions of copies. Microsoft went on to confirm that the future belonged to Windows: the operating system of the future would be Windows NT (a future, 32-bit version of Windows), not OS/2. Not surprisingly, these events seem to have put a damper on the formerly close and cordial relationship between IBM and Microsoft.

In reply to Microsoft's moves with Windows, IBM seized control of OS/2 development and announced a radical upgrade. The new OS/2, Version 2.0, runs MS-DOS and Windows applications perfectly, as well as OS/2 applications, and what is more, it takes full advantage of the 32-bit architecture of 80386 and later microprocessors. It also offers a new graphical user interface, one that—as it turns out—much more closely resembles the screen of a NeXT workstation than the Macintosh-like Windows display (see fig. O.5). Released in early 1992, IBM's Version 2.0 of OS/2 was widely acclaimed as a major technological achievement. Whether OS/2 can stop Windows' astonishing momentum, however, remains to be seen. See *Microsoft Windows, protected mode,* and *real mode.*

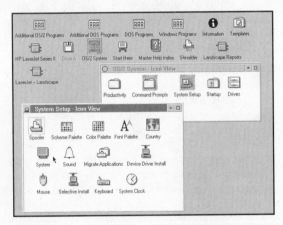

**Fig. O.5.** The OS/2 Presentation Manager interface.

**optical character recognition (OCR)**   The machine recognition of printed or typed text. For example, the postal service uses OCR to route mail.

**optical disk**   A secondary storage medium for computers in which you store information of extremely high density on a disk in the form of tiny pits, the presence or absence of which corresponds to a bit of information read by a tightly focused laser beam.

Optical storage technologies are expected to play a significant role in the secondary storage systems of the 1990s. CD-ROM disks and CD-ROM disk drives offer an increasingly economical distribution medium for read-only data and programs. Write-once, read-many (WORM) drives enable organizations to create their own huge, in-house databases.

Erasable optical disk drives, such as the 256M drive included with the NeXT computer, offer more secondary storage than hard disks, and the CDs are removable.

Optical storage disk drives, however, are more expensive and much slower than hard disks. See *CD-ROM*, *interactive videodisk*, and *write-once, read-many (WORM)*.

**optical scanner**   See *scanner*.

**optimal recalculation**   In Lotus 1-2-3 and other advanced spreadsheet programs, a method that speeds automatic recalculation by recalculating only those cells that changed since the last recalculation. See *automatic recalculation*.

**option button**   See *radio button*.

**ORACLE**   A program developed by Oracle Corporation, the maker of mainframe and minicomputer relational database programs, that enables users of Macintosh computers and IBM PC compatibles to access data on large corporate databases.

Many people in the mainframe and minicomputer world know ORACLE as one of the leading relational database management systems (DBMS). In its personal

computer form, ORACLE is a connectivity platform—
a program designed to enable personal computers to
access data kept in large corporate mainframe databases.

Using one of the several versions of ORACLE for
personal computers, anyone running Lotus 1-2-3,
HyperCard, SuperCard, 4th Dimension, or dBASE III
Plus can access the following mainframe databases:
ORACLE, DB2, and SQL/DS. Perhaps the most innovative of these programs is ORACLE for the Macintosh,
which transforms HyperCard into an exceptionally
user-friendly front end for corporate databases. See
*connectivity platform* and *relational database management system (RDBMS)*.

**organization chart**   In presentation graphics, a text chart
you use to diagram the reporting structure of a multilevel organization, such as a corporation or a club
(see fig. O.6).

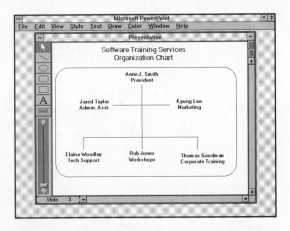

**Fig. O.6.** An organization chart.

**orientation**   See *landscape orientation* and *portrait orientation*.

**original equipment manufacturer (OEM)**   The company that actually manufactures a given piece of hardware, unlike the value-added reseller (VAR)—the company that modifies, configures, repackages, and sells the hardware.

For example, only a few companies such as Canon, Toshiba, and Ricoh make the print engines used in laser printers. These engines are configured and sold by VARs.

**orphan**   A formatting flaw in which the first line of a paragraph appears alone at the bottom of a page.

Most word processing and page-layout programs suppress widows and orphans; the better programs enable you to switch widow/orphan control on and off and to choose the number of lines for which the suppression feature is effective. See *widow*.

**OS/2**   See *Operating System/2*.

**outline font**   A printer or screen font in which a mathematical formula generates each character, producing a graceful and undistorted outline of the character, which the printer then fills in at its maximum resolution.

Mathematical formulas, rather than bit maps, produce the graceful arcs and lines of outline characters (see fig. O.7). You can easily change the type size of an outline font. Unlike bit-mapped fonts, scale outline fonts can be scaled up and down without introducing distortions. (You may need to reduce the weight of small font sizes by using a process called *hinting*, which prevents you from losing the fine detail.)

Because mathematical formulas produce the characters, you need only one font in the printer's memory to use any type size from 2 to 127 points. With bit-mapped fonts, however, you must download into the printer's memory a complete set of characters for each font size, and you cannot use a type size that you have not downloaded.

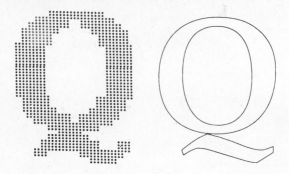

**Fig. O.7.** A bit-mapped character (left) and an outline character (right).

Outline fonts are available as built-in fonts in many laser printers and as downloadable fonts provided on disk. The leading supplier of outline fonts is Adobe Systems, Inc., which encrypts these fonts (using a proprietary technique) by transforming them into instructions phrased in the Adobe's page description language (PostScript). Adobe's fonts print only on laser or high-resolution printers specifically licensed (at a fee) to contain PostScript decoders. Such fonts are called *Type 1 fonts*, and PostScript laser printers give these fonts priority in processing operations. See *bit-mapped font* and *hinting*.

**outline utility**   In some full-featured word processing programs, a mode that assists you in planning and organizing a document by equating outline headings with document headings. The program enables you to view the document as an outline or as ordinary text.

This convenient feature is useful for anyone who writes lengthy, complex documents segmented by internal headings and subheadings (scholarly articles, technical reports, and proposals, for example). When you view the document in Outline mode, the headings and subheadings appear as they would in an outline (see fig. O.8). The text beneath the headings collapses (disappears) so that only the headings and subheadings are visible.

In Outline mode, you can move the headings and sub-headings vertically; if you move a heading, all the hidden text positioned beneath it also moves. The Outline mode provides the tools necessary for reorganizing large text in a document by using only a few keystrokes. After you switch back to Document mode, the outline format disappears, and the document appears as normal (see fig. O.9).

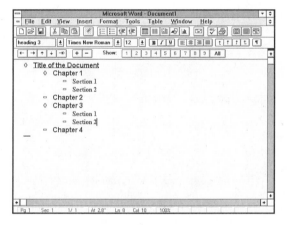

**Fig. O.8.** Document headings viewed in Outline mode.

**output**   The process of displaying or printing the results of processing operations. See *input*.

**overlaid windows**   In a user interface, a display mode in which windows are allowed to overlap each other. If you zoom the topmost window to full size, it completely hides the other windows. See *cascading windows* and *tiled windows*.

**overlay**   See *program overlay*.

**overlay chart**   In a business graphics program, a second type of chart that is overlaid on top of the main chart, such as a line chart on top of a bar chart. Synonymous with *combination chart*.

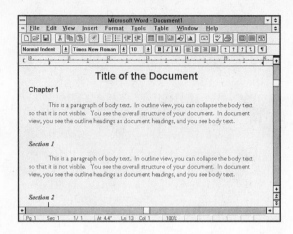

**Fig. O.9.** Document headings viewed in Document mode.

**overstrike** The printing of a character not found in a printer's character set by printing one character, moving the print head back one space, and printing a second character on top of the first. Today's graphics-based computer systems eliminate the need for this printing technique; however, it is sometimes needed by users of character-based DOS programs.

**Overtype mode** An editing mode in word processing programs and other software that enables you to enter and edit text; in Overtype mode, the characters you type erase existing characters, if any. In WordPerfect, the Overtype mode is called Typeover mode. See *Insert mode*.

**overwrite** To write data on a magnetic disk in the same area where other data is stored, thereby destroying the original data.

**package** In Microsoft Windows 3.1, an icon that represents a linked or embedded object that has been reduced to an icon by using the Object Packager utility.

**packaged software** Application programs commercially marketed, unlike custom programs privately developed for a specific client. Synonymous with *off-the-shelf software*.

**page** A fixed-size block of random-access memory (RAM). In word processing and desktop publishing, an on-screen representation of a printed page of text or graphics. See *paging memory*.

**page break** In word processing, a mark that indicates where the printer will start a new page.

In a program that has active, on-screen pagination, such as WordPerfect, the program inserts the page break automatically (often a line of dots or dashes across the screen) when you have typed a full page of text. An automatic page break is called a *soft page break* because the program may adjust its location if you insert or delete text above the break. With most programs, you can enter a hard page break—also called a *forced page break*—which forces the program to break the page at the hard page break's location. A hard page break stays put even if you insert or delete text above the break.

**page description language (PDL)** A programming language that describes printer output in device-independent commands.

Normally, a program's printer output includes printer control codes that vary from printer to printer. A program that generates output in a PDL, however, can drive any printer containing an interpreter for the PDL; a PDL, therefore, is device independent, making it technically superior to ordinary printing techniques. A program that generates output in the PostScript page description language, for example, can drive any printer with a PostScript interpreter, including imagesetters with 1,200 dpi or better resolutions.

PDLs are technically superior to ordinary printing techniques for another reason: the burden of processing the output is transferred from the computer to the printer. To print a circle by using ordinary printing techniques, the computer must transform the screen image into a bit map and send the bit map to the printer. A circle in a PDL, however, is represented mathematically, and the printer is responsible for constructing the actual image. This technique has a drawback: to interpret the PDL output, the printer must have its own central processing unit (CPU) and random-access memory (RAM), which makes PostScript printers expensive. See *PostScript*.

**paged memory**   See *paging memory*.

**paged memory management unit (PMMU)**   In computer hardware, a chip or circuit that enables virtual memory. Virtual memory, a very desirable and advanced feature, allows your computer to use space on your hard disk to expand the apparent amount of random-access memory in your system. With virtual memory, a computer with only 4M of RAM can function as if it were equipped with 8M or more of RAM, enabling you to run several programs simultaneously.

 If you're shopping for a new computer, avoid Macs with Motorola 68000 or 68020 microprocessors, which do not include PMMU circuitry and, therefore, don't let you use System 7's virtual memory capabilities. Choose a Mac that employs the Motorola 68030 or 68040; these microprocessors contain PMMU circuitry and allow you to use System 7's virtual memory features. The same caution applies to IBM PCs or PC compatibles based on the 8088 or 80286 microprocessors, which do not include PMMU circuitry. For Windows computing, a minimal system is based on the Intel 80386SX microprocessor, which permits Windows to implement virtual memory. See *Microsoft Windows, System 7,* and *virtual memory*.

**page layout program**   In desktop publishing, an application program that assembles text and graphics from a variety of files. You can determine the precise placement, sizing, scaling, and cropping of material in accordance with the page design represented on-screen.

Page layout programs such as PageMaker and Ventura Publisher display a graphic representation of the page, including nonprinting guides that define areas into which you can insert text and graphics. See *PageMaker* and *Ventura Publisher*.

**PageMaker**   A leading page layout program for Windows and Macintosh computers that is excellent for generating documents such as newsletters, brochures, reports, and books.

Introduced in 1985 for the Macintosh, PageMaker (Aldus Corporation) and the Apple LaserWriter printer launched desktop publishing—a term that was, in fact, created by Aldus Corporation's president, Paul Brainerd.

**page-mode RAM**   High-performance random-access memory (RAM) that segments the memory into separate units, called *pages*, to enable the computer's central processing unit (CPU) to access data more quickly. Page-mode RAM is found in high-end computer systems. It allows the fast microprocessors of such systems to function at maximum speeds, without the use of wait states. Page-mode RAM should be distinguished from paging memory systems, which employ special memory management circuits to extend memory storage to hard disks. See *paging memory, random-access memory (RAM), virtual memory*, and *wait state*.

**page orientation**   See *landscape orientation* and *portrait orientation*.

**pagination**   In word processing, the process of dividing a document into pages for printing. Today's advanced word processing programs employ background pagination, in which pagination occurs after you stop typing or editing and the microprocessor has nothing else to do.

If you're using a slow computer, such as an 8088-based PC-compatible or a 68000-based Mac, check to see whether your word processing program enables you to disable background pagination. After doing so, the program will run less sluggishly. Pagination will occur when you print. Just remember that the page breaks you see on-screen may not be accurate. See *page break*.

**paging memory**  A memory system in which the location of data is specified by an intersection of column and row on the memory page, rather than by the actual physical location of the data. (A page is a unit of memory of fixed size.) Because the location of the data is specified by a means other than the data's actual physical location in the memory, a paging memory system allows memory pages to be stored wherever memory space becomes available, including disk drives. Paging memory, therefore, is one method you can use to implement virtual memory, in which your computer's hard disk drive functions as an extension of random-access memory (RAM). A chip or circuit called a *paged memory management unit* (PMMU) manages the movement of pages of data in and out of the memory devices. See *page, paged memory management unit (PMMU), random access memory (RAM),* and *virtual memory*.

**paint file format**  A bit-mapped graphics file format found in programs such as MacPaint and PC Paintbrush.

The standard paint file format in the Macintosh environment is the 72-dots-per-inch format originally used by MacPaint, which is linked to the Mac's bit-mapped screen display. In Windows computers, the Windows bit map file format (BMP) is increasingly common. Many programs also recognize the PC Paintbrush file format (PCX). See *file format* and *paint program*.

**paint program**  A program that enables you to paint the screen by switching on or off the individual dots or pixels that make up a bit-mapped screen display.

The first paint program (and the first program for the Macintosh) was MacPaint, the creation of Bill Atkinson at Apple Computer. MacPaint is designed to work with the Mac's bit-mapped display that has a resolution of 72 dots per inch. Graphics created with MacPaint have the same resolution when printed and look rather crude, but you can create some striking effects by varying the patterns of dots on-screen.

MacPaint has many imitators in the Macintosh world, such as SuperPaint (Silicon Beach Software). MacPaint-like applications also exist for IBM PC–compatible computers; a leading program in this category is PC Paintbrush. Windows includes an accessory called Paintbrush. See *MacPaint* and *PC Paintbrush*.

**paired bar graph**    A bar graph with two different x-axes (categories axes).

A paired bar graph is an excellent way to demonstrate the relationship between two data series that share the same y-axis values but require two different x-axis categories. Because the bars mirror each other, variations become obvious (see fig. P.1). See *dual y-axis graph*.

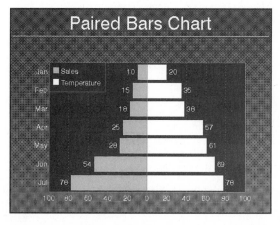

**Fig. P.1.** A paired bar graph.

**pair kerning**   See *kerning*.

**palette**   In computer video displays, the repertoire of colors
that the system is capable of displaying. VGA color
displays offer a palette of 262,144 colors, although each
screen can display a maximum of 256 colors simultaneously. In paint and draw programs, an on-screen
display of options such as color, brush shape, line
width, or pattern. See *draw program, paint program,*
and *video graphics array (VGA).*

**pan**   In multimedia, the capability of a synthesizer or sound
board to alter the left and right channel volumes to
create the illusion of movement of the source of the
sound.

**Pantone Matching System**   A standard color-selection
system for professional color printing supported
by high-end illustration programs, such as Adobe
Illustrator and PageMaker 4.0.

**paperless office**   An office in which using paper for traditional purposes, such as sending messages, filling out
forms, and maintaining records, has been reduced or
eliminated.

When the paperless office was announced as a goal for
the office of the future, the future looked bleak indeed
for paper manufacturers. Yet, over the past 15 years,
paper consumption has exploded and paper manufacturers have experienced record growth and profits. In
most offices, computers generate more paper, not less.

A new application for personal computers is the
business-form program. These programs enable a person who isn't trained in graphic arts to design and
print a business form that can be mass-duplicated using
inexpensive offset techniques.

Paper remains popular as a communication and filing
medium for two important reasons. First, a paper message, after you receive it, keeps on broadcasting its
message unless you throw the message away, file it, or
answer it. In contrast, electronic mail systems enable
you to duck your messages by failing to log on to the

system. Second, paper documents have an entrenched legal status; the exchange of first-class letters, for example, has been recognized by the courts to constitute a legal contract. The legal status of computer-based documents is still unclear. Many people fear the storage of important documents on computer systems without hard-copy backup; wiping out a file is easy to do.

Despite these barriers to the acceptance of the paperless office, many valid reasons exist for businesses to seek to reduce the consumption of paper. Filling out forms directly on computer screens, rather than on paper, can save an organization a great deal of money otherwise spent on filing and other clerical tasks.

**paper-white monitor**   A monochrome monitor that displays black text and graphics on a white background. Paper-white monitors are preferred for word processing and desktop publishing because the display closely resembles the appearance of the printed page.

 When shopping for a monitor, remember that color has its advantages. In a color display, you can more easily locate menu names, accelerator keys, data entry fields, and other on-screen areas. Moreover, most programs permit you to configure the on-screen colors, so that you can simulate a paper-white monitor (black text on a white background) if you want.

**Paradox**   A relational database program originally developed by Ansa Software and offered by Borland International for IBM PC–compatible computers.

Paradox uses query-by-example techniques and an interface reminiscent of Lotus 1-2-3. See *query by example (QBE)*.

**parallel columns**   See *side-by-side columns*.

**parallel interface**   See *parallel port*.

**parallel port**   A port that supports the synchronous, high-speed flow of data along parallel lines to peripheral devices, especially parallel printers.

Essentially an extension of the computer's internal data bus, the parallel port provides a high-speed connection to printing devices. A parallel port also negotiates with peripheral devices to determine whether they are ready to receive data, and reports error messages if a device is not ready. Unlike the serial port, the parallel port provides a trouble-free way to connect a printer to your computer; you usually can install parallel printers easily. As the length of the cable increases, however, so does the risk of crosstalk (interference between the parallel wires). Parallel printer cables, therefore, usually are no longer than 10 to 15 feet.

You can configure the systems of IBM PC–compatible computers with three parallel ports. The device names of the ports are LPT1, LPT2, and LPT3 (*LPT* is an abbreviation for *line printer*). The device named PRN is the same as LPT1.

**parallel printer**   A printer designed to be connected to the computer's parallel port.

 If a printer is available in serial and parallel versions, the parallel version is the better choice unless you must position the printer more than 10 feet away from the computer. Parallel printers usually are easier to install and use than their serial counterparts.

**parallel processing**   See *multitasking*.

**parameter**   A value or option that you add or alter when you give a command so that the command accomplishes its task the way you want. If you do not state a parameter, the program uses a default value or option.

For instance, most programs enable you to type the name of the file you want to work with when you start the program. If you type *WORD report1.doc*, for example, Microsoft Word and the document file REPORT1.DOC load up at the same time. In this case, the file name is the parameter. If you do not type the file name, Word starts and opens a new, blank document file. See *argument*.

**parameter RAM**   In the Macintosh environment, a small bank of battery-powered memory that stores your configuration choices after you switch off the power.

**parent**   In a windowing system like X Windows or an outlining utility like ThinkTank, a unit (such as a window or outline heading) that is superior to lower-level units, which are called *children*. In the following outline, the major heading—ABUNDANT BIRDS OF WEST VIRGINIA—is a parent of three children.

> ABUNDANT BIRDS OF WEST VIRGINIA [parent]
>    Bluejay [child]
>    Cardinal [child]
>    Goldfinch [child]

See *child* and *family*.

**parent directory**   In DOS directories, the directory above the current subdirectory in the tree structure.

You can move quickly to the parent directory by typing *CD..* and pressing Enter.

**parity bit**   In asynchronous communications and primary storage, an extra bit added to a data word for parity checking.

If you are using a communications program, try setting the parity bit option to no parity and the data bits option to 8 bits. If these settings do not work, try even parity with 7 data bits. See *asynchronous communication* and *parity checking*.

**parity checking**   A technique used to detect memory or data communication errors. The computer adds up the number of bits in a one-byte data item, and if the parity bit setting disagrees with the sum of the other bits, the computer reports an error.

Parity-checking schemes work by storing a one-bit digit (0 or 1) that indicates whether the sum of the 1 bits in a data item is odd or even. When the data item is read from memory or received by another computer, a parity check occurs. If the parity check reveals that the parity bit is incorrect, the computer displays an error message. When errors occur in a computer's memory or in data communications, a 50-percent chance exists that the sum of the bits in a one-byte data item will change from an odd to an even number, or vice versa. See *even parity* and *odd parity*.

**parity error**   An error that a computer reports when parity checking reveals that one or more parity bits is incorrect, which indicates a probable error in data processing or data transmission.

**park**   To position a hard drive's read/write head so that the drive is not damaged by jostling during transport.

**parse**   To separate imported data into separate columns so that it appears correctly in a spreadsheet.

When you import data using Lotus 1-2-3's File Import Text command, for example, the program enters each line of the data as a long label—in other words, each line of data appears in just one cell. Because 1-2-3 uses soft-cell boundaries, you can see the entire line on-screen, but you cannot use this data for calculations. To render this data usable, you must use the Data Parse command that separates the data into distinct columns.

**partition**   A section of the storage area of a hard disk. A partition is set aside during initial preparation of the hard disk, before the disk is formatted.

In MS-DOS, every hard disk has at least one DOS partition. Versions of MS-DOS prior to 4.0 require you to set up more than one partition on a single hard disk to use a disk larger than 32M. You also can create a second DOS partition to run another operating system, such as UNIX.

Macintosh users may partition their drives to separate the Macintosh System and the A/UX version of UNIX, but utility programs, such as MultiDisk, are available that enable you to create several system partitions. The operating system treats these partitions as if they were different disks. These utilities are useful for organizing large hard disks. See *directory* and *subdirectory*.

**Pascal**   Pronounced "pass-kal'." A high-level programming language that encourages programmers to write well-structured, modular programs. Pascal has gained wide acceptance as a teaching and application-development language.

Developed by the European computer scientist Nicklaus Wirth in the early 1970s, Pascal—named for the seventeenth-century French mathematician and philosopher Blaise Pascal—expresses the principles of structured programming. Wirth hoped that the language would be widely adopted as a teaching language and a professional program-development language. Pascal is still used for teaching purposes at some colleges and universities.

Pascal is available in interpreted and compiled versions. Pascal resembles BASIC and FORTRAN in that it is a procedural language: its statements tell the computer what to do. In contrast to these earlier languages, however, Pascal was designed to take full advantage of modern control structures, eliminating spaghetti code and improving program readability.

Unlike BASIC, Pascal does not force programmers to express groups of related data items in arrays; instead, the language has a fully developed record data structure, making it far more suitable for professional program development than any language that lacks this data structure. Another important feature of Pascal is the modular structure; you can express important program functions in mini-programs called *procedures*, which are set aside from the main program and called by name (compare to Modula-2).

Unlike BASIC and FORTRAN, Pascal is a strongly type-checked language; the program does not use default data types, but requires that the programmer declare the data type of all variables and that all input conforms to the types declared. The lack of data typing and type-checking in other languages is a major cause of programming errors.

A major disadvantage of Pascal is that its standard version (Standard Pascal) contains many shortcomings. Commercial versions of the language generally include extensions that make them mutually unintelligible. The language's inventor, Wirth, has offered a new language, Modula-2, as a successor to Pascal, and this new language directly addresses Pascal's shortcomings. Professional programmers prefer C or C++. Because Pascal is exclusively a high-level language that does not enable you to include assembly-language statements, the language is too slow for large-scale application program development or systems programming.

In personal computing, Pascal lives on, largely due to the influence of Turbo Pascal (Borland International), a high-performance compiler for Pascal that recognizes a number of important and useful extensions to the language. See *BASIC, C, C++, FORTRAN*, and *Modula-2*.

**password** A security tool used to identify authorized users of a computer program or computer network and to define their privileges, such as read-only, reading and writing, or file copying.

 Computer hackers and saboteurs know that most people choose passwords based on their birthdays, nicknames, children's names, or easily remembered words such as *password, secret,* or even *none.* To secure your system, choose a password randomly, so that there is no chance someone will figure out a way to associate the password with you. Open a nice, thick novel, close your eyes, and run your fingers across a page until you come across a genuinely random word, such as *wolf, porch,* or *capable.* Then write it down somewhere so that you don't forget it. Another suggestion is to misspell your password in an odd way; for example, instead of *garnet,* use *garnit* or *garnete.*

**password protection**   A method of limiting access to a program or a network by requiring you to enter a password.

 Some programs enable you to password-protect your files, but be sure to keep a record of the password. Many users have lost work permanently because they forgot the password and had no means to retrieve it. (If a method for retrieving a password were included in software programs, a clever hacker would quickly discover it, and your data would not be secure.)

**paste**   In text editing, the part of the cut-and-paste operation in which you insert text or graphics at the cursor's location. In Windows and Macintosh systems, you cut or copy the text or graphics from a document. A temporary storage area called the Clipboard stores the cut or copied material while you scroll to the material's new location. When you paste, you copy the material from the Clipboard back into the same document or into another document.

 Bear in mind that the Clipboard stores only one unit of copied or cut text at a time. If you're not careful, you could accidentally delete the Clipboard's contents. Suppose that you cut several pages of text from a document, intending to move this text elsewhere. While scrolling to the text's new location, you notice a wording problem and edit it. This editing includes cutting a sentence of text. When you try to paste the lengthy passage into your document, you find that the Clipboard now contains only the sentence you cut en route. To avoid this problem, don't interrupt cut-and-paste operations. Some programs include commands that permit you to cut and paste without involving the Clipboard. See *block move* and *Clipboard.*

**patch**   A quick fix, in the form of one or more program statements, added to a program to correct bugs or to enhance the program's capabilities.

**path** In DOS, the route the operating system must follow to access an executable program stored in a subdirectory.

The purpose of dividing a disk into subdirectories is that DOS then treats each subdirectory as if it were a disk unto itself. If you type *DIR* and press Enter, you see an on-screen list of the files contained in the current subdirectory, but no others. If you type *ERASE* *.* and press Enter, DOS erases all the files in the current subdirectory, but not others. Creating subdirectories, then, serves to limit directory information—and damage it, if you use the ERASE command thoughtlessly. However, the limitation of DOS actions to the current subdirectory does have one serious disadvantage: by default, DOS examines only the current subdirectory when you issue a command—such as typing *WP* and pressing Enter—to start an executable program. If the program isn't in the current subdirectory, you see the friendly (and ambiguous) message Bad command or file name.

Two strategies circumvent the problem of starting programs located outside the current subdirectory. First, you can type the full path name (such as C:\WP51\WP) so that DOS knows where to find the program. Second, and much better, you can add a PATH command to your hard disk's AUTOEXEC.BAT file, listing all the subdirectories in which programs are stored. After adding the PATH command, you can start your application programs from any subdirectory. Most of today's application programs automatically create or update the PATH command in AUTOEXEC.BAT when you install the program. If you need to add the path statement yourself, use any word processing program or text editor to create or update the PATH command. Type *PATH*, followed by the full path names of all the directories that contain programs, separating the path names with semicolons. Here's an example: PATH C:\WP51; C:\WINDOWS; C:\NORTON; C:\WINWORD. See *AUTOEXEC.BAT, current directory, directory, path name, path statement,* and *subdirectory.*

**path name**   In DOS, a statement that indicates precisely
    where a file is located on a hard disk. When opening or
    saving a file with most applications, you must specify
    the full path name to retrieve or store the file in a direc-
    tory other than the current directory. For example,
    suppose that you're using WordPerfect, and you want
    to store the file REPORT9.DOC in the directory
    C:\DOCS. If C:\DOCS is not the current directory, you
    must type C:\DOCS\REPORT9.DOC to name and store
    the file in the correct location.

 Some applications permit you to define a
    permanent default directory for storing and
    retrieving the data files created by the appli-
    cation. If the application you're using per-
    mits you to define a default data directory, you don't
    need to type the full path name when retrieving and
    storing files.

**path statement**   In DOS, an entry in the AUTOEXEC.BAT
    file that lists the directories in which executable pro-
    grams are listed. The statement begins with the key
    word PATH, which is followed by a list of path names
    separated by semicolons, as shown in the following
    example: PATH C:\WP51; C:\WINDOWS; C:\NORTON;
    C:\WINWORD. After you add the path statement to
    AUTOEXEC.BAT, you need not activate a program's
    directory before starting the program.

**PC**   Abbreviation for *personal computer*. In practice,
    this abbreviation frequently connotes IBM or IBM-
    compatible personal computers, as opposed to
    Macintoshes. See *personal computer*.

**PC DOS**   The version of the MS-DOS operating system pack-
    aged with IBM personal computer systems. See *MS-DOS*.

**PCL**   See *printer control language.*

**PC Paintbrush**   A popular paint program for IBM PC–com-
    patible computers. See *paint program*.

**PC Tools**   A comprehensive, popular package of utility and
    system maintenance programs for IBM and Macintosh
    personal computers (Central Point Software).

DOS contains some tools you need to perform system maintenance and disaster recovery tasks, but at a cost: for example, fussy DOS commands such as BACKUP and RESTORE are not easy to use on a daily basis. On the other hand, PC Tools provides an outstanding, menu-driven backup program and many tools that early versions of DOS omitted, such as file undelete and unformat commands. In addition, PC Tools' current version provides a host of useful functions, such as a word processing module, a telecommunications module, an appointment scheduler, a disk defragmentation program (Compress), a disk repair program that can recover files DOS cannot access, comprehensive virus checking and elimination, and remote computer operation. Windows users will find a Windows-compatible version of the program's backup and undelete features, as well as a clever file-launching utility that automatically modifies the application control icon. See *Microsoft Windows*.

**PDL**   See *page description language*.

**PCM**   See *pulse code modulation*.

**PCX**   A file extension indicating that the file contains a graphic in the PCX graphics file format, which was originally developed for the PC Paintbrush program but now is widely used by other applications.

**peer-to-peer file transfer**   A file-sharing technique for local area networks in which each user has access to the public files of all other network users located on their respective workstations. Each user determines which files, if any, he or she wants to make public for network access. See *TOPS*.

**peer-to-peer network**   A local area network without a central file server and in which all computers in the network have access to the public files of all other workstations. See *client-server network* and *peer-to-peer file transfer*.

**pel**   Abbreviation for *pixel*.

**pen-based computer**   A personal computer equipped with pattern recognition circuitry so that it can recognize human handwriting as a form of data input.

To use a pen-based computer, you "write" on the screen using a special stylus that resembles a pen. But you can't use that elegant cursive you used in school—pen-based computers recognize only printing, and neat printing at that. Using pattern recognition technology, the computer interprets your scribbles and enters words, numbers, symbols, and graphics. You also can use the stylus to choose commands from menus.

The earliest pen-based computers did not perform well, but subsequent models have used more advanced technology. Pen-based computers are expected to find a large market among the many professional and technical workers who need to jot down notes or data as they work with a convenient, portable notebook computer.

Abetting the adoption of pen-based computing is the availability of a special version of Microsoft Windows designed for pen-based computing systems.

**peripheral**   A device, such as a printer or disk drive, connected to and controlled by a computer, but external to the computer's central processing unit (CPU).

**permanent swap file**   In Microsoft Windows, a disk file composed of contiguous disk sectors that is set aside for the rapid storage and retrieval of program instructions or data in the program's 386 Enhanced mode. This storage space is used in virtual memory operations, which use disk space as a seamless extension of random-access memory (RAM). Because the storage areas used in a permanent swap file are contiguous, storage and retrieval operations exceed the normal speed of hard disk operations, which usually distribute data here and there on the disk. The permanent swap file, however, consumes a large amount of space on the disk. See *Microsoft Windows, random-access memory (RAM), swap file, temporary swap file,* and *virtual memory*.

**personal computer**   A stand-alone computer equipped
with all the system, utility, and application software,
and the input/output devices and other peripherals
that an individual needs to perform one or more tasks.

The idea of personal computing, at least initially, was to
free individuals from dependence on tightly controlled
mainframe and minicomputer resources. In a corporate
setting, for example, data processing managers once
had the sole authority to choose the programs and data
formats people used. Even if this choice were made
responsibly, it would suit some employees more than
others. With the rise of personal computing, people
have gained substantially more freedom to choose the
applications tailored to their needs.

In recent years, ample reason has been found to reinte-
grate personal computers (PCs) into the data communications networks of organizations, and this goal can
be achieved without forcing people to give up the
autonomy that personal computing implies.

PCs can serve, for example, as ideal platforms for
common organizational databases, enabling users to
access a huge, central-information storehouse. Smaller
networks can facilitate productivity and work efficiency
among members of a workgroup. By means of electronic
mail, the network can serve as a new way of improving
communication and exchanging information.

Because PCs increasingly are equipped with the
networking and communications hardware they
need to participate in such networks, the boundary
between PCs and professional workstations has blurred
considerably. Professional workstations are powerful,
high-performance computers designed to provide
professionals such as graphics designers, engineers,
and architects with the computing power they need for
calculation-intensive applications, such as computer-
aided design (CAD). Generally equipped with communications hardware, workstations clearly provide the
model toward which high-end PCs, such as those based
on the Intel 80386 and 80486 microprocessors, are
evolving.

Similarly blurred is the distinction between PCs and minicomputers. At one time, PCs were synonymous with microcomputers (computers that have a microprocessor as their CPU). Many minicomputers, however, now use microprocessors. Further blurring the issue, today's high-end PCs can handle a few remote terminals if the PCs have UNIX or some other multiuser operating system. See *professional workstation*.

**personal information manager (PIM)**   A database-management program such as Lotus Agenda that stores and retrieves a variety of personal information, including notes, memos, names and addresses, and appointments.

Unlike a database management program, a PIM is optimized for the storage and retrieval of a variety of personal information. You can switch among a variety of views of your notes, such as people, to-do items, and expenses. PIMs have been slow to gain acceptance, though, because they are hard to learn and people often are away from the computer when they need the information.

**PgUp/PgDn keys**   On IBM PC–compatible computer keyboards, the keys you press to move the cursor to the preceding screen (PgUp) or the next screen (PgDn).

Because the precise implementation of these keys is up to the programmer, their functions vary from program to program. Some word processing programs, for example, use PgUp and PgDn keys for moving to the top of the preceding page, rather than to the preceding screen of text.

**phono plug**   A connector with a short stem. A phono plug connects home audio devices. For example, the jacks on the back of a high-fidelity amplifier are phono plugs. In computers, phono plugs are used for audio and composite monitor output ports. Synonymous with *RCA plug*.

**phosphor**   An electrofluorescent material used to coat the inside face of a cathode ray tube (CRT). After being energized by the electron beam being directed to the inside face of the tube, the phosphors glow for a fraction of a second. The beam must refresh the phosphor many times per second to produce a consistent illumination. See *cathode ray tube (CRT)* and *raster display*.

**phototypesetter**   See *imagesetter*.

**physical drive**   The disk drive actually performing the read/write operations in a secondary storage system.

A disk drive, such as a floppy disk or a hard disk, may have unique electronic and electromechanical characteristics when compared to the other drives in the system, but these unique characteristics of the physical drive are invisible to the user. In an IBM PC–compatible computer equipped with a floppy drive and a hard disk, for example, you follow exactly the same procedure to save a file to drive A and to drive C, even though the two drives are different items of hardware.

From a user's perspective, all the drives seem like logical drives—drives that appear to have exactly the same characteristics, even though they are physically, electronically, and electromechanically different. See *floppy disk*, *hard disk*, *logical drives*, and *secondary storage*.

**physical format**   See *low-level format*.

**physical memory**   The actual random-access memory (RAM) circuits in which data is stored, as opposed to virtual memory—the "apparent" RAM that results from employing the computer's hard disk as an extension of physical memory. See *random-access memory (RAM)* and *virtual memory*.

**PIC**   A file extension indicating that the file contains a graphic in the Lotus PIC format, which Lotus 1-2-3 employs to save business graphs.

**pica**   In typography, a unit of measure equal to approximately 1/6 inch, or 12 points. In typewriting and letter-quality printing, a pica is a 12-point monospace font that prints at a pitch of 10 characters per inch (cpi).

Picas usually describe horizontal and vertical measurements on the page, with the exception of type sizes, which are expressed in points.

Six picas is not exactly equal to 1 inch. In formal typography, one pica is 0.166 of an inch, and 1/6 inch is approximately 0.1667 of an inch. Thirty picas, therefore, is equal to 4.98 inches—a little less than 5 inches. Many word processing and page layout programs, however, break this tradition and define one pica as exactly 1/6 inch.

**pico-**    Prefix for one trillionth ($10^{-12}$). Abbreviated *p.*

**picosecond**    One trillionth ($10^{-12}$) of a second.

**PICT**    A Macintosh graphics file format originally developed by Apple Computer for the MacDraw program. An object-oriented format, PICT files consist of separate graphics objects, such as lines, arcs, ovals, or rectangles, each of which you can independently edit, size, move, or color. (PICT files also can store bit-mapped images.) The PICT format draws on the Mac's built-in QuickDraw graphics toolset and is widely supported by Macintosh application programs. Some Windows graphics applications can read PICT files. See *bit-mapped graphic, file format,* and *object-oriented graphic.*

**pie graph**    In presentation graphics, a graph that displays a data series as a circle to emphasize the relative contribution of each data item to the whole (see fig. P.2).

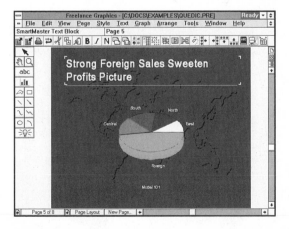

**Fig. P.2.** A pie graph.

Each slice of the pie appears in a distinctive pattern, which can produce Moiré distortions if you juxtapose too many patterns. Some programs can produce paired pie graphs that display two data series. For presentations, exploding a slice from the whole is a useful technique to add emphasis (see fig. P.3). See *linked pie/column graph*, *Moiré distortion*, and *proportional pie graph*.

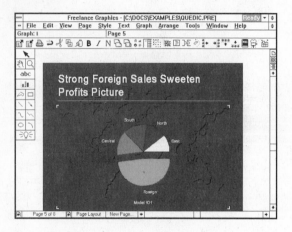

**Fig. P.3.** A pie graph with an exploded slice.

**PIF**   See *program information file*.

**PILOT**   An authoring language for computer-assisted instruction (CAI).

John Starkweather developed PILOT (short for Programmed Inquiry Learning Or Teaching) at the University of California (San Francisco, 1968). PILOT is exceptionally easy to learn because it has very few commands. Used primarily to develop on-screen instructional materials, PILOT is being displaced by new authoring languages that use graphical user interfaces such as HyperTalk. See *computer-assisted instruction (CAI)*.

**PIM**   See *personal information manager*.

**pin feed**   See *tractor feed*.

**pipe**   In DOS and UNIX, a symbol that tells the operating
system to send the output of one command to another
command, rather than displaying this output on the
screen.

In the following example, the pipe (represented by
the ¦ symbol) tells DOS to send the output of the TREE
command to the MORE command, which then displays
the output page by page on-screen:

```
TREE C:\ ¦ MORE
```

See *filter* and *input/output redirection*.

**piracy**   See *software piracy*.

**pitch**   A horizontal measurement of the number of characters per linear inch in a monospace font, such as those
used with typewriters, dot-matrix printers, and daisywheel printers.

By convention, pica pitch (not to be confused with the
printer's measurement of approximately 1/6 inch) is
equal to 10 characters per inch, and elite pitch is equal
to 12 characters per inch. See *monospace*, *pica*, and
*point*.

**pixel**   The smallest element (a picture element) that a
device can display on-screen and out of which the displayed image is constructed. See *bit-mapped graphic*.

**plain text document**   A document that contains nothing
but the standard ASCII text and number characters.

In many applications, you have the option to
save a plain text document in two ways: with
or without Enter keystrokes at the end of
each line.

If you are exporting the document to another word
processor, choose the option that saves the document
*without* Enter keystrokes at the end of each line; after
you import the document, you can insert text within
existing text and have the line breaks reformat automatically. If you choose the option that places Enter

keystrokes at the end of each line, you cannot revise the text without deleting all the Enter keystrokes except those at the end of a paragraph—and that's a tedious operation. Choose the Enter keystroke option only when you need to save plain text for an application, such as uploading a file through telecommunications links. See *ASCII*.

**plasma display**   A display technology used with high-end laptop computers. The display is produced by energizing an ionized gas held between two transparent panels. Synonymous with *gas plasma display*.

**platen**   In dot-matrix and letter-quality impact printers, the cylinder that guides paper through the printer and provides a surface for the impression of the image onto the page.

**platform**   See *hardware platform*.

**platform independence**   The capability of a local area network to connect computers made by different makers, such as connecting an IBM PC–compatible computer with a Macintosh computer.

**platter**   Synonymous with *disk*.

**plot**   To construct an image by drawing lines.

**plotter**   A printer that produces high-quality output by moving ink pens over the surface of the paper. The printer moves the pens under the direction of the computer, so that printing is automatic. Plotters are commonly used for computer-aided design and presentation graphics.

**plotter font**   In Microsoft Windows, a vector font designed to be used with a plotter. The font composes characters by generating dots connected by lines.

**PMMU**   See *paged memory management unit*.

**point**   To move the mouse pointer on-screen without clicking the button. In typography, a fundamental unit of measurement. 72 points equal approximately one inch

(0.9936 inch). Computer programs usually ignore this slight discrepancy, making a point exactly equal to 1/72 inch. See *pica* and *pitch*.

**pointer**   An on-screen symbol, usually an arrow, that shows the current position of the mouse. In database management programs, a record number in an index that stores the actual physical location of the data record.

 If you use Microsoft Windows, learn the meaning of the pointer's shape changes. They tell you when the application is ready to select something, jump to related information, or size a graphic object. See *cursor*.

**pointing device**   An input device such as a mouse, trackball, or stylus graphics tablet used to display a pointer on-screen.

**point-of-sale software**   A program that transforms a personal computer into a point-of-sale system for a small business. Such a system replaces the usual cash register and offers, in its place, computerized invoice printing, automatic retention of customer names and addresses, and sales analysis.

For more than a decade, large businesses have taken full advantage of computerized point-of-sale systems that employ bar code readers and inventory databases. The advantages of such systems are significant: the person working the checkout stand uses a bar code reader to read the product code from each item, and the system automatically looks up the item's name and price. Not only does the computer perform this task more quickly and accurately than even the best checker, but it also automatically adjusts the inventory database as each item is sold. The software warns the manager to reorder an item when stocks fall below a predetermined level, and it enables the manager to analyze sales patterns and trends.

With the arrival of point-of-sale software and bar code readers for personal computers, even a small retail business can take advantage of this technology. A typical point-of-sale software package such as Retail Store Controller (Microbiz) brings virtually all the functionality of the large business systems to a single-user, PC-based point-of-sale workstation. Included are such features as automatic credit card verification, customer history tracking, bar code label printing, sales tracking by employee, reorder reports, flexible sales analysis and reports, and export links to accounting software. Available accessories include a compatible cash drawer and a receipt printer.

**polarity**   In electronics, polarity refers to the negative or positive property of a charge. In computer graphics, polarity refers to the tonal relationship between foreground and background elements. Positive polarity is the printing of black or dark characters on a white or light background, and negative polarity is the printing of white or light characters on a black or dark background.

**polling**   In local area networks, a method for controlling channel access in which the central computer continuously asks or polls the workstations to determine whether they have a message to transmit.

With polling channel access, you can specify how often, and for how long, the central computer polls the workstations. Unlike CSMA/CD and token-ring channel-access methods, the network manager can establish a form of electronic inequality among the networked workstations, in which some nodes have more access to the network than others. See *carrier sense multiple access with collision detection (CSMA/CD)* and *token-ring network*.

**polyline**   In object-oriented computer graphics, a shape created by drawing a straight line to a point, and then continuing the straight line in a different direction, as if you were connecting the stars in a constellation. By continuing this operation, you can create a complex object other than a square, rectangle, circle, or oval. The result is a graphics primitive, which the program treats as a single object. Like the more familiar primitives (squares or circles), the polyline object can be independently edited, sized, moved, or colored. See *graphics primitive* and *object-oriented graphics*.

**pop-up menu**    A menu that appears on-screen anywhere other than in the standard menu bar location at the top of the screen. See *pull-down menu*.

**port**    An entry/exit boundary mechanism that governs and synchronizes the flow of data into and out of the central processing unit (CPU) from and to external devices such as printers and modems. Synonymous with *interface*. Reprogramming an application so that it runs on another type of computer. See *central processing unit (CPU)*, *interface*, *parallel port*, and *serial port*.

**portable**    Capable of working on a variety of hardware platforms.

UNIX is a portable operating system. Most operating systems are designed around the specific electronic capabilities of a given central processing unit (CPU). UNIX, in contrast, is designed with a predetermined, overall structure. Instructions are embedded within the program that enable it to function on a given CPU. See *UNIX*.

**portable computer**    A computer designed to be transported easily from one location to another.

The first portable personal computers, such as the Osborne I and Compaq II, are best described as "luggables." These computers weigh in at well over 25 pounds and cannot be carried comfortably for more than a short distance. Today's battery-powered laptop computers are much more portable. A computer weighing over 10 pounds is too heavy to carry around all day. See *laptop computer* and *notebook computer*.

**portrait monitor**    See *full-page display*.

**portrait orientation**    The default printing orientation for a page of text, with the longest measurement oriented vertically (see fig. P.4). See *landscape orientation*.

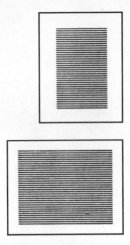

**Fig. P.4.** Examples of portrait orientation (top) and landscape orientation (bottom).

**post**   In database management, to add data to a data record.

**postprocessor**   A program that performs a final, automatic processing operation after you finish working with a file.

Postprocessing programs include text formatters that prepare a document for printing, and page description languages that convert an on-screen document into a set of commands that the printer's interpreter can recognize and use to print the document.

**PostScript**   A sophisticated page description language, widely used in desktop publishing, that is used for printing high-quality text and graphics on laser printers and other high-resolution printing devices.

PostScript, developed by Adobe Systems, Inc., is a programming language that describes how to print a page that blends text and graphics. Because PostScript is a genuine programming language, you can learn to write PostScript instructions and embed them in documents to be printed.

For most users, however, PostScript is invisible and automatic. When you use an application program equipped with a PostScript printer driver, the program

generates the PostScript code that goes to the printer.
At the printer, a PostScript interpreter reads the instructions and follows them to generate an image of
the page in precise accordance with these instructions.
The whole operation is transparent to you.

A major benefit of PostScript is its device independence; you can print the PostScript code generated
by an application on any printer with a PostScript
interpreter. This includes expensive typesetting
machines, such as those manufactured by Linotronic,
Compugraphic, and Varityper, that are capable of resolutions of up to 2,400 dpi.

PostScript printer output always takes full advantage
of the printer's maximum resolution. You can take the
disk containing a document you have created with an
application such as Microsoft Word or WordPerfect to
a service bureau, which can print the document at
resolutions equal to or surpassing those found in professional publications. See *page description language
(PDL)*, *PostScript font,* and *PostScript printer*.

**PostScript font**   An outline font that conforms to Adobe
Software's specifications for Type 1 printer fonts,
which require a PostScript-compatible printer. As opposed to a bit-mapped font, which often prints with
unacceptably crude edges and curves, PostScript's
outline font technology produces smooth letters that
your printer renders at its maximum possible resolution. A PostScript font comes with a screen font, which
simulates the font's appearance on-screen, as well as a
printer font, which you must download to the printer
before you print. Most PostScript laser printers come
with several PostScript fonts built into the printer's
permanent memory; downloading is not necessary
before using these fonts.

PostScript fonts are scalable, which means that you
need not have a separate font for every font size you
want to print (as you must with bit-mapped fonts); you
can choose any font size you want within a specified
range (for example, from 4 to 72 points), and you will
get smooth-looking type at the printer. Note, though,
that the type may look jagged on-screen unless you

purchase Adobe Type Manager, which brings PostScript scalable font technology to the display screen.

For personal computer users who do not want to blend text with high-quality EPS (Encapsulated PostScript) graphics, TrueType font technology, jointly developed by Apple Computer and Microsoft Corporation, provides a cost-effective alternative to PostScript fonts and PostScript laser printers. Like PostScript fonts, TrueType fonts are outline fonts, so they print a high resolution with smooth edges, and they are scalable, so you can choose any font size within the specified range and get good results. But TrueType fonts are much more economical: TrueType fonts do not require the printer to have an expensive interpreter (which requires a microprocessor). Moreover, if you're using TrueType with Microsoft Windows 3.1, or with the Mac's System 7, you do not need Adobe Type Manager to see scalable fonts on-screen. The scaling technology is built into Windows 3.1 and System 7. See *outline font, PostScript, PostScript printer, scalable font,* and *TrueType.*

**PostScript printer**   A printer, generally a laser printer, that includes the processing circuitry needed to decode and interpret printing instructions phrased in PostScript, a page description language (PDL) widely used in desktop publishing.

Because PostScript printers require their own microprocessor circuitry and at least 1M RAM to image each page, they are more expensive than non-PostScript printers.

PostScript laser printers such as the Apple LaserWriter have several advantages over non-PostScript laser printers such as the Hewlett-Packard LaserJet. PostScript printers can print text or graphics in subtle gradations of gray. They can use Encapsulated PostScript (EPS) graphics and outline fonts, both of which you can size and scale without introducing distortions. PostScript printers also can produce special effects, such as rotation and overprinting. However, the TrueType font technology, jointly developed by Apple Computer and Microsoft Corporation, offers a cost-effective alternative to PostScript fonts and printers. TrueType technology does not require the printer to possess a microprocessor, so you can print TrueType fonts on virtually any printer. See *PostScript*.

**posture**   The slant of the characters in a font. Italic characters slant to the right, but the term *italic* is reserved by conservative typographers for custom-designed (as opposed to electronically produced) serif typefaces.

**PowerBook**   A series of portable Macintosh notebook computers. Introduced in 1992, the PowerBook line—jointly manufactured by Sony and Apple—was well received, in contrast to the bulky Macintosh Portable introduced in 1989 (and now discontinued). PowerBooks feature a built-in trackball so that you don't need a mouse to use the system.

**power down**   To turn off the computer's power switch.

**power line filter**   An electrical device that smoothes out the peaks and valleys of the voltage delivered at the wall socket.

Every electrical circuit is subject to voltage fluctuations, and if these fluctuations are extreme, they may cause seemingly random computer errors and failures. Flickering lights are a good sign of uneven voltage. If you are using a computer in a circuit shared by heavy appliances, you may need a power line filter to ensure error-free operation. See *surge protector*.

**PowerPoint**   A full-featured presentation graphics program for the Macintosh that can produce 35-mm transparencies, overhead transparencies, business charts, and flip charts.

Like Harvard Graphics, a similar program available for IBM PC–compatible computers, PowerPoint includes a word processor, spelling checker, and an object-oriented draw program.

**PowerPoint for Windows**   A presentation graphics program developed by Microsoft Corporation for Microsoft Windows. Drawing on Windows' graphical user interface, PowerPoint can take full advantage of Windows' multiple on-screen fonts and capability to import graphics from other Windows applications. The program includes a slide-show mode, which makes the program ideal for desktop presentations. See *desktop presentation, presentation graphics program,* and *slide show*.

**power supply**   The electrical component of a computer system that converts standard AC current to the lower voltage DC current used by the computer. The amount of current a power supply can provide is rated in amperes (amps).

 The power supply of early IBM PC–compatible computers (63.5 watts) often proved inadequate after users added several adapters, a hard disk, and other system upgrades. An overloaded power supply can cause erratic operations, such as read or write errors, parity errors, and unexplained system crashes. For systems with hard disks and several adapters, users should have a power supply of at least 200 watts.

**power surge**   A brief and often very large increase in line voltage caused by turning off appliances, by lightning strikes, or by the re-establishment of power after a power outage. See *surge*.

**power up**   To switch on the computer's power switch.

**power user**   A computer user who has gone beyond the beginning and intermediate stages of computer use. Such a person uses the advanced features of application programs, such as software command languages and macros, and can learn new application programs quickly.

**ppm**   Abbreviation for *pages per minute*. A crude and often inaccurate measurement of page printers, such as inkjet and laser printers. A laser printer that is said to print eight pages per minute may do so only if you choose the built-in Courier font and print a document with no graphics. If you use a different font or include graphics, the document will print more slowly.

**PRAM**   See *parameter RAM*.

**precedence**   The order in which a program performs the operations in a formula. Typically, the program performs exponentiation, such as squaring a number, before multiplication and division; the program then performs addition and subtraction.

**precision**   The number of digits past the decimal that are used to express a quantity. See *accuracy*.

**presentation graphics**   The branch of the graphics profession that is concerned with the preparation of slides, transparencies, and handouts for use in business presentations. Ideally, presentation graphics combines artistry with practical psychology and good taste; color, form, and emphasis are used intelligently to convey the presentation's most significant points to the audience. See *analytical graphics*.

**presentation graphics program**   An application program designed to create and enhance charts and graphs so that they are visually appealing and easily understood by an audience.

A full-featured presentation graphics package such as Lotus Freelance Graphics for Windows includes facilities for making text charts, bar graphs, column graphs, pie graphs, high/low/close/open graphs, and organization charts.

The package also provides facilities for adding titles, legends, and explanatory text anywhere in the chart or graph. A presentation graphics program also includes a library of clip art, so you can enliven charts and graphs by adding a picture related to the subject matter—for example, an airplane for a chart of earnings in the aerospace industry. You can print output, direct output to a film recorder, or display output on-screen in a computer slide show.

**Presentation Manager**   A graphical user interface and application programming interface (API) for OS/2, jointly developed by Microsoft Corporation and IBM.

Presentation Manager brings to IBM PC–compatible computers running the OS/2 operating system many of the graphical user interface features associated with the Macintosh—multiple on-screen typefaces, pull-down menus, multiple on-screen windows, and desktop accessories.

Presentation Manager is not a version of Microsoft Windows. Presentation Manager clearly reflects its joint development by Microsoft and IBM. Unlike Windows, Presentation Manager conforms to IBM standards such as SAA (Systems Application Architecture). The application programming interface standards are set by SAA, not by Windows, and programs developed for Windows do not run under Presentation Manager without very substantial modification.

The lack of an easy upgrade path from Windows applications to Presentation Manager is one of the many factors that has delayed the development of programs for OS/2. See *Microsoft Windows* and *Operating System/2 (OS/2)*.

**primary storage**   The computer's main memory directly accessible to the central processing unit (CPU), unlike secondary storage, such as disk drives.

In personal computers, primary storage consists of the random-access memory (RAM) and the read-only memory (ROM).

**print engine**   Inside a laser printer, the mechanism that uses a laser to create an electrostatic image of a page and fuses that image to a cut sheet of paper.

You can distinguish print engines by their resolution, print quality, longevity, paper-handling features, and speed.

- *Resolution.* The print engine used in most laser printers generally produces resolutions of 300 dpi, although the trend is toward 400-dpi printers. High-end laser printers available for professional typesetting purposes contain engines capable of resolutions up to 600 dpi. (Professional typesetting machines called *imagesetters* use chemical photo-reproduction techniques to produce resolutions of up to 2,400 dpi.)

- *Print Quality.* Write-white engines expose the portion of the page that does not receive ink (so that toner is attracted to the areas that print black) and generally produce deeper blacks than write-black engines, but this quality varies from engine to engine. Although dozens of retail brands of laser printers are on the market, the print engines are made by just a few Japanese original equipment manufacturers (OEM), such as Canon, Ricoh, Toshiba, and Casio. Canon engines are highly regarded within the desktop publishing industry.

- *Longevity.* Most print engines have a life of 300,000 copies, but the life span ratings among brands vary from 180,000 to 600,000 copies. Because printer longevity is estimated from heavy use over a short period of time, you should consider a printer's longevity rating only if the printer will be used in heavy-demand network applications.

- *Paper-Handling Features.* Early laser printers vexed users with thin paper trays capable of holding only 50 or 60 sheets of paper. For convenient use, you should consider a paper tray capacity of at least 100 sheets; 200 or 250 is better.

- *Speed.* Print engines often are rated (optimistically) at speeds of up to 10 pages per minute. Such speeds, however, are attained only under ideal conditions; the same sparse page of text is printed over and over again. When printing a real manuscript with different text on each page, the printer must pause to construct the image, and output is substantially slower. Also, if the printer encounters a graphic, printing may grind to a halt for as long as a minute. For real-world applications, what determines a print engine's speed is the processing prowess of the controller's microprocessor. The speed demons of laser printing use third-generation microprocessors

(such as the Motorola 68020) running at clock
speeds of up to 16.7 MHz.

**printer**   A computer peripheral designed to print computer-
generated text or graphics on paper.

Printers vary significantly in their quality, speed, noise,
graphics capabilities, built-in fonts, and paper usage.
The ideal printer would cost much less than $1,000,
print text and graphics at resolutions approaching
those produced by professional typesetting machinery
(such as 300 or 400 dpi, or dots per inch), churn out
several printed pages per minute, operate quietly,
blend text and graphics seamlessly, offer a variety of
built-in fonts and font sizes, and use standard, office-
quality xerographic bond paper (or your company's
printed letterhead).

How does your printer—or the printer you're thinking
about buying—measure up to the ideal? A given printer's
capabilities are strongly shaped by the printing technology it uses. The following list provides a brief overview
of print technology options in personal computing.

- *Letter-quality printers* (also called *daisywheel printers*) form an image the same way office typewriters
do—by hammering a fully formed image of a character against a ribbon, thus producing an inked image
on the paper. Formerly the mainstay of professional
computing in settings such as law offices or academic departments, letter-quality printers have been
all but pushed out of the market by laser printers.
The best letter-quality printers can print up to 50
characters per second or more, but they have two
major disadvantages: to change fonts, you must halt
printing and physically change the print wheel, and
these printers cannot print graphics. Letter-quality
printers equipped with cut-sheet feeders can use
xerographic bond paper or letterhead; otherwise,
you're stuck with continuous tractor-fed paper, and
you must manually separate the sheets and remove
the snaf (the narrow strips of hole-punched paper
necessary to pull the paper through the printer).

- *Dot-matrix printers* form an image by extruding
  a pattern (or matrix) of wires against a ribbon,
  producing an inked image on paper. Unlike letter-
  quality printers, however, the image is not fully
  formed; you can see the dots, and the result, often,
  is unsightly and hard to read. The best dot-matrix
  printers employ as many as 24 pins so that there is
  very little space between the dots. Dot-matrix printers print rapidly (100 or more characters per second), but printing speeds degrade considerably
  when you choose high-resolution modes, in which
  the printer goes back over a character, printing
  another set of dots slightly out of register so that
  the character appears to be fully formed. Some
  dot-matrix printers come with several fonts and font
  sizes, and all can print graphics. Many dot-matrix
  printers are extremely noisy. Dot-matrix printers
  are still widely sold, but comparably priced inkjet
  printers, which operate silently and produce better
  output, may soon push dot-matrix technology off
  the market.

- *Inkjet printers* form an image by spraying ink
  directly on the paper's surface, producing what
  appears to be a fully formed image. Inkjet printers,
  which often are rated at 4 to 6 ppm (pages per
  minute), are slower than laser printers, but they
  produce text and graphics output that, to the unsophisticated eye, seems comparable to laser printer
  quality. In reality, the characters are somewhat less
  distinct than those formed by a laser printer. Inkjet
  printers, however, are less expensive than laser
  printers, and unlike dot-matrix printers, they produce little noise. Like laser printers, most inkjet
  printers come with a selection of built-in fonts and
  can use font cartridges or downloadable fonts.
  Popular inkjet printers include Hewlett-Packard's
  DeskJet (for IBM PCs and PC compatibles) and
  DeskWriter (for Macs), and Apple Computer's
  StyleWriter, which has supplanted the dot-matrix
  ImageWriter as the entry-level printer in Apple's
  Macintosh line.

- *Laser printers* employ copy-machine technology to fuse powdered ink to paper, producing high-quality output. Laser printers produce high-quality output at relatively high speeds (most are rated at 8 or more pages per minute), use cut sheets or letter-head, and operate quietly. Most come with a selection of built-in fonts and can easily accommodate font cartridges or downloadable fonts. Their major drawback, until lately, was high cost, but laser printers are now available for less than $700. Note, though, that laser toner cartridges, filled with enough toner for 2,500 to 4,000 pages, can cost $100 or more; you can save some money on toner costs by purchasing refilled cartridges. Popular laser printers include Hewlett-Packard's LaserJet printers and Apple Computer's LaserWriters.

- *LED and LCD printers* closely resemble laser printers, except that these printers do not employ lasers to form the image. LED printers employ an array of light-emitting diodes (LEDs) for this purpose; LCD printers employ a halogen light, the illumination of which is distributed by means of liquid crystal shutters.

- *Thermal printers* operate quietly, but that is their only advantage. They operate by pushing a matrix of heated pins against special heat-sensitive paper, which means that you must use the right kind of paper. They produce output that resembles that of a cheap dot-matrix printer, except that the paper's surface is shiny and smells bad; even worse, they print slowly. Thermal printers are deservedly relegated to minor applications in calculators, fax machines, and portable computer systems.

What's the best printer for you? Because inkjet and laser printers are quiet and well supported by most application programs, one of these is probably your best bet. For a home system or for light office use, an inkjet printer may prove ideal. For a busy office, you'll need a laser printer's faster printing speed. See *dot-matrix printer*,

*inkjet printer, laser printer, letter-quality printer, light
emitting diode (LED) printer, liquid crystal display
(LCD) printer*, and *thermal printer*.

**printer control language**   The command set used to control a printer of a given brand. Common printer control
languages include the Epson command set for dot-
matrix printers, the Hewlett-Packard Printer Control
Language (HPPCL) for IBM-compatible laser printers,
and the Diablo command set for letter-quality printers.

Printer control languages should be distinguished from
page description languages such as PostScript, which
are true programming languages in their own right.
Printer control languages are often little more than
proprietary implementations of the higher-order ASCII
control codes, which programs send to the printer to
toggle features such as boldfaced printing on and off.

**printer driver**   A file that contains the information a program needs to print your work with a given brand and
model of printer.

A major difference between the DOS environment and
Macintosh/Windows environments is the way printer
drivers are handled. In IBM PC–compatible computing,
printer drivers are the responsibility of application
programs; each program must come equipped with a
printer driver for the many dozens of printers available.

These printer drivers work only with the program
for which they were written. The WordPerfect printer
driver for the HP DeskJet, for example, does not help
Microsoft Word print with the DeskJet. If a program
does not include a driver for your printer, you may be
out of luck. Microsoft Windows, fortunately, cures the
printing deficiencies of DOS by providing printer drivers for all Windows applications.

Printer drivers also are part of the operating environment in the Macintosh. Individual programs do not
have printer drivers; instead, they are designed to take
advantage of printer drivers provided at the operating
system level and stored in the System Folder.

A significant advantage of this method for handling printer drivers is that all programs can use the printer, not just the programs that have included a printer driver.

**printer emulation**   A printer's recognition of a different printer brand's printer control language. Widely emulated are Epson, Hewlett-Packard, and Diablo printers.

**printer font**   A font that does not display on-screen and is available for use only by the printer. When using a printer font, you see a generic screen font on-screen; you must wait until printing is complete to see your document's fonts.

Ideally, screen fonts and printer fonts should be identical; only then can a computer system claim to offer what-you-see-is-what-you-get text processing. Today's systems are often far from the ideal. Character-based programs running under DOS cannot display typefaces on-screen other than those built into the computer's ROM. In WordPerfect for DOS, for example, you can choose many different printer fonts in a document, but you cannot see the font changes on-screen. Many users are quite satisfied with this technology and get excellent results. For others, seeing the fonts on-screen is necessary to avoid printing errors.

With Microsoft Windows and Macintosh systems, you can use TrueType or Adobe Type Manager (ATM) outline (scalable) fonts, which appear on-screen the way they appear when printed. See *Adobe Type Manager (ATM)*, *outline font*, and *TrueType*.

**printer port**   See *parallel port* and *serial port*.

**print queue**   A list of files that a print spooler prints in the background while the computer performs other tasks in the foreground.

**print server**   In a local area network, a PC that has been dedicated to receiving and temporarily storing files to be printed, which it doles out one-by-one to a printer. The print server runs print spooler software, which establishes a print queue, and is accessible to all the workstations in the network. See *local area network (LAN)*, *print queue*, and *print spooler*.

**print spooler**   A utility program that temporarily stores files to be printed in a print queue and doles them out one-by-one to the printer. See *background printing*, *print queue*, and *print server*.

**print spooling program**   A utility program that prints a file while you continue to work with an application.

**procedural language**   A language such as BASIC or Pascal that requires the programmer to specify the procedure the computer has to follow to accomplish the task. See *declarative language*.

**processing**   The execution of program instructions by the computer's central processing unit (CPU) that in some way transforms data, such as sorting it, selecting some of it according to specified criteria, or performing mathematical computations on it.

**ProComm Plus**   A popular and well-conceived telecommunications package, marketed by Datastorm, for IBM and IBM-compatible personal computers. ProComm Plus had its origins in a shareware product. It facilitates telecommunications functions, such as terminal emulation, file transfer using the XMODEM protocol (and other popular protocols as well), on-line chatting, a host mode for interactive dial-in operations, and automatic log-on procedures.

**Prodigy**   An on-line information service jointly developed by Sears and IBM that offers (via modem) personal computer users home shopping, news, stock quotes, hobbyist conferences, and so on.

Innovative features of Prodigy include the use of a bit-mapped graphical user interface and unlimited use of the system for a flat fee. An exception is electronic mail usage, for which a surcharge is added.

Prodigy, however, has no provisions for software up-loading or downloading, and many users complain about its sluggish speed. Also, part of the screen is occupied by commercial advertisements. See *on-line information service*.

**professional workstation**  A high-performance personal computer optimized for professional applications in fields such as digital circuit design, architecture, and technical drawing.

Professional workstations typically offer excellent screen resolution, fast and powerful processing circuits, and ample memory. Examples include the workstations made by Sun Microsystems and NeXT, Inc. Professional workstations are more expensive than personal computers and typically use the UNIX operating system. The boundary between high-end personal computers and professional workstations, however, is eroding as personal computers become more powerful.

**Professional Write**  A word processing program, marketed by Spinnaker, for IBM Personal Computers and compatibles. Designed for executives and professional workers, the program is easy to use and does not burden you with unnecessary features. A new version is now available for Microsoft Windows.

**program**  A list of instructions, written in a programming language, that a computer can execute so that the machine acts in a predetermined way. Synonymous with *software*.

Computer programmers use a variety of programming languages, such as BASIC, C, C++, FORTRAN, and SmallTalk, to create programs. Some programming languages, such as the ones just listed, are high-level languages, in which the programmer can express the program using symbols and sequences that resemble English; at some point, though, the program must be converted to the machine language that the computer can execute. This conversion can be accomplished by an assembler, an interpreter, or a compiler.

The world of computer programs can be divided into system programs, utility programs, and application programs.

- *System programs* refer, collectively, to all the programs the computer requires to function effectively, including the operating system, memory management software, and command-line interpreters. The MS-DOS operating system is an example of system software.

- *Utility programs* include all the programs provided so that you can maintain the computer system. MS-DOS includes several utility programs, such as CHKDSK; most users equip their systems with utility packages (such as Norton Utilities or PC Tools) that go beyond the basics that MS-DOS provides.

- *Application programs* transform the computer into a tool for performing a specific kind of work, such as word processing, financial analysis (with an electronic spreadsheet), or desktop publishing.

Additional software categories include games, programming languages, educational programs, and a variety of vertical-market programs. See *executable program, high-level language, machine language, programming language,* and *vertical market program.*

**program generator**   A program that enables nonprogrammers to use simple techniques to describe an application. The program generator then creates the code automatically.

In database management programs, for example, you can use program generation techniques to describe the output format graphically. The program generator then uses your input as a set of parameters by which to construct the output program code.

**program information file (PIF)**   A file provided with many non-Windows application programs that tells Windows how to run them. Windows can still run an application, even if it lacks a PIF file. See *Microsoft Windows* and *non-Windows application.*

**program item**   In Microsoft Windows, an icon representing an application.

**programmable**   Capable of being controlled through instructions that can be varied to suit the user's needs.

**programmable read-only memory (PROM)**   A read-only memory (ROM) chip programmed at the factory for use with a given computer.

The alternative to PROM is a ROM chip in which the information is expressed in the actual design of the circuits internal to the chip. This approach is inflexible because the chip can be modified only with difficulty, and if the programming has a bug or the firm decides to add a feature to the computer, redesigning and manufacturing the chip is expensive and time-consuming.

A programmable ROM chip gets around this problem by offering the computer manufacturer a write-once chip—a chip that can be programmed just once, after which the programming becomes permanent. The process of programming the chip is called "burning the PROM." If it becomes necessary to change the programming, making the alterations and burning the new PROMS with the modified information is simple. See *erasable programmable read-only memory (EPROM)*.

**programmer**   A person who designs, codes, tests, debugs, and documents a computer program.

Professional programmers often hold B.S. or M.S. degrees in computer science, but a great deal of programming (professional and otherwise) is done by individuals with little or no formal training. More than half the readers of a popular personal computer magazine, for example, stated in a survey that they regularly programmed their personal computers using languages such as BASIC, Pascal, and assembly language.

**programmer's switch**   A plastic accessory included with pre-1991 Macintosh computers that, when installed on the side of the computer, enables you to perform a hardware reset and access the computer's built-in debugger.

If you use the MacPlus, SE, or SE/30, you should install the programmer's switch, even if you don't perform programming. The programmer's switch enables you to restart the computer after a system crash without flipping the power switch on and off and subjecting your system to the stress of a start-up power surge. You can perform a soft boot by choosing Restart from the Finder menu, but only if you can get to the Finder. After a crash that freezes the system, the programmer's switch provides the only means to restart the system short of flipping the switch off and on. More recent Macs enable you to restart the system from the keyboard.

**programming** The process of providing instructions to the computer that tell the microprocessor what to do.

Stages in programming include design, or making decisions about what the program should accomplish; coding, or using a programming language to express the program's logic in computer-readable form; testing and debugging, in which the program's flaws are discovered and corrected; and documentation, in which an instructional manual for the program is created.

 If you would like to give programming a try, begin with an event-driven language such as HyperTalk (Macintosh systems) or Visual BASIC (Windows systems). In an event-driven language, you embed a few lines of programming code in an on-screen object, such as a window or button. Using an event-driven language, you can produce impressive results in short order. Along the way you will learn many of the basic concepts of programming, including variables and control structures.

Your next step is to tackle a well-structured high-level language such as QuickBASIC or Pascal. (A well-structured language includes a full set of control structures so that you don't have to resort to excessive use of the

GOTO command, which results in "spaghetti code": poorly organized programs that are difficult to debug.) By learning how to use a well-structured high-level language, you will learn more about creating a complete, ready-to-run program that performs a task flawlessly.

If you're interested in developing professional programming expertise, you'll need to learn the details of specific hardware environments, including the capabilities of specific microprocessors. The best way to do so is to learn some assembly language programming or C, a high-level language in which you can embed assembly language instructions. Many professional programming houses are making the transition to object-oriented programming languages, such as C++, so gaining expertise in this area is also desirable. See *C, C++, event-driven environment, HyperTalk, QuickBASIC, object-oriented programming language, Pascal, spaghetti code, Visual BASIC,* and *well-structured programming language.*

**programming environment**   A set of tools for program development, debugging, and maintenance that is commonly provided with a computer's operating system. Minimally, the tools include a line editor, a debugger, and an assembler to compile assembly language programs. These tools may not be sufficient for professional program development, however, and often are replaced by an application development system. See *application development system.*

**programming language**   An artificial language, consisting of a fixed vocabulary and a set of rules (called *syntax*), that you can use to create instructions for a computer to follow. Most programs are written by using a text editor or word processing program to create source code, which is then interpreted or compiled into the machine language that the computer can actually execute.

Programming languages are numerous, and most computer scientists agree that no single language will ever suffice to serve the needs of all programmers.

Conventionally, programming languages are divided into high-level languages and low-level languages.

- *High-level programming languages,* such as BASIC, C, or Pascal, allow the programmer to express the program using keywords and syntax that crudely resemble natural human language. These languages are called "high level" because they free the programmer from detailed concerns about just how the computer will physically carry out each instruction; the language's interpreter or compiler takes care of these details when the original source code is converted into executable machine language. Each statement in a high-level language corresponds to several machine language instructions, so you can write programs more quickly in high-level programming languages than in lower-level languages, such as assembly language. But there is a cost to using a high-level language: the translation is inefficient, so that programs written in high-level languages run more slowly than programs written in low-level languages.

- *Low-level programming languages,* such as assembly language, allow the programmer to code the instructions with the maximum possible efficiency. But using low-level languages requires detailed expertise in the exact capabilities of a given computer system and its microprocessor. In addition, assembly language programming requires far more time.

The popularity of the C programming language, originally developed at AT&T's Bell Laboratories, can be attributed to the fact that it combines the benefits of high-level and low-level programming languages. With C, a programmer writes most of the program in high-level code, but can strategically embed assembly language instructions in the program so that the program executes more efficiently.

Another way of differentiating programming languages is to distinguish between procedural and declarative languages. In a procedural language, the programmer must spell out, to varying degrees, the procedure the computer will follow to accomplish a given goal. Examples of procedural languages include all the ones mentioned thus far in this discussion, including assembly language, BASIC, C, FORTRAN, and Pascal. In a declarative language (also called a *non-procedural language*), the language defines a set of facts and relationships and allows you to query for specific results. Examples of declarative languages include PROLOG and Structured Query Language (SQL). Procedural languages are not about to be pushed aside, however. The use of declarative languages is restricted, in practice, to expert systems and database query applications.

A key issue in professional programming development is the modularity of the language—that is, the extent to which the programming task can be divided among the members of a programming team, with the result that the various parts will function together properly when each individual's assignment is finished. A modular programming language such as Modula-2 or an object-oriented language such as C++ permits each programmer to concentrate on coding, compiling, and debugging a separate program module, which can function (and be tested) on its own. When all the individual modules are working correctly, they can be combined without catastrophic results. See *BASIC, C, C++, COBOL, FORTRAN, compiler, declarative language, expert system, high-level language, interpreter, Modula-2, modular programming language, object code, object-oriented programming language, Pascal, procedural language, PROLOG,* and *source code.*

**program overlay**   A portion of a program kept on disk and called into memory only as required.

**project management program**   Software that tracks individual tasks that make up an entire job.

Managing a big project, like building a submarine or the World Trade Center in New York, is far from easy. Thousands of little jobs must be coordinated so that they're finished at the same time that thousands of other little jobs are finished, because both groups of little jobs are prerequisites for the next phase of the project. To help project managers cope with the problems caused by having so many activities going on at once, project management techniques called CPM (critical path method) and PERT (Program Evaluation and Review Technique) were created. Both methods try to help managers discern the critical path—that is, the jobs that *must* be completed on time if the whole project is to be finished as scheduled. When the critical path becomes clear, the manager can allocate the resources necessary to complete these tasks in a timely fashion.

Project management software brings to PCs the analytical tools of CPM and PERT, but whether many personal computer users will benefit from managing projects with these techniques is doubtful. CPM and PERT are cost-effective only for large projects where a manager or team of managers cannot keep track of all the tasks involved without some record-keeping assistance. Few PC users are likely to engage in tasks of that size, and the value of CPM and PERT for smaller projects is not clear, even when a computer takes care of the formerly troublesome calculations involved in these techniques.

**PROLOG**  A high-level programming language used in artificial intelligence research and applications, particularly expert systems.

PROLOG (short for PROgramming in LOGic) was developed by French computer scientist Alain Colmerauer and logician Philippe Roussel in the early 1970s. Like LISP, PROLOG is a declarative language; PROLOG does not tell the computer what procedure to follow to solve a problem, as a procedural language does, but enables the programmer to describe the problem to be solved.

The language resembles the query language of a database management system such as SQL in that you can use PROLOG to ask a question such as "Is Foster City in California?" But an important difference exists between PROLOG and a database management system (DBMS).

A DBMS query language searches the database to try to match the query terms, using a simple pattern-matching algorithm. PROLOG, however, provides tools by which the programmer can state knowledge about the world as well as a set of rules by which conclusions can be drawn from this knowledge. A database contains information you can retrieve; a PROLOG program, in contrast, contains knowledge, from which the program can draw inferences about what is true or false.

An example should clarify the significance of this difference between PROLOG and database retrieval systems. In PROLOG, you declare a fact about the world (Tina likes rock music) in the following way:

```
likes(tina, rock music)
```

You can create a database of such facts about the world:

```
likes(tina, rock music)
likes(howard, tina)
likes(howard, blues)
likes(tina, howard)
```

Query operations initiate logical inferences from the knowledge base. For example, you can ask, "Does Tina like Howard?" The answer is yes; a rule specifies that Tina likes Howard. You also can ask, "Does Howard like rock music?" The answer is no, or more accurately, no evidence in the database infers a yes answer.

Rules embedded in the database specify how you can draw further inferences from the data. For example, you can specify the following rule:

```
X and Y like each other if X likes Y and
Y likes X
```

You can ask, "Do Howard and Tina like each other?" The answer is yes, because Howard likes Tina and Tina likes Howard.

Programmers often use PROLOG to develop expert systems at the research system level. A great deal of effort and time is involved in developing a PROLOG expert system. For the development of commercial systems, most expert system programmers prefer to use expert system shells, which free programmers from the task of developing user interfaces, input/output operations, and other procedures tedious to program in PROLOG.

**PROM**   See *programmable read-only memory*.

**prompt**   A symbol or phrase that appears on-screen to inform you that the computer is ready to accept input.

**property**   In Microsoft Windows and MS-DOS Shell, an item of information associated with a program. Properties include the program's start-up directory, the application shortcut key, and a password. See *application shortcut key*, *Microsoft Windows*, and *MS-DOS Shell*.

**proportional pie graph**   In presentation graphics, a paired pie graph in which the size of the two pies is adjusted to reflect the difference in their overall magnitude. Proportional pie graphs are useful for comparing two pies when one is significantly larger than the other.

**proportional spacing**   The allocation of character widths proportional to the character shape, so that a narrow character such as *i* receives less space than a wide character such as *m*. See *kerning* and *monospace*.

**proprietary**   Privately owned; based on trade secrets or privately developed technology or specifications that the owner refuses to divulge, thus preventing others from duplicating a product or program unless an explicit license is purchased. The opposite of proprietary is *open* (privately developed but publicly published and available for emulation by others).

In personal computing, the Macintosh employs a proprietary architecture; no other company may produce a Macintosh clone without a license from Apple Computer. In contrast, IBM did not view the IBM Personal Computer's architecture as proprietary, with the exception of the code stored in the computer's read-only memory (ROM). Other companies were able to emulate this code without actually copying IBM's code, enabling many companies, such as Compaq, to make computers that were functionally identical (or superior) to IBM's offerings.

Any given company views its technology as proprietary, due to its natural desire to prohibit others from quickly and cheaply profiting from its expensive, time-consuming product development efforts. What is more, insisting on a proprietary architecture may result in the company's technology becoming the de facto industry standard, thus forcing others to pay a license fee for every computer or program they sell. Adobe Systems, for example, regarded its PostScript font technology as proprietary until 1990, when Apple Computer and Microsoft, averse to Adobe's licensing fees, announced the development of TrueType. In reply, Adobe published the information other firms would need to create PostScript-compatible fonts.

Industry experts are divided, however, on the wisdom of proprietary architectures. IBM's willingness to allow others to clone the Personal Computer led to an explosion in IBM-compatible computing, an explosion that—some would argue—ultimately benefitted IBM. Watching its market share dwindling, however, IBM brought out its PS/2 computers with a proprietary bus architecture called MicroChannel, for which only a few clone makers have purchased licenses. Clone makers countered by offering their own, open bus architecture, called EISA (Extended Industry Standard Architecture). IBM's move has not improved the firm's market share.

From the user's perspective, proprietary designs or formats entail risk. If the company prospers and the design or format is widely emulated or accepted, the user benefits. But if the company does not prosper or fails, the user could be stuck with a computer system or with data that cannot be upgraded or exchanged with others. U.S. government historians and archivists speak of a crisis directly attributable to proprietary data architectures: Huge amounts of important historical data, some of which is still of immense strategic value, are about to be lost irretrievably, and all because they are stored on irreparable, incompatible systems made by defunct computer companies. See *clone*.

**proprietary file format**   A file format developed by a firm for storing data created by its products. A proprietary file format usually is unreadable by other firms' application programs. Microsoft Word, for example, cannot read WordPerfect files.

**protected mode**   In 80286 and later Intel microprocessors, an operating mode in which programs running simultaneously cannot invade each other's memory space or directly access input/output devices, preventing system failures during multitasking operations.

The default operating mode of Intel microprocessors (8088, 8086, 80286, 80386, and 80486) is called *real mode*. In real mode, a program can interfere with another program's instructions in memory, and such interference can cause the computer to crash. (That's why crashes are so frequent when you are running several terminate-and-stay-resident [TSR] programs.) Worse, the programs you are running must compete for the limited, 640K conventional memory space, the maximum allowable under MS-DOS.

With the 80286 and later microprocessors, a second operating mode, *protected mode*, became available. In protected mode, the computer can use memory beyond the 640K conventional memory barrier. The best benefits of protected mode processing, however, become available only with 80386 and higher microprocessors. To run MS-DOS programs in this extended memory, 80386 and higher microprocessors are capable of simulating two or more 640K DOS computers, up to the limits of the available extended memory. These simulated "machines" are called *virtual machines*. In protected mode, each program is given what amounts to its own 640K DOS computer in which to run, and each 640K "machine" is protected from interference by

the others. Note that this mode is not available unless
your system is equipped with memory-management
software to switch it on and manage the programs.

By far the most popular software for this purpose is
Microsoft Windows, running in 386 Enhanced mode.
To run your computer in 386 Enhanced mode with
Microsoft Windows, your computer must be equipped
with a minimum of 2M of RAM; in practice, 4M or more
of RAM are required. See *386 Enhanced mode, extended memory, memory-management program,
Microsoft Windows, real mode,* and *terminate-and-
stay-resident (TSR) program.*

**protocol**   A set of standards for exchanging information
between two computer systems or two computer devices. See *communications protocol* and *file transfer
protocol.*

**PrtSc**   On IBM PC–compatible keyboards, a key you can use
to print an image of the screen display.

If the screen display is currently in graphics
mode, you must run the MS-DOS program
GRAPHICS.COM before the screen prints
properly.

**PS/2**   See *IBM Personal System/2.*

**pseudocode**   An algorithm expressed in English to concep-
tualize the algorithm before coding it in a programming
language. See *algorithm.*

**public domain software**   Software not copyrighted that can
be freely distributed without obtaining permission
from the programmer or paying the programmer a fee.
See *freeware* and *shareware.*

**pull-down menu**   An on-screen menu of command options
that appears after you click the command name on the
menu bar. You then drag the mouse pointer down to
choose the command you want (see fig. P.5).

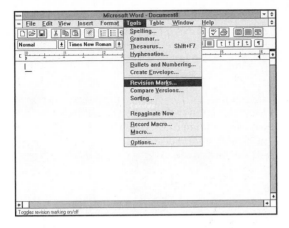

**Fig. P.5.** A pull-down menu.

The term pull-down comes from the Macintosh implementation of this idea, in which the menu doesn't stay
on-screen unless you hold down the mouse button
as you drag the pointer down the menu. In Microsoft
Windows, however, the menu stays on-screen after
you click the menu name.

**pull-out quote**   In desktop publishing, a quotation extracted from the copy of a newsletter or magazine
article and printed in larger type in the column,
often blocked off with ruled lines.

**pulse code modulation (PCM)**   A technique used to transform an incoming analog signal into a noise-free, digital
equivalent. In multimedia, PCM is used to sample
sounds digitally.

**purge**   To remove old, unwanted, or outdated information
from a computer system in a systematic—and ideally
automatic—manner.

**pushbutton**   In industry-standard and graphical user interfaces, a large button in a dialog box that initiates actions after you choose an option. Most dialog boxes
contain the OK button, which confirms your choices

and carries out the command, and the Cancel button, which cancels your choices and closes the dialog box (see fig. P.6). The button representing the option you are most likely to choose, called the *default button*, is highlighted.

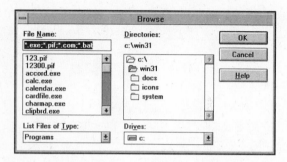

**Fig. P.6.** Pushbuttons in a dialog box (Microsoft Windows).

 In many applications, you can press Enter to choose the default button, usually the OK button. You can press Esc to choose the Cancel button.

**Q&A** An integrated word processing program and flat-file database manager developed by Symantec Corporation for IBM PC–compatible computers.

Designed for novice users, Q&A makes correspondence functions, including mail merging and address label printing, easier. The program also can generate reports and retrieve information based on English-language queries. See *integrated program* and *Microsoft Works*.

**QBasic** See *MS-DOS QBasic*.

**QEMM 386** A memory-management program (Quarterdeck Office Systems) that moves network drivers, disk cache programs, device drivers, and terminate-and-stay-resident programs to the upper memory area, thus freeing conventional memory for DOS programs. See *conventional memory, memory management program*, and *upper memory area*.

**QIC** See *quarter-inch cartridge*.

**quad density** See *high density*.

**Quadra** A series of high-end Macintosh computers powered by the Motorola 68040 microprocessor. Quadras compete directly with professional workstations such as the Sun and NeXT systems. See *Motorola 68040*.

**QuarkXPress** A page layout program, developed by Quark, Inc. for the Macintosh computer, that allows unlimited document length and includes many word processing functions.

Highly regarded for its typographic capabilities and the capability to carry text from a box on one page to a box on another, QuarkXPress is steadily gaining on its chief competition, PageMaker. See *page layout program* and *PageMaker*.

**quarter-inch cartridge (QIC)** A tape cartridge employing quarter-inch magnetic tape widely used for tape backup operations.

**Quattro Pro for Windows**   An innovative, three-dimensional spreadsheet program, developed by Borland International, that introduces a unique concept: a notebook of separate spreadsheet pages, each of which you can name. Using formulas, you can link values on one page with those on another. To display a new page, you can click the index tab at the bottom of the screen (see fig. Q.1). The program also includes excellent graphics capabilities that rival those of presentation graphics programs. See *three-dimensional spreadsheet*.

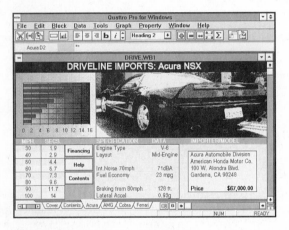

**Fig. Q.1.** Quattro Pro for Windows.

**query**   In database management, a search question that tells the program what kind of data should be retrieved from the database.

The point of an effective database management system is not to display all the information the system contains, but to show only the information you need for a specific purpose.

A query specifies the criteria by which information is extracted from the database. The query guides the computer toward retrieving the required information and eliminating information not required. See *data*

*independence, declarative language, query language,*
and *Structured Query Language (SQL).*

**query by example (QBE)**    In database management programs, a query technique that prompts you to type the
search criteria into a template resembling the data
record.

QBE was developed at IBM's Research Laboratory and
is used in the QBE program. As a retrieval technique,
QBE is emulated by some personal computer database
management programs, such as Paradox.

The advantage of query-by-example retrieval is that you
need not learn a query language to frame a query.
When you initiate the search, the program displays a
screen that lists all the data fields that appear on every
data record; you enter information that restricts the
search to just the specified criteria. The fields left
blank, however, will match anything.

Suppose that you are searching for the titles of all the
Western videotapes rated PG or PG-13 that you have in
stock. Using QBE techniques, you can type the following query:

```
CATEGORY       RATING           TITLE
Western        PG or PG-13
```

This query says, "Find all records in which the
CATEGORY field contains *Western* and the RATING
field contains *PG* or *PG-13.*"

The output of such a query is a list like the following:

```
CATEGORY       RATING       TITLE
Western        PG           Showdown
Western        PG           Tumbleweed
Western        PG-13        Not-So-OK Corral
```

See *database management program, data record,
Paradox,* and *query language.*

**query language** In database management programs, a retrieval and data-editing language that enables you to specify the criteria by which the program retrieves and displays the information stored in a database.

The ideal query language is natural language, such as English. Ideally, you could tell the computer, "Using the database called VIDEOS, show me all the records in which the CATEGORY field contains *Western* and the RATING field contains *PG* or *PG-13*."

A good query language enables you to type queries in a format that, although rigid in syntax, approximates English, as follows:

```
SELECT title
FROM videos
WHERE CATEGORY = Western
AND RATING = PG
OR RATING = PG-13
```

The dot-prompt language of dBASE is a full-fledged query language, although it has quirks and odd nomenclature that make it difficult to use. The up-and-coming query language for personal computing is Structured Query Language (SQL), already widely used for minicomputer and mainframe databases. See *database management program*, *natural language*, *query*, *query by example (QBE)*, and *Structured Query Language (SQL)*.

**queue** See *job queue*.

**QuickBASIC** A high-performance compiler for programs written in Microsoft BASIC. QuickBASIC recognizes modern control structures and enables programmers to omit line numbers.

QuickBASIC was designed to compile any program written in BASICA or GWBASIC, the versions of BASIC supplied with most IBM Personal Computers and compatibles. However, the compiler enables you to create structured programs, complete with indentations and a full set of control structures.

QuickBASIC programs execute much faster than their interpreted counterparts, making the compiler suitable for the creation of commercial software. See *BASIC*, *compiler*, and *control structure*.

**QuickDraw**   The object-oriented graphics and text-display technology built into every Macintosh computer and stored in the computer's read-only memory (ROM). When creating Macintosh programs, programmers draw on the QuickDraw resources to create on-screen windows, dialog boxes, menus, and shapes. For this reason, all Macintosh programs share a common look. Recent versions of QuickDraw offer enhanced color capabilities.

**Quicken**   A checkbook-management program developed by Intuit for IBM PC compatibles and Macintosh computers. Quicken is widely used as a complete system for home and small-business accounting.

Quicken simplifies home and small-business accounting by enabling you to carry out tasks such as check writing, check printing, budgeting, and tax accounting in a familiar way. The program's screens resemble an actual checkbook register. You can automate recurring transactions (the payment of the same amounts every month to utilities or creditors) so that several checks are generated and posted to the register with just one keystroke. The program also can produce a wide variety of reports that enable you to track spending, assess net worth, plan for future cash needs, and list tax-deductible expenditures. You can accomplish all these tasks without learning accounting terminology.

**QuickTime**   An extension to the Macintosh system software that enables applications to display animated or video sequences precisely synchronized with high-quality, digital sound. You can display the sequences in an on-screen window, which can appear within any application that supports QuickTime. In a training document, for instance, you can click an icon to see a QuickTime video sequence (a "movie") that visually shows a specific technique or procedure.

**quit**   To exit a program properly so that all your configuration choices and data are properly saved.

 With many programs, switching the computer off while the program is still on-screen is a bad idea. Not only can you lose configuration choices, but the program won't have a chance to warn you if you failed to save some of your work. In addition, many programs create numerous temporary files, and some of them take up a lot of disk space; normally the program removes these files when you quit the program properly, but if you don't, the files remain and clutter up your disk. Believe it or not, all these cautions apply to Microsoft Windows. Don't end your Windows session by just switching off the computer; choose Exit from the File menu and return to DOS before you switch off the computer.

**QWERTY**   Pronounced "kwerty." The standard typewriter keyboard layout, also used for computer keyboards.

Alternative keyboard layouts, such as the Dvorak keyboard, are said to speed typing by placing the most commonly used letters on the home row. See *Dvorak keyboard*.

**radio button**   In a graphical user interface, the round option buttons that appear in dialog boxes. Unlike check boxes, radio buttons are mutually exclusive; you can pick only one radio button option. See *graphical user interface (GUI)*.

**radio frequency interference (RFI)**   The radio noise generated by computers and other electronic and electromechanical devices during their operation. Excessive RFI generated by computers can severely degrade the reception of radio and television signals; likewise, RFI generated by other sources can cause screen flickering and even data loss in poorly shielded computers. See *FCC certification.*

**ragged-left alignment**   In word processing and desktop publishing, the alignment of each line of text so that the right margin is even, but the left remains ragged. Synonymous with *flush right*.

**ragged-right alignment**   In word processing and desktop publishing, the alignment of each line of text so that the left margin is even, but the right remains ragged. Synonymous with *flush left*.

Typographers say that ragged-right alignment is easier to read and more attractive than full justification, in which the left and right margins are aligned. Personal computer users often choose full justification because it produces a more professional appearance, but full-justified documents may be more difficult to read.

**RAM**   See *random-access memory.*

**RAM cache**   Pronounced "ram cash." A section of random-access memory (RAM) set aside to serve as a buffer between the central processing unit (CPU) and the disk drives.

Because RAM can deliver data and program instructions to the CPU hundreds of times faster than a disk drive, a computer's performance may improve significantly with a RAM cache. A RAM cache stores data and program instructions that an application is likely to require frequently, so that this information can be accessed directly from RAM.

The RAM cache also speeds operations by accepting data to be written to disk as fast as the CPU can send it, rather than forcing the CPU to wait until disk-writing operations are completed at the disk's speed. See *central processing unit (CPU)*, *disk cache*, and *random-access memory (RAM)*.

**RAM disk**   An area of electronic memory configured by a software program to emulate a disk drive. Data stored in a RAM disk can be accessed more quickly than data stored on a disk drive, but this data is erased whenever you turn off or reboot the computer.

Because virtual disk drives operate much faster than real disk drives, placing programs or data in a virtual disk drive can result in major performance improvements, but the benefits come at a stiff price. If you are using a 640K DOS system, you must create the virtual disk out of the available random-access memory (RAM), and because you do not have enough memory to begin with, you may not be able to run your application programs. If you have extended memory or expanded memory, however, you can place the virtual disk in the RAM above 640K, but you still are taking a big risk. When you save work to this disk, you are really writing your work to RAM, and everything in RAM is lost when you switch off the computer. Many computer users have lost hours of important work by failing to copy a document from a virtual disk to a real disk at the end of a session. See *configuration file*, *device driver*, *expanded memory*, *extended memory*, and *random-access memory (RAM)*.

**RAMDRIVE.SYS**   In MS-DOS, a configuration file, provided
    with the operating system, that sets aside part of your
    computer's memory as if it were a disk drive.

 Windows users who have lots of memory
    can use RAMDRIVE.SYS to store Windows'
    temporary (TMP) files, producing noticeable
    improvements in speed. Add the following
command to CONFIG.SYS:

```
DEVICE=C:\WINDOWS\RAMDRIVE.SYS
```

Make sure that the WINDOWS directory contains this
CONFIG.SYS file. Now add the following command to
AUTOEXEC.BAT:

```
SET TEMP=D:
```

Use a drive letter other than D, such as E or F, if
you have connected more than one hard disk to
your computer or if your hard disk has more than
one partition.

**random access**   An information storage and retrieval
    technique in which the computer can access the
    information directly, without having to go through
    a sequence of locations.

This term does not imply that information is stored
randomly in the memory. The computer does not have
to go through a sequence of items (sequential access)
to get to the needed information. A better term is
*direct access*, but the term *random access* has become
enshrined in the acronym RAM, commonly used to
describe a PC's internal memory, or random-access
memory.

To understand the distinction between random and
sequential access, compare a cassette tape (sequential
access) with a long-playing record (random access). To
get to the song you want on a cassette tape, you must
fast forward through a sequence of songs until you
encounter the one you want. To get to the song you

want on a record, however, you can move the arm above the surface of the record and go to the track you want. Precisely the same principle is used in computer disk drives. See *random-access memory (RAM)* and *sequential access.*

**random-access memory (RAM)** The computer's primary working memory in which program instructions and data are stored so that they are accessible directly to the central processing unit (CPU).

To perform computations at high speeds, the computer's processing circuitry must be able to obtain information from the memory directly and quickly. Computer memories, therefore, are designed to give the processor random access to the contents.

Think of RAM as a checkerboard, with each square on the board capable of holding a byte of data or program instructions. Because many personal computers can hold half a million bytes of internal memory, the computer needs some way to find a given memory location with precision. Every square on the checkerboard, therefore, has an address, like a post office box.

Because each location has a unique address, the CPU can access each memory location directly by specifying the address and activating the circuit that leads directly to that address.

RAM often is called *read/write memory* to distinguish it from read-only memory (ROM), the other component of a personal computer's primary storage. In RAM, the CPU can write and read data. Most application programs set aside a portion of RAM as a temporary work space for your data, enabling you to modify (rewrite) as needed until the data is ready for printing or storage on disk.

Almost all computers now use volatile semiconductor memory, which does not retain its contents when the power to the computer is switched off.

Save your work frequently. In the event of a system failure or power interruption, you lose all work in RAM that you have not recorded (saved) on a magnetic medium such as a disk drive. See *primary storage*, *random access*, *read-only memory (ROM)*, and *secondary storage*.

**range**   In a spreadsheet program, a cell or a rectangular group of cells.

Spreadsheet programs would be tedious to use if you could not perform operations, such as formatting, on groups of cells. For example, you can format one column of numbers with the currency format, even though the rest of the worksheet uses a general format.

All spreadsheet programs enable you to identify ranges of cells. A range can include one cell or thousands, with one restriction: the range must be rectangular in shape and consist of contiguous cells. Valid ranges include a single cell, part of a column, part of a row, and a block spanning several columns and several rows (see fig. R.1).

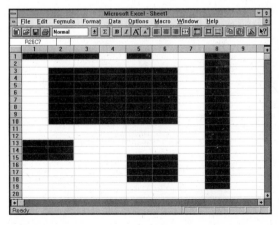

**Fig. R.1.** Valid ranges.

When using a spreadsheet program, you frequently use range expressions in commands and formulas. A range expression enables you to define the boundaries of the rectangular range. See *cell* and *range expression*.

**range expression**   In a spreadsheet program, an expression that describes a range by defining the upper left cell and the lower right cell.

In Lotus 1-2-3, for example, you write a range expression by typing the beginning cell address, two periods, and the ending cell address, as shown in the following example:

    A9..B12

The range expression A9..B12 defines a rectangular block that begins with cell A9. Because the ending cell is B12 (one column right and three rows down) the range includes the following cells:

    A9      B9
    A10     B10
    A11     B11
    A12     B12

See *range name*.

**range format**   In a spreadsheet program, a numeric format or label alignment format that applies only to a range and overrides the global format. See *global format*, *label alignment*, *numeric format*, and *range*.

**range name**   In a spreadsheet program, a range of cells to which you attach a distinctive name.

Remembering a range name is much easier than remembering a range expression. You can name a range of cells and then refer to the range by entering the name. For example, suppose that you create a worksheet in which range E9..E21 contains your company's sales for the first quarter of 1991. After naming the range *FQ1991*, you use the range name, not the range expression, in formulas. In a formula that totals the column, for example, you type *@SUM(FQ1991)*.

A second advantage of range naming is that after you have named the range, the name accurately and precisely refers to the entire range. If you type *FQ1991*, the program unfailingly equates this name with the range E9..E21. If you type this range expression over and over, however, you may make a typing error, such as referring to the range E9..E20 without catching your error. The program cannot detect an error of this sort, and you introduce a significant error into your spreadsheet.

 To avoid errors in range references, name your ranges and then use those names in your formulas. See *range* and *range expression*.

**raster**   On a computer or television screen, the horizontal pattern of lines that forms the image. Within each line are dots that can be illuminated individually.

**raster display**   The display technology used in television sets and computer monitors. Dozens of times each second, the screen is scanned from top to bottom by a tightly focused electron beam that follows a zig-zag pattern as it moves line-by-line down the screen's raster pattern. See *raster* and *vector graphics*.

**raster font**   See *bit-mapped font*.

**raster graphics**   The display of graphic images using a collection of small, separate dots called a *bit map*. The graphic's resolution is limited by the capabilities of the display or printing device. Synonymous with *bit-mapped graphic*.

**raw data**   Unprocessed or unrefined data that has not been arranged, edited, or represented in a form for easy retrieval and analysis.

**RCA plug**   See *phono plug*.

**RDBMS**   See *relational database management system*.

**read**   To retrieve data or program instructions from a peripheral such as a disk drive and place the data into the computer's memory.

**README file**   A text file, often included on the installation disk of application programs, that contains last-minute information not contained in the program's manuals.

   Be sure to look for README files, and read them; they may contain information that can save you trouble and headaches when installing and using a new program. Chances are that the file was placed on the disk after frustrated users besieged the technical support department with complaints and questions.

**read-only**   Capable of being displayed, but not edited, formatted, or otherwise modified. For example, you can view a read-only file, but you cannot delete or modify it. See *file attribute*, *locked file*, and *read/write*.

**read-only attribute**   In DOS, a file attribute stored with a file's directory entry that indicates whether the file can be modified or deleted.

When the read-only attribute is on, you can display the file but cannot modify or erase it. When the read-only attribute is off, you can modify or delete the file. See *file attribute*.

**read-only memory (ROM)**   The portion of a computer's primary storage that does not lose its contents when you switch off the power and that contains essential system programs that neither you nor the computer can erase.

Because the computer's random-access memory (RAM) is volatile (loses information when you switch off the power), the computer's internal memory is blank at power up, and the computer can perform no functions unless given start-up instructions. These instructions are provided by the ROM, which may contain only simple programs that tell the disk drive where to find and load the computer's operating system.

A growing trend, however, is toward including substantial portions of the operating system on ROM chips, instead of providing the bulk of the operating system on disk. In the Macintosh, for example, much of the Macintosh System is encoded on ROM chips, including the graphics routines (QuickDraw) that are part of the Mac's application program interface (API). However, upgrading top ROM is more difficult and expensive than supplying new disks. See *application program interface (API)*, *erasable programmable read-only memory (EPROM)*, *programmable read-only memory (PROM)*, and *QuickDraw*.

**read/write**   The capability of an internal memory or secondary storage device to record data (write) and to play back data (read) previously recorded or saved.

**read/write file**   In DOS, a file whose read-only file attribute is set so that the file can be deleted and modified. See *file attribute*, *locked file*, and *read-only*.

**read/write head**   In a hard disk or floppy disk drive, the magnetic recording and playback device that travels back and forth across the surface of the disk, storing and retrieving data.

**read/write memory**   See *random-access memory (RAM)*.

**real mode**   An operating mode of Intel microprocessors in which a program is given a definite storage location in memory and direct access to peripheral devices.

Real mode is a straightforward way of allocating memory space in a single-user, stand-alone computer system, but causes problems when more than one program is loaded into memory simultaneously; programs can invade each other's memory space or try to access peripheral devices simultaneously. In both situations, a system failure may result.

The Intel 80286, 80386, and 80486 microprocessors therefore offer an additional operating mode—protected mode—that supervises the allocation of memory and governs access to peripheral devices. See *Intel 80286*, *Intel 80386DX*, *Intel 80386SX*, *Intel 80486DX*, *Intel 80486SX*, *memory-management program*, and *protected mode*.

**real time**   The immediate processing of input, such as a point-of-sale transaction or a measurement performed by an analog laboratory device.

**real-time clock**   A battery-powered clock contained in the computer's internal circuitry. The real-time clock keeps track of the time even when the computer is switched off. This clock should be distinguished from the high-speed clock that governs the microprocessor's cycles.

**reboot**   To restart the computer. Rebooting is often necessary after a system crash. In most cases, you can restart the system from the keyboard, but especially severe crashes may require you to perform a hardware reset. In a hard-ware reset, you must push the reset button, or if no such button exists, turn off the computer and turn it back on again. See *programmer's switch*.

**recalculation method**   In a spreadsheet program, the way the program recalculates cell values after you change the contents of a cell. See *automatic recalculation* and *manual recalculation*.

**recalculation order**   In a spreadsheet program, the mode currently in effect for recalculating the values in the spreadsheet after you type new values, labels, or formulas.

Early spreadsheet programs offered two recalculation modes: column-wise recalculation and row-wise recalculation. In column-wise mode, the program recalculates all the cells in column A before moving to column B, and so on. In row-wise recalculation, the program recalculates all the cells in row 1 before moving to the beginning of row 2, and so on.

Programs that offer only these two options, such as very early versions of spreadsheet programs, can produce serious errors. Suppose that you have created a worksheet in which figures are totaled by column. You place data in columns A, B, and C; in cells A15, B15, and C15, you place a formula to calculate the sum of the column. To show the total of all three columns, you place a formula in cell A14; however, the sum displayed in this cell may not be accurate. If the program is set to row-wise recalculation order, cell A14 is recalculated before the column totals are recalculated. In most cases, you obtain the correct answer only by changing the recalculation order to column-wise recalculation.

Today's advanced spreadsheet programs, such as Lotus 1-2-3, get around this problem by offering natural recalculation as the default recalculation order. In natural recalculation, a formula is not calculated until all the formulas to which it refers are calculated. The program scans the entire worksheet to determine the logical order of recalculation as established by creating formulas that reference each other. See *column-wise recalculation*, *natural recalculation*, *optimal recalculation*, and *row-wise recalculation*.

**record** See *data record*.

**record-oriented database management program**    A database management program that displays data records as the result of query operations, unlike a table-oriented program, in which the result of all data query operations is a table. Purists argue that a true relational database management program always treats data in tabular form and that any program that displays records as the result of queries, such as dBASE, does not deserve to call itself relational, even if the program can work simultaneously with two or more databases.

The rationale for such an attitude is partly academic; the relational model of database management is based on a mathematical foundation so that any departure from the relational model's true form (in which data is represented in tables) is an affront to mathematical purity. But the rationale also is practical; a program that retrieves data records as the result of query operations gives you much unwanted information, and because most records take up the whole screen, you must page through them.

A table-oriented program, in contrast, succinctly summarizes data in tables displayed on-screen, eliminating all extraneous data not specifically called for in the search query. See *data retrieval, relational database management, Structured Query Language (SQL)*, and *table-oriented database management program*.

**record pointer** In a database management program, the record pointer is an on-screen status message that states the number of the data record currently displayed on-screen (or in which the cursor is positioned).

**recover** To bring the computer system back to a previous, stable operating state or to restore erased or misdirected data. Recovery, which may require user intervention, is needed after a system or user error occurs, such as instructing the system to write data to a drive that doesn't contain a disk. See *undelete utility*.

**recoverable error** An error that does not cause the program or system to crash or to erase data irretrievably.

**recto** The right-hand (odd-numbered) page in two-sided printing. See *verso*.

**redirection** See *input/output redirection*.

**redirection operator** In DOS, a symbol that routes input or output directions from or to a device other than the console (the keyboard and video display).

You can use the following redirection operators in a DOS command:

> *Output redirection.* Redirects the output of a command from the console to a file or device. The following command, for example, redirects the contents of LETTER.DOC to the printer:

```
LETTER.DOC>PRN
```

>> *Append redirection.* Redirects the output of a command from the console to an existing file and

adds the output to the existing file's contents. The following command, for example, redirects the output to DIR.DOC and appends the information to the end of the file if DIR.DOC exists:

```
DIR B: >> DIR.DOC
```

< *Input redirection.* Changes the input of a command from the console to a file, so that the contents of the file are used instead of data input at the keyboard. The following command, for example, redirects SORT's input to the file TERMS.DOC:

```
SORT < TERMS.DOC
```

See *input/output redirection.*

**redlining** In word processing, an attribute such as a distinctive color or double underlining that marks the text coauthors have added to a document. The redlined text is highlighted so that other authors or editors know exactly what has been added to or deleted from the document.

**reduced instruction set computer (RISC)** A central processing unit (CPU) in which the number of instructions the processor can execute is reduced to a minimum to increase processing speed.

Microprocessors, such as the Intel 80386, recognize well over one hundred instructions for performing various computations, but the more instructions a chip can handle, the more slowly it runs for all instructions.

The idea of a RISC architecture is to reduce the instruction set to the bare minimum, emphasizing the instructions used most of the time and optimizing them for the fastest possible execution. The instructions left out of the chip must be carried out by combining the ones that remain, but because these instructions are needed far less frequently, a RISC processor usually runs 50 to 75 percent faster than its CISC counterpart.

RISC processors also are cheaper to design, debug, and manufacture because they are less complex. However, simplifying the microprocessor places the burden on programmers, who must restore the complexity by writing lengthier programs. In general, software development does not show the same impressive trend of increased efficiency that is evident in the hardware industry—quite the opposite, in fact. The cost of developing a major new application program is so astronomical that all but the biggest companies are being pushed out of the business. For this reason, some argue that it makes much more sense to put the complexity in the hardware, giving programmers a much-needed break. The issue may become moot because today's "ordinary" microprocessors (now called *complex instruction set computers*, or CISC for short) rival the performance of the fastest RISC processors of just two or three years ago. RISC processors may find a niche, however, in special-purpose applications, such as graphics accelerator circuits, in which their speed provides a critical advantage. See *central processing unit (CPU)* and *complex instruction set computer (CISC)*.

**reengineering**   A method of computer-based automation that begins by radically redesigning the way work is done and then choosing computer tools that enhance the redesigned work process.

It's no secret that computer technology hasn't delivered on its promise of higher productivity. Even allowing for the fact that white-collar productivity is notoriously difficult to measure, very few studies have been able to demonstrate that work gets done more efficiently after computers are installed. On the contrary, productivity may even decrease after the installation of a computer system. A northern Virginia drugstore chain, for example, was forced to file for bankruptcy after a multimillion dollar computer-based inventory system functioned so poorly that managers were unable to tell whether an item was in stock.

One of the chief reasons computers bring a puny productivity payoff has to do with old attitudes rather than poor system design. In many firms, the way business is done is based on old, often unspoken beliefs about the "right" way to do things: The credit department handles credit, the receiving department receives goods, the accounting department writes checks. These beliefs date back to the turn-of-the-century innovations in assembly line technology that, for a time, made the United States the world's undisputed technological and economic leader. But breaking down work into specialized, fragmented departments isn't necessarily the best way to get work done, as Japanese firms have amply demonstrated. What is more, bringing computers into poorly organized work settings doesn't produce much improvement. When you automate a mess, you get an automated mess.

A midwestern manufacturing firm's experience with its accounts receivable department shows that reengineering can bring huge productivity payoffs. The company orders parts from suppliers, but invariably, something is missing from the shipment. The company nevertheless is billed for everything that was ordered. Under the old system, clerks had to call the receiving department and find out what was received and what wasn't, and after determining this information, authorized a check. The system was slow and inefficient, to say the least, and equipping the clerks with computers wouldn't help at all. The reengineering strategy? Put computers in the receiving department, so that the receiving staff can confirm what's received and write the checks on the spot.

Reengineering is the latest business buzzword, but the underlying concept is really very simple. You can apply some of the principles of reengineering to your own computer work just by remembering a few simple rules:

- *Avoid reinventing the wheel.* Develop and refine template versions of important letters, memos, reports, worksheets, newsletters, business forms, and data management forms.

- *Capture information at the source.* A sales manager in the field jots down sales results in a notebook, and then spends 15 minutes a day pecking the information into a Lotus worksheet. The cure? A portable computer running Lotus 1-2-3.

- *Never type the same information twice.* Develop macros that, every time you write a letter, automatically enter your correpondent's name and address into a mailing list database and that automatically crank out an addressed envelope.

**reformat**   In operating systems, to repeat a formatting operation on a secondary storage disk, such as a floppy disk or hard disk. In word processing or page layout programs, to change the arrangement of text elements on the page.

**refresh**   To repeat the display or storage of data to keep it from fading or becoming lost. The video display and random-access memory (RAM) must be refreshed constantly.

**relational database management**   An approach to database management in which data is stored in two-dimensional data tables. The program can work with two data tables at the same time, relating the information through links established by a common column or field.

The term *relational* as applied to database management was introduced in 1970 by Edgar Codd to refer to the storage and retrieval of data in the form of tables, in which the table defines the relation between the items listed in rows (data records) and columns (data fields).

Codd founded his database design on a mathematical theory. A true relational database, one designed solely in accordance with this theory, treats all data as tables, and the result of any query is a new table.

Suppose that a video store database lists customer phone numbers and names in a table as follows:

```
PHONE_NO      NAME
325-4321      Smith, Ted
325-4411      Jones, Jane
```

Another table contains the titles of rented videotapes, the phone numbers of the customers who rented those tapes, and the due dates:

```
TITLE         PHONE_NO      DUE_DATE
Blues         325-4321      07/16/92
Danger        325-4411      07/19/92
```

A query may ask, "Show me the names and phone numbers of customers with tapes due on or before July 19, 1992, and print those films' titles." Such a query results in the following table:

```
NAME          PHONE_NO      TITLE
Smith, Ted    325-4321      Blues
Jones, Jane   325-4411      Danger
```

Not all database management programs marketed as relational are true table-oriented programs. Most are record-oriented programs relational only to the extent that they can link data in two databases through a common field. dBASE is such a program; data is stored in records, not tables. However, you can use dBASE as if it were a true relational program.

**relational database management system (RDBMS)** A relational database management program, especially one that comes with all the necessary support programs, programming tools, and documentation needed to create, install, and maintain custom database applications.

**relational operator**   A symbol used to specify the relationship between two numeric values.

In query languages, relational operators frequently are
used in specifying search criteria. For example, a video
store manager may want to tell the computer, "Show
me all the telephone numbers of customers with overdue tapes that are due on a date less than or equal to
May 7, 1992."

In electronic spreadsheets, relational operators are
used to return the number 1 if the expression is true
and 0 if the expression is false. In @IF formulas, you
can use relational operators to perform tests on data
so that different values are displayed, depending on
the results of the test.

Suppose that you are computing sales bonuses. If a
salesperson has sold more than $22,000 in merchan-
dise, the normal bonus (5 percent) is increased to 7.5
percent. In the expression @IF(B14>22000, 0.75, 0.5),
the program tests cell B14 to see whether the number
(total sales) is greater than 22,000. If so, the cell in
which you have placed the formula displays 0.75. If
not, the cell displays 0.5.

To permit the expression of logical operators in the
character-based world of computing, many programs
use the following conventions:

| | |
|---|---|
| = | equal to |
| < | less than |
| > | greater than |
| <= | less than or equal to |
| >= | greater than or equal to |
| <> | not equal to |

**relative addressing**   See *relative cell reference.*

**relative cell reference**   In a spreadsheet program, a
formula's cell reference that the program adjusts when
you copy the formula to another cell or range of cells.

To understand what happens when you copy a relative
cell reference, you need to know how a spreadsheet
program actually records a cell reference. Suppose that
you type the formula @SUM(C6..C8) in cell C10. The
program does not actually record "add cells C6, C7,
and C8" in the file (see fig. R.2). Instead, the program
records a code that means, "add all the values in the
cells positioned in the second, third, and fourth rows
up from the current cell." When you copy this formula
to the next four cells to the right (D10..G10), it still
reads, "add all the values in the cells positioned in the
second, third, and fourth rows up from the current
cell," and sums each column correctly (see fig. R.3).
See *absolute cell reference* and *mixed cell reference.*

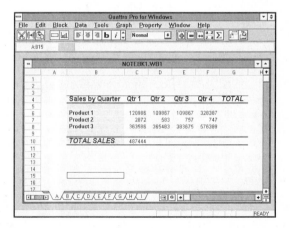

**Fig. R.2.** One column summed by a formula containing a
relative cell reference.

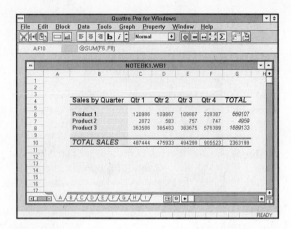

**Fig. R.3.** Formula containing a relative cell reference copied into remaining columns.

**release number** The number, usually a decimal number, that identifies an incrementally improved version of a program rather than a major revision, which is numbered using an integer.

A program labeled Version 5.1, for example, is the second release of Version 5 of the program (the first was Version 5.0). Not all software publishers use this numbering scheme, and competitive pressures sometimes encourage publishers to jump to a new version number when the program being released is in fact only an incremental improvement over its predecessor. See *version*.

**reliability** The capability of computer hardware or software to perform as the user expects and to do so consistently, without failures or erratic behavior. See *mean time between failures (MTBF)*.

**remark** In a batch file, macro, or source code, explanatory text that is ignored when the computer executes the commands. See *batch file*.

**remote control program** A utility program that enables you to link two personal computers so that you can use one to control the operation of the second.

Why would anyone want to control a distant PC? Users of popular remote control programs such as Carbon Copy Plus are using this software to train remote users, to perform tasks at the office while working at home, to install and demonstrate software on clients' computers, and to provide technical support by logging on to the remote computer and determining what went wrong.

**remote terminal**   See *terminal*.

**removable mass storage**   A high-capacity secondary storage medium, such as a Bernoulli box or a tape backup system, in which the magnetic disk or tape is encased in a plastic cartridge or cassette and can be removed from the drive for safekeeping.

By this definition, a high-density floppy disk qualifies as a removable mass storage medium, but the term usually is reserved for cartridge-based backup systems with many megabytes of storage capacity. See *Bernoulli box*.

**removable storage media**   A secondary storage device in which the actual storage medium, such as a magnetic disk, can be removed from the drive for safekeeping.

Floppy disks are removable storage media, but the term is more often applied to tape backup units and Bernoulli boxes that use cartridges that can hold dozens of megabytes of data.

**rendering**   In computer graphics, the conversion of an outline drawing into a fully formed, solid image.

**repagination**   In word processing and desktop publishing, a formatting operation in which pages are renumbered to reflect insertions, deletions, block moves, or other changes to the document's text.

Most programs repaginate automatically as you insert and edit text, but some programs require a manual repagination operation before the page count and specific page numbers are correctly displayed on-screen.

**repeater** In local area networks, a hardware device used to extend the length of network cabling by amplifying and passing along the messages traveling through the network. See *local area network (LAN)*.

**repeating field** A fundamental error of database design that compromises data integrity by forcing you to type the same data item repeatedly.

Consider the following database design:

| TITLE | SUPPLIER | ADDRESS | CITY | STATE | ZIP |
|-------|----------|---------|------|-------|-----|
| Spring Rains | Big Video Supply | 123 Elm | Ivy | VA | 22992 |
| Prince of Doom | Acme Distributors | 695 Thrush | Vista | VA | 22990 |
| Warp Drive | Acme Distributors | 695 Thrush | Vista | VA | 22990 |
| Fast Buck | Acme Distributors | 695 Thrush | Vista | VA | 22990 |
| Big City | Big Video Supply | 123 Elm | Ivy | VA | 22992 |

In this database design, the user must repeatedly type suppliers' names and addresses, creating many possibilities for errors, due to typos or misspellings. The cure for this problem is to use a relational database management system (RDMS), and to create two databases: TITLES and SUPPLIERS. In the TITLES database, you see the following information:

| TITLE | SUPPLIER_ID |
|-------|-------------|
| Spring Rains | BVS |
| Prince of Doom | AD |
| Warp Drive | AD |
| Fast Buck | AD |
| Big City | BVS |

And in the SUPPLIERS database, you see the following:

| SUPPLIER_ID | SUPPLIER | ADDRESS | CITY | STATE | ZIP |
|-------------|----------|---------|------|-------|-----|
| AD | Acme Distributors | 695 Thrush | Vista | VA | 22990 |
| BVS | Big Video Supply | 123 Elm | Ivy | VA | 22992 |

A relational database management program lets you link data in separate databases by means of a field common to both—in this example, the SUPPLIER_ID field in the TITLES database. By typing the supplier IDs in the TITLES database, you link the video titles with the addresses in SUPPLIERS. Although you must type the codes more than once in the SUPPLIERS database, the codes are short and easy to proofread. You need type the full name and address of each supplier only once, in the SUPPLIERS database. See *database design, data integrity*, *data redundancy*, and *relational database management*.

**repeating label**   In a spreadsheet program, a character preceded by a label prefix that causes the character to be repeated across the cell.

For example, Lotus 1-2-3 uses \ to repeat one or more characters across a cell. The entry \– would therefore produce a line of hyphens across the cell.

 You can use repeating labels to create lines across your worksheet. For example, use repeating hyphens to create a single line or repeating equal signs to create a double line. See *label prefix*.

**repeat key**   A key that continues to enter the same character as long as you hold down that key.

**repetitive strain injury (RSI)**   A serious and potentially debilitating occupational illness caused by prolonged repetitive hand and arm movements that can damage, inflame, or kill nerves in the hands, arms, shoulder, or neck.

Also known as *cumulative trauma disorder (CTD)*, RSI occurs when constantly repeated motions strain tendons and ligaments, resulting in scar tissue that squeezes and eventually may kill nerves. RSI has long been observed among meat packers, musicians, and assembly-line workers who repeatedly perform the same hand movements. With the proliferation of computer keyboards, RSI is increasingly noted among white-collar office workers and poses a genuine threat to personal computer users who work long hours at the keyboard. Specific RSI disorders include *carpal tunnel syndrome (CTS)*, which often afflicts supermarket cashiers who must drag items over price-code scanners for extended periods.

Symptoms of CTS include burning, tingling, or numbness in the hands, as well as a loss of muscle control and dexterity. Potentially incapacitating to full-time writers, secretaries, and journalists, CTS and other RSI injuries are estimated to cost U.S. corporations an estimated $27 billion per year in medical bills and lost workdays.

The symptoms of RSI frequently occur after office hours, creating the impression that the pain, numbness, or twinges are not related to computer usage. However, they potentially are signs of a serious and debilitating disease. You should see a doctor immediately if you work at the computer for long hours and experience any of these symptoms.

You can prevent RSI. Adjust your chair height to eliminate any unnecessary extension or flexing of the wrist. Take frequent breaks, use good posture, and vary your daily activities so that you perform a variety of actions with your wrists.

**replace** A text processing utility found in most word processing programs that searches for a string and replaces it with another string.

Unless you are absolutely sure that you know what you are doing, use the replace utility only in the mode that requests your confirmation. If you permit the utility to do its work without confirmation throughout the document, it may perform incorrect substitutions.

Suppose that you want to delete the vague intensifier *very* throughout your document. You perform the replacement without confirmation; however, the utility also removes the string *very* from the word *every*.

With most programs, you can improve the accuracy of the replacement operation by specifying capitalization and whole-word options. If you tell the program to match the capitalization pattern in the search string (such as TREE), the program replaces only those strings that match the characters and the capitalization pattern (TREE is replaced, but not Tree or tree).

If you select the whole-word option when replacing *very*, the program replaces the string only if it stands alone as a whole word, but not if the string is part of a longer word.

**replaceable parameter**    In MS-DOS, a symbol used in a batch file that MS-DOS replaces with information you type. The symbol consists of a percent sign and a number from 1 through 9, such as %1.

Suppose that you create a batch file, PRINTNOW.BAT, that contains the statement *COPY %1 PRN*. If you type the command *PRINTNOW LETTER.DOC*, MS-DOS replaces the %1 symbol with the file name you typed and copies LETTER.DOC to the printer. See *batch file*.

**report**    In database management, printed output that usually is formatted with page numbers and headings. With most programs, reports can include calculated fields, showing subtotals, totals, averages, and other figures computed from the data. See *calculated field*.

**report generator**    A program or program function that enables a non-programmer to request printed output from a computer database.

**Report Program Generator (RPG)**    A programming language for report generation. RPG was developed by IBM.

RPG enables a novice programmer to produce output from a database by describing the format in which the data is to be printed. RPG then generates the necessary programming code.

**research network**   A wide-area computer network, such as ARPANET or NSFNET, developed and funded by a governmental agency to improve research productivity in areas of national interest.

**ResEdit**   Pronounced "rez edit." A Macintosh utility program, available free from Apple Computer dealers, that enables you to edit (and copy to other programs) many program features, such as menu text, icons, cursor shapes, and dialog boxes.

Every Macintosh file is made up of two parts: the data fork and the resource fork. The data fork contains data, such as text or the data in a database; the resource fork contains a variety of separate program resources, such as dialog boxes, sounds, icons, menus, and graphic images.

With ResEdit, you can edit these resources—thereby customizing the program—or copy the resources to other programs, where they become available as programming resources.

If you are modifying a program file, be sure to work on a backup copy of the program. With ResEdit, modifying icons, menus, and dialog boxes is easy, but you accidentally may make a change that corrupts the program. See *utility program*.

**reserved memory**   See *upper memory area*.

**reserved word**   In a programming language or operating system, a word—also called a *keyword*—that has a fixed function and cannot be used for any other purpose. For example, in DOS batch files, the word REM is reserved to indicate the beginning of a remark (a line of text that DOS will ignore when executing the file). You can use a reserved word only for its intended purpose; you cannot use the word for naming files, variables, or other user-named objects. See *keyword*.

**reset button**   A button, usually mounted on the system unit's front panel, that enables you to perform a warm boot if the reset key (Ctrl-Alt-Del) doesn't work. On older Macintoshes, the reset button is part of the programmer's switch. Synonymous with *hardware reset*. See *programmer's switch*, *reset key*, and *warm boot*.

**reset key**   A key combination that, when pressed, restarts the computer. This key combination (Ctrl-Alt-Del on DOS machines) provides an alternative to switching the power off and on after a crash so severe that the keyboard does not respond. See *hardware reset*, *programmer's switch*, and *warm boot*.

**resident program**   See *terminate-and-stay-resident (TSR) program*.

**resolution**   A measurement—usually expressed in linear dots per inch (dpi), horizontally and vertically—of the sharpness of an image generated by an output device such as a monitor or printer.

In monitors, resolution is expressed as the number of pixels horizontally displayed and lines vertically displayed on-screen. For example, a CGA monitor displays fewer lines than a VGA monitor, and therefore, a CGA image appears more jagged than a VGA image. The following table lists the resolutions of common video adapters for IBM PCs and compatibles:

| Adapter | Resolution (pixels x lines) |
| --- | --- |
| Monochrome Display Adapter (MDA) | 720 x 350 |
| Color Graphics Adapter (CGA) | 640 x 200 |
| Enhanced Graphics Adapter (EGA) | 640 x 350 |
| MultiColor Graphics Array (MCGA) | 640 x 480 |
| Video Graphics Array (VGA) | 640 x 480 |
| Super VGA (extended VGA) | 800 x 600 |
| Super VGA (VGA Plus) | 1,024 x 768 |

Macintoshes with 9-inch screens display 512 pixels by 342 lines, whereas Macs with 12- or 13-inch monitors display 640 by 480.

For printers, resolution is typically measured by the number of dots per inch (dpi) that the printer is capable of printing: the higher the number, the sharper the resolution. Low-quality dot-matrix printers print approximately 125 dpi, whereas laser printers can print 300 dpi. Professional typesetting machinery prints at resolutions of 1,200 or more dpi.

**response time** The time the computer needs to respond and carry out a request.

Response time is a better measurement of system performance than access time because it more fairly states the system's throughput. See *access time*.

**retrieval** All the procedures involved in finding, summarizing, organizing, displaying, or printing information from a computer system in a form useful for the user.

**Return** See *Enter/Return*.

**reverse engineering** The process of systematically taking apart a computer chip or application program to discover how it works, with the aim of imitating or duplicating some or all of its functions.

Reverse engineering is a common practice in contemporary industry, but it often raises ethical and moral issues that range from clear-cut to murky. In the clear-cut department, microprocessors and other chips have been reverse engineered and copied outright—a clear violation of applicable U.S. and international law—by firms operating outside North America. In a well-publicized example of a murky area of reverse engineering, Advanced Micro Devices (AMD) employed reverse engineering to discover how the Intel 80386 microprocessor works. With this information, AMD created a logical simulation of the 80386's performance, and used this simulation to design its own microprocessor (the Am386) that duplicates the

80386's performance without duplicating its circuitry. The result is 100-percent compatible with the Intel 80386, but it is not an 80386—or so AMD claims. The legal issues raised by reverse engineering will be decided in the courts, but only after years of expensive litigation. See *Am386*, *Intel 80386DX*, and *Intel 80386SX*.

**reverse video**    In monochrome monitors, a means of highlighting text on the display screen so that normally dark characters are displayed as bright characters on a dark background, or normally bright characters are displayed as dark characters on a bright background. See *highlighting*.

**rewrite**    Synonymous with *overwrite*.

**RGB monitor**    A color digital monitor that accepts separate inputs for **r**ed, **g**reen, and **b**lue, and produces a much sharper image than composite color monitors.

Although the Enhanced Graphics Display uses RGB techniques, the RGB monitor is synonymous in IBM PC–compatible computing with the Color Graphics Adapter (CGA) standard. See *composite color monitor*.

**Rich Text Format (RTF)**    A text formatting standard developed by Microsoft Corporation that enables a word processing program to create a file encoded with all the document's formatting instructions, but without using any special codes. An RTF-encoded document can be transmitted over telecommunications links or read by another RTF-compatible word processing program, without loss of the formatting.

**right justification**    In word processing, the alignment of text along the right margin, producing a superficial resemblance to professionally printed text. The results may be poor, however, if the printer is incapable of proportional spacing; in such cases, right justification can be achieved only by inserting unsightly gaps of two or more spaces between words. For readability, most graphics artists advise computer users to leave the right margin ragged.

**RightWriter**   A style and grammar-checking program offered by Que Corporation that relies on artificial intelligence techniques to find and identify common errors in usage, style, punctuation, and grammar. The program is available for IBM and IBM-compatible personal computers.

**ring network**   In local area networks, a decentralized network topology in which a number of nodes (including workstations, shared peripherals, and file servers) are arranged around a closed loop cable.

Like a bus network, a ring network's workstations send messages to all other workstations. Each node in the ring, however, has a unique address, and its reception circuitry constantly monitors the bus to determine whether a message is being sent. For example, a message sent to a node named Laser Printer is ignored by the other nodes on the network.

Unlike a bus network, each node contains a repeater that amplifies and sends the signal along to the next node. Ring networks therefore can extend far beyond the geographic limits of bus networks, which lack repeaters.

The failure of a single node can disrupt the entire network; however, fault-tolerance schemes have been devised that enable ring networks to continue to function even if one or more nodes fail.

The ring-like electronic structure of the network may not be immediately obvious from its physical layout, which may resemble a star network or multiple stars; the ring is implemented in the actual electronic connections among the computers, which may or may not be reflected in their actual geographic distribution (see fig. R.4). See *file server*, *local area network (LAN)*, *network topology*, and *node*.

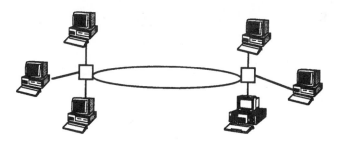

**Fig. R.4.** An illustration of a ring network.

**RIP**  See *raster image processor.*

**ripple-through effect**  In a spreadsheet program, the sudden appearance of ERR values throughout the cells of a spreadsheet after you make a change that breaks the link among formulas.

If you introduce into a spreadsheet a change that corrupts a formula so that it evaluates to ERR (error) or NA (unavailable value), all the formulas linked to (dependent on) the corrupted formula also display ERR, and you see the ERR message ripple through the spreadsheet.

If this happens, you may think that you have ruined the whole spreadsheet, but after you locate and repair the problem, all the other formulas are restored.

**river**  In desktop publishing, a formatting flaw caused by accidental patterns of white space between words, encouraging the eye to follow the flow down three or more lines.

Rivers injure what typographers refer to as the color of the page, which should be perceived by the eye as an overall shade of gray without interruption from white spaces, bad word breaks, poor character spacing, or uneven line spacing. See *desktop publishing.*

**RLL**  See *Run-Length Limited.*

**ROM**  See *read-only memory.*

**Roman**   In typography, an upright serif typeface of medium weight. In proofreading, characters without emphasis. See *emphasis*, *serif*, and *weight*.

**root directory**   On a disk, the top-level directory that MS-DOS creates when you format the disk. See *directory*, *parent directory*, and *subdirectory*.

**root name**   The first, mandatory part of a DOS file name, using from one to eight characters. See *extension* and *file name*.

**rotated type**   In a graphics or desktop publishing program, text that has been rotated from its normal, horizontal position on the page. The best graphics programs, such as CorelDRAW!, permit you to edit the type even after you have rotated it.

**rotation tool**   In a graphics or desktop publishing program, an on-screen command option, represented by an icon, that you can use to rotate type from its normal, horizontal position. See *rotated type*.

**roughs**   In desktop publishing, the preliminary page layouts that the designer creates using rough sketches to represent page design ideas. Synonymous with *thumbnails*. See *desktop publishing*.

**row**   In a spreadsheet program, a horizontal block of cells running across the breadth of the spreadsheet. In most programs, rows are numbered sequentially from the top. In a database, a row is the same as a record or data record.

**row-wise recalculation**   In spreadsheet programs, a recalculation order that calculates all the values in row 1 before moving to row 2, and so on.

If your spreadsheet program does not offer natural recalculation, use row-wise recalculation for worksheets in which rows are summed and the totals are forwarded. Column-wise recalculation may produce erroneous results. See *column-wise recalculation*, *natural recalculation*, *optimal recalculation*, and *recalculation order*.

**RS-232C**   A standard recommended by the Electronic
Industries Association (EIA) concerning the asynchronous transmission of computer data. Most personal
computers are equipped with an RS-232–compatible
serial port, which you can use for external modems,
printers, scanners, and other peripheral devices. See
*modem*, *printer*, *scanner*, and *serial port*.

**RS-422**   A standard recommended by the Electronic
Industries Association (EIA) and used as the serial port
standard for Macintosh computers. RS-422 governs the
asynchronous transmission of computer data at speeds
of up to 920,000 bits per second.

**RSI**   See *repetitive strain injury.*

**rule**   In computer graphics and desktop publishing, a thin,
black horizontal or vertical line.

**ruler**   In many word processing and desktop publishing
programs, an on-screen bar that measures the page
horizontally, showing the current margins, tab stops,
and paragraph indents. Windows and Macintosh programs often permit you to manipulate margins and
indents and to set tabs by manipulating the corresponding on-screen symbols with the mouse.

**run**   To execute a program.

**Run-Length Limited (RLL)**   A method of storing and retrieving information on a hard disk that, compared
to double-density techniques, increases by at least
50 percent the amount of data a hard disk can store.

The improvement in storage density is achieved by
translating the data into a new digital format that can
be written more compactly to the disk. The translation
is achieved, however, only at the cost of adding complex electronics to the storage device. RLL drives therefore are more expensive than their MFM counterparts.
See *Advanced Run-Length Limited (ARLL)* and *Modified
Frequency Modulation (MFM)*.

**run-time version**   A commercial version of an interpreter or windowing environment that enables the creator of an application program to sell a limited version of the interpreter or environment, for the benefit of users who may lack the interpreter or windowing environment.

Not all users have Microsoft Windows, for example, so some software publishers sell their Windows applications with a run-time version of Windows. This version loads each time you use the program, but you cannot use it with other programs. See *interpreter* and *windowing environment*.

**r/w**   A common abbreviation for *read/write*, indicating that the file or device has been configured so that you can write data to it as well as read data from it. See *read/write* and *read/write file*.

**SAA** See *Systems Application Architecture*.

**safe format** A disk format that does not destroy the data on disk if you inadvertently format the wrong disk. Utility packages such as PC Tools and Norton Utilities also can perform safe formats. To format safely with MS-DOS 5.0, use the FORMAT command *without* using the /u switch. You can quickly and easily restore the data on disk that has been formatted safely using the UNFORMAT command (MS-DOS 5.0 and later), as long as you haven't copied more files to the disk.

**sans serif** A typeface that lacks serifs, the fine cross strokes across the ends of the main strokes of a character.

Sans serif typefaces, such as Helvetica, are preferred for display type but, when used for body type, are harder to read than serif typefaces, such as Times Roman. See *body type*, *display type*, *serif*, and *typeface*.

**satellite** In a multiuser computer system, a terminal or workstation linked to a centralized host computer. See *host*.

**save** To transfer data from the computer's random-access memory, where it is liable to erasure, to a secondary storage medium such as a disk drive.

Computers bring powerful new tools to daily tasks, but any tool powerful enough to change the way you work is also powerful enough to cause grief. By far the most common source of computer-assisted grief is work loss resulting from power failures, user errors, or system crashes. As you work with the computer, your work is kept in the computer's random-access memory (RAM), which is volatile—meaning, very simply, that the work may very well evaporate into nothingness should the power fail or the computer crash. Sooner or later, every computer user experiences the sense of shock, dread, dismay, and anger that comes with the realization that hours and hours of work have just been lost, irretrievably.

 Do everything you can to protect yourself against lost work. Save repeatedly while you work; if you save every five minutes, you'll never lose more than five minutes of work. If you're using a program that has an autosave feature, which saves your work automatically at an interval you specify, by all means activate it! When you quit a program, save all the documents you've created, even if you're not sure all of them are valuable. (If you don't want to clutter up your hard disk, save your documents to a floppy disk. Floppies are cheap. Your time isn't.) And bear in mind that, for full protection, you should perform a regular backup procedure. Hard disks fail, too. See *backup procedure, random-access memory (RAM),* and *volatility.*

**sawtooth distortion**   See *aliasing.*

**scalable font**   A screen or printer font you can enlarge or reduce to any size, within a specified range, without introducing unattractive distortions. Outline font technology is most commonly used to provide scalable fonts, but other technologies—including stroke fonts, in which a character is formed out of a matrix of lines— are sometimes used. The most popular scalable fonts for Macintosh and Windows systems are PostScript and TrueType fonts.

 Looking for a Mac or Windows system? If you want scalable fonts, choose a Mac that's System 7 capable, or a Windows system with Windows 3.1. Both systems include TrueType capabilities; you will see scalable TrueType fonts on-screen, and you will get good results from a huge variety of printers, without having to buy an expensive PostScript-compatible printer. See *bit-mapped font, outline font, PostScript font, printer font, screen font, System 7,* and *TrueType.*

**scaling**   In presentation graphics, the adjustment of the y-axis (values axis) chosen by the program so that differences in the data are highlighted.

Most presentation graphics programs scale the y-axis, but the scaling choice may be unsatisfactory (see fig. S.1). Manually adjusting the scaling produces better results (see fig. S.2). See *presentation graphics* and *y-axis*.

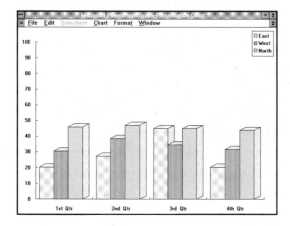

**Fig. S.1.** A column graph with unsatisfactory scaling.

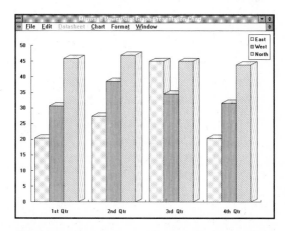

**Fig. S.2.** A column graph with manually adjusted scaling.

**scanner**  A peripheral device that digitizes artwork or photographs and stores the image as a file you can merge with text in many word processing and page layout programs.

Scanners use two techniques for transforming photographs into digitized images (see fig. S.3). The first technique, dithering, simulates a halftone by varying the space between the dots normally used to create a bit-mapped graphic image. Like all bit-mapped images, the digital halftone cannot be sized without introducing crude distortions, and the quality may be too crude for professional applications.

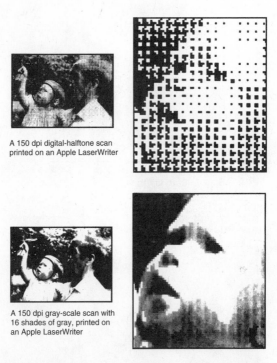

A 150 dpi digital-halftone scan
printed on an Apple LaserWriter

A 150 dpi gray-scale scan with
16 shades of gray, printed on
an Apple LaserWriter

**Fig. S.3.** A digital halftone image (top) and a gray-scale image (bottom).

The second technique, Tagged Image File Format (TIFF), stores the image using a series of 16 gray values and produces better results, but this technique is still inferior to halftones produced by photographic methods. See *bit-mapped graphic*, *halftone*, and *Tagged Image File Format (TIFF)*.

**scatter diagram**   An analytical graphic in which data items are plotted as points on two numeric axes.

Scatter diagrams show clustering relationships in numeric data. In Lotus 1-2-3, for example, a scatter diagram (an x-y graph) can show a clear correlation between sales and advertising funds.

**scatter plot**   See *scatter diagram*.

**scientific notation**   See *floating-point calculation*.

**scissoring**   In computer graphics, an editing technique in which an image is cropped to a size determined by a frame, which is placed over the image.

**Scrapbook**   On the Macintosh, a desk accessory that can hold frequently used graphic images, such as a company letterhead, which you can then insert into new documents as required.

**screen capture**   The storage of a screen display as a text or graphics file on disk.

**screen dump**   A printout of the current screen display.

**screen elements**   In Microsoft Windows, the components of the display screen, such as dialog boxes, borders, buttons, check boxes, and scroll bars.

**screen flicker**   See *flicker*.

**screen font**   A bit-mapped font designed to mimic the appearance of printer fonts when displayed on medium-resolution monitors. Modern laser printers can print text with a resolution of 300 dpi or more, but video displays, except for the most expensive professional units, lack such high resolution and cannot display typefaces with such precision. What you see isn't necessarily what you get.

In character-based IBM PC–compatible machines running under DOS, no attempt is made to suggest the printer font's typeface. In WordPerfect for DOS, for example, you type what appears to be a generic Roman typeface and attach invisible formatting instructions that control the selection of printer fonts.

Early Macintosh systems (before System 7) and Windows systems (before Version 3.1) offer bit-mapped screen fonts that mimic the appearance of high-resolution printer fonts, but at a price: the fonts look good on-screen only if you choose a font size (such as 10, 12, or 14 points) supported by a font on disk. If you choose an unsupported size, you see crude characters with rough edges.

In 1990, Adobe International released Adobe Type Manager (ATM) for both Macintosh and Windows systems. ATM offers scalable type technology that generates on-screen type as well as printer output, even in inexpensive non-PostScript printers. In 1992, Apple and Microsoft incorporated their jointly developed TrueType scalable font technology into Apple's System 7 and Microsoft Windows 3.1. ATM and TrueType both produce excellent results; you can choose any font size, without seeing crude characters on-screen, and the fonts print beautifully on any graphics-capable printer. See *Adobe Type Manager (ATM)*, *bit-mapped font*, *laser printer*, *outline font*, *printer font*, *resolution*, *TrueType*, and *typeface*.

**screen saver utility**   A utility program that prolongs the life of your monitor by blanking the screen while you are away from your computer.

Monitors degrade with use, particularly when an image is displayed on-screen continuously. Such images "burn" into the screen phosphors, resulting in a ghost image. Prolonged use also decreases screen sharpness.

Screen saver utilities help prevent burned-in images and prolong monitor life by blanking the screen while you are away from the computer. You can set the utility so that the blanking occurs after a specified amount of time, such as 5 or 10 minutes.

To alert you that the computer has not been turned off, screen saver utilities display a moving image (such as a clock or stars) on a black background.

 If you're running Microsoft Windows 3.1, don't bother buying a screen saver utility; one is built into this version of Windows. See *utility program*.

**script**  A series of instructions that tells an application program how to perform a specific procedure, such as logging on to an electronic mail system.

Script capabilities are built into some application programs. You must learn how to write the script using what amounts to a mini-programming language. Some programs write the script automatically by recording your keystrokes and command choices as you perform the procedure. In HyperTalk, a script is a HyperTalk program embedded into a card, button, or field. Scripts are similar to macros, except that the term *macro* is reserved for scripts you initiate by pressing a key combination that you define. See *HyperTalk* and *macro*.

**scripting**  The process of creating a handler—a brief program that traps messages you initiate—for an object in an object-oriented programming language, such as HyperTalk. See *handler* and *inheritance*.

**scroll**  To move the window horizontally or vertically so that its position over a document or worksheet changes.

In some programs, scrolling is clearly distinguished from cursor movement; when you scroll, the cursor stays put. In other programs, however, scrolling the screen also moves the cursor.

**scroll arrow**  In a graphical user interface such as Microsoft Windows or the Macintosh Finder, an arrow (pointing up, down, left, or right) you can click to scroll the screen in the desired direction. The scroll arrows are located at the ends of scroll bars (see fig. S.4).

**scroll bar/scroll box** A user interface feature that provides
you with horizontal and vertical scrolling capabilities
by placing rectangular scrolling areas on the right and
bottom borders of the window. You scroll the document horizontally or vertically by clicking the scroll
bars or scroll arrows, or by dragging the scroll boxes
(see fig. S.4).

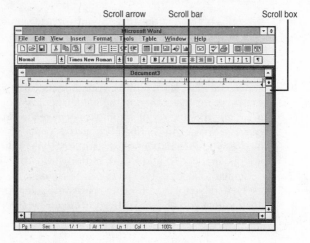

**Fig. S.4.** Vertical scroll arrow, bar, and box.

**Scroll Lock key** On IBM PC–compatible keyboards, a
toggle key that switches the cursor-movement keys
between two different modes with most programs.

The exact function of this key varies from program to
program. In one program, for example, the cursor-
movement keys normally move the cursor within the
screen. After pressing Scroll Lock, however, the left-
and right-arrow keys stop working, and the up- and
down-arrow keys scroll the screen without moving the
cursor.

If the cursor-movement keys seem to be
doing strange things, you may have pressed
the Scroll Lock key accidentally. Toggle it off
and try again. See *toggle key*.

**SCSI**   See *Small Computer System Interface*.

**search and replace**   See *replace*.

**secondary storage**   A nonvolatile storage medium such as a disk drive that stores program instructions and data, even after you switch off the power. Synonymous with *auxiliary storage*. See *primary storage*.

**secondary storage medium**   The specific secondary storage technology used to store and retrieve data, such as a magnetic disk, magnetic tape, or optical disk.

**sector**   In a floppy disk or hard disk, a segment of one of the concentric tracks encoded on the disk during a low-level format.

In IBM PC–compatible computing, a sector usually contains 512 bytes of information. See *cluster*.

**sector interleave factor**   See *interleave factor*.

**security**   The protection of data so that unauthorized persons cannot examine or copy it.

As business and professional people have discovered, a reasonably competent hacker can get into almost any computer system, even those that have been protected through such measures as passwords and data encryption. Sensitive data—such as employee performance ratings, customer lists, budget proposals, and confidential memos—can be downloaded on floppy disks that can be carried right out of the office without anyone knowing.

Mainframe computer systems address this problem by keeping the computer and its mass storage media under lock and key; the only way you can use the data is through remote terminals, equipped with a screen but no disk drives.

On the issue of security, some experts argue that personal computer local area networks should be set up the same way. The server should be kept under lock and key, and the workstations should have no disk drives. These experts forget that the excessive central-ization of mainframe computer systems was one of the main reasons personal computers were developed.

Concern for security should not prevent a manager from distributing computing power—and computing autonomy—to subordinates. Data encryption and pass-word-protection schemes exist that even a talented hacker cannot penetrate.

**seek** In a secondary storage device, to locate a specific region of a disk and to position the read/write head so that data or program instructions can be retrieved.

**seek time** In a secondary storage device, the time it takes the read/write head to reach the correct location on the disk. See *access time*.

**select** To highlight text so that the program can identify the text on which you want the next operation to be per-formed.

**selection** A unit of text, ranging from one character to many pages, highlighted in reverse video for formatting or editing purposes. In programming, a branch or conditional control structure. In database management, the retrieval of records by using a query. See *branch control structure*.

**semiconductor** A material such as silicon or germanium that lies between excellent electrical conductors, such as copper, and insulating materials in its electrical conductivity. When dopants (impurities) are added to the material during manufacture, it is possible to vary the material's electrical resistance with precision. Semi-conductor wafers or chips of varying resistance can be assembled to create a variety of electronic devices. In personal computers, semiconductor materials are used for microprocessors, internal storage, and other elec-tronic circuits. See *integrated circuit*.

**sequence control structure** A control structure that in-structs the computer to execute program statements in the order in which the statements are written.

One of three fundamental control structures that govern the order in which program statements are executed, the sequence control structure is the default in all programming languages. Unless instructed otherwise, the computer carries out the tasks in the order in which they are written. You can use the branch control structure and loop control structure to alter the sequence. See *control structure*.

**sequential access**   An information storage and retrieval technique in which the computer must move through a sequence of stored data items to reach the desired one.

Sequential access media such as cassette tape recorders are much slower than random-access media. See *random access*.

**serial**   See *asynchronous communication*, *parallel port*, and *parallel processing*.

**serial mouse**   A mouse designed to be connected directly to one of the computer's serial ports. See *bus mouse* and *mouse*.

**serial port**   A port that synchronizes and makes asynchronous communication easier between the computer and devices such as serial printers, modems, and other computers.

The function of the serial port is not only to transmit and receive asynchronous data in its one-bit-after-the-other stream; the serial port also negotiates with the receiving device to make sure that transmissions and receptions occur without the loss of data. The negotiation occurs through hardware or software handshaking. See *asynchronous communication*, *modem*, *port*, *RS-232C*, and *Universal Asynchronous Receiver/Transmitter (UART)*.

**serial printer**   A printer designed to be connected to the computer's serial port.

If you are using a serial printer with an IBM PC–compatible system, you must give the correct MODE command to configure your system at the start of each operating session. Almost all users place the necessary command in the AUTOEXEC.BAT file (DOS users) or STARTUP.CMD file (OS/2 users), which the operating system consults when you start up your computer. See your printer's manual for more details.

**serif** The fine cross strokes across the ends of the main strokes of a character.

Serif fonts are easier to read for body type, but most designers prefer to use sans serif typefaces for display type. (The text in this book is serif text.) See *sans serif*.

**server** In a local area network, a computer that provides services for users of the network. The server receives requests for peripheral services and manages the requests so that they are answered in an orderly, sequential manner. Synonymous with *network server*. See *dedicated file server*, *file server*, *print server*, and *workstation*.

**server application** In object linking and embedding (OLE), the application that creates the source document. Data from the source document is pasted in one or more destination documents, created by client applications. To update or edit the source data, the user chooses a command that starts the server application and displays the data in its native environment. See *client application*, *destination document*, *object linking and embedding (OLE)*, and *source document*.

**server-based application** A network version of an application program stored on the network's file server and available to more than one user at a time. See *client-based application* and *file server*.

**service bureau** A firm that provides a variety of publication services such as graphics file format conversion, optical scanning of graphics, and typesetting on high-resolution printers such as Linotronics and Varitypers.

**setup string**   A series of characters that an application program conveys to the printer so that the printer operates
in a specified mode. In Lotus 1-2-3, for example, the
setup string \027G turns on an Epson printer's double-
strike mode.

**shadow RAM**   In 80386 and 80486 computers, a portion of
the upper memory area between 640K and 1M set aside
for programs ordinarily retrieved from read-only
memory (ROM). Because RAM is faster than ROM,
shadow RAM increases performance.

 Computer manufacturers like to equip their
machines with shadow RAM because doing
so improves the machines' performance on
speed measurement tests. However, configuring part of the upper memory area as shadow RAM
could cause problems with applications that try to use
upper memory as extended memory. If you're running
Microsoft Windows, or any other application that uses
MS-DOS 5.0 or requires extended memory, consult
your computer manual to determine how to disable
shadow RAM. See *random-access memory (RAM),
read-only memory (ROM),* and *upper memory area.*

**shareware**   Copyrighted computer programs made available
on a trial basis; if you like and decide to use the program, you are expected to pay a fee to the program's
author. See *public domain software.*

**sheet feeder**   See *cut-sheet feeder.*

**shell**   A utility program designed to provide an improved
(and often menu-driven) user interface for a program
or operating system generally considered difficult to
use. See *user interface* and *utility program.*

**Shift-click**   A mouse maneuver accomplished by holding
down the Shift key when you click the mouse. Applications implement Shift-clicking differently, but in most,
the action extends a selection.

**Shift key**   The key you press to enter uppercase letters or
punctuation marks.

On early IBM keyboards, the Shift key is labeled only with a white arrow. Later IBM keyboards and most compatible keyboards label this key with the word *Shift*. See *Caps Lock key*.

**shortcut key** A key combination that provides rapid access to a menu command or dialog box option. Using a shortcut key can save you time by removing the need to display two or more menus before you reach the option you want.

**side-by-side columns** Unequally sized blocks of text positioned side-by-side on a page, so that the first block is always positioned next to the second one.

Side-by-side columns, often called *parallel columns*, include paragraphs meant to be positioned adjacent to one another. Newspaper column formats cannot handle this formatting task, because no relationship exists between the paragraphs in one column and the paragraphs in another.

An easy way to create side-by-side paragraphs is to use the table utilities included in some word processing programs (see fig. S.5). See *newspaper columns* and *table utility*.

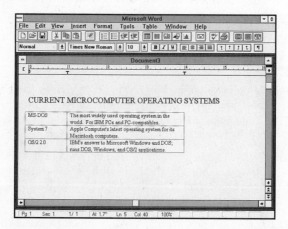

**Fig. S.5.** Side-by-side columns.

**SIG**   See *special interest group*.

**signal**   The portion of a transmission that coherently represents information, unlike the random and meaningless noise that occurs in the transmission channel.

**silicon chip**   See *chip*.

**Silicon Valley**   An area in California's Santa Clara Valley with one of the largest concentrations of high-technology businesses in the world. The word *Silicon* suggests the area's prominence in silicon chip design and manufacturing.

**SIMM**   See *single in-line memory module*.

**simple list text chart**   In presentation graphics, a text chart used to enumerate items in no particular order, with each item given equal emphasis (see fig. S.6). See *presentation graphics*.

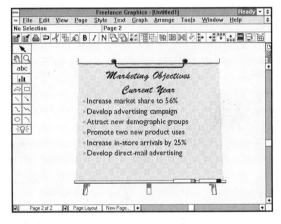

**Fig. S.6.** A simple list text chart.

**simulation**   In computer applications, an analytical technique in which an analyst investigates a phenomenon's properties by creating a model of the phenomenon and exploring the model's behavior.

One of the most important contributions of the computer lies in its provision of new, useful tools for simulation. In aeronautical engineering, for example, the aerodynamic properties of a proposed aircraft could be simulated only through the time-consuming and expensive construction of a series of physical models, which were subjected to wind-tunnel tests.

Now, however, you can use computer simulation techniques to design and test thousands of alternative models quickly. The wind tunnel, therefore, is becoming an anachronism in modern aerospace firms.

In education, simulation techniques are enabling schools that cannot afford laboratory equipment to offer students a chance to engage in simulated, on-screen versions of classic laboratory experiments.

Simulation also is found in computer games, such as Microsoft Flight Simulator. This program is so realistic in its simulation of powered flight that it has been used as a prelude to professional flight instruction in many flight schools.

Users of spreadsheet programs frequently use simulation techniques to create a model of a business. Using simulation, a manager can ask what-if questions such as, "What is the effect on market share if we spend 20 percent more on advertising?"

As with any model, however, a simulation is only as good as its underlying assumptions. If these assumptions are not correct, the model does not accurately mimic the behavior of the real-world system being simulated.

**single density**  A magnetic recording scheme for digital data that uses a technique called *frequency modulation* (FM). Single-density disks, common in early personal computing, have low storage capacity, such as 90K per disk, and are rarely used today.

Disk drives designed for FM recording, therefore, could use disks (single-density disks) with relatively large-grained magnetic particles. Single-density recording disks have been superseded by double-density storage devices that use modified frequency modulation (MFM) storage techniques, double-density disks with finer grained partitions, and high-density disks with even finer partitions. See *double density, frequency modulation (FM) recording, Modified Frequency Modulation (MFM),* and *single density.*

**single in-line memory module (SIMM)**   A plug-in memory module containing all the chips needed to add 256K or 1M of random-access memory to your computer.

**single in-line package (SIP)**   A plastic package, designed to house and protect an electronic circuit, with a single row of pins extending from one side of the package. See *dual in-line package.*

**single-sided disk**   A floppy disk designed so that only one side of the disk can be used for read/write operations. Single-sided disks have low storage capacities and are used infrequently in today's personal computer systems.

**SIP**   See *single in-line package.*

**site license**   An agreement between a software publisher and an organization that enables the organization to make unlimited copies of the publisher's software program for internal use. Often a company using a local area network purchases a site license for a program so that all the users on the LAN can access the program. Most site licenses stipulate a numeric limit on the number of copies the organization can make. The cost per copy is much less than buying individual copies.

**sixteen-bit**   See *16-bit computer.*

**skip factor**   In a graphics program, an increment that specifies how many data points the program should skip as it constructs a chart or graph.

Use a skip factor when a graph looks cluttered with too many thin, spindly columns or when the categories axis is too crowded with headings. A skip factor of 3, for example, displays every third data item, reducing the graph's complexity.

**slide show**   In presentation graphics, a predetermined list of on-screen charts and graphs displayed one after the other.

Some programs can produce interesting effects, such as fading out one screen before displaying another. You can add buttons that allow the viewer to alter the sequence in which the slides are displayed, jump to a specific slide, or exit the slide show. See *presentation graphics*.

**slot**   See *expansion slot*.

**slug**   In word processing and desktop publishing, a code inserted in headers or footers that generates page numbers when the document is printed.

**Small Computer System Interface (SCSI)**   Pronounced "scuzzy." An interface standard for peripheral devices such as hard disk drives and laser printers.

The most common SCSI device in use is the SCSI hard disk. Unlike ST506 and ESDI drives, the drive contains most of the controller circuitry, leaving the SCSI interface free to communicate with other peripherals. SCSI drivers generally are faster than ST506 drives. See *Enhanced System Device Interface (ESDI)* and *ST-506/ST-412*.

**SmallTalk**   A high-level programming language and programming environment that conceptualizes computations as objects that send messages to one another.

Developed by Alan Kay and others at Xerox Corporation's Palo Alto Research Center (PARC),

SmallTalk is unlike all other programming languages because all programming functions are expressed in terms of the dominant metaphor of objects sending messages to one another.

A declarative language, SmallTalk encourages the programmer to define these objects in terms relevant to the intended application, and the language is highly extensible because objects can be created quite easily.

More than a programming language, SmallTalk is a complete programming environment that features a graphical user interface with pull-down menus and mouse support. A major goal of SmallTalk was to make computer programming more accessible to nonprogrammers.

SmallTalk is an important innovation in programming language design and is used in research and development settings. Because the language requires a great deal of memory to produce efficient, fast-running programs, however, professional programmers continue to prefer languages such as assembly language and C. But SmallTalk inspired HyperTalk, the software command language of HyperCard, an application provided with every Macintosh sold since 1987.

Thousands of hobbyists and professional programmers are learning the object-oriented programming philosophy as they use HyperTalk to create HyperCard applications. In its new guise, SmallTalk has fulfilled its goal of making computer programming more accessible; tens of thousands of Macintosh users have learned to program in HyperTalk. See *declarative language*, *high-level programming language*, *HyperCard*, and *object-oriented programming language*.

**smart machine**   Any device containing microprocessor-based electronics that enable the device to branch to alternative operating sequences depending on external conditions, to repeat operations until a condition is fulfilled, or to execute a series of instructions repetitively.

Microprocessors are so inexpensive that they can be embedded in even the most prosaic of everyday devices, such as toasters, coffee makers, and ovens. At the University of Virginia, an undergraduate engineering student created a microprocessor-controlled barbecue oven that slow-roasts a side of beef at the optimum temperature. A temperature sensor tells the microprocessor whether the beef is too hot or cool, and adjusts the electric heating element. An analysis program calculates the optimum cooking time. Taste testers agreed that the results were impressive indeed.

**smart terminal**   In a multiuser system, a terminal containing its own processing circuitry so that it not only retrieves data from the host computer, but also carries out additional processing operations and runs host-delivered programs.

**snaf**   The messy strips of waste paper that litter the office after the perforated edge is removed from continuous, tractor-fed computer paper.

The term *snaf* was the winning entry in a contest sponsored by National Public Radio's "All Things Considered." The runner-up, *perfory,* is worthy of mention.

**snaking columns**   See *newspaper columns*.

**snapshot**   See *screen dump*.

**SNOBOL**   A high-level programming language designed for text-processing applications.

Developed at AT&T's Bell Laboratories in 1962, SNOBOL (StriNg-Oriented symBOlic Language) arose from the frustration of its creators (Ralph Griswold, David Farber, and Ivan Polonsky) with numerically oriented programming languages. They sought to create a programming language that could manipulate text, and they hoped to create a language that would interest people who were not mathematicians.

The language they created is especially strong in its textual pattern-matching capabilities and has been used for research work in fields such as language translation, the generation of indexes or concordances to literary works, and text reformatting.

SNOBOL shares with BASIC and FORTRAN, its contemporaries, a lack of structure and an overreliance on GOTO statements and, therefore, is little more than a curiosity. SNOBOL4 is available for IBM PC–compatible computers. See *BASIC* and *FORTRAN*.

**soft**   Temporary or changeable, as opposed to hard (permanently wired, physically fixed, or inflexible). Compare a soft return, a page break inserted by a word processing program and subject to change if you add or delete text, to a hard return, a page break you insert manually and which remains fixed in place despite further editing.

**soft cell boundaries**   In a spreadsheet program, a feature that enables you to enter labels longer than the cell's width (unless the adjacent cells are occupied).

**soft font**   See *downloadable font*.

**soft hyphen**   A hyphen formatted so that the program does not use it unless the hyphen is needed to improve the spacing on a line. Synonymous with *optional hyphen*. See *hard hyphen*.

**soft page break**   In a word processing program, a page break inserted by the program, based on the current state of the text; the page break may move up or down if you make insertions, deletions, margin changes, or page size changes. See *forced page break*.

**soft return**   In a word processing program, a line break inserted by the program to maintain the margins. The location of soft returns changes automatically if you change the margins or insert or delete text. See *hard return* and *word wrap*.

**soft-sectored disk**   A disk that, when new, contains no magnetic patterns of tracks or sectors. The patterns must be added in a process called *formatting* before you can use the disk. See *formatting*.

**soft start**   See *warm boot*.

**software**   System, utility, or application programs expressed in a computer-readable language. See *firmware*.

**software command language**   A high-level programming language developed to work with an application, such as a spreadsheet or database management program.

Software command languages vary from the simple macro capabilities of word processing programs to full-fledged programming languages, such as the dBASE command language. The best software command languages enable programmers to create custom applications, complete with iteration, logical branching, and conditional execution of operations.

These languages give the programmer enormous leverage because the package already handles all details related to disk input/output, the user interface, data structures, error handling, and so on. A relatively simple program, therefore, can produce an extremely powerful custom application. See *control structure*, *dBASE*, and *HyperTalk*.

**software compatibility**   The capability of a computer system to run a specific type of software. The Commodore 64, for example, is not software-compatible with software written for the Apple II, even though both computers use the MOS Technology 6502 microprocessor.

**software engineering**   An applied science devoted to improving and optimizing the production of computer software.

**software license**   A legal agreement included with commercial programs. The software license specifies the rights and obligations of the individual who purchased the program and limits the liability of the software publisher.

**software package**   A computer application program delivered to the user in a complete and ready-to-run form, including all necessary utility programs and documentation. See *application program*.

**software piracy**   The unauthorized and illegal duplication of copyrighted software without the permission of the software publisher.

Software can be duplicated in a matter of seconds. To the consternation of software publishers, software piracy is extremely common and seems to be an endemic problem of personal computing.

As early as 1976, Bill Gates, a cofounder of Microsoft Corporation, complained that he could not remain in the business of selling a BASIC interpreter for the Altair computer if people kept on making illegal copies of his program. Worse, people who seldom break other moral or legal rules engage in software piracy without hesitation. The computer revolution appears to have happened so quickly that cultural norms and moral values have not had time to adjust accordingly.

Those who defend software piracy, however, present arguments that seem to amount to little more than thinly veiled excuses for self interest. Some argue, for example, that software piracy has a beneficial effect on the software industry: to motivate people to become registered users, or so the argument goes, software publishers are forced to make constant improvements to a program. But most software revisions are motivated almost exclusively by competitive pressures.

Others argue that software piracy is a way of previewing a program—and a justifiable way, considering that most software retailers don't let you return a program after you have opened the package. If the pirate really likes the program, argue the defenders of piracy, the pirate will become a registered user, seeking the benefit of upgrades and documentation. But few pirates ever purchase the upgrades.

Attempts to stop software piracy through copy-protection schemes backfired on the companies that tried them. Such schemes prevented a casual, unsophisticated user from copying a disk, but they also imposed penalties on valid, registered users of the program. Legitimate users therefore avoided buying copy-protected programs, so the major software publishers gave them up.

 Software piracy is immoral and illegal when it occurs at home, but prosecution is far from likely. Don't let this fact lull you into security when it comes to using computers in businesses and organizations. More than a few companies have been sued for damages attributable to unauthorized software duplication, and an industry consortium has established a toll-free hotline through which whistle blowers (or disgruntled employees) can report offenders. A wise manager establishes a policy that absolutely no unauthorized copies of software are to be kept near, or used with, company computers.

**software program**   An application program. Despite its redundancy, this term is used frequently, especially in advertisements, articles, books, and manuals written for a computer-illiterate audience. See *application program* and *software*.

**software protection**   See *copy protection*.

**sort**   An operation that rearranges data so that it is in alphabetical or numerical order.

Most application programs can perform sorts. Full-featured word processing programs, such as WordPerfect, provide commands that sort lists, and electronic spreadsheets provide commands that sort the cells in a range.

In database management programs, sorts are distinguished from index operations. A sort physically rearranges data records, resulting in a new, permanently sorted file—consuming much disk space in the process. You can use the permanently re-sorted records later, without repeating the sort operation, but you now have two copies of your database. If you forget to erase the first one, you can become confused about which copy you used to update the data. An index operation, however, does not physically rearrange the records. Instead, an index operation creates an index to the records and sorts the index rather than the records. The index consumes less disk space than a new copy of the whole database.

Even if you have a huge hard disk, however, indexing provides a much more important advantage; a good database management program (such as dBASE) preserves data integrity by updating all the indexes whenever you add records or update old ones. See *data integrity* and *sort order*.

**sort key**   In database management, the data field that determines the order in which data records are arranged.

In an employee database, for example, you can use the LAST_NAME field or SOCSECNO (Social Security number) field to arrange the records in alphabetical or numerical order. See *multilevel sort*.

**sort order**   The order in which a program arranges data when performing a sort. Most programs sort data in the standard order of ASCII characters. Synonymous with *collating sequence*. See *ASCII sort order*, *dictionary sort*, and *sort*.

**sound board**   An adapter that adds digital sound reproduction capabilities to an IBM or IBM-compatible personal computer.

A major drawback of IBM-format computing is the wholly inadequate sound; the tinny, three-inch speaker can reproduce only a limited range of irritating beeps, honks, and squawks. In the future, high-quality sound, including beautiful stereo reproduction of voices and music, probably will be considered a minimal component of a useful and friendly computer system.

One technological advantage of the latest Macintosh computers is their stereo digital sound reproduction capabilities. Programmers can add a fuller dimension of sound to their programs, knowing that all Macintoshes can reproduce them. The Macintosh LC II comes equipped with a microphone and software that enables you to record your own brief sounds and voice messages.

MS-DOS and Microsoft Windows programmers must assume that users will not possess a sound board, because this adapter is not often provided as standard equipment. In consequence, they rarely include many sounds with their programs. Some programs, however, are designed to detect the presence of a sound board automatically and to switch to a richer sound palette if a sound board is found.

 Windows users should look for a sound board that is fully supported by Windows' multimedia extensions. These sound boards include Ad Lib Gold Card, Soundblaster, Soundblaster Pro, and Thunderboard. See *adapter* and *multimedia.*

**Sound Recorder**    A Microsoft Windows 3.1 accessory that enables you to record and play back sounds (see fig. S.7). To operate Sound Recorder, your system must be equipped with an MPC-compatible sound board with recording capabilities, including a microphone. Sound Recorder serves as a control device, turning your computer into a digital tape recorder. Sound Recorder places the recorded sound into a file with the extension WAV, a file that other MPC-compatible programs can access. See *Multimedia Personal Computer (MPC)* and *sound board.*

**Fig. S.7.** Sound Recorder window (Microsoft Windows 3.1).

**source** The record, file, document, or disk from which information is taken or moved, as opposed to the destination. See *destination*.

**source code** In a high-level programming language, the typed program instructions that people create, before the program has been compiled or interpreted into machine instructions that the computer can execute.

**source document** In dynamic data exchange (DDE), the document containing data that has been dynamically linked to copies of that data in other documents, called *destination documents*. See *destination document* and *dynamic data exchange (DDE)*.

**source file** In many DOS commands, the file from which data or program instructions are copied. See *destination file*.

**source worksheet** In Microsoft Excel, a worksheet containing a cell or range that has been dynamically linked to one or more dependent worksheets. The changes you make to the source worksheet are automatically reflected in the dependent worksheets. See *dependent worksheet*.

**spaghetti code** A poorly organized program that results from excessive use of GOTO statements. As the use of GOTO statements proliferates, the program becomes almost impossible to read and debug. The cure is to use a well-structured programming language, such as QuickBASIC, C, or Pascal, that offers a full set of control structures. See *C, Pascal, QuickBASIC,* and *structured programming*.

**special interest group (SIG)** A subgroup of an organization or computer networking system, consisting of members who share a common interest. Common SIG topics include software, hobbies, sports, literary genres such as mystery or science fiction, and artifact collecting of every kind. See *user group*.

**speech synthesis** Computer production of audio output that resembles human speech.

Computer voice recognition technology is still primitive. Even the best systems can recognize only a few hundred words, and they do so only after a lengthy training session in which the computer becomes familiar with an individual's specific voice patterns.

Speech synthesis technology, however, is quite well developed. Existing and inexpensive speech synthesis boards can do an impressive job of reading virtually any file containing English sentences in ASCII script—although, to some listeners, the English sounds as though it is being spoken with a Czech accent.

Speech synthesis is improving the lives of blind people by making written material more accessible to them; blind writers can proof and edit their own written work by having the computer read their work to them.

**spell checker**   A program, often incorporated in word processing programs, that checks for the correct spelling of words in a document. Each word is compared against a file of correctly spelled words.

A good spell checker displays the correct spelling of a misspelled word and enables you to replace the misspelled word with the correct one. You usually can add words to the spell checker's dictionary.

**spike**   See *power surge.*

**split bar**   In a graphical user interface such as Microsoft Windows or the Macintosh Finder, a bar you can drag to split the window horizontally or vertically.

**split screen**   A display technique in which the screen is divided into two windows. In word processing programs that have split screen capabilities, independently displaying two parts of the same document is usually possible, as is displaying two different documents. Splitting the screen is useful when you want to refer to one document, or part of a document, while writing in another. It also facilitates cut-and-paste editing.

Most Microsoft Windows applications can display more than one window. You can display different documents in each window, or if you prefer, you can display two or more sections of the same document. In figure S.8, for example, Document3 is displayed in two windows: Document3:1 and Document3:2. Many applications also allow you to split a window into two panes. To do so, you drag the split bar—a thick black line—down the vertical scroll bar. In this example, the Document2 window is split into two panes.

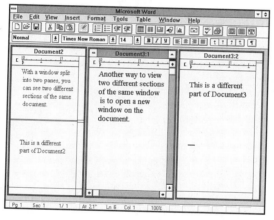

**Fig. S.8.** Split screens.

**spooler**   A program, often included with an operating system's utility programs, that routes printer commands to a file on disk or in RAM instead of to the printer, and then doles out the printer commands when the central processing unit (CPU) is idle.

A print spooler provides background printing; your program thinks it is printing to a super-fast printer, but the printer output actually is being directed to RAM or a disk file. You can continue working with your program, and the spooler guides the printer data to the printer during those moments when the CPU is not busy handling your work. See *background printing*.

**spreadsheet** See *worksheet*.

**spreadsheet program** A program that simulates an accountant's worksheet on-screen and enables you to embed hidden formulas that perform calculations on the visible data.

In 1978, a Harvard Business School student named Dan Bricklin got tired of adding up columns of numbers—and adding them up all over again after making a few changes, just to assess the effect of a merger. Bricklin, who knew a little about computers from summer jobs at Wang and other firms, came up with the idea of a spreadsheet program running on a personal computer.

Bricklin's teachers thought the idea was nonsense, but he and a programmer friend, Bob Frankston, produced VisiCalc, a program for the Apple II computer, and launched an important new chapter in American enterprise.

A spreadsheet program presents you with a matrix of rows (usually numbered) and columns (usually assigned alphabetical letters) that form individual cells. The on-screen display is called a *spreadsheet*. Each cell has a distinctive cell address, such as B4 or D19. Into each cell, you can place a value (a number), a hidden formula that performs a calculation, or a label (a heading or explanatory text).

Formulas make a spreadsheet powerful. A formula can contain constants, such as 2+2, but the most useful formulas contain cell references, such as D9+D10. By placing formulas in a spreadsheet's cells, you can create a complex network of links among the parts of a spreadsheet. You don't see the formulas, which are hidden behind the cell, but you see the values they generate.

The point of creating a spreadsheet isn't just to find the answer to a problem. After you complete your spreadsheet, you can enter new values, and the spreadsheet is recalculated. In seconds, you can see how a change in one value ripples through the spreadsheet and affects the outcome.

This form of sensitivity testing—changing values to see how they affect the outcome— is called *what-if analysis* and is one of the main reasons spreadsheet programs have sold so well. Using what-if analysis, you can examine the potential effect of a decision.

VisiCalc was a huge success; more than 700,000 copies of the program eventually were sold, and VisiCalc was almost single-handedly responsible for the success of the Apple II personal computer. But VisiCalc met stiff competition from Lotus 1-2-3 in the IBM PC environment and, by 1984, had disappeared from the market. VisiCalc may be gone, but its influence lives on in many ways; almost all spreadsheet programs use VisiCalc's slash key ( / ) command to display the command menu.

Spreadsheets have acquired many new features since VisiCalc's time. Lotus 1-2-3 is an integrated program that combines analytical graphics and database management with what is clearly a clone of VisiCalc's spreadsheet. Recent trends in spreadsheets include the three-dimensional spreadsheet programs, such as 1-2-3 Release 3.1, and Windows spreadsheets, such as Microsoft Excel, which bring high-quality fonts and graphics to spreadsheets.

As useful as spreadsheets are, remember that they are prone to error. Because you cannot see the formulas, you may not notice when one contains a serious error. Also, during what-if analysis, you may type a constant into a cell containing a formula and destroy the links among cells without realizing what you have done. Both errors are very common and occur even among people who should know better.

A spreadsheet is just a model of a business; any model includes only some of the significant determinants of a firm's behavior, and manipulating the model—as is commonly done in what-if analysis—may lead to serious errors in decision making, even if all the formulas are correct. People may be tempted to tweak the assumptions so that they get the right answer.

A particularly unjustified "tweak" may be partly responsible for the huge U.S. budget deficit of the last decade. David Stockman, the director of President Reagan's Office of Management and Budget, was instructed to produce a model of the American economy that would show the results of the President's tax cuts. According to William Greider's book *The Education of David Stockman*, Stockman found that the model suggested huge budget deficits. Because this answer was not the one he was looking for, he introduced a swift decline in prices and a rapid rise in productivity into the model, which then produced the "right" answer.

Do not make business decisions based on a spreadsheet without carefully thinking through what you are doing.

- Check all the formulas to see whether they are correct. Many programs include a command that displays the formulas on-screen. Third-party programs such as Spreadsheet Auditor (Cambridge Software) are available for the programs without this command.

- Use cell protection on every cell containing a formula.

- Never place constants in a formula. Place all the constants in your spreadsheet in a special area at the top of the spreadsheet that contains the key variables.

- Bear in mind the limitations of a model; a model can never mimic reality, only part of it.

- Remember that all good decisions aren't necessarily defensible on purely quantitative grounds. A model that suggests saving money may do so at the sacrifice of employee or community good will or market share, and even though the results look good, they may wind up being catastrophic in the end.

**SQL**   See *Structured Query Language*.

**ST-506/ST-412**   A hard disk interface standard widely used in IBM and IBM-compatible computers.

These drives are slower and cheaper than drives using more recent interface standards, such as ESDI, IOE, and SCSI. MFM and RLL encoding methods are used with the ST-506/ST-412 interface. MFM has a 5-megabit-per-second transfer rate, and RLL has a 7.5-megabit-per-second rate. ST-506/ST-412 is still the most common interface using the MFM encoding and is standard on 80286-based computers.

 If you use an 80386- or 80486-based computer with an IDE (Intelligent Drive Electronics) interface, don't install an ST-506/ST-412 drive; it probably won't coexist with the IDE controller. Get an IDE drive instead. See *Enhanced System Device Interface (ESDI)*, *Intelligent Drive Electronics (IDE)*, *interface standard*, *Modified Frequency Modulation (MFM)*, *Run-Length Limited (RLL)*, and *Small Computer Systems Interface (SCSI)*.

**stack**   In programming, a stack is a data structure in which the first items inserted are the last ones removed. This data structure is used in programs that use control structures; a stack enables the computer to track what it was doing when it branched or jumped to a procedure. In HyperCard, the term *stack* refers to a file containing one or more cards that share a common background. See *control structure* and *HyperCard*.

**stacked column chart**   See *stacked column graph*.

**stacked column graph** A column graph in which two or more data series are displayed, not adjacent to one another, but on top of one another (see fig S.9). See *histogram*.

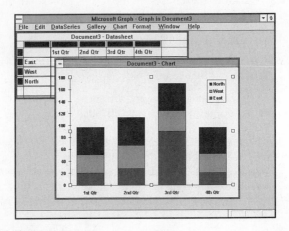

**Fig. S.9.** A stacked column graph.

**staggered windows** See *cascading windows*.

**stand-alone computer** A computer system dedicated to meeting all the computing needs of an individual. The user chooses just the software needed for his or her daily tasks.

A stand-alone system contains only the hardware and software a user requires, and it is tailored to that person's needs. Links with other computers are incidental to the system's chief purpose. See *distributed processing system*, *multiuser system*, and *professional workstation*.

**Standard mode** In Microsoft Windows, an operating mode that takes advantage of extended memory in 80286 and higher computers, but does not allow full use of the technical capabilities of 80386 and higher microprocessors. Standard mode runs Windows applications well, and it is faster than 386 Enhanced mode. The disadvantages of Standard mode are apparent only when you try to run DOS applications. In Standard mode, DOS applications take over the screen, and virtual memory and multitasking are not available. In 386 Enhanced mode, you can run two or more DOS applications in their own windows, and each has 640K of clear, unobstructed memory.

 If you have an 80386 or higher microprocessor and at least 2M of RAM, you can run Windows in 386 Enhanced mode, which makes true multitasking and virtual memory available. See *386 Enhanced mode, extended memory, Microsoft Windows, multitasking, real mode*, and *virtual memory*.

**star network**   In local area networks, a centralized network topology with the physical layout of a star. At the center is a central network processor or wiring concentrator; the nodes are arranged around and connected directly to the central point.

Wiring costs are considerably higher because each workstation requires a cable that links the workstation directly to the central processor (see fig S.10).

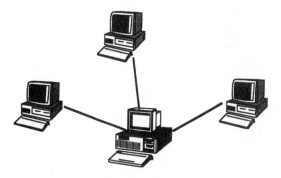

**Fig. S.10.** An illustration of a star network.

**start bit**   In serial communications, a bit inserted into the data stream to inform the receiving computer that a byte of data is to follow.

**startup disk**   The disk containing portions of the operating system that you normally use to start your computer. Synonymous with *boot disk* and *system disk*. See *hard disk*.

**startup screen**   A Macintosh graphics file that, when correctly named and placed in the System Folder, displays when you turn on or restart the computer.

Most Macintosh users are content with the "Welcome to Macintosh" message, but you can see virtually anything you want when you turn on your machine; you can save any bit-mapped graphic image as the startup screen. For example, you can display a bird, a volcano, or even a picture of yourself.

**statement**   In a high-level programming language, a command that trained programmers can read and understand. A statement successfully generates machine language instructions when the program is interpreted or compiled. See *high-level programming language* and *instruction*.

**state-of-the-art**   A technically sophisticated item containing the latest technology and representing the highest possible level of technical achievement.

**static object**   A document or portion of a document pasted into a destination document by using normal, Clipboard copy-and-paste techniques. If the object was created by an application other than the client application, you cannot change or edit the object. The only way to change a static object is to delete it, make changes to the source document, and copy the source document again. Object linking and embedding (OLE) provides a way to insert dynamic objects (linked objects and embedded objects) into documents. Linked objects automatically reflect the changes you make to the source documents, and you can edit embedded objects from the destination document. See *embedded object, linked object,* and *object linking and embedding (OLE)*.

**static random-access memory (RAM)**   A random-access memory (RAM) chip that holds its contents without constant refreshing from the CPU.

Although as volatile as DRAM chips, static RAM does not require the CPU to refresh its contents several hundred times per second. These chips, therefore, are substantially faster and preferable for high-speed computers based on microprocessors such as the Intel 80386. They also are significantly more expensive than DRAM chips. See *dynamic random-access memory (DRAM)*, *random-access memory (RAM)*, and *volatility*.

**station**   See *workstation*.

**statistical software**   An application program that makes the application of statistical tests and measures to computer-readable data easier.

**status line**   A line of an application program's display screen that describes the state of the program.

Often included in status lines are the name of the file you currently are modifying and the name of any toggle keys you have pressed, such as Num Lock or Caps Lock.

**stem**   In typography, the main vertical stroke of a character.

**stickup initial**   An enlarged initial letter at the beginning of a paragraph that rises above the top of the first line.

 You can create initials with many word processing and page layout programs, but to avoid a common formatting error, make sure that the letter aligns precisely at the base of a line of text. See *drop cap* and *initial*.

**stop bit**   In serial communications, a bit inserted into the data stream to inform the receiving computer that the transmission of a byte of data is complete.

**storage**   The retention of program instructions, initial data, and intermediate data within the computer so that this information is available for processing purposes. See *primary storage* and *secondary storage*.

**storage device**   Any optical or magnetic device capable of secondary storage functions in a computer system. See *secondary storage*.

**stored program concept**   The idea, which underlies the architecture of all modern computers, that the program should be stored in memory with the data.

An insight of the late physician and scientist John von Neumann as he beheld the hard-wired programs of the ENIAC (North America's first digital electronic computer), this concept showed how a program could jump back and forth through instructions instead of executing them sequentially. With this insight, virtually the entire world of modern computing was launched. See *von Neumann bottleneck*.

**streaming tape drive**   A secondary storage device that uses continuous tape, contained in a cartridge, for backup purposes.

**strikeout**   An attribute, such as type, struck through with a hyphen to mark text; for example, ~~this text has strikeout formatting~~.

Strikeout often is used to mark text to be deleted from a coauthored document so that the other author can see changes easily. See *overstrike, Overtype mode,* and *redlining*.

**string**   A series of alphanumeric characters.

**string formula**   In a spreadsheet program, a formula that performs a string operation such as concatenation.

**string operation**   A computation performed on alphanumeric characters.

Computers cannot understand the meaning of words, and they therefore cannot process them like people do; however, computers can perform simple processing operations on textual data, such as the following:

- *Comparison.* Comparing two strings to see whether they are the same.

- *Concatenation.* Joining two strings together.

- *Length calculation.* Calculating the number of characters a string occupies.

- *Sorting.* Arranging strings in ASCII order.

**structured programming**   A set of quality standards that make programs more verbose but more readable, more reliable, and more easily maintained.

The essence of structured programming is to avoid spaghetti code, the untrackable links in a program that result from an overreliance on GOTO statements. Spaghetti code programs are difficult to read and can be difficult to debug.

To avoid spaghetti code, structured programming insists that the overall program structure logically reflects what the program is supposed to do, beginning with the first task and proceeding logically. Indentations are used to make the logic clear to anyone reading the program. The programmer is encouraged to use loop and branch control structures and named procedures instead of GOTO statements. A properly designed program does not require line numbers, and the function of the program should be immediately obvious to anyone trained in the language. Languages such as C, Pascal, Modula-2, and the dBASE software command language are inherently structured and encourage the programmer to adopt these good habits.

Early versions of languages such as BASIC and FORTRAN are not inherently structured and are seldom used for serious professional program development. See *modular programming*.

**Structured Query Language (SQL)**   In database management systems, an IBM-developed query language widely used in mainframe and minicomputer systems. SQL increasingly is being implemented in client/server networks as a way of enabling personal computers to access the resources of corporate databases.

Originally developed by D. D. Chamberlin and other researchers at IBM Research Laboratories, SQL is the up-and-coming query language for microcomputers because the language can be used with a variety of database management packages.

SQL is data independent; the user does not have to worry about the particulars of how data is accessed physically. In theory, SQL also is device independent; the same query language can be used to access databases on mainframes, minicomputers, and personal computers. Currently, however, several versions of SQL are competing.

Because of its data and device independence, SQL is a fast-rising star on the personal computer scene. Many companies have purchased hundreds or even thousands of personal computers, which function well as stand-alone workstations, but the problem faced by many companies is how to enable users to access data on corporate minicomputers and mainframes.

SQL, therefore, rapidly is becoming a common language for computerized database management. Anyone who knows how to use a personal computer database that uses SQL has already learned the necessary commands and syntax, and the same query language is useful for accessing a database stored on a corporate mainframe.

SQL is an elegant and concise query language with only thirty commands. The four basic commands (SELECT, UPDATE, DELETE, and INSERT) correspond to the four basic functions of data manipulation (data retrieval, data modification, data deletion, and data insertion, respectively).

SQL queries also approximate the structure of an English natural-language query. For example, the request, "Show me the title and rating of those videotapes in the inventory database in which the CATEGORY field contains the word *children*, and put the result in order by title," is represented by the following SQL query:

```
SELECT title, rating
FROM inventory
WHERE category = "children"
ORDER BY title
```

SQL is table-oriented; SQL queries do not display individual data records. Instead, the queries result in the on-screen display of a data table, consisting of columns (corresponding to data fields) and rows (corresponding to data records). See *data deletion*, *data insertion*, *data manipulation*, *data modification*, *data retrieval*, *natural language*, and *table-oriented database management program*.

**style sheet**   In some word processing and page layout programs, a stored collection of user-created text-formatting definitions containing information such as type style, alignment, and line spacing specifications.

In the old days of professional typists, the typist interviewed the author and filled out a style sheet, listing the author's preferences for all formats (such as titles, footnotes, body text paragraphs, and the like). In word processing software, however, the term describes an on-disk collection of formatting definitions you create. For example, you can have a style sheet entry for normal body text paragraphs that includes the following formats: Palatino, 10-point type size, ragged-left indentation, single line spacing, and 1/2-inch first line indentation.

 When used properly, style sheets can enhance productivity by greatly speeding the reformatting of a document. Suppose that you decide to use New Century Schoolbook instead of Palatino for the body type. If you have not defined the body paragraph style in a style sheet, you must go through the document and manually change the style of all body paragraphs, carefully skipping over display type and other formats. If you *have* defined a body paragraph style, however, you make just one change to the style sheet, and the program automatically changes all the text linked to this style.

**stylus**   A pen-shaped instrument used on a monitor's screen or on a graphics tablet to draw line art or select menu options.

**subdirectory**   In DOS and UNIX, a directory listed within a directory that, when opened, reveals another directory containing files and additional subdirectories.

The directory you see when you use MS-DOS's DIR command is an effective guide to a disk's contents until you create more files than one screen can display. With MS-DOS, you operate under stringent limitations on the number of files you can place in one directory. You can place only 112 files in one directory on a 360K or 720K disk. You can place only 512 files in one directory on a hard disk. Subdirectories enable you to create a tree-like, hierarchical structure of nested directories in which you can store many more than 512 files.

To understand how subdirectories are linked, look at a typical root directory:

```
Volume in Drive A has no label
Directory of A:\
LETTER1   DOC    1651    3-24-92    12:01a
REPORT1   DOC    1102    3-24-92    12:01a
MEMO1     DOC    6462    3-24-92    12:00p
LETTER2   DOC    1651    5-24-92    12:01a
REPORT2   DOC    1102    5-24-92    12:01a
MEMO2     DOC    6462    5-24-92    12:00p
LETTER3   DOC    1651    7-24-92    12:01a
REPORT3   DOC    1102    7-24-92    12:01a
MEMO3     DOC    6462    7-24-92    12:00p
9 File(s) 280576 bytes free
```

Like most of the directories MS-DOS creates, this
sample directory is organized haphazardly. (Imagine
what the directory would look like if you had 350 files.)
Grouping the LETTER files, REPORT files, and MEMO
files would be better than mixing them. You can create
three subdirectories—called LETTERS, REPORTS, and
MEMOS—and place these files into them.

After you create the subdirectories and move the files
into them, the directory looks different. The DIR command now reveals the following directory:

```
Volume in Drive A has no label
Directory of A:\
LETTERS        <DIR>       9-24-92      1:14p
REPORTS        <DIR>       9-24-92      1:15p
MEMOS          <DIR>       9-24-92      1:16p
0 File(s) 280576 bytes free
```

This directory now contains three subdirectories. Using
the CHDIR command, you can open one of these
subdirectories.

Directories are linked in a tree structure. Think of an
upside-down tree. The main directory is like the root
and trunk, and the subdirectories are like branches.
The main directory created by MS-DOS is therefore
called the *root directory*. The entire directory structure
of the disk grows from this directory.

You also can create subdirectories within subdirectories.
In this way, you can organize a huge hard disk so that
you never see more than a few files after typing DIR.
See *root directory*.

**submenu**   A subordinate menu that may appear when you
choose a command from a pull-down menu. The
submenu lists further choices (see fig. S.11).

Not all menu commands display submenus. Some carry
out an action directly; others display dialog boxes.

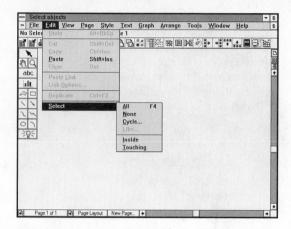

**Fig. S.11.** The submenu that appears after choosing the menu option **Select**.

 In Microsoft Windows applications, you can tell which commands display submenus by the ▶ symbol next to the command name. Command names followed by an ellipsis (...) display dialog boxes.

**subroutine**   A portion of a program that performs a specific function and is set aside so that it can be used by more than one section of the program.

A subroutine takes care of tasks needed frequently, such as writing a file to disk. In BASIC programs, subroutines are referenced by GOSUB statements.

**subscript**   In text processing, a number or letter printed slightly below the typing line, as in this example: $n_1$. See *superscript*.

**suitcase**   In the Macintosh environment, an icon containing a screen font or desk accessory not yet installed in the System Folder.

**supercomputer**   A sophisticated, expensive computer designed to execute complex calculations at the maximum speed permitted by state-of-the-art technology. Supercomputers are used for scientific research, especially for modeling complex, dynamic systems, such as the world's weather, the U.S. economy, or the motions of a galaxy's spiral arms.

**SuperDrive**   An innovative 3 1/2-inch floppy disk drive now standard on Apple Macintosh computers. SuperDrives can read all Macintosh formats (400K, 800K, and 1.4M). With the aid of Apple's Apple File Exchange software, included with all Macintosh system software, the drive can read and write to 720K and 1.44M DOS disks. It also can format disks in the DOS format.

 Thanks to SuperDrive, you can move data files easily between IBM PC and Macintosh systems. To achieve a higher level of data compatibility, choose the same applications for both systems. For example, suppose that you run the Macintosh version of Microsoft Word on your Mac and the Windows version on your PC. The Mac version of Word can read and write to the Windows format without losing any formatting.

**SuperPaint**   An illustration program for Macintosh computers that combines the bit-mapped graphics of MacPaint with the object-oriented graphics of MacDraw.

Introduced in 1986, the innovative SuperPaint (Silicon Beach Software) separated the paint and draw functions by placing them in separate layers: one in a background layer and the other in a foreground layer. The two layers are independent but superimposed, so that you can create a drawing, send it to the background, and add transparent paint effects in the foreground.

Because SuperPaint combined the best aspects of MacPaint and MacDraw, this program quickly emerged as the program of choice for amateur illustration purposes. Professional illustrators prefer programs such as Adobe Illustrator and Freehand, which can create Encapsulated PostScript (EPS) graphics.

**superscript**   A number or letter printed slightly above the typing line, as in this example: $a^2$. See *subscript*.

**Super VGA** An enhancement of the Video Graphics Array (VGA) display standard for IBM Personal Computers; Super VGA boards and monitors can display at least 800 pixels horizontally and 600 lines vertically, and up to 1,024 pixels by 768 lines with 16 or 256 colors simultaneously displayed, although as much as 1M of video memory may be required for high performance.

 Do you really need 1,024 by 768 resolution? With most Windows application programs, the higher resolution doesn't show you a sharper version of the same image; instead, it shows you *more* of the image—as much as 50 percent more than an 800-by-600 resolution VGA system can display. However, the type will be smaller. The higher resolution may be welcomed by spreadsheet users who want to see more of their worksheet in one window, writers who want to see several paragraphs of text at a time, and desktop publishers who want to lay out an entire page.

**support** See *technical support*.

**surge** A momentary and sometimes destructive increase in the amount of voltage delivered through a power line.

**surge protector** An inexpensive electrical device that prevents high-voltage surges from reaching a computer and damaging its circuitry. See *power line filter*.

**SVID** Abbreviation for *System V Interface Definition*.

**swap file** A file used to store program instructions and data that will not fit in the computer's random-access memory (RAM). See *permanent swap file, temporary swap file,* and *virtual memory*.

**swash** A character that sweeps over or under adjacent characters with a curvilinear flourish.

**switch** An addition to an MS-DOS command that affects the way the command performs its function. The switch symbol is a forward slash, which is followed by a letter (such as /s or /a).

**symbolic coding**   The expression of an algorithm in coded
form by using symbols and numbers that people can
understand (rather than the binary numbers that computers use). All modern programming languages use
symbolic coding.

**Symphony**   See *integrated program.*

**synchronous communication**   The transmission of data at
very high speeds by using circuits in which the transfer
of data is synchronized by electronic clock signals.
Synchronous communication is used within the computer and in high-speed mainframe computer networks. See *asynchronous communication.*

**syntax**   All the rules that specify precisely how a command,
statement, or instruction must be given to the computer so that the machine can recognize and process
the instruction correctly.

**syntax error**   An error resulting from the expression of a
command in a way that violates a program's syntax rules.

**SYSOP**   Pronounced "siss'-op." Acronym for *system operator.* A person who runs a bulletin board.

**system**   See *computer system.*

**System**   The operating system for Apple Macintosh computers, contained in the Macintosh's read-only memory
and the System File in the System Folder.

**System 7**   A 1991 version of the Macintosh operating system
software that maintains Apple Computer's technological lead in graphical user interfaces.

Among System 7's benefits are long-overdue improvements to Finder (the program and file-management
system), true multitasking (rather than multiple program loading), program launching from menus, true
virtual memory (with 68030 microprocessors), outline
(scalable) fonts that work on the screen as well as the
printer, peer-to-peer file sharing on networked Macs
without the need of a file server, external database
access, and hot links across applications that instanta-
neously update copied data.

System 7 is a state-of-the-art operating system, and the applications developed for it will redefine the way people work with application programs, especially when they are running more than one program. System 7 requires a minimum of 2M of RAM, but most users find that 4M is required to get the full benefit of System 7's advanced features.

 Not all existing Mac applications are compatible with System 7. Apple dealers can run a diagnostic program that informs you whether any of your programs are incompatible with System 7. See *file server, Finder, hot link, Macintosh, multiple program loading, outline font, peer-to-peer network,* and *virtual memory.*

**system date** The calendar date maintained by the computer system and updated while the system is in operation.

Not all personal computers maintain the system date after you switch off the computer. To do so, the system must be equipped with a battery. Computers without such batteries on their motherboards must be equipped with a clock/calendar board. If you are using an IBM PC–compatible computer that lacks battery-powered system date circuitry, you can use the DATE command to set the system date manually.

 Be sure to set the system date. When you create and save files, the operating system records the date and time you saved the file. This information can be important when you are trying to determine which version of a file is the most recent.

**system disk** A disk containing the operating system and all files necessary to start the computer.

Hard disk users normally configure the hard disk to serve as the system disk.

**system file** A program or data file that contains information that the operating system needs—distinguished from program or data files that the application programs use.

**System Folder**   A folder in the Macintosh desktop environment that contains the System and Finder files, the two components of the Mac's operating system.

In addition to the System and Finder files, the System Folder also contains all the desk accessories, INITs, CDEV, screen fonts, downloadable printer fonts, and printer drivers available during an operating session.

Because the System Folder is the only folder that the Finder consults when searching for a file, many applications require you to place configuration files, dictionaries, and other necessary files in this folder so that the Finder can access them. See *blessed folder, control panel device (CDEV), desk accessory (DA), downloadable font, Finder, INIT, printer driver*, and *screen font*.

**system prompt**   In a command-line operating system, the prompt that indicates the operating system's availability for system maintenance tasks such as copying files, formatting disks, and loading programs. In DOS, the system prompt (a letter designating the disk drive, followed by a greater-than symbol) shows the current drive. When you see the prompt C>, for example, drive C is the current drive, and DOS is ready to accept instructions. You can customize the system prompt by using the PROMPT command. See *command-line operating system*.

**systems analyst**   A person who designs specifications, calculates feasibility and costs, and implements a business system.

**Systems Application Architecture (SAA)**   A set of standards for communication among various types of IBM computers, from personal computers to mainframes.

Announced in 1987, SAA was IBM's response to criticisms that its products did not work well together, and to the competitive pressure exerted by Digital Electronic Corporation (DEC), which claimed that its products were optimized for easy interconnection.

Although SAA is little more than an evolving set of standards for future development, SAA calls for a consistent user interface and consistent system terminology across all environments. SAA influenced the design of

Presentation Manager, the windowing environment jointly developed by Microsoft and IBM for the OS/2 operating system. See *Operating System/2 (OS/2)*, *Presentation Manager*, and *windowing environment*.

**system software**   All the software used to operate and maintain a computer system, including the operating system and utility programs—distinguished from application programs.

**system time**   The time of day maintained by the computer system and updated while the system is in operation.

Not all personal computers maintain the system time after you switch off the computer. To do so, the system must be equipped with a battery. Computers without such batteries on their motherboards must be equipped with a clock/calendar board. If you are using an IBM PC–compatible computer that lacks battery-powered system date circuitry, you can use the TIME command to set the system time manually.

 Be sure to set the system time. When you create and save files, the operating system records the date and time you save each file. This information can be important when you are trying to determine which version of a file is the most recent.

**system unit**   The case that houses the computer's internal processing circuitry, including the power supply, motherboard, disk drives, plug-in boards, and a speaker. Some personal computer system units also contain a monitor.

The system unit often is called the *central processing unit* (CPU), but this usage is inaccurate. Properly, the CPU consists of the computer's microprocessor and memory (usually housed on the motherboard) but not peripherals, such as disk drives.

**System V Interface Definition (SVID)**   A standard for UNIX operating systems, established by AT&T Bell Laboratories and demanded by corporate buyers, based on UNIX Version 5. See *Berkeley UNIX* and *UNIX*.

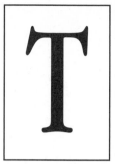

**tab-delimited file**   A data file, usually in ASCII file format, in which the data items are separated by tab keystrokes. See *ASCII file* and *comma-delimited file*.

**Tab key**   A key used to enter a fixed number of blank characters in a document. The tab key often is used to guide the cursor in on-screen command menus.

In a word processing program, don't enter indentations on the first line of paragraphs by pressing Tab, unless you have no other way of performing this task. Some programs include first-line indent commands that you should use, because if you change your mind about the amount of the indentation, you can change all of the first-line indentations in one keystroke by resetting the command. If you enter the indentations manually, you must change them all manually.

**table**   In a relational database management program, the fundamental structure of data storage and display in which data items are linked by the relations formed by placing them in rows and columns.

The rows correspond to the data records of record-oriented database management programs, and the columns correspond to data fields. See *table-oriented database management program*.

**table of authorities**   A table of legal citations generated by a word processing program from in-text references.

**table-oriented database management program**   A database management program that displays data tables (rather than records) as the result of query operations. See *data retrieval, record-oriented database management program*, and *Structured Query Language (SQL)*.

**table utility**   In a word processing program, a utility
that makes the typing of tables easier by creating a
spreadsheet-like matrix of rows and columns, into
which you can insert text without forcing word
wrapping.

When you create a table with tab stops, you must type
the table line-by-line. If you later want to add a few
words to one of the items, the words may not fit, and
you succeed only in forcing the rest of the line to wrap
down to the next line, ruining the column alignment.
Table utilities solve this problem by making the cell,
not the line, the unit of word wrapping (see fig. T.1).

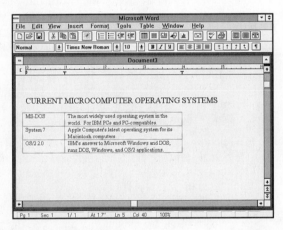

**Fig. T.1.** A table utility.

**tab stop**   The place where the cursor stops after you press
the Tab key.

Most word processing programs set default tab stops
every 1/2 inch, but you can set tabs individually anywhere you want or redefine the default tab width. In
addition, most programs permit you to set flush-right,
centered, and decimal tab stops in addition to the
default flush-left tab stops, as shown in the following
examples:

| *flush right* | *centered* | *decimal* |
|---|---|---|
| aligns at right | aligns at center | $2,110.56 |
| | | .50986 |
| | | 54 |

Note that although a decimal tab stop aligns numbers at the decimal point, it aligns text flush right.

**Tagged Image File Format (TIFF)**   A bit-mapped graphics format for scanned images with resolutions of up to 300 dpi. TIFF simulates gray-scale shading. See *bit-mapped graphic*.

**Tandy Corporation**   A Texas-based manufacturer of computer devices and electronic products generally sold through the company's franchised Radio Shack stores.

The Radio Shack TRS-80 Model 1 was one of the first personal computers, and the firm has remained active in the personal computer marketplace. The firm's low-end IBM PC–compatible computers have won broad market acceptance, partly attributable to the provision with each computer of a DeskMate, an easy-to-use DOS shell that includes desk accessories.

**tape**   A strip of thin plastic coated with a magnetically sensitive recording medium. In mainframe and minicomputing, tape is widely used as a backup medium. Thanks to a dramatic price drop in cartridge tape backup units, tape will become increasingly common in personal computing.

A major drawback to using tape for secondary storage purposes is that it is a sequential storage medium— that is, you must access all the data in a sequence, a process contrary to using random-access devices such as disk drives. Consequently, accessing data requires much more time. Every time you fast forward a cassette tape to find the song you want, you experience the delay sequential access causes; in contrast, you can access a given track on a compact disk (a random-access medium) almost instantly. As a medium for backup purposes, however, tape is widely and appropriately used. See *backup, backup procedure, backup utility, quarter-inch cartridge (QIC), random access, sequential access,* and *tape drive.*

**tape drive**   A secondary storage medium that employs magnetic tape and is commonly used for backup purposes.

In personal computing, by far the most popular drives for backup purposes are quarter-inch cartridge (QIC) drives, which fit in a standard, half-height drive bay. With prices below $300, these drives are fast becoming standard equipment for business and professional computing. Also available are 8-mm VCR cartridge drives, which use VCR tapes, and 4-mm digital audio tape (DAT) drives. The latter two options are significantly more expensive. Widely used in mainframe and minicomputing applications are half-inch tape drives, which use large, nine-track tape wheels and cartridges. Nine-track tape technology is available for personal computers from specialty suppliers listed in the classified advertising sections of popular personal computer magazines.

**technical support**   The provision of technical advice and problem-solving expertise to registered users of a hardware device or program.

**technocentrism**   An overidentification with computer technology, often associated with a preference for factual thinking, denial of emotions, a lack of empathy for other people, and a low tolerance for human ambiguity. First noted by the psychotherapist Craig Brod, technocentrism stems from the stress individuals encounter as they try to adapt to a computer-driven society.

Resembling the character Mr. Spock on the television series *Star Trek*, a technocentric individual shows an inordinate preference for factual thinking, coupled with poor access to feelings. At the extreme, the technocentric individual regards himself or herself, as well as others, as machines and treats people accordingly.

**telecommunications**   The transmission of information,
whether expressed by voice or computer signals, via
the telephone system. See *asynchronous communication* and *modem*.

**telecommuting**   Performing your work at home while
linked to the office by means of a telecommunications-
equipped computer system.

The arguments for telecommuting are compelling: It
reduces pollution and job stress, reinforces familial
bonds, saves time, and offers a pleasant work environment. Nevertheless, firms have been slow to adopt
telecommuting. Managers distrust the idea, naturally,
because telecommuting employees cannot be directly
supervised; many prefer to use telecommuting for
contract-based work rather than risk employees taking
time off at the company's expense. Employees, too,
have been slow to adopt telecommuting; many workers
find that they miss the office, which—despite the harsh
realities of a boss, Sherman Tank–type coworkers, and
irritable customers—offers social contact. As urban
transport becomes increasingly difficult and expensive
due to crowding, crumbling roads, clogged traffic, and
pollution controls, more and more people will work
one or more days per week at home.

**Telenet**   A commercial wide-area network with thousands of
local dial-up numbers. Telenet provides log-on services
to a variety of commercial on-line computer services,
such as Dialog Information Services and CompuServe.

**teletype (TTY) display**   A method of displaying characters
on a monitor in which characters are generated and
sent, one by one, to the video display; as the characters
are received, the screen fills, line by line. When full, the
screen scrolls up to accommodate the new lines of
characters appearing at the bottom of the screen.

The teletype display mode should be familiar to DOS
users. This mode uses a teletype display for accepting
commands and displaying messages. See *character-
mapped display*.

**template**   In an application program, a document or
worksheet that includes the text or formulas needed
for some generic applications and that is available
repeatedly for customization.

In word processing, templates frequently are used for
letterheads; the on-screen version of the file contains
the corporate logo, the company's address, and all the
formats necessary to write the letter, but no text. You
use the template by loading the file, adding the text,
and printing.

In spreadsheet programs, templates are available for
solving a number of common problems, such as calculating and printing a mortgage amortization schedule.

**temporary swap file**   In Microsoft Windows, a disk file that
is set aside for the storage and retrieval of program
instructions or data in the program's 386 Enhanced
mode. This storage space is used in virtual memory
operations, which use disk space as a seamless extension of random-access memory (RAM).

If Windows cannot find a permanent swap file, it creates a temporary one in which to store program instructions or data that will not fit in RAM. A temporary
swap file consumes less disk space than a permanent
swap file, but storage and retrieval operations are
slower.

 You can improve Windows' performance
considerably by creating a permanent swap
file. Doing so has an additional payoff because it enables Windows' virtual memory
capabilities for 80386- and 80486-based machines. The
amount of disk space Windows can assign to this task,
however, is limited by the largest area containing contiguous empty sectors. To make the maximum amount
of virtual memory available, run a disk defragmentation
program before setting up the permanent swap file.
See *defragmentation*, *Microsoft Windows*, *permanent
swap file*, *random-access memory (RAM)*, *swap file*,
and *virtual memory*.

**tera-**   Prefix indicating one trillion ($10^{12}$).

**terabyte**   A unit of memory measurement equal to approximately one trillion bytes (actually 1,099,511,627,776 bytes).

One terabyte is equal to 1,000 gigabytes, or one million megabytes. See *byte*, *gigabyte*, and *megabyte (M)*.

**terminal**   An input/output device, consisting of a keyboard and video display, commonly used with multiuser systems.

A terminal lacking its own central processing unit (CPU) and disk drives is called a *dumb terminal* and is restricted to interacting with a distant multiuser computer. A smart terminal, on the other hand, has some processing circuitry and, in some cases, a disk drive so that you can download information and display it later.

A personal computer is in many ways the opposite of a terminal. A terminal centralizes computing resources and denies you autonomy, whereas a personal computer distributes computing resources and enables you to make your own software choices. As a personal computer user, however, you may have many valid reasons for wanting to take advantage of centralized computer resources. To do so, you need to transform your computer into a smart terminal, which is the function of communications software.

Many different brands and models of terminals exist, and their electronic characteristics and capabilities differ. A given on-line service usually expects those contacting its computer to use a specific brand and model of terminal, such as the DEC VT100. One important function of a communications program, therefore, is to configure the personal computer so that it communicates on-line as a specific terminal would. The better communications programs provide several terminal emulations, including TTY (a teletype terminal), DEC VT52, DEC VT100, and Lear-Siegler ADM/3A.

If you are contacting an on-line information service or a bulletin board for the first time, use TTY emulation. See *terminal emulation*.

**terminal emulation** The use of a communications program to transform a personal computer into a terminal for the purpose of data communications.

**terminate-and-stay-resident (TSR) program** An accessory or utility program designed to remain in the computer's random-access memory (RAM) at all times so that you can activate it with a keystroke, even if another program also is in memory.

If you are using MS-DOS, use TSR programs with caution. Don't use TSR programs at all if you are working with valuable data or documents.

Using a TSR program all but guarantees a system crash sooner or later because DOS does not operate in protected mode. DOS has no provisions for keeping one program from invading the memory space of another, and such invasions cripple the invaded program or cause crashes.

With its protected-mode processing, OS/2 enables the simultaneous execution of two or more programs, without the peril of system crashes. See *multitasking*, *protected mode*, and *real mode*.

**Texas Instruments Graphics Architecture (TIGA)** A high-resolution graphics standard for IBM and IBM-compatible personal computers. TIGA boards and monitors display 1,024 pixels horizontally by 786 lines vertically with 256 simultaneous colors.

**text** Data composed of the standard ASCII characters, without any special formatting codes. A text file, therefore, contains nothing but the standard ASCII characters (even if it contains only numbers separated by commas).

**text chart**   In presentation graphics, a slide, transparency, or handout that contains text, such as a bulleted list. See *bulleted list chart, column text chart, free-form text chart, organization chart*, and *simple list text chart*.

**text editor**   In computer programming, a program designed for creating, editing, and storing object code.

A text editor resembles a word processing program in many respects; a text editor makes the entry and editing of words and numbers easier. Because a text editor is designed for writing computer programs, text editors generally contain only the most primitive facilities for text formatting and printing.

**text file**   A file consisting of nothing but standard ASCII characters (with no control characters or higher order characters).

**text mode**   An operating mode of IBM PC and PC–compatible video boards in which the computer displays only those images that can be constructed using the standard, 254-character IBM character set. Although this character set includes a limited number of graphics characters, text mode can display simple graphic images such as boxes and lines. In addition, text can be displayed in bold and reverse video. Text mode cannot display bit-mapped graphics, italic characters, fonts other than the standard display font, font sizes, or characters positioned above or below the baseline.

Text mode is one of two standard modes supported by most IBM PC–compatible video systems; the other mode is called *graphics mode*. Text mode is significantly faster than graphics mode because the computer can rely on the built-in, ready-to-use character set rather than having to construct the image bit by bit on-screen. On older systems based on the Intel 8088, 8086, and 80286 microprocessors, the text mode's performance advantages are so considerable that most users avoid graphics mode, except when necessary to display graphics. Character-based programs such as Lotus 1-2-3 and WordPerfect 5.1 are designed to function in text mode normally, and to shift into graphics mode when graphics displays are required. For example, choosing Graph View in Lotus 1-2-3 shifts the display to graphics mode so that you can display a graph on-screen.

**thermal printer**   A nonimpact printer that forms an image by moving heated styluses over specially treated paper.

Although quiet and fast, thermal printers have one disadvantage: most of them require specially treated paper that has an unpleasant, waxy feel.

**third-party vendor**   A firm that markets an accessory hardware product for a given brand of computer equipment.

**thirty-two bit computer**   See *32-bit computer*.

**three-dimensional graph**   A business or scientific chart that depicts information using three axes: width (x-axis), height (y-axis), and depth (z-axis). In Microsoft Excel, the vertical axis—the one that measures the data items—is called the value (y) axis, and the horizontal axis is called category (x) axis (see fig. T.2). The axis that shows depth—the one that seems to go "back" into the page—is the series (z) axis. 3-D graphs are very useful when you're portraying more than one data series.

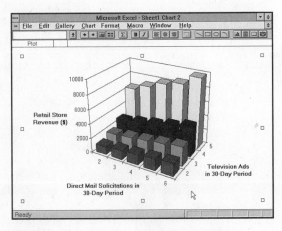

**Fig. T.2.** A three-dimensional business graph.

A two-dimensional business graph can show the relationship between two values, such as advertising expenditures and sales. A three-dimensional graph, however, can show the relationship among *three* values, as shown in figure T.2. This graph reveals the effectiveness of coupling five minutes of television advertising in a 30-day period with direct mail solicitation. In general, the more television advertising, the better the revenue; sending two mailings and purchasing five minutes of TV time is better than sending six mailings with four minutes of TV time.

**three-dimensional spreadsheet**   A spreadsheet program that can create a worksheet file made up of multiple stacked pages, each page resembling a separate worksheet.

Suppose that your organization, XYZ Corporation, has two divisions, each with its own income statement. You create two spreadsheets (called Sheet1 and Sheet2), one for each division. To sum the quarterly income amounts, you create a third spreadsheet, Sheet3. In this spreadsheet, you place formulas that use three-dimensional statements (see fig. T.3). In this illustration, the statement in cell B4 of spreadsheet Sheet3 (as shown in the line above the spreadsheet window) is

```
=Sheet2!$B$4+Sheet1!$B$4
```

This statement says, "Sum the amounts shown in cell B4 of spreadsheets Sheet2 and Sheet1, and place the total here."

**throughput**   A computer's overall performance as measured by its capability to send data through all components of the system, including secondary storage devices, such as disk drives.

Throughput is a much more meaningful indication of system performance than some of the benchmark speeds commonly reported in computer advertising, which involve the execution of computation-intensive algorithms.

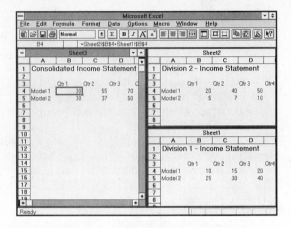

**Fig. T.3.** A three-dimensional spreadsheet.

A computer equipped with an Intel 80386 microprocessor and running at 25 MHz, for example, has good benchmark speed but may have less-than-spectacular throughput if equipped with slow random-access memory (RAM) chips, no cache memory, and a slow hard disk. Under Windows, screen updating may be sluggish unless you install a graphics accelerator.

 Before you make a purchasing decision based on benchmarks, find out whether the benchmark includes a full range of computer tasks. *PC Magazine*, for example, tests CPU instruction mix, floating-point calculation, conventional memory, DOS file access (small and large records), and BIOS disk seek. But remember that these benchmarks may not appropriately measure the system's performance under Windows, for which video speed is critical.

**thumbnail**   See *roughs*.

**TIFF**   See *Tagged Image File Format*.

**tiled windows**   In a user interface, a display mode in which the windows overlap each other (see fig. T.4). If you open additional windows, the others are automatically sized so that you still see all of them. See *cascading windows* and *overlaid windows*.

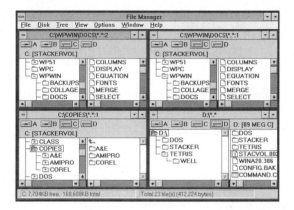

**Fig. T.4.** Tiled windows (Microsoft Windows).

**timed backup**   A desirable application program feature that
saves your work at a specified interval, such as every
five minutes.

Power outages occur during storms, during periods of
heavy demand, and when essential maintenance must
be performed on a local circuit. If you don't have an
uninterruptible power supply (UPS) or you haven't
saved your work to disk, your work is gone forever.
Your keyboard also can freeze if you are using a
terminate-and-stay-resident (TSR) program that doesn't
get along with the current application package.

Because power outages and system crashes can destroy
many hours of work, good computer practice calls for
saving your work at frequent intervals, but software can
perform saves for you. The best word processing programs include timed backup features that enable you to
specify the interval.

Using a timed backup feature is no substitute
for saving your work to disk at the end of a
working session. The files created by timed
backup utilities are temporary files, designed
to restore your work after a system crash or power outage. Use timed backups, but don't forget to save your
work. See *backup procedure*, *save*, and *tape drive*.

**time division multiplexing**   In local area networks, a technique for transmitting two or more signals over the same cable by alternating them, one after the other. Time division multiplexing is used in baseband (digital) networks. See *baseband*, *frequency division multiplexing*, *local area network (LAN)*, and *multiplexing*.

**time-sharing**   A technique for sharing a multiuser computer's resources in which each user has the illusion that he or she is the only person using the system.

In the largest mainframe systems, hundreds or even thousands of people can use the system simultaneously without realizing that others are doing so. At times of peak usage, however, system response time tends to decline noticeably.

**Timeslips III**   A time-tracking and billing program marketed by Timeslips Corporation and widely used by accountants, attorneys, consultants, and other professionals who charge clients by the hour. Timeslips III is available for IBM and Macintosh personal computers.

**title bar**   In graphical user interfaces such as Microsoft Windows, a bar that stretches across the top of a window, indicating the name of the document displayed in that window. When you activate the window, the title bar is highlighted. See *graphical user interface (GUI)*.

**toggle**   To switch back and forth between two modes or states. On the IBM PC and PC–compatible keyboard, for example, the Caps Lock key is a toggle key. When you press the key the first time, you switch the keyboard into a caps-entry mode, in which the letters you type will appear in uppercase letters on-screen. When you press the key the second time, you switch the keyboard back to the normal mode, in which you must press the Shift key to type capital letters.

Programs may implement additional toggles at the keyboard level. Many programs use the Ins key, for instance, to toggle between two text-entry modes called Insert mode and Overtype mode.

If you're shopping for an IBM PC–
compatible system, look for one equipped
with a keyboard that has indicator lights for
the Caps Lock key, Num Lock key, and Scroll
Lock key. Without these lights, you may not realize that
you've pressed one of these keys accidentally.

**toggle key**   A key that switches back and forth between two
  modes. See *Caps Lock key*, *Num Lock key*, *Scroll Lock
  key*, and *toggle*.

**token passing**   In local area networks, a network protocol
  in which a special bit configuration, called a *token*, is
  circulated among the workstations. A node gains access
  to the network only if the node can obtain a free token.
  The node that obtains the token retains control of the
  network until the message has been received and
  acknowledged.

  The token can have two values: free or busy. Any
  workstation wanting to transmit captures a free token,
  changes the value to busy, and attaches to the token
  the address of the destination node and the data to be
  transmitted. Every workstation constantly monitors the
  network to catch a token addressed to that workstation.

  When a workstation receives a token, it attaches an
  acknowledgment message to the token. When the token
  comes back to the source node, the token's value is set
  back to free.

  Because token passing rules out the data collisions that
  occur when two devices begin transmitting at the same
  time, this channel access method is preferred for large
  networks that experience high volume. See *carrier
  sense multiple access with collision detection
  (CSMA/CD)*, *contention*, *local area network (LAN)*,
  and *polling*.

**token-ring network**   In local area networks, a network
  architecture that combines token passing with a hybrid
  star/ring topology.

  Developed by IBM and announced in 1986, the IBM
  Token-Ring Network uses a Multistation Access Unit at its

hub. This unit is wired with twisted-pair cable in a star configuration with up to 255 workstations, but the resulting network is actually a decentralized ring network. See *local area network (LAN)* and *token passing*.

**toner**   The electrically charged ink used in laser printers and photocopying machines. To form the image, toner is applied to an electrostatically charged drum and fused to the paper by a heating element. See *laser printer* and *toner cartridge*.

**toner cartridge**   In laser printers, a cartridge containing the electrically charged ink, called *toner*, that the printer fuses to the page.

You can save up to 50 percent of the retail cost of new toner cartridges by using recycled toner cartridges. See *toner*.

**toolbar**   In recent applications designed for Microsoft Windows and Macintosh systems, a bar across the top of a window containing buttons, each with a distinctive icon (see fig. T.5). These icons represent frequently accessed commands. Microsoft Excel was the first application to offer a toolbar, now widely imitated in other programs.

**Fig. T.5.** A toolbar.

**toolbox**   A set of programs that helps programmers develop software without having to create individual routines from scratch.

**top-down programming**   A method of program design and development in which the design process begins with a statement (in English) of the program's fundamental purpose. This purpose is broken into a set of subcategories that describe aspects of the program's anticipated functions. Each of these subcategories corresponds to a specific program module that can be coded independently.

Structured programming languages, such as Pascal, C, and Modula-2, and object-oriented programming languages, such as C++, are especially amenable to the top-down approach. See *C*, *C++*, *Pascal*, and *structured programming*.

**topology**   See *network topology*.

**TOPS**   A file-serving program for local area networks that enables IBM PC–compatibles and Macintosh computers to be linked in one distributed processing system. TOPS is designed to work with AppleTalk and EtherNet networks.

File-serving software provides peer-to-peer file transfer in which each user has access to the public files located on the workstations of all other users in the network. Each user determines which files, if any, are to be made public for network access.

When a TOPS user decides to make a file public, he or she publishes the file on the network. Every node on the network, therefore, is potentially a file server.

A significant advantage of TOPS is that, when the user of an IBM PC–compatible computer accesses a file on a Macintosh, TOPS displays the file as if it were in a directory on a DOS disk. When the user of a Macintosh computer accesses a file on an IBM PC–compatible machine, the file appears as it normally would on the Finder's desktop display: as an on-screen icon.

Users of IBM PC–compatible computers, therefore, need not learn Macintosh skills, and Macintosh users need not learn IBM PC–compatible skills. See *file server*.

**touch screen**   See *touch-sensitive display*.

**touch-sensitive display**   A display technology designed with a pressure-sensitive panel mounted in front of the screen. You select options by pressing the screen at the appropriate place.

Hewlett-Packard championed the touch-sensitive display concept in the mid-1980s, but users disliked it. The screen quickly becomes smudged and unreadable. Touch-sensitive displays are currently used for public-access information purposes in such settings as museums, supermarkets, and airports. Synonymous with *touch screen*.

**tower case**   A computer system unit case designed to stand vertically on the floor rather than sit horizontally on a desk. Tower cases usually have much more room for accessories—including expansion boards, tape drives, and disk drives—than desktop cases. Tower cases permit you to move noisy components, including cooling fans and hard disks, away from the immediate work area, but they are inconvenient if you must frequently insert floppy disks into your system.

**tpi**   See *tracks per inch*.

**track**   In a floppy disk or hard disk, one of several concentric rings that is encoded on the disk during the low-level format and that defines a distinct area of data storage on the disk. See *cluster* and *sector*.

**trackball**   An input device, designed to replace the mouse, that moves the mouse pointer on-screen as you rotate a ball embedded in the keyboard or in a case adjacent to the keyboard.

Unlike a mouse, a trackball does not require a flat, clean surface to operate; in consequence, trackballs are often used with portable or notebook computers. Apple Computer's PowerBook systems include the trackball in the keyboard's case.

**tracks per inch (tpi)**   A measurement of the data-storage density of magnetic disks, such as floppy disks. The greater the tpi, the more data the disk can hold. In DOS, double-density 5 1/4-inch disks are formatted with 48 tpi, and high-density 5 1/4-inch disks are formatted with 96 tpi. High-density 3 1/2-inch disks are formatted with 135 tpi.

**tractor feed**   A printer paper-feed mechanism in which continuous (fan-fold) paper is pulled (or pushed) into and through the printer by using a sprocket wheel. The sprockets fit into prepunched holes on the left and right edges of the paper.

A disadvantage of tractor-feed mechanisms is that when printing is complete, you must tear off the sides of the paper and separate the sheets. For a long document, this job can become tedious, and you can easily tear a page by accident. Dot-matrix printers normally come with tractor-feed mechanisms.

**traffic**   The volume of messages sent over a communications network.

**transactional application**   In a local area network, a program that creates and maintains one shared database that contains a master record of all the transactions in which network participants engage, such as filling out invoices or time-billing forms. See *nontransactional application*.

**transfer rate**   The number of bits of data transferred per second between a disk and the computer after the drive head reaches the place where the data is located.

The maximum transfer rate is controlled by input/output standards such as ESDI or SCSI. See *access time*, *Enhanced System Device Interface (ESDI)*, and *Small Computer System Interface (SCSI)*.

**transient**   See *power surge*.

**transient command**   See *external command*.

**translate**   To convert a program from one programming language or operating system to another, or to convert a data file from one file format to another. See *file format*.

**transparent**   In computing, a hidden computer operation or entity that programmers have made invisible so that you do not have to deal with it.

A transparent computer function is present, but you can't see it; a virtual computer function *isn't* present, but you *can* see it. For example, Microsoft Word inserts formatting codes in your document, but they are transparent: you see only your formatted text. A RAM disk drive, in contrast, isn't a disk drive at all; it's just part of your computer's memory, set aside to act like a disk drive. But this virtual drive appears to you, the user, as if it were a real disk drive. See *virtual*.

**transpose**   To change the order in which characters, words, or sentences are displayed on-screen. Some word processing programs include commands that transpose text. These commands are useful when characters, words, or sentences are in the wrong order.

**trapping**   See *error trapping*.

**tree structure**   A way of organizing information into a hierarchical structure with a root and branches. See *directory* and *subdirectory*.

**Trojan Horse**   A computer program that appears to perform a valid function but contains, hidden in its code, instructions that cause damage (sometimes severe) to the systems on which it runs.

A spectacular Trojan Horse made headlines in late 1989. More than 10,000 copies of a computer disk purportedly containing information about AIDS were mailed from a prestigious London address to corporations, insurance companies, and health professionals throughout Europe and North America.

Ostensibly, the program would help users calculate
their risks of exposure to AIDS. Professionally prepared
and packaged, the disk and its accompanying documentation cost an estimated $150,000 to prepare and
mail. Recipients who loaded the disks into their computers, however, quickly found that the software was a
particularly vicious Trojan Horse that completely wiped
out the data on hard disks.

Trojan Horses, unlike computer viruses, cannot repli-
cate themselves, but that may provide small satisfaction
indeed to someone who has just lost days or weeks of
work. See *virus*.

**troubleshooting**   The process of determining why a
computer system or specific hardware device is
malfunctioning.

 When a computer fails, most people panic
and assume that a huge bill is on the way.
Most likely, however, the problem is a minor
one, such as a loose connection. Turn off the
power and carefully inspect all the cables and connections. Remove the computer's lid and press down on
the adapter boards to make sure that they are well
seated in the expansion slots. You also should check
connections at peripheral devices.

**True BASIC**   A modern, structured version of the BASIC
programming language developed by its originators,
John Kemeny and Thomas Kurtz, in response to criticism of earlier versions of BASIC.

With modern control structures and optional line numbers, True BASIC is a well-structured language used to
teach the principles of structured programming. The
language, which is interpreted rather than compiled, is
not frequently used for professional programming
purposes.

**TrueType**   A font technology, provided gratis with Apple
Computer's System 7 and Microsoft Windows 3.1 (and
later), that brings scalable fonts to the screens and
printers of Macintosh and Windows systems. Jointly

developed by Apple Computer and Microsoft Corporation, TrueType offers a cost-effective alternative to
PostScript font technology. TrueType does not require
an add-on utility program (such as Adobe Type
Manager) to display scalable fonts on-screen; nor does
it require the printer to be equipped with an expensive,
microprocessor-driven interpreter.

In the Macintosh world, System 7 users will find that
Apple Computer packages the TrueType versions of
standard Macintosh fonts with the system: Chicago,
Courier, Geneva, Helvetica, Monaco, New York,
Symbol, and Times. With Windows 3.1, you receive
Arial (a sans serif font similar to Helvetica), Courier
New, Symbol, and Times New Roman. Font suppliers
such as Fontek and Bitstream are making many addi-
tional TrueType fonts available commercially.

The TrueType fonts you see on-screen are exactly the
same as the ones you see when you print your document. If you choose the Arial font, for instance, you see
exactly the same Arial on-screen that you see on your
printed document. Furthermore, TrueType fonts are
scalable, which means (in brief) that no matter what
font size you choose—even if you choose huge, odd-
numbered font sizes, such as 63 or 109 points—you
will see that exact font size choice on-screen.

Unlike PostScript fonts, TrueType fonts will print on
most printers—no special cartridge, soft font, or built-
in font support is necessary. The "intelligence" needed
to print the font attractively is built into the equations
that produce the font; therefore, a "smart" printer (one
equipped with an expensive microprocessor to interpret printing instructions) is not needed. For this reason, documents you create with TrueType are more
portable than documents you create with PostScript
fonts. The document that printed so nicely on your
Hewlett-Packard LaserJet prints just as attractively on
your DeskJet at home. With TrueType, your documents
become much more portable. You can exchange your
document with colleagues and coworkers, who can
then print the document on their systems without
going through the hassle of reformatting the fonts.

If you already have Adobe Type Manager and a PostScript-compatible printer, should you abandon PostScript for TrueType? Experienced desktop publishers agree that TrueType does not offer a decisive technological advantage over PostScript. On Macintosh systems, Adobe Type Manager images screen fonts somewhat more quickly than System 7, and TrueType documents print more slowly than their PostScript counterparts. PostScript is still an excellent choice for professional typesetting, desktop publishing, and newsletter production.

 If you're shopping for a system, consider buying one powerful enough to run System 7 or Windows 3.1, which include TrueType capabilities and a starter font set. For Macs, such a system is a 68030-based system with at least 4M of RAM. For IBM PS/2 systems or IBM PC compatibles, look for systems with at least an 80386SX microprocessor and a bare-bones minimum of 2M of RAM (4M is better). See *Adobe Type Manager (ATM), Microsoft Windows, scalable font,* and *System 7.*

**truncate**   To cut off part of a number or character string.

**truncation error**   A rounding error that occurs when part of a number is omitted from storage because it exceeds the capacity of the memory set aside for number storage. See *floating-point calculation.*

**TSR**   See *terminate-and-stay-resident program.*

**TTY**   See *teletype display.*

**Turbo Pascal**   A high-performance compiler developed by Borland International for Pascal. The compiler comes with a full-screen text editor.

Outperforming compilers that cost 10 times as much, Borland International's Turbo Pascal took the world of DOS programming by storm when released in 1984 and is now one of the most popular compilers ever written.

Although a compiler, Turbo Pascal is an excellent tool for teaching because it contains a fully integrated, full-screen

text editor. If an error is encountered during program compilation, the editor returns on-screen and the cursor points to the error's location.

Turbo Pascal has many of the advantages of an interpreter for teaching, but it creates executable programs (object code). This compiler is used in hobby and academic environments, and some professional programmers use Turbo Pascal to prepare short- to medium-sized programs. See *interpreter*.

**turnkey system** A computer system developed for a specific application, such as a point-of-sale terminal, and delivered ready-to-run, with all the necessary application programs and peripherals.

**tutorial** A form of instruction in which the student is guided step by step through the application of a program to a specific task, such as developing a budget or writing a business letter. Some application programs come with on-screen tutorials that use computer-based training techniques.

**twisted-pair cable** In local area networks, a low bandwidth connecting cable used in telephone systems. The cable includes two insulated wires wrapped around each other to minimize interference from other wires.

**Type 1 font** A PostScript-compatible font that includes Adobe Systems' proprietary font-scaling technology, which improves type legibility at low resolutions and small type sizes. See *PostScript font*.

**typeface** The distinctive design of a set of type, distinguished from its weight (such as bold), posture (such as italic), and size.

Today's typefaces stem from the columns of ancient Rome, the workshops of Gutenberg and Garamond, and the ultra-modern design philosophy of the Bauhaus school in twentieth-century Germany. Thanks to desktop publishing, personal computer users can lay claim to and use this heritage as another element in an overall communication strategy.

Many laser printers come with as many as a dozen or more typefaces available in the printer's ROM, and literally hundreds more can be downloaded. With this enhanced communicative power, however, comes the responsibility to use typefaces with good taste.

One of the best ways to get help in the selection of typefaces is to look at books, magazines, and brochures from a new viewpoint—the viewpoint of the publication designer. Notice which fonts are used for body type and display type, the message being conveyed by the typeface, the appropriateness of the type for the publication's message, the use of white space as a design element, and the overall "color" of each page. Books in which the design team takes pride often include a colophon—a brief note (often on the last page) that indicates the typefaces chosen and the names of the principal designers.

Typefaces are grouped into two categories, serif and sans serif. Serif typefaces frequently are chosen for body type because they are more legible; sans serif typefaces are preferred for display type. This rule, however, often is broken by designers who, striving for unity of design, prefer to use the same typeface (or closely related typefaces) for both display and body type.

 Even if your system includes dozens of type-faces, professional graphic artists rarely use more than two typefaces in one document. Choose one typeface for display type and a second for body type. See *body type*, *display type*, *font*, and *font family*.

**typeover**    See *Overtype mode*.

**typeover mode**    See *Overtype mode*.

**typesetter**    See *imagesetter*.

**typesetting**    The production of camera-ready copy on a high-end typesetting machine such as a Linotronic or Varityper.

The current crop of office-quality PostScript laser printers can produce 300-dots-per-inch (dpi) output, which
is considered crude by professional typesetting standards, but which may be acceptable for applications
such as newsletters, textbooks, instructional manuals,
brochures, and proposals. See *resolution*.

**type size**    The size of a font, measured in points (approximately 1/72 inch) from the top of the tallest ascender
to the bottom of the lowest descender. See *ascender*,
*descender*, and *pitch*.

**type style**    The weight (such as bold) or posture (such as
italic) of a font—distinguished from a font's typeface
design and type size. See *attribute* and *emphasis*.

**typography**    The science and art of designing aesthetically
pleasing and readable typefaces.

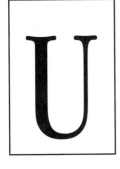

**undelete utility** A utility program that can restore a file that was accidentally erased from disk as long as no other data has been written to the disk since the erasure occurred.

Available from commercial and shareware sources, undelete utilities work because disk drives do not actually erase the file; they delete the file's name from the file allocation table (FAT).

The clusters used for the file, however, become available to the operating system for additional write operations, and if such operations occur, the file can be erased irretrievably.

If you have just deleted a file by error, *stop!* Perform no additional work with your computer that may result in write operations. Use the undelete utility immediately; if you don't have one, stop working and go buy one. See *Norton Utilities*.

**undo** A program command that restores the program and your data to the stage they were in just before the last command was given or the last action was initiated. Undo commands enable you to cancel the often catastrophic effects of giving the wrong command.

**unformatted text file** See *plain text document*.

**unformat utility** A utility program that can restore the data on an inadvertently formatted disk. If the disk has been formatted using a safe-format technique, the data is restored quickly. If the disk has not been safe formatted, you can recover the data if you have been using the MIRROR utility, provided with MS-DOS 5.0, or certain utility programs, such as PC Tools. See *safe format*.

**uninterruptible power supply (UPS)**   A battery capable of supplying continuous power to a computer system in the event of a power failure.

The battery, charged while your computer is switched on, kicks in if the power fails and provides power for up to 10 minutes or more, during which time you can shut down the computer to preserve the integrity of crucial data.

An uninterruptible power supply is mandatory equipment if a sudden power outage will result in the loss of crucial data.

**Universal Asynchronous Receiver/Transmitter (UART)** An integrated circuit that transforms the parallel data stream within the computer to the serial, one-after-the-other data stream used in asynchronous communications.

In early IBM Personal Computers, the UART was contained on the Asynchronous Communications Adapter, but the UART now is found on the motherboard in most designs. Serial communication requires, in addition to the UART, a serial port and modem. See *asynchronous communications, modem, motherboard*, and *serial port*.

**UNIX**   Pronounced "yoo'-nicks." An operating system for a wide variety of computers, from mainframes to personal computers, that supports multitasking and is ideally suited to multiuser applications.

UNIX is written in the highly portable programming language C and, like C, the product of work at AT&T Bell Laboratories during the early 1970s. Originally developed by highly advanced research scientists for sophisticated work in computer science, UNIX is a comprehensive programming environment that expresses a unique programming philosophy.

Creating software tools, each of which performs one—and only one—function, and making these tools part of the operating system is better than writing very large programs, each of which performs all functions. Application programs need not rely on their own features to accomplish functions, but can take advantage of the software tools in the programming environment. This philosophy helps programmers keep application programs in manageable bounds.

As appealing as this philosophy may be to programmers, it exacts a heavy toll on end users. The communication of data from one software tool to another is accomplished using a pipe, a user command that couples the output of one command to the input of another. Pipes are highly flexible and enable you to control virtually every aspect of the operating environment; you can extend the command set to create commands for situations not anticipated in the operating system's development.

With more than 200 commands, inadequate error messages, and a cryptic command syntax, however, UNIX imposes heavy burdens on people who do not use the system frequently and have little or no interest in gaining precise control over every conceivable operating system feature. With the development of UNIX shells, the operating system may play a much wider role in computing.

NeXTStep, a UNIX shell for the NeXT workstation, is as easy to use and as versatile as the Macintosh Finder. NeXTStep aids programmers because it includes an application program interface (API) that handles virtually all screen routines, freeing programmers from the tedious programming required to generate screen images from within an application program. IBM is expected to offer NeXTStep on its own UNIX workstations. NeXTStep is by no means tied to the NeXT workstation and can be made available for 80386 and 80486 computers. Another widely used UNIX shell is X Windows, which is currently being developed in academic computing centers.

When the user is insulated from the peculiarities of using UNIX at the system level, the operating system's other advantages quickly become apparent. Unlike most personal computer operating systems, UNIX was designed as a multiuser system. With its multitasking capabilities, UNIX can perform more than one function at a time.

In the past, these features have been in little demand by personal computer users who use stand-alone machines to run one application at a time. UNIX, therefore, is seldom used on personal computers. If the future of personal computing lies in linking workstations to corporate minicomputers and mainframes, however, UNIX operating systems—particularly when equipped with a shell such as NeXTStep—stand a chance of displacing DOS and even OS/2.

Because Bell Laboratories was prohibited from marketing UNIX by the antitrust regulations then governing AT&T, UNIX—the first version to gain significant distribution—was provided without charge to colleges and universities throughout North America, beginning in 1976.

In 1979, the University of California at Berkeley developed an enhanced and technically sophisticated version of UNIX for VAX computers. Much preferred in technical and engineering environments, Berkeley UNIX led to other versions made available commercially. In the early 1980s, AT&T gained the right to market the system and released System V in 1983.

As a result of these independent lines of UNIX development, many alternative and mutually incompatible versions of the system are in use; however, a standard UNIX version clearly is emerging. Although many thought that Berkeley UNIX would establish a standard, AT&T's System V caught up technically with Berkeley UNIX.

With the release of System V, AT&T established a set of UNIX standards called System V Interface Definition

(SVID). SVID established a standard toward which most UNIX systems are migrating, especially now that major corporate purchasers are requiring this standard. IBM adopted the SVID standard for its own versions of UNIX. See *input/output redirection*, *NeXT, pipe, shell, System V Interface Definition (SVID)*, and *X Windows*.

**unrecoverable application error (UAE)**  In Microsoft Windows, a system crash that results from one program invading another program's memory space, thus wiping out part of the other program's code. UAEs were common in Microsoft Windows 3.0, but subsequent versions are more stable.

**update**  In database management, a fundamental data manipulation that involves adding, modifying, or deleting data records so that data is brought up to date.

**upgrade**  To purchase a new release or version of a program, or a more recent or more powerful version of a computer or peripheral.

**upload**  To transmit a file by telecommunications to another computer user or a bulletin board.

**upper memory area**  In an IBM-compatible computer running MS-DOS, the memory between the 640K limit of conventional memory and 1M. In the original PC system design, some of the memory in this area was reserved for system uses, but most was never assigned for such purposes and can be used by programs. Memory management programs, as well as MS-DOS 5.0, can configure the upper memory area so that it is available for system utilities and application programs. One such program, HIMEM.SYS, comes with Microsoft Windows. See *conventional memory*, *HIMEM.SYS*, and *Microsoft Windows*.

**UPS**  See *uninterruptible power supply*.

**upward compatibility**  Software that functions, without modification, on later or more powerful versions of a computer system.

**USENET**   The news distribution and bulletin board channel of UUCP, an international wide-area network that links UNIX computers. See *UUCP* and *wide-area network*.

**user**   See *end user*.

**user default**   A user-defined program operating preference, such as the default margins for every new document that a word processing program creates.

**user-defined**   Selected or chosen by the user of the computer system.

**user-friendly**   A program or computer system designed so that individuals who lack extensive computer experience or training can use the system without becoming confused or frustrated.

A user-friendly program usually includes the following elements: menus are used instead of commands you have to memorize; on-screen help is available at the touch of a key; program functions are mapped to the keyboard in a logical order and do not contradict established conventions; error messages contain an explanation of what went wrong and what to do to solve the problem; intermediate and advanced features are hidden from view so that they do not clutter the screen and confuse beginners; commands that erase or destroy data display confirmation messages that warn you of the command's drastic consequences and provide a way to escape without initiating that operation; and clear, concise documentation that provides tutorials and reference information.

**user group**   A voluntary association of users of a specific computer or program who meet regularly to exchange tips and techniques, hear presentations by computer experts, and obtain public domain software and shareware.

**user interface**   All the features of a program or computer that govern the way people interact with the computer. See *command-driven program* and *graphical user interface (GUI)*.

**utility program**   A program that assists you in maintaining and improving the efficiency of a computer system.

In the best of all possible worlds, the operating system would provide all the utility programs you need, but this scenario is rarely the case. MS-DOS, for example, provides many external commands, including utilities such as BACKUP and RESTORE, but many MS-DOS users purchase utilities such as file compression utilities, defragmentation utilities, shells, undelete utilities, and vaccines, which DOS doesn't provide. Because MS-DOS can be difficult to use, many users purchase utilities more user-friendly than existing MS-DOS utilities. MS-DOS 5.0 remedies this deficiency in part by providing MS-DOS Shell, a user-friendly shell for basic DOS functions. See *shell*.

**UUCP**   An international, cooperative wide-area network that links thousands of UNIX computers in the United States, Europe, and Asia. UUCP has electronic mail gateways to BITNET. See *BITNET* and *USENET*.

**vaccine** A computer program designed to detect the presence of a computer virus in a system. Synonymous with *antivirus program*.

A vaccine detects a virus by checking for unusual attempts to access vital disk areas and system files and by searching for specific viruses known to afflict many computer systems.

The malevolent authors of computer viruses are aware of vaccines and are busy creating new viruses to thwart them. If you use your computer for vital business or professional applications, protect your data by using only fresh, previously unopened copies of software obtained directly from computer software publishers.

**value** In a spreadsheet program, a numeric cell entry.

Two kinds of values exist. The first kind, called a *constant*, is a value you type directly into a cell. The second kind of value looks like a constant, but it is produced by a hidden formula placed into a cell.

On-screen, the values you enter directly (constants) and the values produced by formulas look alike. You easily can destroy a spreadsheet, therefore, by typing a constant on top of a formula. You probably see no apparent difference in the spreadsheet, but because you have removed a formula, recalculation produces errors. Before changing a value you see on-screen, be sure to check the entry line in the control panel to find out whether a formula is in the cell. See *cell protection* and *label*.

**value-added reseller (VAR)** An organization that repackages and improves hardware manufactured by an original equipment manufacturer (OEM).

A value-added reseller typically improves the original equipment by adding superior documentation, packaging, system integration, and exterior finish. Some VARs, however, do little more than put their name on a device.

**vaporware**   A program that is still under development and heavily marketed even though no one knows whether its development problems will be solved.

The most celebrated vaporware fiasco was Ovation, an integrated program like Symphony or Framework that received a great deal of press attention in 1984. The developer, however, could not overcome development problems, and the program was never released.

**variable**   In computer programming, a named area in memory that stores a value or string assigned to that variable.

**VDT**   Abbreviation for *video display terminal*. Synonymous with *monitor*.

**VDT radiation**   The electromagnetic radiation emitted by a video display terminal.

Debate continues in the scientific community about whether VDTs are safe. Computer monitors produce x-rays, ultraviolet radiation, and electromagnetic fields; however, whether their emissions are dangerous is unknown. Most laboratory studies of these emissions show that they are so minimal that they cannot be distinguished from the background radiation present in an average work environment.

Some studies have demonstrated a correlation between VDT use and health problems, particularly miscarriages among pregnant users. Job-related stress, however, may be responsible for these problems. Labor unions continue to charge that the scientific research on VDT radiation is flawed and biased because the research has been conducted by the computer industry or on behalf of the computer industry.

Recent debate focuses on extremely low frequency electromagnetic radiation fields, created by strong electrical currents in power lines and electrical equipment. Correlations between the very strong fields emitted by high-voltage electrical power distribution lines and an increased risk of cancer have been demonstrated by a number of studies, although other studies show no increased risk.

Some studies indicate that risk may be involved for much more modest fields, such as those emitted by electric blankets and waterbed heaters. A careful study conducted by *PC Magazine* (December 12, 1989) demonstrated that although computers and monitors emit such radiation, the level was below background radiation levels at a distance of 18 inches from the computer and display.

 The evidence so far compiled does not prove that prolonged use of computers and CRT displays is dangerous. To be on the safe side, however, keep your face and body at least 18 inches from the computer and display. If your computer displays varying font sizes, work with a large font (such as a 14-point font) while writing, and reformat to a smaller font for printing purposes. To avoid repetitive strain injury (RSI), take frequent breaks. See *cathode ray tube (CRT)* and *repetitive strain injury (RSI)*.

**VDU**   Abbreviation for *video display unit*. Synonymous with *monitor*.

**vector font**   See *outline font*.

**vector graphics**   See *object-oriented graphic*.

**vector-to-raster conversion**   A utility available with many professional illustration programs, such as CorelDRAW!, that transforms object-oriented (vector) graphics into bit-mapped (raster) graphic images. See *bit-mapped graphic* and *object-oriented graphic*.

**Vectra**   A line of IBM PC–compatible computers, developed and marketed by Hewlett-Packard, Inc., that features a windowing environment.

**vendor**    A seller or supplier of computers, peripherals, or computer-related services.

**Ventura Publisher**    A page layout program for IBM PC–compatible computers considered excellent for long documents. See *PageMaker*.

**verify**    To determine the accuracy and completion of a computer operation.

**version**    A specific release of a software or hardware product.

A large version number indicates a later product release. For example, MS-DOS 4.0 is a more recent product than MS-DOS 3.3. In many cases, version numbers are skipped, such as 3.4–3.9 in the MS-DOS example. Other products, such as FileMaker, have different versions, not necessarily in sequential order: FileMaker Plus, FileMaker 4, and FileMaker II.

Users are often wary of Version 1.0 products because such releases may lack extensive hands-on testing. Revisions that repair minor bugs, called *bug fixes*, often have even smaller intermediate numbers such as Version 1.02 or 1.2a.

**verso**    The left-side (even-numbered) page in two-sided printing. See *recto*.

**vertical application**    An application program created for a narrowly defined market, such as the members of a profession or a specific type of retail store.

**vertical centering**    The automatic centering of graphics or text vertically on the page. WordPerfect, for example, includes a Center Top to Bottom command that centers text vertically.

**vertical justification**    The alignment of newspaper columns by means of feathering (adding vertical space), so that all columns end evenly at the bottom margin.

A page layout program capable of vertical justification inserts white space between frame borders and text, between paragraphs, and between lines to even the columns at the bottom margin.

Vertical justification is by no means necessary. Vertical justification is common, but not universal, in newspapers and magazines, but many newsletter designers prefer to leave the bottom margin ragged. See *newspaper columns*.

**vertical market program**   An application program designed for use in a specific career or profession, such as real estate, law, or architecture. Timeslips III, for example, is a time expense and billing program ideal for a small law office. See *Timeslips III*.

**very large scale integration (VLSI)**   A level of technological sophistication in the manufacture of semiconductor chips that allows the equivalent of up to 100,000 transistors to be placed on one chip.

**VGA**   See *Video Graphics Array*.

**video adapter**   The adapter that generates the output required to display computer text and graphics on a monitor.

Most video adapters support a variety of video modes, including outmoded standards. This support is needed in case you want to run an older program that may not support the newer standards. Before you purchase a video adapter, check your programs' manuals to find out which video standards your software requires.

When you select a video adapter, you also must choose a compatible monitor. An EGA monitor will not respond to the signals from a VGA video adapter. Some monitors, called *multiscanning monitors*, are designed to detect the incoming signal and adjust to it automatically.

Even if you're planning to use your computer for nothing but word processing, there is still a good argument for choosing a color-capable video adapter and a color monitor. Programmers have learned to use color intelligently to cue the eye to important screen features, such as menu names, accelerator keys, and dialog boxes. If you use Microsoft Windows with a color adapter and monitor, you can choose your own color design for your screen. You can create color combinations that are quite beautiful and that add to the aesthetic enjoyment of your computer system.

Most computer systems are sold with a choice of video adapters, so if you're looking for a system, you will be wise to think through your options. For Windows systems, many of the older standards are no longer supported, including CGA and MDA; therefore, if you're planning to run Windows, you should choose a video adapter that Windows supports. The VGA standard, with its 640 by 480 resolution, is the current standard, although systems beyond the entry level are usually sold with Super VGA adapters, offering resolutions of 800 by 600 or 1,024 by 768. Also supported by Windows 3.1 are the following video standards: 8514/A, EGA, Hercules Graphics Adapter (HGA), TIGA, Super VGA, and a variety of proprietary standards for notebook and portable computers.

 Beware of "bargain" VGA video adapters designed to fit the older, 8-bit bus of 8088- and 8086-based computers. These video adapters will work in 80286, 80386, and 80486 systems, but at the cost of sluggish performance. For a few dollars more, you can get a true, 16-bit VGA adapter. See *Color Graphics Adapter (CGA)*, *Enhanced Graphics Adapter (EGA)*, *Extended VGA*, *Hercules Graphics Adapter*, *IBM 8514/A display adapter*, *monochrome display adapter (MDA)*, *MultiColor Graphics Array (MCGA)*, and *Video Graphics Array (VGA)*.

**videodisk**   An optical disk used for the storage and retrieval of still pictures or television pictures and sound. A videodisk player is required to play back the videodisk on a standard television monitor.

Coupled with a computer that can control the videodisk player, a program called *interactive video* becomes possible; the program enables you to gain controlled access to the information stored on the

videodisk for instructional, presentation, or training
purposes. A standard videodisk can hold approximately
50,000 still frames or up to two hours of television
pictures.

**Video Graphics Array (VGA)**   A color bit-mapped graphics
display standard, introduced by IBM in 1987 with its
PS/2 computers. VGA adapters and analog monitors
display as many as 256 continuously variable colors
simultaneously, with a resolution of 640 pixels horizontally by 480 lines vertically.

Built into the motherboard of some PS/2 computers,
VGA circuitry is downwardly compatible with all previous IBM display standards, including CGA, MDA, and
EGA. VGA is superior to the EGA standard not only
because of the apparently modest increase in resolution (perceptually, the increase is much more significant than the numbers indicate), but also because,
unlike EGA adapters, VGA technology preserves the
aspect ratio of on-screen graphic images.

VGA's analog input technology also produces an unlimited number of continuously variable colors; the EGA is
a digital monitor technology locked into a fixed number of color intensity levels.

The IBM VGA standard has been pushed to new heights
by third-party vendors, who offer VGA adapters that can
display two additional graphics modes—an enhanced
Super VGA resolution of 800 pixels by 600 lines and
even more advanced adapters with a resolution of
1,024 by 768—with up to 256 colors displayed simultaneously. See *analog monitor, aspect ratio, bit-mapped
graphic, Color Graphics Adapter (CGA), digital monitor, Enhanced Graphics Adapter (EGA),* and *monochrome display adapter (MDA).*

**video monitor**   See *monitor.*

**video RAM**   Specially designed random-access memory
(RAM) chips that maximize the performance of video
adapters. Synonymous with dual-ported memory, these
chips allow one port to write to the memory while
another one reads from the same memory. In

consequence, the read process is not delayed by the writing process. Video RAM chips are employed in high-end video adapter boards. See *random-access memory (RAM)* and *video adapter*.

**video standard**    A standard for computer displays that was developed so that software developers will know how their programs will appear on-screen.

In IBM and IBM-compatible personal computing, most of the video standards were originally established by IBM, with the exception of the Hercules graphics adapter standard. New standards for high-resolution displays are being established by the Video Electronics Standards Association (VESA), of which IBM is a member.

Table V.1 lists the most popular video standards for IBM and IBM-compatible computers. Note that most standards call for downward compatibility—that is, including the video circuitry modes that conform to earlier standards. The EGA standard, for instance, includes some of the earlier CGA modes. Many VGA and SVGA adapters will respond to virtually any previous mode, including the HGA (Hercules Graphics Adapter) mode. Note, also, that most of these standards assume two basic operating modes, the text mode (which employs only the characters provided in IBM's built-in character set) and a bit-mapped graphics mode. The graphics mode runs much more slowly, but today's 386- and 486-based computers are up to the task.

A complete video system includes not only a video adapter, but also a monitor, and both must be designed to work together. When you select a monitor, make sure that it is designed to work with the video adapter you've selected.

Numerous proprietary standards exist in addition to those listed in table V.1. These standards generally call for high-resolution displays for special-purpose applications, such as multimedia or computer-aided design. If you choose a video system that employs a proprietary standard, be aware that some of your programs may not support the standard.

Table V.1
Video Standards for IBM and IBM-Compatible Computers

| Standard | Horizontal Resolution | Vertical Resolution | Mode | Colors Displayed Simultaneously |
|---|---|---|---|---|
| CGA | 640 | 200 | text | 16 |
| | 160 | 200 | graphics | 16 |
| | 320 | 200 | graphics | 4 |
| | 640 | 200 | graphics | 2 |
| EGA | 640 | 350 | text | 16 |
| | 720 | 350 | text | 4 |
| | 640 | 350 | graphics | 16 |
| | 320 | 200 | graphics | 16 |
| | 640 | 200 | graphics | 16 |
| | 640 | 350 | graphics | 16 |
| 8514/A | 1,024 | 768 | graphics | 256 |
| HGA | 720 | 348 | graphics | 1 |
| MCGA | 320 | 400 | text | 4 |
| | 640 | 200 | text | 2 |
| | 640 | 400 | graphics | 2 |
| | 320 | 200 | graphics | 256 |
| MDA | 720 | 350 | text | 1 |
| SVGA | 800 | 600 | graphics | 16 |
| | 1,024 | 768 | graphics | 256 |
| VGA | 720 | 400 | text | 4 |
| | 360 | 400 | text | 2 |
| | 640 | 480 | graphics | 2 |
| | 320 | 200 | graphics | 256 |
| XGA | 640 | 480 | graphics | 65,536 |
| | 1,024 | 768 | graphics | 256 |
| | 1,056 | 400 | text | 16 |

Before choosing a video standard for your
computer, examine your software's documentation to find out which video modes
the programs support. If possible, buy a
video board that's supported by all the programs
you're currently using. Note, too, that a 1,024 by 768
resolution isn't really needed on a standard, 14-inch
monitor; if you use this mode, the only result may be
that you see smaller text on-screen and, therefore,
more information. The Super VGA standard (800 by
600 resolution) is sufficient for most applications. See
*color graphics adapter (CGA), enhanced graphics
adapter (EGA), extended graphics array (XGA), Extended VGA, Hercules Graphics Adapter, Multi-Color
Gate Array (MCGA), Super VGA*, and *video graphics
array (VGA)*.

**videotext**   The transmission of information, such as news
headlines, stock quotes, and current movie reviews,
through a cable television system. See *on-line information service*.

**view**   In database management programs, an on-screen
display of only part of the information in a database—
the part that meets the criteria specified in a query.

Most programs enable you to save a view that can be
useful for certain purposes. Suppose that you have
created a database of all the videotapes available in
your video store. A printout of all the titles is long and
expensive to duplicate. Rather than listing all the tapes
in every category, you decide to make different printouts, sorted by category. The SQL command that produces a view of children's videotapes, for example, is as
follows:

```
SELECT title, rating
FROM inventory
WHERE category = "children"
ORDER BY title
```

Most database management programs enable you to save views, and the best ones update each view every time you add or edit records.

**virtual**  In computing, the on-screen representation of a computer entity or object (such as a disk drive) that does not exist. See *transparent*.

**virtual device**  The on-screen simulation of a computer device or peripheral, such as a hard disk drive or port, that does not exist.

In a local area network, a two-drive computer might appear to have an enormous hard disk, which actually is made available to the workstation by means of the network links to the file server. See *file server, local area network (LAN),* and *workstation*.

**virtual machine**  An on-screen simulation of a separate computer, as if the computer really exists and can run programs independently.

This simulation is made possible by a computer with the necessary processing circuitry and a large random-access memory (RAM). The Intel 80386DX and 80386SX microprocessors, for example, can run two or more virtual MS-DOS machines, each of which can run MS-DOS programs concurrently in their own 640K memory space.

**virtual memory**  A method of extending the apparent size of a computer's random-access memory (RAM) by using part of the hard disk as an extension of RAM.

Virtual memory has been around in personal computing for a long time; many application programs, such as Microsoft Word, routinely use the disk instead of memory to store some data or program instructions while you're running the program. A true virtual memory system, however, is implemented at the operating system level, so that the memory is available to any and all programs. Under virtual memory, even a program such as WordPerfect, which insists that the current document be placed in RAM, can work with

documents of unlimited length (or length limited by
the capacity of a hard disk rather than the capacity of
RAM). See *virtual memory management*.

**virtual memory management**    The management of virtual
memory operations at the operating system level rather
than the application level.

Many personal computer programs use virtual memory.
When the computer doesn't have enough memory to
store all the program instructions and data, the program automatically creates a swap file (a temporary file)
and stores the data or instructions on disk. However, a
significant advantage to implementing virtual memory
at the operating system level rather than the application level is that any program can take advantage of the
virtual memory, with the result that memory extends
seamlessly from RAM to the computer's secondary
storage. To take advantage of virtual memory at the
operating system level, however, the computer must be
equipped with a microprocessor capable of extending
memory addresses into secondary memory in this way.
The Intel 8088, 8086, and 80286 microprocessors lack
this capability, but the 80386 and 80486 microprocessors have it. In 386 Enhanced mode, Microsoft Windows can take full advantage of the virtual memory
capabilities of these microprocessors. In the Macintosh
world, Apple's System 7 makes virtual memory management available for users of 68030-based Macintoshes.

 To implement virtual memory with Microsoft
Windows, set up a permanent swap file. See
*386 Enhanced mode, Intel 80386DX, Intel
80386SX, Intel 80486DX, Intel 80486SX,
Microsoft Windows*, *permanent swap file*, and *temporary swap file*.

**virus**    A computer program, designed as a prank or as
sabotage, that replicates itself by attaching to other
programs and carrying out unwanted and sometimes
damaging operations.

When embedded in its host, the virus replicates itself by attaching to other programs in the system, including system software. Like a human virus, the effects of a computer virus may not be detectable for a period of days or weeks, during which time every disk inserted into the system comes away with a hidden copy of the virus.

Eventually, the effects manifest themselves. The consequences range from prank messages to erratic system software performance or catastrophic erasure of all the information on a hard disk.

 To protect your system from computer viruses, observe the following rules:

- Do not download executable programs from public bulletin boards unless you are certain they are virus free (you actually have seen someone else use the program without problems).

- Do not obtain executable programs from mail-order vendors of public domain or shareware programs unless they specifically promise to check each program they sell.

- Never download a recently uploaded program on a bulletin board until the SYSOP has checked it. When you do download the program, download it to a dual-floppy system so that the program cannot get near your hard disk.

- Don't copy pirated disks of commercial programs, because these disks may contain viruses.

- Purchase and use a vaccine.

See *Trojan Horse* and *vaccine*.

**VLSI**   See *very large scale integration*.

**voice mail**   In office automation, a communications system in which voice messages are transformed into digital form and stored on a computer network. When the person to whom the message is directed logs on to the system and discovers that a message is waiting, the system plays the message. Synonymous with *voice store and forward*.

**voice recognition**   Computer recognition of human speech and transformation of the recognized words into computer-readable, digitized text.

Computers and people share an unfortunate characteristic: they talk much better than they listen. In the most advanced research systems, computers can recognize only about one or two hundred words, and even this capability is achieved only after the speaker has trained the system to recognize his or her specific voice pattern.

Voice recognition involves some extremely complex pattern-recognition capabilities in the human brain— capabilities that are not well understood. See *voice synthesis*.

**voice store and forward**   See *voice mail*.

**voice synthesis**   The audible output of computer-based text in the form of synthesized speech that people can recognize and understand.

Voice synthesis is much easier to achieve than voice recognition; you can equip virtually any personal computer to read ASCII text out loud with a minimum of errors. This capability has helped many blind people gain increased access to written works not recorded on cassette tape. See *voice recognition*.

**volatility**   The susceptibility of a computer's random-access memory (RAM) to the complete loss of stored information if power is interrupted suddenly.

**volume label**   In MS-DOS, the unique, identifying name assigned to a disk and displayed on the first line of a directory. The name must be no more than 11 characters. You assign the volume label when you format the disk.

**von Neumann bottleneck**   The limitation on processing
   speed imposed by a computer architecture linking a
   single processing unit with memory.

   This architecture is the product of John von Neumann's
   discovery of the stored program concept, but its limitations are now apparent. You can create very fast central
   processing units (CPU) and huge, fast memories, but a
   seemingly inescapable limitation has emerged: the
   processor is going to spend more time fetching instructions and data than actually processing the data.

   One proposed solution to the von Neumann bottleneck is parallel processing, in which a program's tasks
   are divided among two or more CPUs. Existing programming languages and techniques, however, cannot
   handle parallel processing very well, and new languages that can handle parallel processing involve the
   programmer in the nitty-gritty procedural details of
   allocating tasks to the processors.

**VRAM**   See *video RAM*.

**wait state**   A microprocessor clock cycle in which nothing occurs. A wait state is programmed into a computer system to allow other components, such as random-access memory (RAM), to catch up with the central processing unit (CPU).

A microprocessor with a fast clock speed, such as 25 MHz, can outrace the main memory, particularly if the memory is composed of dynamic random-access memory (DRAM) chips. Wait states, therefore, are programmed into the machine to rule out the serious errors that can occur if DRAM does not respond to the microprocessor fast enough.

Wait states can be eliminated—resulting in a "zero wait state" machine—by using fast (but expensive) cache memory, interleaved memory, page-mode RAM, or static RAM chips. See *cache memory, central processing unit (CPU), interleaved memory,* and *random-access memory (RAM)*.

**wallpaper**   See *desktop pattern*.

**warm boot**   A system restart performed after the system has been powered and operating; a restart is the electronic equivalent of turning on the system, because it clears the memory and reloads the operating system.

A warm boot is preferable to a cold start because a warm boot places less strain on your system's electrical and electronic components. With IBM PC–compatible computers, you press Ctrl-Alt-Del to restart the system, although this method does not always unlock the system. You also can perform a warm boot by pressing the reset button (IBM computers or compatibles) or the programmer's switch (older Macintosh computers). Newer Macintoshes have a Restart button on the keyboard. See *cold boot, programmer's switch,* and *reset button*.

**warm link**   In object linking and embedding (OLE) and dynamic data exchange (DDE), a dynamic link that has been modified so that it is updated only when you explicitly request the update by choosing the appropriate command. See *hot link*.

**weight**   The overall lightness or darkness of a typeface design, or the gradations of lightness to darkness within a font family.

A type style can be light or dark, and within a type style, you can see several gradations of weight: extra light, light, semilight, regular, medium, semibold, bold, extrabold, and ultrabold. See *typeface*.

**Weitek coprocessor**   A numeric coprocessor, created for computers that use the Intel 80286 or 80386 microprocessors. This coprocessor offers significantly faster performance than the Intel 80287 and Intel 80387 and is widely used for professional computer-aided design (CAD) applications.

Unlike the Intel 80287 and 80387, however, the Weitek coprocessor cannot be used by programs unless you modify the programs to use it. See *computer-aided design (CAD)* and *numeric coprocessor*.

**well-structured programming language**   A programming language that encourages programmers to create logically organized programs that are easy to read, debug, and update. Modular programming languages encourage clear, logical code by permitting the programmer to break down the program into separate modules, each of which accomplishes just one function. More recently, object-oriented programming (OOP) languages, such as SmallTalk and C++, have introduced another approach to modularity. The languages are structured by a hierarchy of objects, ranging from small objects, such as option buttons, to larger ones, such as dialog boxes and windows. A hidden unit of programming code, called a *script*, is linked to each object. The script tells the computer what to do when the object is manipulated. Well-structured languages are a needed alternative to their predecessors, which allowed programmers to create illogically organized programs that were almost impossible to debug or alter. See *modular programming, object-oriented programming language, spaghetti code,* and *structured programming.*

**what-if analysis**   In spreadsheet programs, an important form of data exploration in which you change key variables to see the effect on the results of the computation.

What-if analysis provides businesspeople and professionals with an effective vehicle for exploring the effect of alternative strategies, such as "What will my profits look like if I invest another $10,000 in advertising, assuming that past trends hold true?"

**what-you-see-is-what-you-get (WYSIWYG)**   Pronounced "wizzy wig." A design philosophy for word processing programs in which formatting commands directly affect the text displayed on-screen, so that the screen shows the appearance of the printed text. See *embedded formatting command.*

**white space**   The portion of the page not printed. A good page design involves the use of white space to balance the areas that receive text and graphics.

**wide-area network**   A computer network that uses high-speed, long-distance communications networks or satellites to connect computers over distances greater than the distances—one or two miles—traversed by local area networks.

**widow**   A formatting flaw in which the last line of a paragraph appears alone at the top of a new column or page.

Most word processing and page layout programs suppress widows and orphans; better programs enable you to switch widow/orphan control on and off and to choose the number of lines for which the suppression feature is effective. See *orphan.*

**wild card**   Characters, such as asterisks and question marks, that stand for any other character that may appear in the same place.

MS-DOS employs two wild cards: the asterisk (*), which stands for any character or characters, and the question mark (?), which stands for any single character. Note the following examples:

| Wild card | Stands for |
|---|---|
| REPORT1.* | REPORT1.DOC |
| | REPORT1.BAK |
| REPORT?.DOC | REPORT1.DOC |
| | REPORT2.DOC |
| | REPORT3.DOC |

**Winchester drive** See *hard disk*.

**window** A rectangular, on-screen frame through which you can view a document, worksheet, database, or other application.

In most programs, only one window is displayed. This window functions as a frame through which you can see your document, database, or worksheet. Some programs can display two or more parts of the same file, or even two or more different files, each in its own window.

A windowing environment carries multiple windowing even further by enabling you to run two or more applications concurrently, each in its own window. See *application program interface (API)*, *graphical user interface (GUI)*, and *Microsoft Windows*.

**windowing environment** An applications program interface (API) that provides the features commonly associated with a graphical user interface (such as windows, pull-down menus, on-screen fonts, and scroll bars or scroll boxes) and that makes these features available to programmers of application packages. See *application program interface (API)*, *DESQview*, *graphical user interface (GUI)*, and *Microsoft Windows*.

**Windows**   See *Microsoft Windows*.

**Windows application**   An application specifically designed
to run in the Microsoft Windows windowing environment, taking full advantage of Windows' application
program interface (API), its ability to display fonts and
graphics on-screen, and its ability to exchange data
dynamically between applications. See *non-Windows
application*.

**Windows Metafile Format (WMF)**   An object-oriented
(vector) graphics file format for Microsoft Windows
applications. All Windows applications that support
object-oriented graphics can read graphics files saved
with the WMF format. See *file format*.

**WMF**   A file name extension indicating that the file contains
a graphic saved in the Windows Metafile Format. See
*Windows Metafile Format (WMF)*.

**WordPerfect**   A full-featured word processing program
devolped by WordPerfect Corporation for a variety of
computers, including the Macintosh, DOS, and
Windows systems.

Emphasizing portability and a consistent command
structure across a wide variety of computer formats,
WordPerfect is the most widely used word processing
program. Its phenomenal success in the IBM PC–compatible marketplace is attributable to its power.

The program includes more features than any other
program, with the possible exception of Microsoft
Word. WordPerfect also is fast (the entire document is
kept in random-access memory, so that scrolling occurs
at high speed), and the company's responsiveness to
user suggestions is good.

Essentially an on-screen formatting program that operates in a character-based environment, the DOS version
of WordPerfect displays most text formats as they appear when printed. The hidden codes that tell the
printer how to print these formats, however, can be
edited by the user—an unusual feature in this type of
program.

WordPerfect strives to make all of its features accessible to the user who wants to gain complete control over the program. The program's critics, however, point out that the user frequently must perform manual edits of these hidden codes when, for one reason or another, the program fails to delete an extraneous code.

In most versions, WordPerfect relies heavily on function keys for the command interface, and this choice also has attracted criticism. In response, WordPerfect Version 5.1 for IBM PC–compatible computers introduced the use of the mouse and pull-down menus.

The program is available for a wide variety of computers, including mainframe and minicomputers, and one of its strengths lies in its provision of a consistent user interface and file structure across a variety of computing environments. This consistency appeals greatly to organizations, because costs rise as people use a variety of computers to produce documents with mutually unintelligible file formats.

The emphasis on portability, however, has been achieved at some sacrifice; WordPerfect often has been criticized for not taking full advantage of graphical user interfaces. The Macintosh version of WordPerfect, for example, has been criticized because it does not take full advantage of the Mac's graphical user interface, nor does the program recognize many tacit conventions of program functionality that users have come to expect. But Version 2.0 for the Mac thoroughly addressed these criticisms and received acclaim from reviewers. WordPerfect for Windows disappointed initial reviewers and faces stiff competition from Microsoft Word and Ami Pro.

**word processing**   Using the computer to create, edit, proofread, format, and print documents.

By a wide margin, word processing is the most popular computer application. Word processing software enables you to use word processing applications with a personal computer. The most popular word processing programs include WordPerfect, Microsoft Word, and WordStar.

What makes word processing so appealing is the ease with which you can alter the text before you print it. With typewriters, you have to type the document correctly the first time; if you inadvertently omit a paragraph, you must manually retype the page on which you made the error, as well as all subsequent pages. With a word processing program, you merely insert the missing paragraph. Other editing operations, such as deleting words or sentences, are comparably easy, and you also can move text from one location in a document to another.

Although word processing technology greatly speeds the revision process, some writing experts worry that the technology adversely affects the quality of writing. The author Joan Didion, for example, argues that word processing makes writing too easy: instead of completely rewriting a flawed paragraph, you can simply insert words or phrases here and there in an attempt to clarify the muddled thought. The result, as the editors of many publishing houses complain, is a phenomenon called "word processor bloat." Other writing experts criticize the small screen, which tends to focus revision efforts at the word and sentence level while disguising the overall flow of logic in the document. They point out that good writing begins with good organization, but word processing makes your document's organization harder to see.

Judging from huge increases in the number of articles and books submitted to publishers in the last decade, word processing no doubt has increased writers' productivity. But the productivity benefits of word processing technology are far from automatic. With today's Windows and Macintosh programs, the boundary between word processing and desktop publishing has narrowed, so that writers are tempted, as never before, to think about the design of the printed document. The time gained from not having to retype the document may be squandered as a writer fusses with unnecessary font changes, graphics embedded within text, and other desktop publishing niceties.

 Today's best word processing technology provides strategies for overcoming these drawbacks. A full-page display, for example, provides a better view of your document's paragraph-by-paragraph logic. Outlining utilities that are fully embedded within your document's structure can help you see and restructure your document's overall organization. Microsoft Word features a fully embedded outline utility. Bear in mind, as you write, that the best cure for a poor sentence or paragraph isn't to add more words: delete the offending passage and rewrite it from scratch. As for wasting time with fonts and formatting, just remember to keep it simple.

**word processing program**   A program that transforms a computer into a tool for creating, editing, proofreading, formatting, and printing documents.

Word processing programs top the best-seller lists, and for a simple reason: of all computer applications, people have found word processing the most useful.

Word processing software was initially developed in two entirely different settings: the corporate word processing pool and the programmer's bench. Beginning in the late 1960s, word processing programs were developed for corporate typists—programs that simulated, as far as possible, the behavior of a fine office typewriter. These programs were designed to ease typists' transition into the new world of computing, in which they would do the same, old job: typing someone else's work.

Key firms that developed corporate word processing systems include Wang, which dominated the word processor market in the 1970s, and IBM, which successfully marketed its DisplayWrite system during the 1970s and early 1980s as a word processing system. In personal computing, programs such as MultiMate (a personal computer version of the Wang word processing software) and DisplayWrite show the influence of this setting.

Although office word processing programs of the MultiMate or DisplayWrite type have found many buyers, today's most popular programs—WordPerfect and Microsoft Word—stem from a different origin: the programmer's bench. During the same period that dedicated word processors started appearing in offices, computer programmers were busy developing a totally different kind of word processing technology, and for two purposes: to create and edit computer programs and to print documentation for their programs. For the first job, they created text editors, which had few printing features but included many other features, such as search and replace, that are helpful when writing programs. To print manuals for the programs they wrote, they developed formatting programs, which produced paginated manuals with automatically generated tables of contents and indexes.

Early formatting programs, such as the famed EMACS formatter at MIT, were completely separate from the text editing program; to print the document, you had to use the text editor to go through the document and embed formatting commands, which in turn instructed the printer how to print the document. Often you would find out that you had made a mistake only *after* you had printed the document. An early CP/M word processing program, widely packaged with Z-80 based microcomputers such as the Kaypro and Osborne, included an EMACS-influenced text editor and formatter package called Perfect Writer, which was very far from perfect, as many writers found.

So that writers could see the results of a formatting mistake on-screen before printing the document, programmers merged text editors and formatters into one program. The result was what-you-see-is-what-you-get (WYSIWYG) software, which displays the results of most formatting commands on-screen. One of the first WYSIWYG programs, called Bravo, was created at Xerox's Palo Alto Research Center (PARC) in the 1970s. WordStar, the first popular implementation of WYSIWYG technology for personal computers, quickly dominated the CP/M market. After the 1981 debut of the IBM Personal Computer, WordPerfect, another WYSIWYG program, quickly rose to prominence.

During the 1980s, numerous technical improvements were made to word processing programs, such as the inclusion of spelling checkers and electronic thesauruses, mail merging, and the capability to work with all of a printer's font and font size resources. By the late 1980s, leading word processing programs were incorporating features formerly found only in page layout programs, features such as the capability to anchor a graphic or a unit of text to an absolute position on the page so that text flows around it. With the rise of graphical user interface (GUI) systems such as the Macintosh and 386 PCs running Microsoft Windows, programs acquired the capability to display fonts and font size choices on-screen. Today's word processing software, such as Microsoft Word for Windows or WordPerfect for Windows, is capable of taking on light desktop publishing duties, such as newsletter production, while still offering a writer all the necessary tools for the creation, editing, proofing, formatting, and printing of text.

 If you're shopping for a word processing program, bear in mind that some programs include features that may have special appeal to people working in specific professions. WordPerfect, for example, is a mainstay in legal offices, thanks to its case-citation capabilities, and Nota Bene, a version of XyWrite marketed by the Modern Language Association, appeals to scholars trying to cope with all those footnotes and bibliographic citations. WordPerfect 5.1 for DOS, which includes many very desirable features for office typing, will be found for years to come on clerical workers' desks. Newsletter writers greatly esteem Ami Pro for Windows, and screenwriters, who often must format their scripts with bizarre indentations, prefer Microsoft Word, with its user-definable style sheets. Newspaper people like XyWrite, thanks to XyWrite's capability to interface with the typesetting technology that most newspaper offices use. Talk to people in your line of work to see which program they prefer.

**WordStar**    A WYSIWYG word processing program originally developed by MicroPro International (now WordStar International) for CP/M, DOS, and Windows systems.

WordStar originated the term *what-you-see-is-what-you-get*, although its WYSIWYG ("wizzy wig") features are by no means complete; embedded commands still are required for many functions. The program is still preferred by writers with good touch-typing skills because almost all commands can be given without taking your fingers off the home position, as you must do with most function keys or a mouse.

**word wrap**    A feature of word processing programs, and other programs that include text-editing features, that wraps words down to the beginning of the next line if they go beyond the right margin.

If you are just getting started in word processing, remember that you should not press Enter until you are ready to start a new paragraph. If you press Enter at the end of every line, you may find that changing the margins or performing editing operations is difficult after you type the text.

**workgroup**    A small group of employees assigned to work together on a specific project.

Much of the work accomplished in contemporary corporations is done in workgroups, and if this work is to be done well and in a timely fashion, the workgroup needs to communicate effectively and share resources.

Personal computer technology, especially when linked in a local area network (LAN), is thought to enhance workgroup productivity by giving the group additional communication channels (in the form of electronic mail), facilities for the group editing of technical documentation (such as redlining and strikeout), and shared access to a common database. See *redlining* and *strikeout.*

**worksheet**   In spreadsheet programs, the two-dimensional matrix of rows and columns within which you enter headings, numbers, and formulas. The worksheet resembles the ledger sheet used in accounting. Synonymous with *spreadsheet.*

**worksheet window**   In spreadsheet programs, the portion of the worksheet visible on-screen (see fig. W.1).

With up to 8,192 rows and 256 columns, modern electronic spreadsheets are larger than a two-car garage in size. The worksheet window displays only a small portion of the total area potentially available.

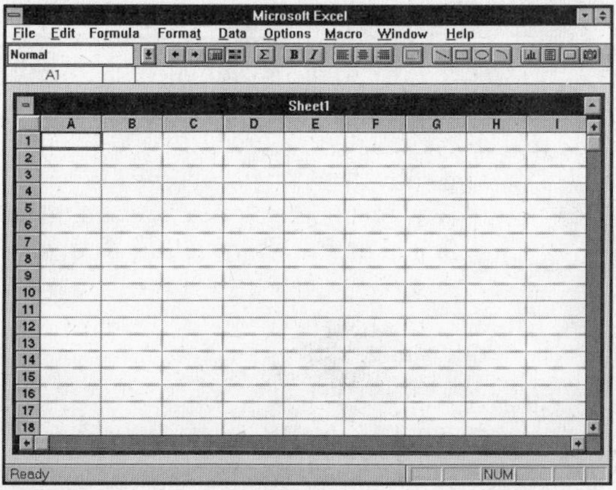

**Fig. W.1.** A worksheet window.

**workstation**   In a local area network, a desktop computer that runs application programs and serves as an access point to shared network resources. See *file server, personal computer*, and *professional workstation.*

**WORM** See *write-once, read-many*.

**wrap-around type** Type contoured so that it surrounds a graphic (see fig. W.2). Because wrap-around type is harder to read than noncontoured type, use wrap-around type sparingly.

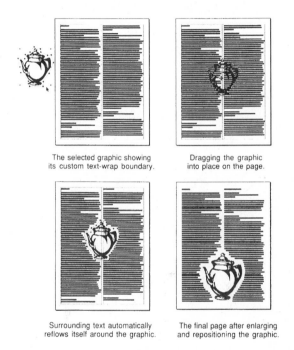

The selected graphic showing its custom text-wrap boundary.

Dragging the graphic into place on the page.

Surrounding text automatically reflows itself around the graphic.

The final page after enlarging and repositioning the graphic.

**Fig. W.2.** Text wrapped around a graphic.

**write** A fundamental processing operation in which the central processing unit (CPU) records information in the computer's random-access memory (RAM) or the computer's secondary storage media, such as disk drives. In personal computing, the term most often refers to storing information on disks.

**write-black engine** See *print engine*.

**write head** See *read/write head*.

**write-once, read-many (WORM)**    An optical disk drive with storage capacities of up to 1 terabyte. After you write data to the disk, it becomes a read-only storage medium.

WORM drives can store huge amounts of information and have been touted as an excellent technology for organizations that need to publish large databases internally (such as collections of engineering drawings or technical documentation). The advent of fully read/write-capable optical disk drives, however, has greatly diminished the appeal of WORM technology. See *CD-ROM* and *erasable optical disk drive*.

**write-protect**    To modify a file or disk so that no one can edit or erase its data.

**write-protect notch**    On a 5 1/4-inch disk, a small notch cut out of the disk's protective jacket that, when covered by a piece of tape, prevents the disk drive from performing erasures or write operations to the disk.

**write-protect tab**    On a 3 1/2-inch disk, a tab located in the disk's upper right corner as you hold the disk with the label up. When you slide the tab down to cover the hole, you have write-protected the disk.

**write-white engine**    See *print engine*.

**WYSIWYG**    See *what-you-see-is-what-you-get*.

**x-axis**   In a business graph, the x-axis is the categories axis, which usually is the horizontal axis. See *bar graph, column graph, y-axis,* and *z-axis.*

**XCFN**   See *external function.*

**XCMD**   See *external command.*

**XENIX**   An operating system developed by Microsoft Corporation that conforms to the UNIX System V Interface Definition (SVID) and runs on IBM PC–compatible computers. See *System V Interface Definition (SVID)* and *UNIX.*

**XGA**   See *Extended Graphics Array.*

**x-height**   In typography, the height of a font's lowercase letters, measured from the baseline up.

Because many fonts have unusually long or short ascenders and descenders, the x-height is a better measurement of the actual size of a font than the type size, measured in points. In figure X.1, for example, notice the variation in x-height in the letter *y*. See *ascender, baseline,* and *descender.*

AyAyAyAyAyAy *Ay*

**Fig. X.1.** Letters with the same nominal type size that have different x-heights.

**XMODEM**   An asynchronous file-transfer protocol for personal computers that makes the error-free transmission of computer files through the telephone system easier.

Developed by Ward Christiansen for 8-bit CP/M computers and placed in the public domain, the XMODEM protocol is included in all personal computer communications programs and commonly is used to download files from computer bulletin boards.

**XMS**   See *eXtended Memory Specification*.

**XMS memory**   In computers based on the Intel 80286 and higher microprocessors, memory that a memory management program has configured as extended memory. Some DOS programs can use XMS memory to break the 640K RAM barrier. Synonymous with *extended memory*.

**XON/XOFF handshaking**   See *handshaking*.

**XT**   See *IBM Personal Computer XT*.

**X Windows**   A network windowing environment commonly used on UNIX-based workstations.

Originally developed at MIT and distributed freely to the academic community, X Windows is a device-independent API that can run under operating systems ranging from a disk operating system to a mainframe operating system. However, it is used most frequently on UNIX machines. Unlike Microsoft Windows and other PC-based windowing environments, X Windows is designed for use on a minicomputer-based network.

Many different research labs and computer science departments have adopted and separately developed the freeware version of X Windows, with the unfortunate result that many incompatible versions of X Windows exist. As a result, a consortium of UNIX vendors joined with MIT in 1987 to establish an X Windows standard; however, application development with X Windows is a formidable undertaking. For this reason, several vendors have developed proprietary toolkits for X Windows application development, with inevitable compatibility problems. See *UNIX* and *windowing environment*.

**x-y graph**   See *scatter diagram*.

**y-axis** In a business graph, the y-axis is the values axis, which normally is vertical. See *bar graph*, *column graph*, *x-axis*, and *z-axis*.

**YMCK** Abbreviation for *yellow, magenta, cyan, and black*. See *color separation*.

**zap** Synonymous with *erase* and *delete*.

**Zapf Dingbats** A set of decorative symbols developed by Herman Zapf, a German typeface designer (see fig. Z.1).

**z-axis** In a three-dimensional graphic image, the third dimension of depth. See *three-dimensional graph*, *x-axis*, and *y-axis*.

**zero-slot LAN** A local area network designed to use a computer's serial port instead of requiring the user to purchase a network interface card.

Zero-slot LANs are considerably slower than systems that use network interface cards, which take advantage of the computer's high-speed internal bus. Zero-slot LANs are therefore best used for applications in which network applications are limited to occasional access to an infrequently used shared peripheral (such as a plotter) or electronic mail. See *network interface card* and *serial port*.

**Fig. Z.1.** Zapf Dingbats.

**zero wait state computer**    An IBM PC–compatible computer with memory optimized by using a scheme such as cache memory, interleaved memory, page-mode random-access memory (RAM), or static RAM chips, so that the microprocessor does not have to wait for the memory to catch up with processing operations. See *cache memory, interleaved memory, page-mode RAM, static random-access memory (RAM)*, and *wait state*.

**zone**    In a local area network (LAN), a subgroup of networked computers set aside and named by the network administrator so that these computers can be treated as a group. If an administrator sets up zones called *Marketing, Design*, and *Manufacturing*, for example, someone in manufacturing can address an electronic mail message to everyone in marketing by sending the message to the Marketing zone.

**zoom**    To enlarge a window so that it fills the screen.

**zoom box**    In a graphical user interface, a box—usually positioned on the window border—that you click with the mouse to zoom the window to full size or restore the window to normal size. See *graphical user interface (GUI)*.

## Add terms to

### *Que's Computer User's Dictionary*

*Que's Computer User's Dictionary* defines and describes terms of interest to the typical user of personal computers. We have tried to include all terms appropriate to a general audience, but we know that we must have missed some that you think should be in this book. Please help us improve the next edition. Write down the terms you think we should include, and send the list to

Que's Computer User's Dictionary
Que Corporation
c/o Julia D. Blount
11711 N. College Avenue
Carmel, IN 46032-5634

Your feedback is important to us. Thanks for your help!